Courage &
Commitment

Courage & Commitment

~An Autobiography~

MARGARET ALVA

RUPA

Published by
Rupa Publications India Pvt. Ltd 2016
7/16, Ansari Road, Daryaganj
New Delhi 110002

Sales centres:
Allahabad Bengaluru Chennai
Hyderabad Jaipur Kathmandu
Kolkata Mumbai

ISBN: 978-81-291-3956-6

First impression 2016

10 9 8 7 6 5 4 3 2 1

The moral right of the author has been asserted.

This edition is for sale in the Indian subcontinent only.

To Niranjan, my husband,
the cornerstone of my life

CONTENTS

After days and nights of thunder and rain, I woke up to a bright, sunny morning—the sunlight gleaming through the glass of my large bay windows. I instinctively opened them for fresh air. The sound of birds chirping in the tall trees around this castle called the Summer Raj Bhavan at Nainital, the flower beds abloom with rich colours, and the luscious lawns spread out before me like an unending carpet—it was all so beautiful. I stared, alone at my window, in that early morning silence. I felt like a queen imprisoned in a castle, far away from the world I knew, far removed from the reality of the life I had led.

And my thoughts wandered to the days gone by—my early childhood; the growing-up years in a closely knit family; my university life where, as an activist, I met Niranjan Alva; my marriage, children, life in the Alva household in Delhi; the tragedy of my mother-in-law's sudden passing away; and the transition from a young homemaker in a joint family to the world of politics. I thought of my years in the party, then in Parliament; my days in government, followed by the defeat and the days in the opposition; the shift to the Lok Sabha and then to the AICC (All India Congress Committee); the bitter battles for survival, as I juggled home and work; and finally, the acceptance of defeat and the departure from Delhi, leaving family, friends and associations spanning more than forty years.

The tears rolled down my cold cheeks as I stood at the window. This was my life, my struggle, my ups and downs, my highs and lows, my successes and failures. But through it all, I stood brave and bold, never faltering in my commitment to speak up for what I believed was right, and never afraid to defend the truth.

I dried my face with my cold hands and shut the window—the past behind me; the present staring me in the face; the future unknown.

The Wonder Years

Chapter 1

BACK TO THE DISTANT PAST: CHILDHOOD

My life began on the South-west coast of India, in what was then a small town—Mangalore, in the district of South Canara. My father was posted as a Judicial Officer (Munsiff) at Kurnool (now in Andhra Pradesh, but in those days, a part of the Madras Presidency). My pregnant mother went home to her parents—as she did for the birth of every child—to be cared for and pampered at Churchills, the family home.

Churchills was a large, old-world, Portuguese-style house. In the front was a large, open veranda, and the centrepiece was a carved, wooden round table always laden with a big bowl of flowers, and surrounded by chairs. All of us, as children, played 'house-house' under the table's imposing round top, pretending to cook, eat and sleep with all our toys and dolls. There were countless large rooms, one leading into the next. The hall had an imposing carved rosewood altar, benches done up with beautiful rattan work and family photographs on the walls. The doors and windows were carved and the floors had dull mud-pink stone tiles.

My mother was taken to Dr Shiva Rao's hospital at Nandigudda Hill on the evening of 13 April 1942. She was shifted to the labour room in the early hours of the morning. Just about then, there was a loud bang, followed by a total blackout. 'The Japanese have landed! There was an explosion in the port. Mangalore is being bombed; run for shelter!' were the cries all around. It was wartime, and panic spread, with doctors and nurses disappearing into the dark.

My mother, unable to move, looked despairingly at the one woman attendant who remained by her side. 'Will you also leave me to die?' she asked.

'Never! I will stay with you, even if the Japanese reach the hospital. You will be safe. God is with us,' she assured my mother. And so, by candlelight, at around 5 a.m., I was delivered by the attendant and kept on the bare floor. When my mother protested, she was told, 'Nothing will happen to her. I have given her to Mother Earth, who will protect her. She will live to be great.'

I survived.

My mother was disappointed at the birth of another daughter (the third), despite her prayers for a son. Early in the morning, on the way to his office, her father dropped in to see her. She wept, thoroughly upset. 'Never cry over the birth of a child. She is born on my birthday, she will be a great lawyer one day,' he predicted, blessing me with a cross on my forehead.

The first decade of my life was influenced, to a large extent, by my maternal family. It was also shaped by Mangalorean society. School, family get-togethers, weddings, vacations—all revolved around that small town.

Churchills was a home away from home for eleven children—nine girls and two boys—who visited regularly along with their families and were provided for by my grandmother, Bai (as she was affectionately called by all generations). Bai had a heart as large as her house. Family, distant relations, friends, charity seekers—everyone was welcome, no one was left out or neglected. Fruits of the season were bought by the basket, fish and meats of every variety were laid out for lunch and dinner, the mouthwatering sweets of the coast were served at coffee-time (we never had tea) and goodies came out of her locked cupboard every few hours.

Bai ran the household like a Commander-in-Chief. From the kitchen to the locked storeroom, to the garden with fruit and coconut trees, and to the cowshed—she controlled and managed everything, with three faithful women to assist her.

And then there was Mai—her mother in her eighties, with a toothless smile—who lived close by with her son. She was a regular visitor. On holidays, we'd gather around her to hear fascinating stories of days gone by—of Tipu's men who looted and plundered homes and killed those who resisted, hanging their bodies from trees; of tall Afghan and short Japanese men who came selling exquisite wares; and of Sadhus and mendicants with knotted hair who brought rare herbs and medicines to cure any ailment.

My mother had been married to my father at the age of sixteen-and-a-half, while still in the fifth form (eleventh standard by today's yardstick). Apart from being fluent in English, she was an artist who drew beautifully. She motivated us, made us ambitious, and ensured that we did well at school. My father, a lawyer, came from a rural agricultural family based in

Shirva in the South Canara district. He was an only son and had a sister. Their mother had passed away while they were kids. Their father—my grandfather, Abba—was a landlord, respected and feared by his tenants. He was known to be not only a tough taskmaster, but also a patriarch who cared only for the male inheritors of his property. So he sent his son to a boarding school—St Aloysius School—and then to a college in Mangalore. He refused to sell his surplus land though land reforms were coming. And so, after he was gone, most of it went to the tenants, ending the saga of the family inheritance in Shirva.

We spent some wonderful holidays in the village, although they were few in number since my town-bred mother did not enjoy that life. The tenants loved my father, who listened to their problems and pleaded with his father to be more generous with them.

My maternal grandfather, Pascal D'Souza, was a well-known and respected lawyer, who worked tirelessly to keep a lavish lifestyle going for his large family. We called him Baba and loved him dearly.

In 1949, Baba was struck by tuberculosis—a dreaded disease in those days—that confined him to his room, with only my grandmother and mother attending to him, apart from the family doctor. On 23 June 1951, we were picked up from school in a horse carriage and brought home, to see candles and white flowers by the altar, and Baba laid out in a dark suit with white socks and gloves. He was dead. An eerie silence prevailed, broken only by mourners coming in with flowers to offer their condolences. The next day, we were made ready for the funeral. This was my first experience of a funeral. I was at once sad and nervous. I watched silently as the coffin was lowered into a grave in the church and sobbed as I threw a fistful of mud over it. When we returned home, there was a speech in praise of the departed, and then everyone left, as I sat watching the candles flicker and slowly die in front of a picture of Baba. My grandfather was gone and life at Churchills would never be the same again.

◆

My schooling was a chequered affair. While my siblings, Corinne, Joan and Alan, were left with our grandmother at Churchills for schooling, I, being a sickly child, stayed with my parents, going where my father was posted. Thus I was home-schooled for most of the first eight years of my life, though my travels with my parents ensured that I picked up local languages without any effort—Telugu, Kannada and Konkani, among others.

When my father was posted as a Sub-Judge at Ottapalam, I was sent to the neighbourhood convent school, where Sister Marina used to teach me. She also prepared me for my first communion. Here I joined the local children for sports, art and dance. They all spoke Malayalam—another language that I soon absorbed.

I recall an afternoon in 1948 in Ottapalam. Ours was a lovely house with many bedrooms, a large garden (infested with snakes) and a wicket gate. Suddenly, policemen with guns appeared at the gate and in the compound. My father returned home early and was very agitated. We were asked to stay indoors. All the doors and windows were shut. We could hear loud shouts on the road outside as processions went through the streets. I was frightened. As I sat on my father's lap, I asked, 'What has happened? Why is everyone scared?' My father told me, 'Mahatma Gandhi, our great leader, has been killed. And now, the people are angry and are screaming.' It was an earth-shattering event, no doubt, but it made no sense to me back then. I did not ask any more questions, sensing the mood around me.

My sister, Corinne, was beautiful, with two long plaits. She was loved by all at home and in school (where she became the head girl). In December 1950, sixteen-and-a-half-year-old Corinne was married to a smart and good-looking lawyer from Bangalore (now Bengaluru) named Gladwyn Rego. The wedding took place at Churchills. When Corinne left, it felt like a big branch of the family tree had been cut.

1952 saw the first election for the Madras (now Tamil Nadu) Legislative Assembly. Bai's brother, my grandfather's partner in the law office, the late L.C. Pais, was the Congress candidate from our area. His party's symbol was a pair of bullocks. So what better mode of canvassing than using a bullock cart with a hand-held loudspeaker, and throwing coloured handbills asking for votes?

Even as the neighbourhood was swept by election frenzy, Bai remained rather uninterested in the electoral process and the Congress. In fact, when her other brother, Lawrence, came to visit her, she is said to have spoken disparagingly about L.C. Pais' politics and his ambitions. This was promptly carried back to him. And so, early one morning, there was a loud knock at the door, and in marched the two brothers to Bai's bedroom. They gave her a lecture on the Congress, and told her to hold her tongue and vote for the party. Having had their say, they marched out. Bai sat in her nightgown under her mosquito net, peering through the mesh, speechless and stunned by this early morning intrusion! I do not know whom she voted for, but she was among the first to go to the booth and vote as ordered by her brothers. L.C. Pais won the election, but Bai never forgot the early morning knock and the obnoxious behaviour of her brothers, whom she referred to as the Congress bullocks on a rampage!

Over that summer of 1952, we were in Gooty (Anantapur district) for our vacations. There was great excitement when the visit of Pandit Jawaharlal Nehru to Anantapur was announced. As the District Magistrate, my father was in charge of the law and order arrangements. He decided to take my brother, sister and me to the public meeting. The crowds were frightening—in bullock carts and tongas, cycles, buses, lorries or on foot. They came in countless numbers, in the heat and dust of that summer night. We were seated in the front row, which was meant for the 'officials'.

As Pandit Nehru walked in, there were cheers, slogans and garlands. Nothing made sense to me. He climbed up to the high stage, waved, and spoke, and departed as the cheering crowds began to disperse. We drove back—tired, hungry, dusty and sleepy—down those kutcha roads and into the dark wilderness, to reach home in the early hours of the morning. This was the Congress' Parliamentary election campaign—the country's and my first!

In April 1954, I moved to a new world, when my father was transferred to Coimbatore as an Additional District Judge. My parents took my siblings and me along as Coimbatore had English-medium education. I went to the SSLC (Secondary School Leaving Certificate) section of St Francis Convent in the second form. For me, it was a huge jump—from Malayalam and Kannada to English. Since I was diagnosed with trachoma, and was advised minimum strain to my eyes, during those early years in Coimbatore, my mother would sit with me for hours and read to me, helping me memorize my spellings and revise each subject, chapter by chapter. Thanks to her tireless efforts, I overcame the language hurdle and stood first in my class in my first quarterly examination. I excelled in sports as well, and was selected for the school basketball and throwball teams.

Coimbatore also opened a window to Tamil culture and its nuances. I picked up the language, changed my attire from dresses to graceful pavadai-chokkas (later adopting the half-saree), grew my hair for plaits and dabbed a small red bindi on my forehead.

In March 1956, my mother's youngest sister arrived, armed with a proposal for my sister, Joan—aged seventeen—who was shy and studious, and in her second intermediate. Michael Peres—from the wealthy Peres family which had business interests in Kerala and Karnataka—was the groom. In no time, everything was settled. The engagement took place that week and the wedding in Mangalore in May.

In March, my father retired to settle in Bangalore. Here he started his law practice. We lived on his pension, as clients were slow to come. While my father managed to buy a lovely house from an old Irish lady, getting her to vacate the place proved to be a Herculean task!

Those were trying times. After the big bungalows we had lived in, we found ourselves packed into a wing of my Aunt Mary's damp, old house, where we felt like unwanted guests. Thankfully, this was a passing phase. Things began to change. My father's reputation was his asset. His practice grew, and we soon moved to our house on Ware Road, with a huge garden.

Chapter 2

A NEW CHAPTER:
GROWING UP AND MEETING THE ALVAS

I passed out of school in May 1958 and joined Mount Carmel College, where my grand-aunt, Sister Imelda, was the Vice Principal. It was here that I honed my debating skills, winning every debate I participated in—much to the pride of my Principal and my father, who'd drive me to every debate, sit through it and watch me receive my prize. Thanks to my reputation, when Indira Gandhi (not yet Prime Minister) came to the college to address us, I was selected to present her with flowers, and was introduced as the 'ace debater'.

Mount Carmel College is situated on Palace Road, with the tall steel gates of the Mysore Maharaja's palace around the corner. Pandit Jawaharlal Nehru always stayed there when in Bangalore. He'd drive in an open sedan with a siren jeep and two security vehicles. The moment we heard the siren, we would dash out onto the road, leaving our lecturers staring in disbelief. The car would halt and we would surround it to grab Panditji's hands—even as he'd shake our hands, pinch our cheeks and pull our noses, before driving on. The especially lucky students would solemnly vow not to wash the hand he had shaken!

While Alan was preparing for his civil services exams in Bangalore, he became friends with Isobel Colaco, a beautiful, young Mangalorean teacher, the daughter of a retired senior railway officer. They would walk back from church every morning and would often be seen together. My parents kept cautioning him against making any commitment at such an early age. Alan, however, was a man in love, and before leaving for Japan, on his first posting in the Foreign Service, informed the family that he intended to marry her. He then persuaded my mother to go with him to Japan for a year.

In the year my mother was away, my life changed dramatically. I participated in a range of student activities, especially in the Catholic

Students' Union and, along the way, by a quirk of fate, met its dynamic all-India President.

We were attending a meeting of delegates to the state leadership camp to be held in Mysore during the Dussehra holidays. A slim, rather dark-complexioned newcomer happened to be addressing us, delivering an impressive speech. The Mount Carmel Unit President, my friend Eleanor, and I were sitting together and exchanging slips and an occasional word on the arrangements for the trip to Mysore. I saw the President give us a nasty look a couple of times to silence us.

When the meeting ended, we walked out, only to discover that my umbrella had disappeared. There was a lot of commotion, but it could not be traced. In the middle of this, a voice cut through: 'That comes of talking too much.'

It was the all-India President.

'Thank you,' I snapped back and walked out into the drizzle to catch an auto. I was more than upset with his remark. Back then, I did not know that the day's events would influence and change my life permanently.

For the President was none other than Niranjan Alva.

With his brilliant oratory, bubbling nationalistic fervour, and penchant for shervanis and bandhgalas—which happened to be quite a novelty in the student world of that time—Niranjan, or Niru as he was called, represented the new post-Independence ethos of the youth, as against the old-world approach of the Catholic establishment.

After the rather unpleasant first encounter in Bangalore, I met Niru at the Mysore leadership training camp, which he inaugurated with a most impressive speech, dressed in a white shervani. I was fascinated by his ideas and oratory, as were most of the delegates. We later went to the Dussehra exhibition where l bumped into him while he was accompanying his mother with an entourage of officials and security men. We were told that she was a Minister in Delhi. Niru, rather embarrassed, introduced the group to her and decided to join us for the rest of the evening.

Violet Alva, Niru's mother, was a short, smart Gujarati, with dark rings round her eyes and a smile that lit up her face. Dressed in a well-starched, white khadi saree, she appeared warm, friendly and without pretensions.

Niru and I subsequently met at student camps, at times by chance and sometimes by design. But it was essentially a courtship by correspondence which lasted over four years. There were quarrels, letters of apology, misunderstandings, greetings, birthday wishes, doubts and differences of opinion, besides long political discourses meant to educate me—all on paper—as Niru studied at Loyola College, Madras (now Chennai), and went on to work in Bombay (now Mumbai), while I continued studying in Bangalore.

One day, in March 1962, the unexpected happened. During an evening mass at the Cathedral church, at the communion rails, a chill went down my spine. I realized that Niru's father, Joachim Alva, was kneeling next to me. When I came out, he greeted me and said he would like to visit my parents. He took me home in his car, telling me that he knew my father from his school days in St Aloysius College.

My feet were cold and my hands trembled as I rang the doorbell. Carmine, our cook, opened the door. I seated him and rushed in to tell my parents. He chatted with them for a while, sharing old memories, and then, patting me on the back, left. Not surprisingly, my parents were left wondering why he had suddenly thought of them after all these years.

It was only when Niru later told me that his father had come across a couple of my letters in his room, and had asked if they had been left for him to see, that I put two and two together. Having checked us out, he told Niru he was impressed to see me at mass on a weekday! I seemed to have passed the first test.

In May 1962, I was at a seminar on 'The Emerging Catholic Woman' at Sophia College, Bombay; I had been invited as the General Secretary of AICUF (All India Catholic University Federation), and my mother had allowed me to go.

I spent a week with my aunts before and after the seven-day seminar. Niru, who was working in Bombay, would pick me up with his childhood friend, Jimmy Pinto, after office hours, and take me to Cuffe Parade or Marine Drive or Kemps Corner, where we would walk, have coffee, and sample chaat or ice creams. My aunts soon became suspicious and began asking veiled questions, which I would answer without hesitation—as General Secretary, AICUF, I was in the city for a seminar, and had to prepare for it!

A couple of days before I was to leave, I was out for lunch with Niru; it was a Sunday. In the restaurant, he suddenly blurted out, 'My mother wants to meet you. I want to take you home today!'

I was stunned. 'No question!' I replied. 'My parents know nothing about this. I cannot go without telling them.'

'There is nothing formal about this,' Niru pleaded. 'Baba [Joachim Alva] has told my mother about you and she asked me last night. I told her the truth. Please do not say no to me. I beg of you!'

I could not refuse.

So, I went with Niru and Jimmy. I was terrified, almost in tears. 'Please relax! She is such a lovely, informal, lovable lady!' said Jimmy. But I could not relax. Niru seemed just as nervous. We stared at each other but said nothing. When we reached Queen's Court, Niru rang the bell; the door opened. My heart was pounding.

It was a large hall-cum-dining room, with heavy, old-world furniture and a couple of paintings on the walls. Niru's mother was seated, reading a newspaper. 'Come, come, sit here!' she said, the moment I entered, while beaming at me. Before I could go up to her, Niru dashed into a corridor and disappeared behind the curtains. I liked his mother instantly. She was warm and charming. Niru later told me that his mother thought I was a 'pretty, unspoilt girl'. As for me, while I was happy to have met the Alva family, I had no idea what I was going to tell my parents!

I returned home that week and told my mother of my visit to Queen's Court and all that followed. There was no response, but no reprimand either. I was relieved. I seemed to be crossing the hurdles one by one.

In the meantime, I completed my graduation with a degree in economics and political science (though only with a second class). There was a family debate on the course I should pursue. If there was any consensus within the household, it was that Central College was a better place for girls than the Government Law College, which had a reputation for being a rather troublesome place. After much thought, I opted for English at Central College.

Then came a long lecture from Niru in a ten-page letter, telling me that I should go in for law as I was best suited for that profession. I changed my mind and decided to devote myself to law, which pleased my parents as well.

For someone who had been educated all along in institutions run by nuns, entering the Government Law College in July 1962 for an LLB (Bachelor of Law) degree was absolutely terrifying. In a class of 180 boys, we were all of fourteen girls, and we would cluster together in the first two rows, next to the door.

But with time, I adapted and settled down. I became popular with the staff and students. I participated in debates, mock Parliaments, assemblies and UN (United Nations) sessions of the university, always getting important 'portfolios'. I got elected to the students' union as a Joint Secretary. I also continued to climb the AICUF ladder with support from Niru's team at the headquarters.

Since classes were part-time, I took up a job in the convent school across the road where I had secured my SSLC, teaching 'Higher English' for an hour-and-a-half in the afternoons to the fifth and sixth forms (presently the eleventh and twelfth standards). There were only twelve students in each class and 1 enjoyed what I did, earning ₹200 a month, which paid for my fees, bus fare and books.

Around June 1962, the state government came out with a bill on minority educational institutions, which united all minority groups; they were vehemently against it. A silent march through the city followed, which culminated in a massive protest meeting in the heart of the city. I was one of the speakers. I made an emotional and fiery speech. My father shed tears of joy and pride when I left the stage, and my mother hugged me. The next day, I hit the headlines of both secular and Christian media outlets; 1 was called the 'new star on the horizon'. I had been 'noticed'. My initiation into public life in Bangalore had begun.

The war with China in 1962 ignited a patriotic spark in every Indian. There was massive mobilization of resources; money poured in from the rich and poor alike, and thousands of youth flocked to recruitment centres to join the defence forces. A university mobilization committee was set up in which I played a prominent role as Joint Secretary of the Law College Union.

I recall attending one of the big meetings in the university addressed by Niru's mother. She spoke with great zeal and confidence about our strength and ability to overcome this temporary military setback. One of the journalists covering the meeting intervened to ask, 'This is what the government will keep saying until the Chinese knock on the doors of Delhi. What will happen then?' She answered calmly, 'Every conqueror who reached Delhi settled down to become an Indian. There was no way any of them could return. In any case, India is too large and united to be conquered by anyone today.' There was nothing more to be said. That was the end of the meeting.

By mid-1962, Niru made it to the first batch of ten senior management trainees, after a rigorous selection process by DCM (Delhi Cloth Mills) in Delhi. He was thrilled; so were his parents. Due to this appointment, Niru failed to make it to Alan's wedding in September.

However, he was aware of the pressures on me to consider the many 'proposals' coming my way. So he decided to propose himself. One morning, in late August, when the house was full of relations, a letter came from Niru. I read it in the bathroom. Then I took my sister Joan aside and showed it to her. She was thrilled and hugged me. 'How will I tell Daddy?' I nervously asked. 'Don't worry, I will handle it!' she said, confidently. Dad was in his office room. Joan talked to him quietly and showed him the letter. By the time he had finished reading it, Joan had announced the news to the entire household, relations and all. While everyone congratulated me, my mother simply said, 'I had suspected something ever since I returned! I went with my son to keep him away from being hooked by a Japanese girl, but returned to find my daughter hooked instead!'

My father, after processing the contents of Niru's proposal letter, commented that this was precisely why he had been objecting to all those outstation camps! All the same, he seemed happy, especially because Niru was the son of Joachim Alva—a man he held in awe.

Since I had said 'yes' to Niru, his parents felt they should formally meet my parents. So they came. Niru also arrived for a long weekend. The formalities were completed over a family meal. It was decided that the engagement would be in Delhi on my twenty-first birthday in April 1963, with the wedding scheduled for the following May in Bangalore, after I completed my law course. Everyone was pleased.

Chapter 3

ANOTHER WORLD: TO DELHI

My parents and I travelled to Delhi for the engagement, which was a small but elegant affair on the lawns of 3, Ashoka Road, in Lutyens' Delhi. Niru was happy with his new job. Life seemed perfect, perhaps too perfect, for all at once there came a bolt from the blue. I realized something was awry only when I was taken to call on Morarji Desai (whom the family called Kako) as the prospective bahu of the house. He had brought both the Alvas into elective politics in Bombay. Baba and he had been in Yerwada Central Jail together for three-and-a-half long years during the freedom struggle.

Kako was seated for his meal—a silver plate with dry fruits, milk in a silver glass, some dal, dahi and fresh fruit. He received us with great affection and blessed me with the words, 'You must imbibe Joachim's courage and Violet's wisdom.' Then he turned to Niru and asked him what he was doing. Before Niru could answer, his father intervened, 'Your DCM "lalas" have turned the screws on him. They want him to leave a week after his engagement. This is what your capitalist culture brings!'

I was stunned. Kako turned to Niru again and asked what had happened. Niru explained that as part of their training, the senior management trainees were asked to prepare a report with suggestions for the unit they were assigned. Niru was working at the Daurala Sugar Mills. His report contained a chapter on the labour force at the factory which he felt was underpaid and exploited. He enumerated their grievances and suggested measures to improve their lot, claiming that a happier and satisfied workforce would enhance the atmosphere at the workplace, and increase production and profits. The old-fashioned, conservative management—headed by Bharat and Charat Ram—thought this was blasphemy. Niru was branded a communist and told that such recruits, despite their merits and background, were not acceptable in their organization.

'You have begun to talk like your father already,' Kako smiled wryly, scratching his bald head.

On our way back, there was stunned silence in the car. As we entered the gate, Niru's mother asked me, 'So now? Does the engagement stand? What will your parents say?'

'The engagement stands. I am marrying Niru, not his job. And please say nothing to my parents for now,' I pleaded.

We left for Bangalore soon after. My mother had noticed the change of mood in the house, but asked no questions till we had boarded the train. 'Is something wrong? Any misunderstanding? Why was Niru avoiding us over the last three days? Did we upset him?' I assured both her and my father that there was nothing wrong and slept most of the journey back.

All too soon, we were back in Bangalore, with visitors, friends and relations coming to congratulate me and get the 'gossip.' I was in no mood to meet anyone, worried about what Niru was going through.

Then came Niru's long letter, thanking me for having stood by him in his hour of crisis and giving me the news that he was back at work. Morarji Desai had called Charat Ram, given him a piece of his mind and ordered him to let Niru stay. While Niru felt humiliated at being called back and told, 'These are the Finance Minister's orders and we have to comply,' his father had insisted he go back—first, because he needed a job after getting engaged and second, because Morarjibhai had intervened and asked for Niru to be sent back to DCM. Subsequently, Niru was shifted to a new division.

In June 1963, the Prime Minister asked Niru's mother to head to Kerala as there were complaints that the E.M.S. Namboodiripad government was creating problems for minority institutions and the Congress was clamouring for its dismissal. She was asked to assess ground realities and report back. She took her daughter, Maya, and me with her. This was my first introduction to real politics, involving discussions and meetings with a variety of groups. It was Violet Alva's report that ultimately led to the dismissal of the first communist government in Kerala.

It is a strange coincidence that four decades later, I was sent (along with Congress General Secretary R.L. Bhatia) by the Congress President, Sonia Gandhi, to study the situation in Kerala after the Congress had lost every Parliamentary seat in the state in the 2004 elections. I will say more about this later.

With my final law exams done, the wedding loomed large. The Papal

Nuncio, His Eminence Ronald Knox, who later became Cardinal, flew down from Delhi to bless our nuptials on 24 May 1964 at the Holy Ghost Church. He was assisted by the Archbishop of Bangalore, Lourd Swamy (who also became a Cardinal later). It was the first marriage service in India to be conducted fully in English (as opposed to the traditional Latin) under the new dispensation following the Second Vatican Council.

There was one special guest in the front row with the Alva family. Dressed in a spotless white Kerala dhoti-kurta and angavastram was V.K. Krishna Menon, the renowned diplomat, statesman and Minister who had flown in from Bombay that afternoon to bless us. He did everything the others did during the service, even kneeling down. As the late Father Long, who conducted the service from the pulpit, later commented, 'I did something that neither Nehru nor the UN could do. I brought Krishna Menon down on his knees!' I especially recall one sentence from Krishna Menon's toast at the reception at the Glass House—'I am told the bride, like the groom, is a great orator; how that qualification will help a happy marriage I do not know!' On the family's insistence I also replied to the toast—breaking tradition. After the reception, Baba insisted that we thank Krishna Menon at his hotel. He kept talking as we sat listening—till Niru quietly pointed out that it was almost midnight on our wedding day. We always joke that we spent the best part of our wedding night with Krishna Menon.

Niru and I caught the train back to Delhi a couple of days later. It was a sad and tearful farewell to family and friends, and to Bangalore. We arrived in Delhi to the tragic news of Pandit Nehru's death. His message for our wedding was probably among the last he had signed. The whole family was at the station to greet us. As I entered the house, they blessed me and Mummy handed over a bunch of keys, telling me to run the house and look after the family.

Niru was back at work the next day. He was still unhappy at DCM but was biding his time till something better came along. I started settling into my new world, content staying home, attempting to cook from the recipes I had taken down from Carmine (sometimes successfully and sometimes with disastrous results), sewing and knitting. I joined various courses like interior decoration, Ikebana and international cooking at the YWCA (Young Women's Christian Association), and expanded my circle of friends as well. I had turned into a traditional bahu in the Alva household, with no intention of ever taking up a job or practising law.

Chapter 4

KEEPING HOME: THE BAHU

The next five years were among the happiest of my life. We lived at 3, Ashoka Road, with well-kept lawns and a doting staff. I was a happy homemaker, part of a nurturing joint family. Niret, our firstborn, whom we affectionately called Choku, arrived on 23 August 1965, and became the centre of my world. Petted and pampered, he was a bundle of joy, always smiling, full of energy. As days passed, I found myself totally immersed in my role as a mother, looking after my son.

However, soon I began to get bored with the routine; I was also lonely. Mummy tried to coax me to join a law firm and start legal practice. 'What a waste of a brilliant mind!' she often said when she caught me knitting or sewing. 'If educated and qualified girls do this, what will those in need of such jobs do?' At one of the dinners she hosted for important dignitaries, while gracefully acknowledging my cooking prowess, she said, 'Shall I be selfish and keep her at home or send her out to practise law? This is my dilemma!' Despite her persistent hints, I chose to stay at home like my mother and sisters had done. Later, I took up a part-time job at the newly set up co-operative store, Super Bazaar, as Special Assistant to the Chairman, L.C. Jain, and earned ₹300 a month. I oversaw Board meetings, prepared progress reports and supervised staff training. I gradually got involved in social activities—becoming Secretary of the Catholic Women's League; being elected a delegate from the Delhi Diocese to the Church in India conclave; helping organize the International Conference of Women Lawyers (Mummy was the President); and participating in the international conference against apartheid.

Mummy and I grew really close; taking long walks together in the evenings on the lawns of India Gate, or eating chaat from the family chaatwala on the steps of our residence. I admired her and learnt a lot from her. She was a loving mother, a devoted wife and a doting grandmother. Her ways were simple, and her principles, her guiding stars. I have always followed the advice she gave me: 'Get dressed for the day in such a way that you are ready to go anywhere...'

During those early years in Delhi, I cultivated some lasting friendships. One of them was with Mother Teresa. Back then, we grew a lot of vegetables as part of the 'Grow More Food' campaign. I used to drive to Mother Teresa's home in Old Delhi with extra produce. On one occasion, the sister in charge told me that Mother Teresa was around, then asked, 'Would you like to meet her?' I jumped at the opportunity. Mother, when I approached her, thanked and blessed me, placing her hand on my head. This was the beginning of a long and warm friendship that I have ever since cherished. When she was ill in hospital in Calcutta (now Kolkata), I flew with Rajivji and Sonia to see her. When I told her she must recover as she had much to do, she replied, 'You are the one to do that,' and blessed me. I had the unique privilege of flying with Prime Minister I.K. Gujral to pay homage to her when she died.

Another friend I made was Aung San Suu Kyi, who studied with Maya in the Convent of Jesus and Mary, and went to college in New Delhi. Her mother, Khin Kyi, the widow of the Burmese patriot Aung Sang, was Burma's (now Myanmar) Ambassador to India. The family lived at 24, Akbar Road, and Khin Kyi was a great friend of Mummy. We used to meet often, have Sunday lunches in each other's homes, and even go to the movies together. Years later, in 2012, on her visit to India to deliver the Jawaharlal Nehru Memorial Lecture, after receiving the Jawaharlal Nehru Award for International Understanding, I met Aung San Suu Kyi in Bangalore with the family to recall those happy days.

◆

Lal Bahadur Shastri died in January 1966 in Tashkent under what people claimed were 'mysterious circumstances'. Mummy had served as his Deputy in the Home Ministry from 1957 to 1962, and Shastri had been very fond of her. We attended his funeral carrying Choku along.

Indira Gandhi succeeded Shastri as Prime Minister, after having served in his Cabinet as Information and Broadcasting Minister. In 1966, Mummy was up for re-election to the Rajya Sabha. The leaders in Karnataka began creating hurdles, on the ground that husband and wife were cornering two seats to Parliament from the state. Fortunately, B. Basavalingappa, the fiery SC (scheduled caste) leader and a Minister of the state, was a great supporter. Despite the efforts made by some to sabotage her election, she made it. (Ironically, my fate would be no different in an election to the Rajya Sabha years later.) Mummy was re-elected as Deputy Chairperson of the Rajya Sabha for a second term, with glowing compliments paid by the Prime Minister and other leaders across the political spectrum. We watched the proceedings from the gallery with great pride. At that point, I had not the faintest premonition that, one day, I would sit in the same chair and conduct the proceedings of the Rajya Sabha as a member of the Panel of Presiding Officers!

In the election of 1967, the Congress' strength depleted significantly to 283 from 361 in 1962.[1] Internal dissent surfaced, and there was general unrest due to the drought caused by failed monsoons. Indiraji, though in command, was hemmed in by a powerful group headed by S. Nijalingappa, the party's President, and the old-timers popularly known as the 'Syndicate'. The Congress, under Kamaraj Nadar, was routed for the first time in 1967 in Tamil Nadu, with the Dravida Munnetra Kazhagam (DMK) forming the government. In Kerala, the same year, the Communist Party of India-Marxist (CPM), under E.M.S. Namboodiripad, was voted to power. In Bengal, too, the Congress was voted out, to be replaced by the United Front. Overwhelmed by food shortages, Indiraji was compelled to seek US food assistance under Public Law 480[2] under humiliating conditions. (It was then that she declared, 'We will never beg for food again' and launched the 'Green Revolution'.) To complicate matters, the Indian rupee had been devalued in June 1966. The situation seemed dim and gloomy for the party and the country.

Morarji Desai, the Finance Minister, close to the Syndicate, was not happy playing second fiddle to the pro-Socialist Prime Minister. But Baba had come out openly in support of Indira Gandhi's progressive steps in his magazine, *Forum*, much to the annoyance of Nijalingappa, a Desai supporter.

---

[1]See Indian General Election results, in <http://www.elections.in/parliamentary-constituencies/1967-election-results.html> and <http://www.elections.in/parliamentary-constituencies/1962-election-results.html>, accessed on 14 April 2016.

[2]President Dwight D. Eisenhower of the US signed into law the Agricultural Trade Development and Assistance Act of 1954, commonly known as Public Law 480, PL-480 or Food for Peace. This permitted the President to authorize the shipment of surplus commodities to 'friendly' nations, either on concessional or grant terms. See Office of the Historian, US Department of State, in <https://history.state.gov/milestones/1961-1968/pl-480>, accessed on 14 April 2016.

So, in the 1967 elections, Nijalingappa denied him a ticket from his Lok Sabha constituency of Karwar—a constituency in coastal Karnataka that he had won thrice. Indiraji was helpless. However, soon after the elections, she sent Dinesh Singh, then the External Affairs Minister and part of her inner circle, to enquire from Baba if he would like to be Ambassador or a nominated member of the Rajya Sabha. Baba chose the latter, entering the House in which his wife was the Deputy Chairperson. On one occasion, when he refused to pay heed to her repeated call for silence in the House, Bhupesh Gupta of the Communist Party of India (CPI) is said to have admonished him, telling him she was the 'boss' in this House. 'Here or at home, I am the "boss",' was his answer.

Both Houses of Parliament were going through turbulent times. Often, Mummy would come home exhausted and upset after a harrowing day in the chair. Raj Narain, a lifelong socialist, was a law unto himself. On a couple of occasions he had to be named and carried out of the House, even as he hit and kicked the staff.

The AICC met on 10 July 1969 at the Glass House in Bangalore, where our wedding reception had been held. It was a historic session during which Indiraji presented a manifesto for radical reforms, which included bank nationalization and the abolition of privy purses. The battle lines were drawn. Mummy and Baba were clearly with Indiraji, who also received the overwhelming support of MPs (Members of Parliament) and party leaders.

After the session, Morarji Desai, who was opposed to the radical reforms agenda, was shifted out of the Ministry of Finance, following which he resigned. Subsequently, there came an ordinance nationalizing fourteen commercial banks. Other reforms followed.

President Zakir Husain had died suddenly on 3 May 1969. Vice President V.V. Giri, also a socialist trade union leader, became Acting President, with Mummy moving in soon after, as the Officiating Chairperson of the Rajya Sabha. Now arose the question of the new President. The Syndicate chose Neelam Sanjiva Reddy, who had been the Speaker of the Lok Sabha, but Indiraji opted for V.V. Giri, whom she could trust. When the Syndicate refused to accept her nominee, she asked for a conscience vote.[3] V.V. Giri

---

[3]A conscience vote allows legislators to vote according to their own personal views or conscience rather that according to an official line laid down by their political party.

won the election in August 1969. This signalled an open challenge to the party hierarchy by the Prime Minister. A split became inevitable.

Then came the question of filling the post of Vice President. Mummy, prior to accepting the post of Officiating Chairperson, had served as Deputy Chairperson of the Rajya Sabha under three Presidents/Acting Presidents—S. Radhakrishnan, Zakir Husain and V.V. Giri. She now set her sights on the post of Vice President, even as support for her cut across party lines.

But when the announcement for Vice President came, Mummy was left heartbroken; it was G.S. Pathak, the nondescript Governor of Karnataka and a former Judge of the Allahabad High Court, whom Indiraji chose. It was presumed that Mummy and Baba's proximity to Morarji Desai had gone against her, besides Indiraji's reluctance to let another woman overtake her in protocol.

Mummy kept calm, continuing to chair the Joint Parliamentary Committee (JPC) on bank nationalization and submitting its report to Parliament.

Then, on 17 November 1969, she resigned from her post, returning home in an auto, refusing the official car. Though she was subsequently offered the post of Governor by the Prime Minister, she refused to accept it, saying she was 'neither a discredited nor a doddering politician'.

On 19 November, during the formal farewell, glowing tributes were paid to her in the House by Indira Gandhi and the leaders of all parties. She presided over a public function to mark Indiraji's birthday that day, and praised her leadership and courage. That was Mummy's last public appearance.

Chapter 5

SHE IS GONE

It was the morning of 20 November. Niru and l were in Bangalore for the birth of our second son, Nikhil. At around 9 a.m., I received a call from Gopinath, Mummy's Private Secretary from Delhi. 'I have some shocking news. Where is Niranjan sir?' he asked. Half asleep, I presumed there had been some kind of mishap—Niru had left that morning by train.

'Why? What has happened?' I shouted back.

'Madam is dead,' he said in a low voice.

'Which madam? Who?' I asked, my voice choked with suspense.

'Madam Alva. She died in her sleep. The doctors have just declared her dead,' he replied.

I dropped the phone in shock and called out to Mummy. I do not know what happened next; I blacked out. On regaining consciousness, I cried till my tears ran dry. My world had collapsed. Mummy had been my friend, philosopher and guide, and I adored her. Indeed, after Maya and Chittu (Chittaranjan, Niru's brother) had left to study abroad, we had been the only ones at home. We would spend long hours in each other's company. And now, Mummy was gone—without a farewell—on her thirty-second wedding anniversary...

We learned that the previous day, Mummy had come back tired and emotionally upset after presiding over the meeting to mark Indiraji's birthday.

At night she had phoned—asking how Nikhil's christening went, seeking news about Niru's departure and speaking to Choku. We wished both Mummy and Baba for their wedding anniversary, as Niru was to leave early the next morning. Mummy seemed as she always did—full of life.

Soon after, she had welcomed a stream of visitors, including a group of senior Karnataka leaders, who wished to discuss the emerging political crisis. Once they left, she had a cup of milk and went to bed. Baba was alone with her in the house, with Eppa—the maid. Late in the night, she got up with a splitting headache and called out to Baba. The doctors were called in. Dr Coroli of the Lady Wellington Hospital showed up with a colleague, examined her, said there was nothing serious, gave her a tablet to help her sleep and left. Baba slept on the bed by her side.

Early in the morning, Baba went to Mummy and kissed her, wishing her a happy anniversary. But there was no response. He tried to wake her, shook her, but to no avail. Gopinath and the doctors were summoned. But it was too late. She was dead. She had suffered a massive brain haemorrhage. Many questions were asked: What was the tablet that was administered to her? Why was she not rushed to the hospital for emergency care? Why was she put to sleep when she complained of a severe headache? But there were no answers.

By the time I recovered from the shock, our home was a madhouse. Neighbours, relations, friends and journalists thronged the premises, hugging me, weeping, asking the same set of questions and offering their sympathies—none of which I wanted. I just wanted to be left alone. Everyone advised me not to travel to a cold Delhi, given my weak condition with a eleven-day-old baby in my arms. But I had made up my mind. I had to go; I *would* go. There was no one with Baba; Maya and Chittu were abroad, and Niru was on a train. I was the only one who could offer strength and support to the shattered family. It was my duty. Besides, Choku and I had to see Mummy a last time.

So, with whatever I could put together, and with Daddy accompanying me, we flew that evening by the only flight from Bangalore.

As we reached the house in Delhi, the same story we had witnessed in Bangalore unfolded. People, known and unknown, friends and associates, began milling around, getting in and out of the hall where Mummy lay. There were all the signs of a Christian funeral—a cross, flickering candles by the altar, white flowers and wreathes and the smell of incense. I stood at the door with my two children, unable to move.

Then I saw Baba slowly rise from his chair by Mummy's side. I approached him, and put Nikhil in his arms. He looked at the boy, tears streaming down his face. 'She would have lived if she had these children here,' he sobbed.

The visitors and mourners kept coming all through the night. The President, Vice President, Indiraji, Cabinet Ministers, opposition leaders, Ambassadors—they all arrived and had to be met. Indiraji, looking quite shaken, came again in the morning and spent some time with us. She returned for the funeral in the evening, as did the President.

Niru was picked up at Madras station and flown to Delhi. He arrived late at night, shattered. Chittu and Maya arrived in the morning. Their presence provided us succour. Despite their immense sorrow, they received guests calmly, met the VIPs and worked out all arrangements.

Parliament was adjourned on the day of her funeral. The carriage carrying her body went through the gates of Parliament House, with a brief halt for wreathes to be placed. There was a beautiful service in the Cathedral Church of the Redemption, a Protestant cathedral, since Mummy belonged to the Church of England.

The next morning, the papers were full of columns detailing Mummy's contribution to the freedom struggle and the nation, to Parliament and the Congress, and to the women's movement. There were anecdotes detailing her life as a journalist and a lawyer. There were editorials describing 'this tiny woman with a heart large enough to embrace the world'. There were excerpts of condolence speeches in Parliament and messages from different parts of the country and the world. Almost all the articles hinted that it was the refusal to recognize her service and loyalty, and the denial of the post of Vice President, that had led to her untimely death at the age of sixty-two.

In the meantime, Niru was at a crossroads. He had been unhappy at DCM, and had decided to move. He applied to the Fertilizer Corporation of India (FCI), which had advertised a host of posts. While interview letters went to several people he knew, he failed to get a call. On enquiring, he was told that there was a secret understanding between DCM and FCI that they would not pick each other's officers! Baba, now recovering in hospital from a heart attack, was livid on hearing this.

As luck would have it, the Minister of Chemicals and Fertilizers, Dr Triguna Sen—a close friend of the family—came to visit him. Baba spoke to Dr Sen of the injustice done to Niru by FCI despite the fact that he fulfilled all required qualifications. Within a week, Niru received a call and was interviewed. He accepted his appointment letter as Sales Manager, with a posting in Bangalore! The light at the end of the tunnel was at last in sight.

And thus began a new life. We prepared to move—packing, shifting and organizing the new house (28, Rajendra Prasad Road) allotted to Baba, training and briefing Eppa, etc. In the middle of all this, Niru received a strange letter from an old associate, with a prediction from his astrologer friend in Barabanki, Uttar Pradesh: 'Your late mother will be reborn. You will have a daughter this year.' We were horrified. 'This man and his astrologer are mad!' Niru declared and we forgot all about it.

We left for Bangalore by train with mixed feelings. As I sat in my berth in the train, while Niru and the boys slept, memories of the past came crowding back—my childhood; my marriage; my new life as a wife and bahu in the Alva household; my exposure to the glamour of Lutyens' Delhi; the arrival of our firstborn, Choku; my special connection with Mummy, my guide and role model, who I regretted leaving at a crucial time, and whose loss pained me deeply; the birth of Nikhil after years of waiting; and now, this shift back to Bangalore.

The security of the past was gone. We had no home of our own; no savings to fall back on. Worse, Niru had been diagnosed with an unexplained growth in his chest cavity during a routine check-up, which we had kept a secret. What could it be? Who would we go to for guidance, without causing panic in both our families?

There were so many questions: Would Niru settle into his new job in the public sector easily? Would Baba, who was still unwell, manage, with only Chittu and Eppa to care for him? How would I cope with this spate of changes?

I looked out of the window of the speeding train into the darkness outside. I saw my role clearly. I had to help Niru and the boys adjust to their new lives in fresh surroundings by serving as their link to Bangalore. I had to gift Choku, shaken by Mummy's death, a sense of security—reassuring him with promises of the joys that awaited him in Bangalore—grandparents, cousins, a wonderful school and, best of all, a dog. I had to find a way of cheering him while my heart ached within.

Was I strong enough for this new life when I was emotionally and physically drained? 'Help me, Lord. In my weakness, give me the strength I need,' I pleaded. And suddenly, up in the sky, I saw the full moon emerge out of the clouds. 'This is a sign,' I told myself. Things would work out.

It was June 1970. I was just twenty-eight years old. I had to transform from a bahu cocooned in the shadows of the Alva household, to a woman at the threshold of a new life, with fresh responsibilities, struggles and challenges.

The Indira Gandhi Years

Chapter 6

HITS AND MISSES: CLIMBING THE RUNGS OF THE CONGRESS LADDER

Niru joined FCI. He began to enjoy his work after the stifling 'babudom' of DCM. We bought a new Fiat car with a company loan—our first wholly independent acquisition. Niru wished to have a home of his own, not wanting to be a 'ghar-jamai', so we spent most weekends house-hunting. We finally bought a three-bedroom house under construction on Milton Street with an LIC (Life Insurance Corporation) loan. Manira, our daughter, arrived on 6 January 1971, as predicted!

My father and Niru were keen that I start practising law in the family office. So I began spending my mornings there assisting my father, only engaging with chamber work. I refused to go to court. The petty corruption in the lower court offices used to annoy me. Everyone had to be tipped—'mamool' they called it. Whether a document copy had to be procured, or a sale deed registered, a katha transferred, or a refund released—everything came at a price. Since I refused to fall in line, my papers kept getting delayed. Eventually, the clients requested my father to send one of the clerks instead of me, as they were prepared to pay!

About this time Baba, on one of his visits to Bangalore, took us to meet Basavalingappa, a Dalit leader and a close friend, as also D. Devaraj Urs, the State Congress President. They both suggested that I become a member of the party. And so I did in 1970, and became active in the party. I was made President of the Bharatinagar Block Congress Committee—the only woman in the state to hold that post.

Then came the Bangladesh war. The support for Indiraji's decision to assist (what was then) East Pakistan was instantaneous—all parties backed her. And when victory came, she was hailed as 'Durga' not only by the Bengalis but also by the entire nation. It was, therefore, not surprising that the Congress swept the General Election of March 1971 with 352 seats in Parliament.[4]

Fresh on the back of the resounding victory of the 1971 Lok Sabha elections, when elections for thirteen state assemblies, including Karnataka, were announced, I was keen to contest from Bharathi Nagar in Bangalore, where we lived. The sitting MP was K. Hanumanthaiah, a veteran Vokkaliga leader. Baba had taken me to meet him and Kollur Mallappa, a member of the Central Parliamentary Board. Both had blessed me, saying Indiraji was looking for young new faces, and she would definitely be happy to have me contest. In December 1971, while we were visiting Delhi, Baba also took me to meet Uma Shankar Dikshit, the Treasurer of the Congress and a trusted advisor to Indiraji, and Chandrajit Yadav, the General Secretary in charge of Karnataka. Both of them assured their support, advising me to quietly start working in the constituency.

When the time came, my name was cleared at all levels in the state. It appeared in the first list published in the local newspapers. Congress workers began to collect in our house. Posters were drafted and were ready for printing. Everything seemed to be on track.

Then came the bombshell. My name was substituted a week before the last day for nominations by that of C. Sharada, who had served as Secretary to Yashoda Dasappa, a veteran Congresswoman and social worker. She had not been active in the party, so the nomination remained a mystery, until it turned out that Eva Vaz, who belonged to my community and was the State Convener of the women's front, did not want another Christian woman to contest as she did not want a competitor for a Minister's berth. Vaz and Dasappa had flown to Delhi, met Indiraji, and told her that I had just come out of hospital with a ten-day baby in arms, which made it impossible for me to campaign. So Indiraji had directed the change, and Sharada's name was announced.

We were stunned. Baba was hopping mad. 'She seems determined to finish the Alva women!' was his immediate response. He asked to meet her, rushing from Bombay to Delhi the next day. But he was too late—Indiraji had left for Calcutta to see Sheikh Mujibur Rahman off to Dacca (now Dhaka), after his release from a jail in Pakistan.

Thus two days were lost. When Indiraji returned, she met Baba. It

---

[4]See Statistical Report on General Elections, 1971, in <http://eci.nic.in/eci_main/StatisticalReports/LS_1971/Vol_I_LS71.pdf>, accessed on 15 April 2016.

was the last day for nominations. He is said to have blown his top. 'You killed my wife by knocking her out of the Vice President's chair, and now you want to destroy my daughter-in-law also? What do you have against us?' he thundered. Indiraji was unfazed. 'I was told she had a baby ten days ago,' she explained. 'It is a lie,' he replied. She immediately phoned Chandrajit Yadav and asked him to announce my name for Udupi, which was still open. Baba thanked her and returned home.

Having waited for news from Delhi for the whole week, I had given up hope. To avoid the unending stream of concerned party workers and supporters, I decided to get out with the kids. When I returned home, I was told there had been frantic calls for me from Baba. I got through to him by 12 noon.

Baba ordered me to get to Udupi and file my nomination. But where was the time? The distance between the two cities was over 400 kilometres! We went to Devaraj Urs, who, too, had no idea how we could make it there on time, and directed me to the Chief Election Officer. It was now past 1 p.m. I was told that the only option was to get someone on the Udupi electoral rolls to propose my name and submit my forms.

Anxiously, we got through to a friend in Manipal, and gave him all the necessary instructions and information. It was 2 p.m. by then. He did not have an extract of his roll, and had to run around to get it. He reached the election office, with filled forms. But he was 15 minutes too late. We had lost out, thanks to my not staying at home that morning. Manorama Madhwaraj, who had filed her nomination, and had been awaiting final clearance, became the official candidate.

It was God's will. My political career would have taken a totally different turn had I contested that Assembly election in March 1972 or succeeded in my attempt for an MLC (Member of Legislative Council) seat a month later.

When Indiraji received the news that I had been left out of the candidates' list on account of facts being misrepresented to her, she was upset. As 'compensation', she had me replace Eva Vaz as the State Convener of the women's front.

Maragatham Chandrasekar, who had taken over as the General Secretary in charge of Karnataka, arrived in Bangalore to review the campaign. All reports from Bharathi Nagar were negative—workers were not prepared to campaign and the candidate remained helpless. To add insult to injury, she put me in charge of the constituency. Much against my will, I had to accompany the candidate and address meetings which were poorly attended. So we decided to cover the constituency standing in an open jeep. Everywhere people kept asking me, 'Why are you not contesting? Why has "thoong moonji" ('sleepy face', as Sharada was called) been put up?' I had no answers.

The elections over, the results came in. While the Congress (I) under Devaraj Urs swept the state, Bharathi Nagar remained one of the big losses. Eva Vaz had succeeded in her plan. She became the only woman Minister in the government under the Chief Ministership of Devaraj Urs. (Urs himself had not contested.)

I continued my work in the women's wing. The by-election from Hunsur to elect Devaraj Urs to the Assembly was an exciting event. Party workers, Ministers and MLAs (Members of Legislative Assembly) descended in their thousands; it was a festival. We ate in the local hotels or in the homes of our workers. Everywhere we went, I was mistaken for one of Urs' daughters. I was told not to deny it. Devaraj Urs was elected by a huge margin, as expected. There was jubilation everywhere, with receptions to greet him.

◆

Two important events took place in Bangalore in 1974. One was the silver jubilee of Mount Carmel College, my alma mater. The Karnataka Governor was the chief guest. I was invited to speak as a former student. I seemed to have made an impression, as the Governor enquired who I was. He congratulated me during the tea that followed.

The second significant event was a conference Devaraj Urs organized in Bangalore to focus on the upliftment of the weaker sections of society. An Organizing Committee was set up, with me as one of the Secretaries of the South Zone's backward classes, SC/STs (scheduled castes and tribes) and minorities' federation. Kemparaj Urs, the Chief Minister's brother, was the convener. The conference, held at the Glass House, was a thundering success. Many AICC stalwarts and leaders of the Congress in the Southern states participated.

The highlight was the inaugural session, with Indiraji as the chief guest. I was one of those chosen to speak, and was predictably nervous. I delivered my speech in English and emphasized the importance of social justice and the need to reach out to the county's neglected sections—the poor, women, minorities and SC/STs.

It was a six-minute speech. But it changed my political fortune. Devaraj Urs was pleased and Indiraji was impressed. On her way to her car, she stopped, patted me and said, 'Well done!'

Devaraj Urs tried to tell her who I was, but she interrupted him saying, 'I know.' Then, with a fleeting smile, she departed.

That day, Indiraji is said to have mentioned my speech at lunch at Raj Bhavan. The Governor, Mohan Lal Sukhadia, in turn, agreed with her, praising my performance at the Mount Carmel celebrations. He is supposed to have said, 'She has talent and promise, which should be nurtured.'

The Governor's comments stayed with India's Prime Minister. For, a couple of months later, when the Rajya Sabha seats from Karnataka were to be decided, Indiraji remembered me, though not my full name. The little she recollected was enough to change the direction of my life.

◆

John, my younger brother, had returned from the US in June 1970 with an MA (Master of Arts) in International Affairs from Columbia University. The family was keen that he have a go at the All India Services (AIS) and follow his brother to the Foreign Service; John, on the other hand, had plans to go back to America. Under considerable pressure, he finally decided to appear for the exam—starting long hours of study that aggravated a back injury, which necessitated surgery and a body plaster for weeks. Studying for the exams ended right there. At the end of September, while still in a plaster, he was taken by my mother, Niru and me to Mangalore for a holiday and a wedding in the family, where he saw the pretty Meena Pinto of the famed Pinto tiles family. John and Meena were married in Mangalore in February 1972. In the meantime, John had joined the Tata Administrative Services.

◆

Even as my political career saw ups and downs, my personal life saw challenges I had least anticipated. The Budget session of 1971 heard questions in Parliament about FCI selling imported fertilizers above stipulated prices in the South-western region; the corporation was charged with black marketing. The Minister of Fertilizers, Dev Kant Barooah, without ascertaining facts, bowed to the farmers' lobby and announced in Parliament that he would order a Central Bureau of Investigation (CBI) inquiry into the matter. The truth was that the corporation faced huge arrears from farmers who had been given credit to popularize Sufala, a new indigenous fertilizer. So, when the imported fertilizer became available, the arrears due from the farmers were added in instalments to the cost of the new fertilizer. Some farmers, who were compelled to pay their dues, complained to their MPs, who created a furore in the House.

Worse, honest marketing officers of the South-western regional office—who had collected crores of rupees of bad debts by cheque for the corporation at the behest of the top management and the Board—now found themselves under the CBI scanner, with their integrity questioned. The CBI could not find anything to pin them down with, but as is customary with CBI and government inquiries, the harassment continued unabated. The inquiry started in Delhi, shifted to Bombay, the company headquarters, in mid-1971, with Bangalore and Hyderabad offices investigated in mid-1972.

Then started Niru's nightmare—long hours of questioning in our sitting room and in the office, and a scrupulous examination of bank accounts, tour bills, house and car purchase agreements, even club receipts. There were whispers in the club, in the bank, among friends and colleagues, that the Alvas were under investigation. The new house, the car, the fridge and radiogram—all bought over time through hire, purchase or loans, became suspect. Not a scrap of evidence could be found against us, but till the truth could be established, we found ourselves defending the honest acquisition of each of our possessions.

About this time, Niru had to undergo surgery for the growth in the chest cavity which kept developing. Though it was a traumatic period, it ended well—it was his liver that had pierced his diaphragm and moved into his chest cavity. Niru returned home for recuperation from the CMC (Christian Medical College) Hospital in Vellore. Then something very unusual happened. FCI had given Niru extraordinary medical leave for the operation as the diagnosis had been 'suspected malignant growth in the chest cavity'. When the post-operative reports came, FCI ruled that the ailment did not fall under its list of health conditions that permitted such medical leave. As a result, FCI wanted him to rejoin duty immediately or stay on leave without pay. It was unbelievable! But there was a bigger shock awaiting us. Unable to find any evidence of corruption in the transactions of FCI's Southern region, yet unwilling to close the inquiry, the ministry, to satisfy the farmers' lobby, ordered a general reshuffle of all the officers of the region. Niru was posted to Varanasi. He could not possibly comply and went on leave. Promptly, his salary was stopped.

We did not tell anyone of the situation we were in. I hardly earned anything from my law practice. So, each month, I would go to the Russell Market Square and quietly dispose of a wedding gift to run the house. Our electricity was cut because we had forgotten that FCI was no longer paying for it. Those were difficult times. But we survived.

I finally told Baba about Niru's transfer to Varanasi and the 'leave without pay' option that we had taken. He was stunned. He intervened, and on health grounds, got Niru's transfer changed to Delhi. So, in January 1974, Niru shifted to the capital to stay with Baba, hoping that it would only be a temporary posting. Little did we know that God had other plans.

◆

My capacity to sleep has been a family joke. And, strangely, the most significant events of my life are connected with my sleeping hours.

It was February 1974. I was in my parent's home with the children (when Niru moved to Delhi, we had put our home on rent). It was past midnight when the phone rang in the hall. I rushed out, as I was always worried about Niru driving at night. The voice at the other end, however, was unfamiliar: 'Congratulations, Margaret. You are one of the party candidates for the Rajya Sabha election.' I was confused as I had neither applied for nor sought a Rajya Sabha seat at that stage. I refused to believe the news.

'This is hardly the time for a practical joke,' I told the caller.

'Margaret, I am Ananthakrishnan, the Mayor. Do you think I would joke with you at this time of night? I am sitting at the PTI (Press Trust of India) office. Your name is the first on the ticker. Please believe me.'

I was shocked. 'I am sorry, Mr Ananthakrishnan,' I said. 'Please forgive me, but I still cannot believe it. I do not know how this has happened.' Then, too confused to pull my thoughts together, I abruptly added, 'Thank you and good night.'

I rang Niru, who said he knew nothing about the matter, and that he would call me in the morning. I spent a restless night. In the morning, I saw my face staring out of the front pages of the newspapers. The phone calls started pouring in. I did not know what to say. I was shocked, terrified and, most of all, unhappy about what was to happen to me—this meant a drastic change in my life, not least because I'd have to shift to Delhi again.

What was I getting into at thirty-one years of age?

Everyone else, though, was delighted. Baba called to say that the news made him more than happy, and told me to thank Devaraj Urs and seek his blessings and support.

When I met Urs, he said, 'Don't thank me. Go to Delhi and thank the lady. It is her decision.'

'I did not ask for this, sir. I wanted to be here. You remember my request to you to get my husband back to Bangalore on deputation?' I replied.

'Well, instead of bringing Niranjan here, we are sending you to him,' he smiled. He gave instructions to his staff to assist me with all nomination formalities and wished me success.

Hectic days followed. I met every member of the Assembly, both from the Congress and from the opposition, to seek their support. A meeting of the Legislature Party was called, all party candidates introduced and papers filed.

We then learnt that M.S. Gurupadaswamy, the Congress (O) candidate, had decided to challenge my age—he claimed that I was under thirty years.

My family was away at our village, Shirva, to attend my aunt's funeral. Who could get my birth certificate from Mangalore at such short notice? I went to my old school, R.T.C. Girls High School, and requested them for help. It was a Saturday morning, but they opened the office and, after a long search, retrieved the old school register which documented my high school exam entries of 1958. They gave me an extract which showed my date of birth as 14 April 1942. With that piece of evidence, Gurupadaswamy's claims were overruled.

The election that followed was managed smoothly by Devaraj Urs; he had his own unique strategy for managing 'secret ballots' that ensured 100 per cent compliance of the whip. I wore my mother-in-law's khadi mustard saree with a black border (as a tribute to her) and stood outside the voting booth, greeting each MLA. Baba and Niru had come down from Delhi to be there with me.

At 5 p.m., the results were out. I had won.

I could not believe that it had actually happened. I was an MP at the age of thirty-one, having spent only ₹200 as a refundable deposit.

When we got home, there were family, friends, relations, well-wishers and party workers in their hundreds, waiting with flowers, sweets and good wishes. Dinner was laid out for everyone. It was a moment of thanksgiving and remembrance of all those who had helped me reach there. Celebrations and receptions followed.

Then the packing started all over again. Niru was on transfer—so all our belongings could go at FCI cost. The furnished house had already been rented out. Whatever had to be sent, with the car, went in a wagon.

We were back on the train to Delhi in March 1974, almost four years after we had left in June 1970. Our lives had changed all over again. For me, it was a new world opening up…a leap into the unknown.

Chapter 7

A YOUNG WOMAN IN THE HOUSE:
THE PRE-EMERGENCY YEARS

I entered Parliament in April 1974—among the youngest to be elected to the Rajya Sabha. There were loud cheers and some desk-thumping when my name was called. Bhupesh Gupta, the doyen of the Rajya Sabha, stood up to welcome the 'daughter-in-law of the House'.

I settled down to life as an MP quite easily. Baba introduced me to Pranab Mukherjee, one of Indiraji's most trusted lieutenants; Om Mehta, Minister for Parliamentary Affairs and a powerful aide of the Prime Minister; and several other friends and colleagues of his. I was the only first-time MP to be allotted the small bungalow in which Baba lived, at 28, Rajendra Prasad Road. I was told by the Chairman of the House Committee that this was at Indiraji's suggestion, as 'Madam does not want to disturb Mr Alva'.

Within Parliament, there were many stalwarts such as Chandra Shekhar, Mohan Dharia, I.K. Gujral, Atal Bihari Vajpayee, Piloo Mody, C.N. Annadurai and Purabi Mukherjee. While it was undoubtedly an education and a pleasure listening to them, I was initially so nervous when I saw the political crowd in Central Hall that I avoided going there. I had a seat on the last bench with three others—a Sikh from Punjab, a Muslim from Kashmir and a Hindu from Himachal Pradesh. We were referred to as the 'secular bench'. Here, I'd sit for long hours with the rule book in my hand, noting the references of senior leaders to the rules, the points of order, etc., and listening to debates. The early days were of learning, watching, listening, absorbing and understanding the rules of the game.

Everyone around—the MPs, the House staff, the watch and ward—treated me with great affection and were very protective. The women MPs, particularly Sushila Adivarekar, Aziza Imam and Pratibha Singh, befriended me from the day I entered the House. On seeing me in white khadi every day, they commented, 'Why do you come looking like a young widow? You must wear coloured sarees!' They got my white sarees printed, so I was in for a complete makeover from the next session!

At home, there were problems to be sorted out. The boys were in a new school with few friends in the neighbourhood. They missed Bangalore and would march around the house with little placards, shouting, 'Dirty Delhi, dirty Delhi, let's go back'. Helping them settle in, dropping them to school and picking them up, and sending them to Bal Bhavan for the afternoons, attending to Baba's special needs, keeping Manira occupied and cared for at home while Niru was at work, kept me on my toes from morning to night. The weekends were spent grocery shopping for the week, cleaning and teaching the boys who had missed their first term. I was driver, cook, cleaner, teacher, MP and hostess all rolled into one, with little time for myself.

Eventually, my initial nervousness in the House faded. While my early silence in the Rajya Sabha had given the impression that I was no speaker, I had the opportunity to prove myself towards the end of the first session.

The railway strike, spearheaded by George Fernandes and supported clandestinely by Socialist International, was playing havoc across the country. The movement of foodgrains and essential commodities was affected, sending prices soaring. The Constitution (33rd Amendment) Bill to amend Articles 101 and 190 (dealing with the right of a member of either a House of Parliament or a State Legislature to resign) was listed. Om Mehta, then the Minister for Parliamentary Affairs, casually asked me if I would like to speak. I gladly agreed. I went to the Parliament library and scanned material to prepare for the debate. Even as I sat immersed in the material I had gathered, Om Mehta seemed to grow increasingly unsure of my capacity to speak; he came to me twice to offer an exit.

'Sir,' I finally said, 'I am fine. Please do not make me nervous. Have faith in me'.

My maiden speech was applauded by all sections of the House. Om Mehta and many senior leaders congratulated me. Purabi Mukherjee, who was in the chair, got someone else in and came to hug me, saying, 'You were brilliant.'

At last, I had established myself as an orator. I was asked to open debates and speak on many important subjects during the turbulent days that followed. The press gallery began taking note of me, prominently reporting my interventions and speeches. More confident now, I started going to Central Hall regularly, which helped me enlarge my circle of friends.

Over the next twenty-four years, I moved from the backbench to the Treasury benches, from the government to the opposition and on to the panel of Vice Chairmen presiding over sessions. I spearheaded discussions on a range of subjects, including the need to change the character of our army to make it an integrated national army, the Patton tanks scam (more in Chapter 14) and why the informal banking system had to be reformed. I defended the Amul Cooperative and questioned the continuation of the Concordat (a treaty between the Vatican and Portugal) for church appointments in Goa. I challenged the Morarji Desai government on so many issues that finally he told me in the House, rather acerbically, 'I wish you had the wisdom to match your speaking capacity.' I held the distinction of causing the resignations of Ministers of the Union government—among them P.C. Sethi and C.P.N. Singh. As a Minister I moved bills, defended the government and championed the cause of women. I joined or led Parliamentary delegations, and I managed the House from the chair, and later, as Parliamentary Affairs Minister. Gradually, I became a known and respected face in the political circles of Delhi.

◆

In the early days, among other things, I raised important issues during Question Hour, joining the pool of women MPs filing questions. This created an unexpected problem for me. Rajni Kumar, the Chairperson of Springdales School, approached me with a simple question, 'Why are you after my school? What do you have against us?'

I was shocked. 'Why do you ask?' I enquired.

Then came her story. Our pool of questions in Parliament were repeatedly seeking details about her school—the acquisition of land, admissions, etc.—for which she had to furnish answers to the Rajya Sabha Secretariat. I knew nothing of the school. I apologized, promising to look into why and how this had happened.

Upon investigating further, I discovered that the person in the Rajya Sabha Secretariat, whom we were paying to draft, file and follow-up on our pool questions, had been repeatedly demanding seats from the school management. When Rajni Kumar discovered that the seats were going for a 'price', she refused to help. This started the incriminating questions from the women's pool.

I promptly withdrew from the pool and began filing my own questions. Rajni Kumar and I became friends, and have worked together on many issues over the years.

◆

When I entered the Rajya Sabha, Indiraji was the Leader. She had emerged out of the shadow of her father; no longer a 'gungi gudia', as the opposition called her, she was now acknowledged as a force in her own right. She had an aura about her—confident in dress and demeanour—and her observant eye missed nothing. Her determination to overcome the challenges her government faced, and her calm response to personal attacks, set her far above the men around her. Her 'garibi hatao' slogan, the victory in the 1971 war, the progressive reforms she attempted, all generated an atmosphere of hope. The nation was truly proud of her, or so it seemed, as indicated by the General Election results of 1971 and the Assembly election results of 1972.

Despite these sweeping victories, trouble started brewing outside, with concerns being raised about corruption and rising prices. The situation was more complex than it appeared. On the one hand, there was a clear shift to left-of-centre politics. On the other, several progressive and pro-poor initiatives that had been attempted were thwarted by court judgements. The unfavourable judgments delivered by the apex court in the bank nationalization and privy purses cases had made Indiraji and her trusted advisors—Dev Kant Barooah, Om Mehta, Siddhartha Shankar Ray, P.N. Haksar, D.P. Dhar, Romesh Thapar, Rajni Patel and Nandini Satpathy, among others—a determined lot who wished to put in place a judiciary responsive to the changing needs of the common citizen. As a result, 1973 witnessed the supersession of three Supreme Court Judges and the appointment of A.N. Ray as the Chief Justice. Soon after, the coal and oil industries were nationalized with no judicial obstruction.

Just before the monsoon session of 1974, Perin Romesh Chandra and Putul Ghosh, the inseparable duo of the Left movement in the capital, approached me to join an Indo-USSR (Union of Soviet Socialist Republics) friendship delegation to Moscow to participate in the Indian Independence Day celebrations. I was just settling down and getting used to Parliamentary work. How could I take off on a trip for a week during the monsoon session? I was advised to seek the Prime Minister's permission. Rather apologetically, I mentioned the invitation to Indiraji. 'You should go. You will learn more there than in Parliament,' she told me.

So I went.

It was a great experience, and my first exposure to a truly socialist world. Ours was a three-member delegation—an old Congress MP from Orissa (now Odisha), Mohanty; a young CPI MLA from Punjab, Raj Kumar; and me. The function on 15 August was at the Indian Embassy. I was the main speaker and got a standing ovation from a packed hall after my speech, which I ended with a couple of Russian greetings.

We were put up at a hotel, which was an old palace in Leningrad that had served as Napoleon's headquarters. The notice board still showed an invitation to a victory ball which had been planned there. Huge doors, heritage beds into which one could sink, plush curtains—the place carried markers of an old world. The huge portraits of dead kings and generals on the walls, however, scared me at night. I knocked at Mohanty's door at 11 p.m. with my pillow and blanket, and asked him if I could sleep on the sofa in his sitting room. He looked embarrassed, offered to sleep in the hall himself—which I did not accept—and finally let me in. I was up and back in my room by 6 a.m.

This was the first of many trips to the USSR over the years, which reinforced my socialist leanings.

◆

Another very interesting trip I made was to Warsaw, for a Peace Council-sponsored meeting. We were a mixed delegation, but I received special attention when my communist hosts discovered that I was a Catholic. I was received by the Speaker in Parliament House and taken on a special trip to visit the ancient churches and monasteries, with the Chief Architect of Poland as my guide. He told me two interesting stories. The first detailed how, to save the building plans of the heritage structures of the city—which the people feared the Nazis would destroy—the architects had the plans buried in airtight coffins in regular cemeteries and accompanied this with mock funerals. They were thus able to reconstruct every damaged building after the war. The second story explained why every visitor was taken to the top of the tallest building in the heart of Warsaw—'because,' the architect chuckled, 'you can see from here the beautiful original city, without this

Soviet-constructed monstrosity!' It was obvious to me that there were very strong anti-Soviet feelings in this part of the world.

◆

My involvement with the North-east started almost simultaneously with my entry into Parliament. The first committee I was nominated to, in April 1974, was the Joint Select Committee on the Children's Adoption Bill (in my father-in-law's vacancy). And the first visit of my Parliamentary career was to the North-east with this committee. The fact that it was a troubled region caused my family, particularly my mother, a significant amount of worry. I reassured them that I would be safe as there was adequate security.

Sushila Adivarekar, Aziza Imam and Marjorie Godfrey were the other women with me. We started with Assam, and then set off by road to Nagaland—two MPs, a security officer and a driver in each car, with armed men in-between in jeeps, because of the Naga insurgency. Luckily for us, Basumatari, an old tribal MP from Assam, decided to get into the car with Sushila and me. It was a Saturday afternoon. We set off after lunch, moving swiftly into the forests, and stopped at Golaghat for tea before resuming the journey. Soon, our car began to splutter and rattle—and came to a halt. Since ours was the last car in the motorcade, we were not noticed. Then started the search for a workshop which could fix the fault. After what seemed like an eternity, the car was set right and we set off again—unescorted, into the dark forests, to cross the troubled border into Nagaland. More difficulties followed. We were forced to turn around and head back to Golaghat as two trucks had just collided, effectively blocking the road.

Past midnight, we were on a train to Dimapur. Tired but safe, we made our way to the place where the others were staying—to discover, to our dismay, that we had not been missed! We then proceeded to Kohima. That night I received a message through a local pastor. A group of underground youth wanted to meet me. I was terrified, and sought advice from Basumatari. He told me I should meet them and that he would be around in case there was any need.

It was an interesting meeting. The source of their frustration was the fact that while they were educated, there were no jobs in Nagaland, and they were not trusted when they went to 'India'. They wanted a better life and, according to them, the only option was to join the 'underground'—where they got a uniform, a designation, a monthly pay packet, a weapon and, most of all, status, besides two foreign trips a year. The group members reiterated that they did not wish to fight or kill, but circumstances compelled them to join these outfits. Their concern seemed genuine—they were angry young men driven by desperation to this situation. I reasoned with them, and told them that Naga problems could be solved, and that their leaders should have a dialogue rather than fight. This conversation went on for two hours. I promised to convey their feelings and fears to the Prime Minister, and reassured them that she would certainly look into their concerns. Then they got up, saluted me, and disappeared into the dark night.

Early next morning, there was an invitation to tea from the well-known Ranu Saiza, who guided and spoke for the underground leaders. Nervous, I went to her home. There was a middle-aged armed Naga guard at the gate, who led me to the door of a beautiful cottage surrounded by a well-kept garden in bloom. At the entrance stood the petite Ranu draped in a Naga shawl and in an intricately embroidered white blouse. The house matched Ranu's elegance: white lace curtains, beautiful old-world English decor, flowers in vases, carpets. As we sat down, a maid appeared with tea and snacks, and perfect silver and porcelain service. After some rudimentary polite conversation, the gentle-looking lady became tough: 'We cannot tolerate this suppression. Our people want their freedom, their land for themselves. Our boys will fight to the end. They are trained and prepared for battle!'

On my part, I tried to reason with her and asked her why we couldn't co-exist and live as friends, as one nation. I went on to say that once peace was established, jobs would automatically follow.

Ranu interrupted me, and told me to 'tell your leader [Indira Gandhi] that the people are losing patience; that the suppression must end; that we must talk and find a solution'.

I promised to convey her views. Ranu then put a Naga shawl around me, embraced me with a 'God bless you' and saw me to the door. This was the beginning of a long friendship with Ranu, who, after the Emergency, came to the Lok Sabha as an elected member, took her oath, and promised to defend the Indian Constitution. Scatu Swu, who challenged the Indian Army for fourteen years as the 'general' of the underground movement, was also brought by Indiraji, in 1974, as a nominated member of the Rajya Sabha, and served two full six-year terms. He was a quiet, reticent man, always dressed in a suit and tie, and proud of his past.

On my return from the North-east, I went to Indiraji to report on my meetings. Before I could begin, a stern Mrs Gandhi looked over her glasses and said, 'You've had encounters with the Naga underground!'

'Not really, ma'am,' I replied. Then for a whole fifteen minutes, I reported my conversations with them.

'If they want to negotiate they must be prepared to lay down arms and accept the Constitution,' she said.

But when I spoke of the youth taking to arms on account of inadequate alternative employment opportunities, Indiraji became responsive. 'We can attend to that. We can absorb them into the army or the paramilitary forces,' she said, while making notes in her writing pad. I understand that, on instructions from her office, a second Naga regiment came into existence.

Since then, and to date, talks have continued, ceasefire agreements made and violated, and innocent lives sacrificed, even as democratic processes— elections, political parties and administrative initiatives—take root. There have also been surrenders and the laying down of arms.

Later, between 6 and 8 February 1976, the North-east regional camp was organized at Shillong. As most of the regional party outfits in the North-eastern states had a loose relationship with the INC (Indian National Congress), a common camp was organized for all of them. Purabi Mukherjee, who inaugurated the camp, and I, were deputed as AICC representatives. The next morning, I spoke about the Congress' history and commitments, its ethos and programmes. All the senior leaders of the North-east who were present sat enthralled during my hour-long speech. To date, there are many who remember it.

This was, in a way, my introduction to the politics of the North-east. My relationship with the region has endured, and I've remained involved with each of its states for over thirty-five years.

◆

My entry into the AICC happened in an unexpected way. One afternoon in October 1974, I was summoned by the newly appointed Congress President, Dev Kant Barooah. Surprised and a little nervous, I went to the AICC office in a crisp white khadi saree. Barooahji was a lovable father figure— short, podgy, fair, balding, always dressed in a pure white dhoti-kurta, and perpetually smiling. In fact, he was referred to as the 'Laughing Buddha'. This veteran politician from Assam was a match to today's Pranabda (Pranab

Mukherjee). He could reel off dates, events, incidents and political data like a talking encyclopaedia; also, much like Pranabda, he loved smoking his pipe.

When he saw me, he rose from his desk, escorted me to the sofa and came straight to the point. 'Indiraji and I have been considering giving you some responsibility—you are doing well in Parliament and have also been active in the party. Indiraji wanted to make you a Deputy Minister. I have persuaded her to let you work in the party…what do you say?'

'That is for you both to decide, sir,' I replied, adding rather nervously, 'but I have no idea how the party functions outside Karnataka.'

'You will learn,' he said. 'In fact, I want you to work in the North-east. You will be very popular there!' Barooahji laughed his usual laugh, clearing his throat. I remained silent. 'You can go now. You will receive a formal letter of appointment.' As I turned to leave, he added, 'I have known Joachim and Violet for a long time. You must prove to be a worthy successor to their progressive nationalist credentials.'

'Yes, sir,' I replied as I left his large room. At that moment, little did I know that a decision taken earlier by this smiling old man was to have a disastrous impact on my family.

Barooahji's appointment as AICC President was ratified at the plenary session of the party in December 1974, at Khamgaon Nagar in Punjab; I missed it as I had to go to Bangalore for a family function. The formal announcement of the new AICC team of four General Secretaries followed—Purabi Mukherjee of Bengal, Maragatham Chandrasekar of Tamil Nadu, V.B. Raju of Andhra Pradesh and A.R. Antulay of Maharashtra—and then came the list of four Joint Secretaries—Tarun Gogoi of Assam, Hari Shastri (Lal Bahadur Shastri's son) of Uttar Pradesh, Naval Kishore Sharma of Rajasthan and me. At the age of thirty-two, I had entered the national headquarters of the INC, becoming a part of the undivided Congress' High Command for the first time.

My office was in one of the back rooms of the sprawling AICC headquarters, at 5, Rajendra Prasad Road; it was reasonably comfortable, with a visitor's and a PA's (Personal Assistant) room. On my first day in office, however, the place appeared bare. Then came the Permanent Secretary, K.N. Joshi, with an apology: 'We do not have a PA for you but we will find someone soon. In the meantime, we have a young boy from Kerala who can be of some help. He has no experience. He has just joined us. He can sit here to attend to your phone calls, though his Hindi proficiency is nil.'

I decided to give him a chance. In a few minutes, in came a shy, Malayali boy, in tight trousers, who introduced himself rather awkwardly: 'I am George. I have been sent to work with you.'

'How long have you worked here?' I asked.

'Two months, but I do not know anything about work here,' he replied.

'Do you type?'

'Yes, a little. But my shorthand is not too good.'

My heart sank. But then, it occurred to me that it might be wise to get a newcomer, so as to train him my way. I told George, 'We are both new here. We are both from the South. Let us learn together, with only one condition: I do not want you getting involved in office politics. You will sit here and work with me. If you have a problem, come to me and I will help. I expect you to be loyal, to keep my confidence. Are you prepared?'

'Yes, sir!' he fumbled.

And so, George became my PA—over the years, growing to become one of the party's and the country's most important 'backroom boys', and building a reputation for himself as V. George. Both of us saw many ups and downs together.

From the outset, George was brilliant. He spoke little, learnt fast, had political acumen, was pleasant, well-mannered and always punctual. His English improved under my scrutiny. The NSUI (National Students' Union of India) leaders—among them Kumaramangalam, Mohan Gopal, Anand Sharma and Geetanjali Sharma—would come to my office regularly to clear their bills or get sanctions for their activities; they would sit with George and get themselves refreshments before meeting me.

I was attached to two General Secretaries—A.R. Antulay and Purabi Mukherjee—for different subjects. Purabi Mukherjee was a towering personality, literally and figuratively. Generally dressed in a clumsily draped khadi saree, matched with a loose blouse, she had a thundering voice, and a firm grip over men and matters. I got to witness this first-hand, when at a meeting of the Central Election Committee, at which I was assisting her, the name of a lady came up. There was absolute silence, until a member spoke, claiming there were rumours about the 'reputation' of the lady in question. The men nodded.

Purabidi got up, standing tall over the leaders squatted on the floor, her hands on her hips. She challenged them: 'Shall I speak about the reputation some of you have?' She pointed to each of the men seated in a semi-circle. 'Do you think I do not know about your reputations? How dare you treat a woman in this manner? Because she is helpless and weak, you condemn her?'

There was silence. The woman's name was cleared without another word. Little wonder that no one dared defy her.

Purabidi had a special fondness for me. She guided and encouraged me, and assigned several tasks to me that gave me experience and exposure. While she, as the person in charge of the Department of Foreign Affairs, prepared background material for all party delegations going abroad, I briefed them about table manners, the use of forks and spoons, clothing, Western toilets, the political system of the country, and the topics to be discussed and avoided. I enjoyed the assignment, and the delegations appreciated my work. In fact, the Department of Foreign Affairs was the most active department of the party with the Ministry of External Affairs providing support and guidance.

My fluency as an English-speaker (with my Hindi proficiency fast improving) was noticed both in the party and in Parliament. Consequently, I found myself delivering regular lectures at training camps and at friendship society meetings of many countries, especially the socialist, Arab and African nations. One day, on noticing my interest in Africa, the Congress President told me, 'I am going on a goodwill visit to three African countries. I am taking you with me. You will meet interesting people and learn a lot. It will be educational.'

I was thrilled. I had never been to Africa. Besides, going as part of the Congress President's delegation was a great honour. Until now, I had briefed party delegations, and picked and wrapped their gift items (with the help of Gayatri Rai and Manju Choudhury, who were attached to the department). Now it seemed I would be the one heading overseas. I anxiously waited for a formal confirmation. To my utter surprise and disappointment, the delegation, when announced, had the name of Maragatham Chandrasekar instead of Margaret Alva!

When I went to the President's house a day before his departure, to deliver the gifts we had packed, Didi—as we affectionately called the affable Mrs Barooah—whispered to me, 'I am so disappointed that you are not going with us, Margaret. Barooahji is also upset. But Indiraji changed the name. What could he do?'

I was stunned. Why would Indiraji do this to me? What did she have against me?

At that moment, Barooahji entered, placed his hand on my shoulder, and said philosophically, 'President proposes, Prime Minister disposes. Better luck next time.'

I smiled, beating back my tears. I kept my mouth shut, but decided I would find out why this had happened.

As I walked out, I bumped into Purabidi, and found myself walking back with her to the Barooah residence. She looked over all the details, and asked me to get into her car. Here, she whispered to me in her usual maternal way, 'You must be upset. But Indiraji has her own reasons to keep you back. You will get a chance, do not worry.'

'But why has this happened?' I asked, still in shock.

'You are young and new to the world of politics. You must trust Indiraji's judgement,' she said.

The matter ended there.

Soon, I was at the airport with the other office bearers to see off the delegation with a smile on my face and watch Maragatham Chandrasekar trudge along with her handbag to board the plane.

Apart from this disappointment, my years in the AICC brought me close to national politics. Early on, I witnessed negotiations for the merger of G.K. Moopanar's Kamaraj Congress in Tamil Nadu with the national arm of the Congress. Om Mehta was to finalize the arrangements, and since I knew Tamil, I was sent with him. I helped Om Mehta with the information I had collected from workers who only spoke Tamil. Moopanarji later organized a massive rally in Trichy to mark the event, at which I was the AICC representative. It went on for hours. My legs ached and my hands went stiff waving from the high dais. I had begun to experience the travails of party 'leadership'!

Around this time, a decision was taken to revitalize the party through camps at the national, state and district levels. Background papers were carefully prepared, and the camps were meticulously planned—starting with the Narora Camp in the Bulandshahar district of Uttar Pradesh (22–24 November 1974). This brought the national leadership to a closed-door conclave to discuss the challenges facing the party and the government. Indiraji, the Congress President and all important policy makers were there.

As a follow up, it was decided that three-day-long state camps would be organized. This would bring the government and party leaders together, and allow Indiraji and the Congress President to interact with state players and listen to their problems, assessments and suggestions. Warring factions would be brought together, making way for a more cohesive state apparatus. I especially recall the Karnataka camp, organized on 3, 4, 5 December 1974; The Congress President insisted that 'ragi mudde' (a special dish in Karnataka made with finger millet and water, and a favourite of Devaraj Urs) be served.

Then came two-days-long district-level camps, which the Chief Ministers and Pradesh Congress Committee (PCC) Presidents would attend.

The entire exercise was completed in a year, with the AICC office bearers monitoring the agenda, attendance, background papers and reports. It was a useful exercise that allowed the grassroots to communicate with the central leadership, and helped rekindle their loyalty and involvement.

◆

As Joint Secretary, AICC, I was, to begin with, put in charge of the Indian Youth Congress (IYC), while Tarun Gogoi was handed the NSUI. This, I was not prepared for. Ambika Soni, the articulate wife of a diplomat, was now the all-powerful President of the IYC, with Sanjay Gandhi, Indira Gandhi's son, her patron. I did not want to get dragged into their politics.

I went to Barooahji and pleaded, 'Please save me from the IYC, sir! I cannot handle it. Let me handle the NSUI.'

Barooahji laughed, 'Difficult for two women to work together, eh?' He paused, and then to my utter relief, said, 'Okay, let us ask Tarun to handle the lady.'

And so it was—Tarun was put in charge of the IYC, and I was given the NSUI.

Those were turbulent days in the IYC. Only Tarun, with his mild manners and affable smile, could survive the onslaught. Most others fell by the wayside. As for me, I was happy doing my job in the Department of Foreign Affairs, as part of the team handling the Twenty Point Programme's implementation and working with the NSUI.

Yet, every post comes with its initial hiccups. One of the first visits I made, while in charge of the NSUI, was to Bombay. Murli Deora, the industrialist-cum-politician, and Rajni Patel invited me to the city for the

NSUI university election campaign; Suresh Shetty was then the Mumbai NSUI President. Murli first took me for the launch of a 'Clean Bombay' campaign. It was my first public function in the city. Dressed in pure white khadi, I was taken to Bhendi Bazaar—a crowded market in Bombay—and given a long broom with which to sweep the road and launch the campaign. The crowds cheered, the cameras clicked. Not another broom appeared; none of the organizers joined me. I was most embarrassed, though the event did get me wide publicity in the press.

The next event I attended was the NSUI rally. To my utter dismay, when I reached the venue, there was a mile-long line of bullock carts filled with NSUI volunteers holding placards and banners seeking votes. They insisted I get into the lead cart, decorated in party colours. I hesitated. With no alternative in sight, deferring to the pleas of the students, I found my way into a bullock cart, and led the NSUI rally! It took over two hours to get to the public meeting venue, where all the leaders were sitting pretty on the stage, waiting for me. Not one had got into the carts. It was truly an unforgettable experience. The only satisfaction I had was that the NSUI swept the Bombay University elections that followed!

I also recall an invitation to a Kerala Students' Union rally. It was a big and impressive affair. Vayalar Ravi, A.K. Antony, Oommen Chandy and a host of state youth and senior leaders were present on the dais. The students marched in their thousands for three hours, shouting slogans, beating drums and waving banners. The IYC did not really exist in Kerala at that time and the state was proud of its student movement. The students' enthusiasm was a sight to behold, and reminded me of how important my role as the Secretary in charge of the NSUI was.

◆

1974 saw the launch of the Navnirman Agitation in Gujarat, which sought the dismissal of the Chimanbhai Mehta government on grounds of rampant corruption. The agitation gained momentum. The government was dismissed and President's Rule imposed. Thereafter, events began to snowball.

Jayaprakash Narayan—or JP as he was popularly called—and his clarion call against corruption and personality-driven politics had many takers. Chandra Shekhar and Mohan Dharia, the Young Turks within the Congress, were sympathetic to JP's message, and called for a national dialogue on rising prices, corruption and unemployment—issues mentioned in the Congress' election manifesto.

I recall Mohan Dharia's emotional speech in the Rajya Sabha around that time, calling for introspection and patience with those who had another point of view. 'I am a true friend. I will speak to you face-to-face...not stab you from behind. I wish you success, but I cannot and will not compromise on principles I hold dear.' The rumblings within the Congress were growing. Yet no one was prepared to speak openly and add to Indiraji's woes.

On 2 March 1975, Mohan Dharia made his exit from the government, and was later expelled.

An emergency meeting of the Parliamentary Party Executive, with Indiraji in the chair, was called to discuss Chandra Shekhar's anti-party activities (he was then the Secretary of the Congress Parliamentary Party [CPP]). V.C. Shukla, then the Minister for Parliamentary Affairs, had come with a resolution for Chandra Shekhar's expulsion. As usual, no one wanted to oppose the coterie.

I asked innocently, 'Doesn't the Constitution of the CPP require a notice to be issued to a member before such drastic action is taken?'

Everyone looked around. Some said that this was a special situation, others that we ought to reconsider the matter carefully.

I added my bit: 'I am not against action being taken. But I want to know under what circumstances and for what reason I can be expelled without notice tomorrow.'

'She is right,' said Indiraji.

The resolution was kept in abeyance. The meeting ended.

As I walked out of the meeting, a furious Shukla approached me and thundered, 'What was the need for you to act so smart? When we decide to expel you, you will go, without discussion or notice.' This was a clear warning.

◆

The Twenty Point Programme had its repercussions. A small farmer from Gulbarga, Karnataka, landed at my door with his family of four, seeking relief from Indira Gandhi. His land, hypothecated to a rich farmer for a small loan, had been forcibly occupied by the lender after the rural debt moratorium had been announced. He was attacked and had fled to Delhi. Despite all my efforts, her could not return to his land immediately—there were court cases filed and records manipulated in which he had signed away his land. So he became my 'house guest' for the next three years, living in my enclosed verandah at Rajendra Prasad Road, fed and clothed by me. Father and son became daily wage earners at a construction site, while the two small girls became Nivedith's inseparable companions. I finally moved them to the quarters of my ministerial bungalow in 1985, and got the son a job in NIPCCD (National Institute of Public Cooperation and Child Development) under the Ministry of Women and Child Development.

◆

The agitation of JP and his group spread, and law and order started breaking down. The distance between Indiraji and JP grew. An effort at reconciliation was made in November 1974 when they met in Delhi, but it failed. This was followed by JP's call for a 'second freedom struggle' that rattled Congressmen across ranks.

Indiraji's insecurity seemed to grow. She increasingly spoke of the movement being an attempt to finish her, her party and the nation. In January 1975, the death of L.N. Misra, the Union Railway Minister, in a bomb blast at Samastipur railway station, was seen as the first strike in this game of violence unleashed by a united opposition under JP.

On 6 March 1975, a massive rally at the Delhi Boat Club showcased the swelling ranks of the opposition. This show of strength further shook the Congress leadership, and Indiraji's insecurity began to show.

In the midst of all this, there was an even more worrying development— the gradual emergence of the new centre of power in the Prime Minister's house—Sanjay Gandhi.

Morarji Desai went on a hunger strike in April 1975 for an end to President's Rule in Gujarat. The Central government had to concede his demands and declare elections. Emboldened by the developments in Gujarat, the agitation spread to Bihar, with JP at the helm. On 5 June, at a rally in Patna, JP called for a 'total revolution', appealing to opposition parties to unite and carry the struggle to all states.

Those were desperate times, and they called for desperate responses.

Chapter 8

AROUND THE WORLD:
TO THE UNITED NATIONS CONFERENCE

I was in Bangalore on 12 June 1975, having a leisurely breakfast with the kids, when I got the news that Indiraji had lost her election case, and the Allahabad High Court had ruled against her.[5] Making arrangements for the children to move to my parents', I left for Delhi—arriving on the night of 14 June. Niru was on tour and the house was locked. So I spent the night at Karnataka Bhavan and went to Safdarjung Road the next morning. I made my way through milling crowds and people shouting slogans, and approached Seshan, Indiraji's Principal Secretary, who was standing in the porch. On seeing me, he asked, 'Where have you been? We have been searching for you all over the country. Go straight to madam!'

I went in, a little nervous, and came face-to-face with a grave-looking Indiraji. 'Where have you been?' she repeated Seshan's question.

'In Bangalore, ma'am, but I had problems getting here.'

The Allahabad High Court judgement that unseated Indira Gandhi from her Lok Sabha seat had rejected many serious charges levelled by the petitioner, Raj Narain, but upheld two points of contention—that government machinery had been used, and that Indira Gandhi's election agent (Yashpal Kapoor) was a government servant (as his resignation had not been accepted) when he assumed that responsibility. Justice Jagmohanlal Sinha therefore disqualified Indiraji for six years and declared Raj Narain as the elected representative; he also gave a stay of twenty days for her to appeal to the Supreme Court. This she did.

In the midst of this hustle and bustle, Indiraji moved towards the

---

[5]Raj Narain had contested against Indira Gandhi in the constituency of Rae Bareilly in the Indian General Elections of 1971. Mrs Gandhi won this seat, and Narain filed a petition to appeal against the verdict. *The State of Uttar Pradesh vs Raj Narain* was heard by the Allahabad High Court, which found the then Prime Minister of India, Mrs Gandhi, guilty of electoral malpractices.

porch, with a group of women following her for a photograph. I recognized most of them.

Indiraji suddenly stopped and asked me to meet Seshan. I went back to him. He told me to get ready to join the women's delegation to the first UN conference on women in Mexico City. The delegation was leaving that night.

'It is impossible for me to go at such short notice,' I explained. 'My house is locked, my husband is on tour, my kids are in Bangalore—I have no idea what the conference is about.'

'Not to worry, we will help,' Seshan smiled calmly.

As I walked away, I bumped into Indiraji again. 'I do not know if you can join them today, but you must get ready to leave.' It was an order.

I tried to explain to her my difficulties, but she smiled and said, 'We will find your husband and open your house; be in touch with Seshan.'

I had no time to say what I had planned to convey to her about the political crisis we faced. Indiraji appeared calm and confident, in total control, meeting leaders who kept crowding the lawns and the porch. I went back to Seshan for guidance. He asked me to break the lock of the house, and get him my passport and photographs. The rest, he said, he would take care of.

I did as advised. I had to break the news to Niru, Baba, my parents and, most of all, the kids. They were all most supportive—except for the children, who wanted to get back to Delhi to be with Niru and Baba.

The next morning, I drove to Kasturba Gandhi Marg to pick up my tickets, visas, etc., from the travel agent. A while later, travel papers in hand, I walked back to my car, happy that the job had been done so easily. But then my car wasn't there! It was nowhere to be found. In the heat of the mid-day June sun, I found an auto, came home and rang Niru. Together, we went back, but the trip was in vain. The car was gone, with the keys in my bag. We finally recovered it, but with parts missing.

This was my first trip to the West. Indira Gandhi was to lead the delegation with Nandini Satpathy, Ambika Soni, Purabi Mukherjee and a few others. Once the Allahabad judgement came, the delegation was recast and people like me were packed off to fill the gaps.

I met Indiraji again before I left. I thanked her for the confidence she had reposed in me but told her I was nervous as it was my first trip to the West. She told me not to worry as instructions would be sent to London and New York to look after me.

'I know nothing of this conference, ma'am,' I said.

'Read the papers on the flight. You do not need a briefing, you will manage,' she smiled.

This was my first experience of Air India first class. It was luxury travel of the ultimate kind. The cabin crew pampered me. I read, I rested, I ate and I slept. I felt like a 'country girl come to town,' as Niru used to call me.

After brief pit-stops in London and New York, I reached Mexico and got to work right away. The theme was 'Equality, Development and Peace'. Listening to and meeting women leaders from across the world—Prime Ministers, Presidents, Members of Parliament, leaders of peace movements, women's rights activists, artists, writers, actors, painters and protestors—giving a call to women to unite and fight the oppression of centuries, was most inspiring. I saw, I heard, I absorbed it all.

Every time a leader was hailed or cheered, I thought of Indiraji and how stately and impressive she would have been on this global platform. Not one of those present could hold a candle to her. Many enquired about her as they had received news of the court judgement. We assured them that all would be fine.

But we were concerned. There was very little news from home. The local papers were in Spanish. The Embassy was most unconcerned and unresponsive. The Ambassador happened to be Vijaya Lakshmi Pandit's son-in-law, E.N. Mangat Rai. 'You do your job, I will do mine. Do not answer any questions; say you have no information from home,' was his caustic advice to the delegation.

The conference was interesting, packed with events. I was invited to be a part of a panel organized by the famous women's activist, Bella Abzug of the US; I was to represent 'Asia'—one of six representatives from six continents—and our topic was: 'If I was my country's Prime Minister/President'. I was quite confused. What could I say? Was I to go with the general mood and be a rabble-rousing cheerleader? Or was I to be a sensible, sober voice placing, in proper perspective, the reality of leadership in a tradition-bound patriarchal system? I decided I'd adopt the latter approach.

As I sat on the stage, listening to the first three speakers, I began to realize with greater certainty that I—the youngest member of the panel—was going to be the odd one out. When my turn came, I stood up and said, 'I am here representing the largest democracy already led by a woman democratically elected.' There was loud applause.

But a woman from an Indian NGO (non-governmental organization) shouted, 'What has she done for our women?'

I remained calm. 'Having seen my Prime Minister work efficiently, despite being challenged by the restrictive conventions of a male-dominated, tradition-bound system, I must say without hesitation, that it is difficult, very, very difficult, to change things in a hurry...'

There was silence for a second, then someone shouted, 'Women must change things when they have the power!' 'Yes, yes,' was the response of nearly 500 women jam-packed in the hall.

I continued, undaunted. 'If I wish to become the Prime Minister or President, I will need the support of both men and women to stay there. Laws, to change, must be approved by the Indian Parliament, which is male dominated. Our political parties are male dominated. A woman leader needs their support—so the first thing I would try to do is win them over.'

'You have to chuck them out!' came a voice in response amidst applause.

I refuted the comment. 'I, personally, would strive to carry them along for change, for justice and equal opportunities for our women, as per the rights guaranteed in our Constitution.'

'That will take centuries! You are not fit to become Prime Minister,' came Bella's intervention from the chair.

'We already have a woman Prime Minister who is doing well; I do not aspire to be one myself,' I retorted and sat down. Interestingly enough, at the end of the discussion, I won many friends—Bella being one of them. I imagine, she liked the fact that I stood my ground, despite the provocation. Over the years, we became close associates, championing the cause of women's rights in various fora in different parts of the world. Bella wore long skirts, colourful scarves, large hats with matching bags, besides red lipstick and pink rouge. She was an institution unto herself—bold, with a sense of humour; loved and feared by leaders, people's representatives, as well as women the world over.

Prabha Rau, as the Leader of the delegation, spoke at the plenary session. As we sat there, unable to follow most of her prepared speech, we whispered: 'What a poor replacement to Indiraji!' When I exited the hall, I was stopped by Sirimavo Bandaranaike, then the Prime Minister of Sri Lanka. 'How is Indira?' she asked. 'We are missing her! I hope all is well at home. Give her my good wishes.' 'All is well,' I assured her.

I spoke at a couple of meetings. I also attended a few NGO events—but here I was quite annoyed to see women attacking the government, and ridiculing our claims of having a pro-people, pro-women dispensation under the Congress. The NGOs showed pictures of mothers in slums, prostitutes, riot victims, starving children and beleaguered Dalit women, claiming they were waging a 'battle for justice'. They insisted that the 'truth' had to be brought before the international community so that their fight would garner support on a global platform.

In the midst of this came news of the Emergency. It reached us, not from the Embassy or from back home, but through a BBC (British Broadcasting Corporation) news broadcast. We did not know what to make of it. So, after a quick meeting, we decided to defend it, at least as long as we were at the conference, which was, in any case, drawing to a close. As expected, there were questions from all sides. We said everything that had been done was Constitutional, done to protect the country from chaos and disintegration. It was only a temporary measure.

With the delegates holding hands to sing, 'We shall overcome...,' the curtain came down on this historic meeting of the women of the world (which saw 133 member states participate, and which witnessed, for the first time, NGOs being brought into the UN's decision-making ambit). Each member pledged to work relentlessly for equality, development and peace at the local, national, regional and international levels, forming networks for sharing information and creating advocacy groups.

It was indeed a new birth for me. What I had accepted as part of normal family life or religious tradition suddenly began to seem oppressive, unjust, even unacceptable. Could we really challenge the status quo when we got home? Our minds had opened—we had heard and seen so much, been exposed to the new world of women—things could no longer be the same for me or for the millions of our girls and women, oppressed, suppressed and exploited, simply because of their gender.

◆

I made three stops on my way back. The first was Chicago with Sunanda Bhandare, and then New York. This was my first visit to the US. The cities, the stores, the sights overwhelmed me. From America, I proceeded to Italy—specifically to Rome. It was a pilgrimage which I was determined to make. Soon after my arrival, I walked to St Peter's Square, and joined the thousands waiting for a public audience of the Pope. There was a wave of excitement as His Holiness appeared by the small window in his quarters. 'Papa, Papa!' the cries rose, as he blessed the crowd. In a few minutes the window closed; the pilgrims dispersed. Early next morning, I was at St Peter's for the morning service. After a quick tour of Rome on a sightseeing bus and some brisk souvenir shopping, I was back at the airport, cocooned in the luxury of a first-class seat, on my way home.

◆

The next morning, I woke up to a rather unpleasant breakfast. Baba was angry about the events of the previous week. The Emergency was bad enough, but the detention of political leaders and media persons, and the censorship of the press, shocked him. He was a journalist, first and above all else, who had fearlessly challenged the British during the freedom struggle through his magazine, *Forum*, and faced charges of sedition. Indira Gandhi's Emergency was more than he could take.

'What is she doing? This is her son's influence. You are all destroying this country—is this democracy?' he thundered.

I had no answer. I was not even aware of the full story at that point or of those who had been detained. And then, I learnt, Morarji Desai had been arrested. Desai had been a friend, mentor, benefactor and political colleague, who had brought Baba and Mummy into politics. His detention angered Baba. And now, I was at the receiving end of his wrath—but what could I do?

I went to Indiraji and updated her about everything that had happened abroad—the leaders who had enquired about her, the lukewarm treatment of the Embassy and the responses of the delegation. Then I presented her a gift I had bought her—an onyx horse head. She liked it, but asked why I had to do this. 'Only for you, ma'am,' I replied. She smiled. But I perceived a kind of tension in her.

She wasn't the same person any longer. Something in her had changed.

Chapter 9

TRIAL BY FIRE:
THE EMERGENCY AND SANJAY GANDHI

The Vacation Judge, Justice Krishna Iyer, had heard Indiraji's appeal on 23 June 1975 and had given her a conditional stay—she was allowed to continue as MP and Prime Minister, but did not have the right to participate in debates, vote or draw her salary and allowances until her appeal was finally disposed of. This made her a 'lame duck' Prime Minister— an awkward situation for any head of government.

That day, all senior leaders of the party and government gathered at 1, Safdarjung Road. Indiraji is said to have sounded out a few of them on the advisability of resigning. But everyone, except for three or four (who thought they could plant themselves in her place as a temporary measure), insisted she stay on and await the final disposal of her appeal.

As expected, the opposition got together to fight this. In the face of a relentless campaign spearheaded by JP—who at a public rally in Delhi called on the defence forces to lay down arms and rebel—there was the risk of violence. Rallies, protests and sharply-worded editorials threatened to break down the administrative machinery in many parts of the country.

Despite an overwhelming majority in Parliament (with 516 party MPs of both Houses signing a resolution asking Indira Gandhi to stay); huge support from Congress workers and the general public (with 10,000 signatures in blood in support of the Prime Minister from Karnataka alone!); and the astounding response of ten lakh people to a 'support the Prime Minister' Congress rally—where Dev Kant Barooah coined his famous slogan, 'Indira is India'—turmoil and tension spread, creating unease and nervousness. United opposition rallies kept clamouring for Indiraji's immediate resignation, and Morarji Desai's call for a 'do or die' struggle at the Boat Club added to the chaos.

The situation was becoming increasingly dangerous, raising serious doubts about the ability of the government to contain the anarchy that was spreading. Suddenly, the most powerful leader of the largest democracy in the world seemed cornered and helpless. Her advisors—who strongly believed that the country was precariously positioned—now urged her to seek relief through the imposition of Emergency. 'The Constitution provides for it,' Siddhartha Shankar Ray is said to have told her, quoting Article 352.[6]

After that, things moved quickly. A letter, signed by the Home Minister, was sent to the President, who had been briefed earlier on the developing situation and the contemplated action. President Fakhruddin Ali Ahmed signed the Declaration imposing a state of Emergency at 11.20 p.m. on 25 June 1975. To a sleeping nation, the Emergency came as a bolt from the blue.

The Cabinet met at 6 a.m. on 26 June at the Prime Minister's house to endorse the decision. Later, on the same day, in her address to the nation, Indira Gandhi claimed:

> Emergency was a necessary response to the deep and widespread conspiracy which has been brewing ever since I began to introduce certain progressive measures of benefit to the common man and woman of India [...] threatening the unity of India. This is not a personal matter. It is not important whether I remain Prime Minister or not.[7]

However, despite Indiraji's assertions to the contrary, the general perception was that the Emergency had been declared more to save a chair than a nation. There was an immediate backlash. Those who had hailed Indiraji as 'Durga' in Parliament, and had glorified her after the Bangladesh war, turned into severe critics and foes.

◆

The Emergency was in full swing when I returned from Mexico—with JP arrested, followed by Morarji Desai and Chandra Shekhar, and the list only growing. Press censorship prevented news of the arrests from reaching the

---

[6]Article 352 of the Indian Constitution clearly states: 'If the President is satisfied that a grave emergency exists whereby the security of India or of any part of the territory thereof is threatened, whether by war or external aggression or armed rebellion, he may, by Proclamation, make a declaration to that effect (in respect of the whole of India or of such part of the territory thereof as may be specified in the Proclamation).'
[7]See Ramachandra Guha, *India after Gandhi: The History of the World's Largest Democracy* (UK: Macmillan, 2007).

public. The AICC met in Delhi soon after to endorse the steps taken by the government to protect the unity and integrity of the country. Indiraji's leadership received unanimous support, with the party standing solidly with her, presenting a united front to the opposition, and calling upon the people to support the Prime Minister in this hour of crisis.

On 23 July 1975, Parliament was summoned to ratify the Emergency. A large number of opposition MPs were in jail. The Jana Sangh and CPM MPs who were present attacked the government for an undemocratic response to a popular people's movement, and walked out. Parliament's endorsement was now a foregone conclusion. The Constitutional requirement was fulfilled.

As I witnessed the Emergency take root, I grew increasingly confused, worried and afraid. But I kept mum and fell in line.

Prior to this tumultuous period, Indiraji had shown absolute faith in the rule of law. She had appeared before the Allahabad Court that had summoned her on 19 March, had stood in the witness box for ten hours, and had refused the chair offered to her. The two counts on which she had been unseated were minor and the appeal could well have gone in her favour.

But it was the advice of her trusted team—a team that did not want to take any chances—that had led her to take drastic measures. In August 1975, the Constitution's 39th Amendment was passed, debarring the courts from entertaining petitions challenging the election of an incumbent Prime Minister 'to ensure that an elected government was not destabilized'; a committee of Parliament alone would look into any challenge to a Prime Minister's election. Naturally, her appeal became infructuous. All the same, on 5 November 1975 the Supreme Court upheld Indiraji's election.

Despite this victory, Indiraji seemed silent, withdrawn. I perceived a sense of disquiet creeping into her. She was a committed democrat, with faith in the people of India. Yet, circumstances had driven her to take these extreme steps, to safeguard the unity and stability of the nation.

◆

The Emergency rapidly tightened its grip on the country. The Twenty Point Programme of the Congress and the Five Point Programme of the IYC (for adult education, an end to dowry, the purchase of Indian goods, tree plantation and family planning), though well-meaning in spirit, were pushed too far, with negative responses from the people.

A number of Constitution amendments and laws followed. The important ones were the Maintenance of Internal Security Act (MISA) in August 1975,[8] the suspension of fundamental rights guaranteed in Article 19 of the Constitution in January 1976, the extension of the life of the Lok Sabha by one year with powers to extend it further in February 1976, the 42nd Constitution Amendment—which attempted to reduce the power of the Supreme Court and High Courts to pronounce upon the Constitutional validity of laws, and declared India a socialist secular republic—in November 1976.

As the Emergency spread its tentacles, the assault on the press began to grow. The Press Council was abolished. Newspapers and magazines were threatened, cajoled or marginalized. Government advertising and DAVP (Directorate of Advertising and Visual Publicity) patronage went to those who fell in line. Several journalists were detained.

The arrest of vocal anti-establishment political activists continued. Octogenarian J.B. Kripalani and the portly Parsi MP, Piloo Mody, were sent to jail. It is said that Mody was in agony while trying to use the Indian-style toilet, and would abuse Indiraji loudly in filthy language every time he went in. On hearing of this, she ordered a Western-style toilet to be installed in his cell!

Other political leaders like George Fernandes, too, faced the repercussions of strident protest. Fernandes—who had led the railway strike of May 1974 that brought the economy and country to the brink of collapse—went underground to lead the movement against the Emergency, dressing as a Sikh. His aim was to sabotage vital installations with dynamite. While he managed to send his wife, Leila, and son to the US to protect them from arrest, and while his arrested friend, Snehalata Reddy, got released on parole due to her deteriorating health, he could not save his brother, Lawrence. A totally apolitical man, he was picked up and tortured for information about his brother, which he did not have, then held in jail in Bangalore. His friends and close relatives approached me for his release. I spoke to Devaraj Urs, the then Chief Minister. 'These are orders from Delhi. I cannot do anything,' he said in response. Worried, I spoke to Om

---

[8] Any person who was considered to be a political threat or who could raise the voice of opposition could be detained without trial under MISA.

Mehta, the Internal Security Minister, who asked me to write to him, since I came from Bangalore. I did so. In a week, Lawrence was released, his legs damaged permanently. George Fernandes was arrested in 1976. He was charged in the infamous Baroda dynamite case.

Internationally, there were mixed reactions to the imposition of the Emergency, especially from the UK. British Cabinet Minister, Michael Foot, and socialist politician, Jennie Lee, openly supported Indira Gandhi in her quest to restore normalcy, while Margaret Thatcher, the then Leader of the Tories, visited India and expressed the view that the situation was grave. I was present at the lunch hosted for her by the Foreign Minister, Y.B. Chavan, and was most impressed by the speech she delivered without a piece of paper before her. Then there was *The Observer* painting a gloomy picture, discounting the possibility of India ever returning to democracy.

Faced with scathing criticism, Indiraji turned to Sanjay, who was determined to make his mother stay on and fight back. He became her most trusted advisor.

Sanjay started his political career with IYC. Here he began substituting those in positions of power with his favourites. He found Priya Rajan Dasmunsi, the President of the IYC, rather unresponsive to his ideas, so he had him replaced by Ambika Soni. Ambika and Sanjay became a formidable combination.

With time, he built a hand-picked team to assist him in achieving his ambitions. Among the seniors, he patronized N.D. Tiwari (Uttar Pradesh), P.C. Sethi and V.C. Shukla (Madhya Pradesh), Bansi Lal (Haryana), Ghani Khan Choudhury (West Bengal), and Sitaram Kesri (Bihar). The junior team included F.M. Khan and Gundu Rao (Karnataka), Arjun Das (Delhi), and Janardhan Singh Gehlot (Rajasthan). Among the officers in his good books were Jagmohan, B.R. Tamta, Naveen Chawla, and R.S. Bhinder. Dhirendra Brahmachari was his guru and Rukhsana Sultana, the socialite in dark glasses, the Muslim face he needed to appear inclusive.

Coterie in place, Sanjay became the man who called the shots. The IYC began to assert itself over the party apparatus. Indiraji's trusted advisors began to get sidelined and humiliated. Many were replaced. I.K. Gujral, a Congress loyalist, was considered too soft for the Information and Broadcasting Ministry; he was replaced by the diehard Sanjay Gandhi loyalist, V.C. Shukla. Swaran Singh, the experienced, soft-spoken Defence Minister made room for Bansi Lal, a tough Jat from Haryana (who helped Sanjay with his Maruti project[9]). A common saying in social circles in the capital those days was, 'Sanjay has three loves: Maruti, Mummy and Maneka'.

Everyone was being watched; hostile responses were marked. I remember sitting with Priya Ranjan Dasmunsi in Central Hall one day for a cup of coffee. Never part of Sanjay's inner circle, Dasmunsi had now fallen out with his long-time colleague, Subroto Mukherjee. I was trying to broker peace. A friend, who saw us, later cautioned me, 'You have a bright future. Why are you annoying the "son" by sitting around with marked men like Priya?'

It was all too evident—a fear psychosis of sorts was gripping the government and cutting across party structures. Cabinet and Chief Ministers began dancing to Sanjay's tunes. Even Dev Kant Barooah began to defend the emerging leader, citing examples of young men who had changed the course of world history. Sanjay was referred to variously as the 'rising son', 'the power behind the throne', and 'the Prime Minister-in-waiting', while George Fernandes had code-named him 'SOD'—'son of the dictator'.

A controversial interview by him to *Surge* (a now defunct magazine)—roughly a month after the Declaration of Emergency, snippets of which began to appear selectively in newspapers and magazines—created an embarrassing situation for the Prime Minister. On the one hand, the party was upset since Sanjay had criticized government policies and functioning. On the other, Indiraji's socialist friends were peeved since Sanjay had attacked the public sector and communists, while effusively praising private entrepreneurship—all of which made sense since he was now fully involved with his Maruti car project. A direct fallout was that Indiraji's commitment to socialism was questioned. She had Sanjay issue a statement of clarification, toning down his remarks. But the damage had been done.

If anyone was happy with the Sanjay Gandhi interview, it was the business community—which was also pro-Emergency since unions could now be controlled, productivity improved and bureaucracies forced to run more efficiently. It was rumoured that his interview quotes were framed

---

[9]In 1971, Indira Gandhi's Cabinet proposed the production of a 'people's car'—an indigenous car for middle-class Indians. A company called 'Maruti Limited' was incorporated and Sanjay Gandhi became its first Managing Director. The company did not produce any vehicles during the young Gandhi's lifetime, and the test model released as a showpiece to demonstrate progress was criticized; there were also allegations of cronyism and rampant corruption, of bankers and investors being threatened and blackmailed, and of rules being disregarded.

by industrial establishments.

Khushwant Singh, the Editor of *The Illustrated Weekly*, remained a great admirer of Sanjay. He claimed that Sanjay lived a simple life, free of liquor or cigarettes, and was committed to his job, working at his workshop at Maruti for fourteen to sixteen hours a day. The magazine brought out a special issue, full of pictures of Sanjay and his young bride, listing his activities and declaring him the 'Indian of the year!'

◆

As days passed, the initial euphoria of a country being 'saved' began to fade. With the press gagged, clandestine newsletters and pamphlets began to get distributed, and the underground movement grew in strength. Stories of forced sterilization of old and even unmarried men, of dubious vaccines being administered to children, and of a concerted effort to sterilize the minorities began to surface, as also reports of the demolition of houses and shops, and of firing if protests risked turning violent.

The South was comparatively secure from these excesses as the Chief Ministers did not toe the 'Sanjay line' blindly. Indeed, many of them asked me what they ought to do: Go to Sanjay or stay away? What could I say?

In the midst of this came the news that the jailed JP's kidneys had failed. He was released that month on parole. On 14 November 1975, the Lok Sangharsh Samiti Satyagraha was launched in Bombay. It spread to other states, with slogans against the Emergency resounding loud and clear. Thousands courted arrest.

Nervousness coupled with arrogance and sycophancy led to some rather strange proposals getting drafted. One was for the creation of a Constituent Assembly to review and draft a new Constitution responsive to the needs of a changing polity. Thirty years after Independence, it was argued, the aspirations of the post-1947 generation had to find expression in the Constitution.

There were conflicting views on the subject. Many spoke up and advised against the move—only to become targets of Sanjay's displeasure. Despite opposition from the top leadership, Sanjay managed to get a meeting of Congress MPs convened by A.P. Sharma to endorse his idea.

While Indiraji expressed annoyance at this development on her return from the non-aligned meeting in Africa, we wondered how any of these events could have unfolded without her knowledge. At first, we suspected that she did not oppose Sanjay simply because she couldn't—as she had confessed to close advisors. Yet as days passed, we began to believe that Sanjay had his mother's support for all that he did. It began to dawn on us that Sanjay was being used as the sounding board. The truth emerged when at the Guwahati AICC session Indiraji declared in her address: 'An attack on Sanjay is an attack on me!'

In the midst of all this, I was made a member of the Twenty Point Programme Implementation Committee and the Swaran Singh Committee, with senior leaders like the Law Minister H.R. Gokhale, S.S. Ray and Rajni Patel, to review the Constitution.

In 1975, a bill was introduced in the Rajya Sabha, providing complete immunity for life to the Prime Minister, the President and the Governors, against any criminal proceedings in a court of law for acts committed before, during and after office. There were a couple of speeches, a three-line whip, and a vote which carried it through.

I was horrified. There was shock and anger in the lobbies. Whose idea was this amendment? Why was it rushed through in this manner?

I went to Indiraji. 'Madam,' I said, 'I am new to the House and quite junior in the party. But I have come to you because I am concerned. MPs are upset about this bill we were made to pass today. Others may not have the courage to come and speak out. What was the need for this? Why was it rushed through in this manner?' I asked.

'I do not know the details. I will look into it,' she assured me.

I was surprised at my audacity, but I also had faith that the Prime Minister was prepared to listen and, when convinced, to act.

And she did act—the bill never went to the Lok Sabha and died a natural death.

◆

I stayed as far away from the IYC and the Sanjay-Ambika combine as I could. I was perhaps one of the very few who not only survived avoiding Sanjay, but also got away with challenging his diktats on three occasions.

The first brush was in a meeting of the Youth Advisory Council—a high-powered body chaired by the Prime Minister and attended by the Congress President, the Minister for Education and other key Ministers; representatives of the IYC and the NSUI; and Joint Secretaries in charge of these organizations, besides some Chief Ministers and young MPs and

MLAs. The meeting had been called at the insistence of Sanjay, who had a plan—to get the NSUI to merge with the IYC.

To the left of the Prime Minister sat Sanjay and Ambika. To her right was the Congress President, with me next to him. I recall the presence of Tarun Gogoi (Joint Secretary), Professor Nurul Hasan (Minister of Education) and V.C. Shukla (Minister for Information and Broadcasting), as also A.K. Antony, Vayalar Ravi, F.M. Khan and R. Gundu Rao, among others.

The meeting came to order as Indiraji took her chair. The moment the minutes of the previous meeting were passed, handpicked representatives, as though on cue, said they wished to raise an 'important issue' for consideration. They claimed that in view of the popularity of the IYC under the leadership of Sanjay Gandhi and the student community's desire to join the youth movement under his aegis, the NSUI had become redundant. 'This is the time to consolidate the youth movement under the banner of the IYC and strengthen the party's base among the educated youth,' was repeated by speaker after speaker, with an approving smile and nod from Sanjay.

I was shocked. 'What nonsense!' I muttered to myself. 'The universities are in turmoil and the students will quit the NSUI if the IYC even steps into campuses!' I whispered in Dev Kant Barooah's ears, 'You must stop this...'

He sat silent and smiled hesitantly, quite unwilling to step in.

Indiraji turned to me and said, 'I think Margaret has something to say. Let us hear her.'

I was stunned. Should I or should I not take on the all-powerful IYC and its boss? I smiled and said, 'No, ma'am, everyone is on one side. I should not speak.'

'No, no, let us hear the other point of view,' she insisted.

So I spoke. 'First of all, this item is not on the agenda. Why is it being discussed? Second, it is wrong to believe that university students support what the IYC is doing. The family planning campaign, for instance, is not for students. The IYC is for non-student youth, and merging the NSUI and the IYC will kill campus leadership. Besides, the girls will certainly not feel comfortable working with members from outside the university, belonging to a different age group; even their parents will have reservations. Third, when the IYC is so popular and powerful, why not let the NSUI retain its identity and work in its own space? Let the NSUI bring students to us through campus activities.'

There was dead silence.

'I do not agree,' said V.C. Shukla.

'I agree completely with Margaret,' came the firm voice of Professor Nurul Hasan. 'The universities are in turmoil, the students are against us. They need careful handling. I would strongly oppose any step in the direction of a merger. Please leave the universities alone. The IYC should stay out of them!'

Vayalar Ravi, the Founder-President of the Kerala Students' Union, who wanted his organization to remain independent in Kerala, supported our stand.

'This is not quite correct,' said Ambika.

'Yes, it is,' Professor Hasan asserted firmly.

Indiraji decided to step in. 'I think there is sense in what Margaret has said. I do not know why this discussion was started. Since there are differing views, let us put it off.'

At that stage, Sanjay intervened, 'We must thrash it out today. Everyone is expecting an announcement!'

Indiraji sternly said, 'That is not possible. Students all over the world are anti-establishment. Let us not fool ourselves. I will constitute a group of this committee to look into all the issues and report to us at the next meeting.' With that, Indiraji got up. So did everyone else.

Professor Hasan patted me on the back and said, 'Well done!'

But I just sat there, staring at the wall, not knowing what had hit me. I had actually challenged Sanjay Gandhi and his coterie, and won. Surely that spelt trouble? Was I doomed to become a modern-day Joan of Arc and get burned at the stake?

When I arrived at the AICC office, the NSUI cadres threw garlands and shouted, '*Margaret didi, zindabad Margaret didi, aage bado, hum tumhare saat hain!*' ('Long live, Margaret. Margaret forge ahead, we are with you!') I had to silence them as the office bearers approached me, smiling but afraid to speak, equipped with the real facts. Apparently, trucks full of IYC workers had assembled outside the NSUI office to take control and then march to the IYC headquarters to hail Sanjay and Ambika with banners and drums; that's when news of the meeting being adjourned trickled in. The IYC workers silently dispersed. All was quiet, now, at the IYC office.

Boxes of sweets arrived and a beaming George ordered tea for all of us. Suddenly I was the heroine—Indiraji had supported me and not the powerful Sanjay–Ambika combine. I ought to have been happy, but sensed that daggers would now be drawn to finish me.

Miraculously, I survived—but found myself in the middle of another face-off. On 13 April 1976, the infamous Turkman Gate demolitions[10] shook Delhi. A few days later, at 7 a.m., Subhadra Joshi, the veteran freedom fighter and MP, arrived in tears at my door.

'I do not know where to go, to whom to speak,' she said. 'Sanjay has gone mad, he is destroying us. His mother is a silent spectator. My constituency is ruined. The houses of innocent Muslims around Jama Masjid are being demolished. Curfew has been imposed, innocent women and children are crying for help. You must come with me to see them!' she pleaded.

'I will,' I said. I wore a saree and drove with her to Old Delhi.

Curfew was still on. Subhadraji had a curfew pass as a local MP, while I was driving in an AICC car. This gave us access to the area.

Subhadraji was expected there. Her workers had assembled all the affected women in the hall of an old house in a congested street. As we arrived, a barricaded door opened into a room full of wailing burka-clad women; a frail, middle-aged woman sat in their midst and beat her chest, inconsolable, muttering her tale of sorrow in chaste Urdu. There was silence for a minute when we entered, but this woman would not stop crying. Subhadraji put her arms around her, tried calming her, and told her that Indiraji had sent us to listen to their woes.

At that, someone shouted back, 'Where is she? Why is she doing this to us? Our homes have been bulldozed, our husbands are in jail, we have no food, our possessions are rubble!' There was despair and anger on the faces of these women; they bared their frail bodies—backs, shoulders, legs, arms—to show the blue and red marks of lathi blows inflicted on them. Even children had not been spared.

Then started the wailing, once again, of the frail woman in the centre of the crowd. Her mentally-challenged son, around sixteen years of age, stared blankly. Her young daughter sobbed, her eyes swollen, her cheeks red—she was to be married in a week. Her mother opened a cupboard and pulled out a red skirt, with zari work, and a dupatta. 'We have worked on this for weeks,'

---

[10]Turkman Gate, where Old Delhi meets New Delhi, became the central point of a demolition drive ordered by Sanjay Gandhi to promote urban beautification. In this low-rise slum, residents, who had also experienced forced sterilization, were almost run over by demolition squads and fired at by the police.

she whispered. 'My son, who was our only support, has been killed by the police. I want him back. Bring him back to me!' She wailed and swooned.

We were told the full story of the tragedy. The weeping woman's elder son, all of twenty-one, was employed as a lab assistant in a government hospital. He was at work when the radio announced curfew in the Jama Masjid area. Fearing for his mentally-challenged brother, who often roamed the streets, he rushed home on his bike at lunch time to make sure he was safe. Before he could reach home, he was shot and wounded. His family was not informed. He was dragged into a police van, bleeding, dumped in a hospital and allowed to die.

When news of the boy's arrest and injury reached his mother, she rushed out, pleading with the police to let her see him. But they pushed her away, saying they knew nothing about her son. After two days, his body was released; his clothes soiled with mud and blood. No explanation was offered and no postmortem report arrived.

As Subhadraji and I tried to console this distraught mother—tears were streaming down my own cheeks—the woman started hurling abuses and curses, asking Allah for revenge. The friends around her joined in shouting, 'Amen, amen.'

I was stunned. I pleaded with her not to curse. 'Indiraji does not even know what is happening. She has not ordered the shooting,' I said.

But no one was prepared to listen.

Subhadraji and I decided to leave; we promised that we'd brief Indiraji. On the journey back, I kept crying. I could not believe that this had been allowed to happen under a Congress government in a free, democratic country. I could not believe that the beautification of the Jama Masjid area had taken precedence over human lives and liberty. I could barely digest the fact that now, with fundamental rights abrogated, courts could not be appealed to.

Something was going very badly wrong. But no one was willing to speak. Jagmohan (Vice Chairman of the Delhi Development Authority) and B.R. Tamta (Delhi's Municipal Commissioner), far from stopping the rot, kept implementing orders.

'Only god can save this country,' I muttered

'If there is one!' replied a stoic Subhadraji.

I reached home, flushed and dishevelled, had a quick bath and rang up N.K. Seshan, telling him I had to meet Indiraji most urgently. In ten minutes, he telephoned back, calling me to South Block. The moment I reached, I was called in. My eyes and nose were red.

Indiraji looked at me sternly and asked, 'So you have been in Old Delhi, meeting people with Subhadraji? Are you aware that curfew is on?'

I was a bit unnerved. The Intelligence Bureau (IB) report had reached the Prime Minister before I could even seek an audience. 'Yes, ma'am,' I muttered, 'and I am glad I went. Things are going terribly wrong. The people are angry, women and children are starving, the men are behind bars. Common citizens have lost everything and innocent people have been shot. When will this end?'

'Subhadraji gets agitated about everything. Besides, everyone complains behind my back. When I called a meeting of the local MPs and MLAs of the party to verify facts, not one spoke. In fact, they praised the clean-up drive; they said, we were shifting the residents of Old Delhi to cleaner and better surroundings; they claimed they'd be happy.'

I knew this was only half the truth. The fact was that nobody wanted to criticize the drive and become Sanjay's target. 'They are afraid, ma'am,' I blurted out.

'Of whom?' she snapped back.

I kept silent but tears welled up in my eyes.

Indiraji noticed this and melted. 'I know you are upset. You are young and new to Delhi. I wanted to go to Jama Masjid and look at the situation myself. But I was stopped for security reasons. Some hard decisions have to be taken sometimes. Otherwise nothing can change, right?'

I had no answer. I just said with a breaking voice, 'For your sake, for their sake, I wish you could go, ma'am. They are expecting you.'

With that, I left the room. I thanked Seshan and went to Parliament, where everyone was whispering the details surrounding the gruesome incidents. But nobody was inclined to speak out.

Gradually, opposition to what was happening in Old Delhi began to grow both within and outside the party. Senior leaders close to Indiraji were targeted and eased out. Siddhartha Shankar Ray, Nandini Satpathy and Rajni Patel were replaced, and Dev Kant Barooah was sidelined.

Strangely, I survived this turn of events as well.

The third time I caused Sanjay offence was when I went to a student convention organized by Allahabad University as Joint Secretary in charge of the NSUI. The turn out was huge, and despite the Emergency, the response of students to the speeches being delivered was heart-warming.

Towards the end, H.N. Bahuguna—who had been General Secretary of the AICC in 1969, and was now the Chief Minister of Uttar Pradesh—made an appearance. I later understood that the popular leader had fallen from Sanjay's grace.

As Bahuguna walked in, the entire audience was on its feet, shouting, 'zindabad' and 'aap aage bado, hum tumhare saath hain'. ('Forge ahead, we are with you.') Bahuguna was a brilliant orator. He mesmerized the students with his half-hour speech. Little did I realize then that this event had been organized as a show of strength, so Bahuguna could prove his own popularity!

Consequently, when I returned to Delhi, I had to answer many questions, among them this—why had I accepted an invitation to share the platform with the Chief Minister? Sanjay, I was told, was very upset.

Happily for me, I survived this round, too. As for Bahuguna, support or no support, he made way for N.D. Tiwari in 1976, a man nicknamed 'New Delhi Tiwari' because he spent more time in Delhi than in Lucknow. Tiwari was Sanjay's choice.

As for me—my multiple brushes with Sanjay began to have a ripple effect. People began to respect me, yet were afraid to associate with me openly, even though they were aware that I had a special and direct rapport with Indiraji. Sanjay, I knew, would get back at me one way or another. He did this—or at least tried to—at a later stage.

◆

Niru was still working for FCI in Delhi. We were staying at 28, Rajendra Prasad Road. Baba's seventieth birthday was approaching, so we began to plan a celebration—our guest list comprised mostly Mangaloreans and a few of his political associates.

When I phoned Praxy Fernandes—a close family friend and then the Petroleum and Fertilizer Secretary—to invite him, he mentioned something that stunned me. 'You are planning a celebration,' he said. 'Are you aware that your husband may be in jail by then?'

'For what? What has he done?' I shot back in dismay.

He said he would come home to explain, which he did the next morning on his way to his office.

I learnt that a list of fifteen officers/Directors of FCI had been prepared by the Minister of Chemicals and Fertilizers P.C. Sethi, for violation of the Fertilizer (Control) Order[11]—considered a serious offence under the Defence of India Rules (DIR) in force. Niru's name was number 14 on the list.

This was exactly the matter the CBI had inquired into, back when Niru had been posted in Bangalore as Sales Manager and Dev Kant Barooah had been the Minister. We were under the impression that the matter was closed. But, it turned out, the closure report hadn't been filed.

Now, the matter was reopened for reasons of vengeance. Apparently, Sethi had wanted an FCI contract given to the petrochemical firm, Snamprogetti of Ottavio Quattrocchi, on the orders of Sanjay. S.K. Mukherjee, the Managing Director of FCI, insisted that Snamprogetti did not meet the requirements of the tender. To punish Mukherjee for defying the directions of Sethi (and Sanjay), Sethi, apart from reopening the case, ensured that fifteen officers, who actually had nothing to do with the allotment of this contract, were also put under scrutiny.

Fernandes told us that he had explained the injustice of the plan to Sethi, and, as a final resort, had mentioned that number 14 was Alva—the husband of Margaret Alva, an office bearer at the AICC. However, his pleas had little impact. He advised me to go to the Prime Minister or Seshan immediately, and update them about what was happening.

For me, my only hope was our family friend, Om Mehta, always kind and protective. I visited him in Parliament and explained the situation. He listened. He promised to keep track of developments but insisted that I brief the Prime Minister. I remained hesitant.

I met Rajni Patel and Nandini Satpathy who were in Delhi. I even went to Dev Kant Barooah, and then to Siddhartha Shankar Ray. But no one wanted to annoy Sanjay by intervening. They all urged me to go to the Prime Minister.

Time was running out. The FCI team was in jitters as their office antenna had picked up the news. They were at my door every day. Finally, I decided to meet Indiraji at her South Block office. I related the whole story, told her that I had come for justice, and added, 'If they are guilty, hang them

---

[11]To ensure an adequate availability of fertilizers at the right time and at the right price to farmers, fertilizers were declared as essential commodities and the Fertilizer (Control) Order was promulgated to regulate the trade, price, quality and distribution of fertilizers in India.

at Connaught Place. But if they are innocent, only you can save them!'

'Something is going wrong with Sethi these days. Keep in touch with Om Mehta,' was all Indiraji said. Then she picked up the phone and ordered someone at the other end, 'Keep track of Sethi's file on the FCI officers. Send it to me when you receive it. Margaret is here with me...' I do not know who she spoke to.

'Thank you, ma'am,' I said and left.

Baba sensed something was up, but we kept the news from him. Instead, we went ahead with preparations for his birthday, hoping that Sethi would be compelled to drop his crazy idea.

But this did not happen. One afternoon, while I was in the Rajya Sabha, I received a message that Sethi wanted to see me. He had sent his PA with a car to take me to his office. I hesitated, and went up to Om Mehta in the House for advice. He told me to go and let him know what transpired. So I went.

Sethi welcomed me, and then came straight to the subject. 'Your husband works for FCI?'

'Yes,' I responded.

'Is his name Niranjan?'

'Yes.'

'You are aware that his name is on the list of officers to be punished for a grave offence?'

'They have committed no grave offence! The matter was investigated by the CBI before I came to Parliament. It is closed.'

'Do not get angry with me. You have been speaking to everyone but me. I am a friend of your family. I have known Joachim and Violet Alva, who have been my colleagues and friends, for years. I want to help your husband...'

'But he has committed no crime!' I pleaded.

'Do not argue. I will remove his name from the list but you must promise not to interfere with the others. They will have to go to jail.'

'Why?' I asked.

'Because I say so,' was his caustic reply.

'They will fight legally for justice. I know the law,' I said tactlessly.

'Oh, so you are challenging me? I will detain them under MISA, which keeps the courts out,' he threatened.

'That is for you to decide, sir,' I said, and stood up. 'If my husband is innocent, every one of them is innocent. I am not pleading for a favour for my husband. I am fighting for justice and I am sure they will receive it.' I turned to leave.

Sethi spoke again. 'Tomorrow is Saturday—a holiday. Why don't you, your husband and children join my family for a picnic? We have some friends from Bhopal. You will like the place.'

'It will not be possible, sir,' I replied.

'Okay. Then by the time you go home this evening, your husband will be behind bars with the others,' he announced gleefully, swinging his baton as he saw me to the door.

I looked at my watch. It was 2 p.m.

Sethi's PA dropped me back at Parliament House. I rushed to Om Mehta's office; he was having lunch. I repeated the conversation to him. 'Do not worry, leave the matter to Indiraji's judgement,' he said.

I went home, phoned Niru at his office, and asked him to come home immediately, which he did. We sat down, waiting for the 'knock'. Niru considered it his duty to inform his colleagues of the possibility of arrest. In an hour, they were all at our house, nervously sipping cups of tea. We switched on the evening news, only to hear an announcement we least expected—'Sethi relieved of portfolio'.

Within minutes, Om Mehta was on the line telling me that Sethi had sent him the file for approval of the arrests. As directed, the file went to the Prime Minister, and within minutes, she acted—she made him a Minister without portfolio.

Indraji's commitment to justice had prevailed over Sanjay's might.

Festivities in the house continued past midnight, with FCI officials pouring in. Baba's birthday was a big celebration, attended by Praxy Fernandes, among others.

I had confronted Sanjay once again and won. Trouble was to be expected. But at least Niru was not in jail.

Chapter 10

NEW SHORES:
AT THE UNITED NATIONS

29 March 1976 saw Air India's 'Emperor Akbar' fly to Australia on its inaugural flight, touching Perth and Sydney, via Madras and Singapore. The then Minister for Tourism and Civil Aviation, Raj Bahadur, invited members of the Civil Aviation and Tourism Committees to join this flight with other airline representatives, tour operators, etc., with elaborate guidelines to the MPs—the most important of these being that no liquor would be served or consumed on the flight.

Whatever the reason, Sheila Kaul, the Prime Minister's aunt, and I were nominated by Indiraji to accompany the delegation. Our brief was to keep track of the MPs and make sure that there was no mishap. Instead of the Minister for Tourism and Civil Aviation, Om Mehta, in his capacity as Minister for Parliamentary Affairs, was made Leader of the delegation.

Once on board, there was a virtual revolt. How could MPs be treated like children? How could they be stopped from buying themselves a drink or from accepting one offered to them by the other guests on board? When the bar opened, many of the MPs went to the lounge and drank to their hearts' content. After a stopover at Singapore we landed in Perth.

We were invited to a formal, sit-down welcome dinner in the banquet hall of the hotel that night—with a beautifully laid out table with immaculate linen and silver and cut-glass service. Many MPs drank from soup bowls raised to their mouths, others abandoned the cutlery and ate with their fingers, still others washed their fingers in their plates! Our appeals in Hindi to wait for finger bowls did little to check their hurry to finish the job! We decided that enough was enough. There would be no more formal dinners or lunches; only buffets with small tables and afternoon meals on the lawns with paper napkins.

We then came to Canberra to attend a reception hosted by the Australian Prime Minister at Parliament House. There were so many of us that the reception hall was packed, and guests joked about India's population 'spilling over' into Australia!

Then came an unexpected crisis at the hotel. We were told that we could go down to the coffee shop at our convenience for meals, or call for room service. A few of us decided to venture into town while others stayed back. When we returned, we were called to Om Mehta's room. The hotel staff and our hosts sat glum-faced. I knew at once that something had gone terribly wrong.

It turned out that one of the housekeepers had knocked at the door of an MP, who opened it in his bathrobe.

'Room service, sir, may I turn in your bed?' she asked.

'Yes, yes, come in,' our MP said.

As the housekeeper finished clearing the room, and asked if he required anything, the MP tried to pull her into bed with him! She screamed and ran out, cursing the guest and all Indians. There was a strike—no one would serve the Indians at the hotel

The MP explained what had happened. He was most apologetic. He said that when she knocked and said 'room service', did up the bed and drew the curtains, he presumed she had been 'sent' by the hotel for the night!

It took all the PR (Public Relations) at our disposal to stop the press and the police from getting involved. The MP gave an unconditional oral apology. It was decided that we would leave the hotel by bus early the next morning for a sightseeing trip and drive straight to the airport for our onward journey to Sydney, Melbourne and the Gold Coast.

As part of our trip, we were taken to the oldest wine brewery of the continent. After an educational tour on wine-making, tables at the exit with white and red wine bottles were set for us. It was presumed that each visitor would pick one. But no. Since the bottles came without a price, MPs picked up as many as they could hold, and clutching them, made a merry exit—little realizing that the brewery had invited the media to cover the visit. We were on all the local channels that night and on the front pages of the local dailies, with photographs of MPs hugging bottles to their chests—a good advertisement for the product!

Back in Delhi, Sheilaji and I went to Indiraji to submit a report of the trip. I said, 'It went off well, except for...'

Before I could complete my sentence, Indiraji interrupted, 'Yes, except for the drinking and clutching of bottles for TV channels!' She had already heard about it. So we said nothing more.

The infamous trip with the MPs was the first of my five official visits to Australia, which included a CPA (Commonwealth Parliamentary Association) conference and a week's visit as Minister-in-waiting to Vice President K.R. Narayanan, which took us to places off the tourist map— visiting even the Aboriginal reserve and Ayers Rock, considered sacred by them, in the heart of the continent.

In hindsight, I believe Indiraji was grooming me for Foreign Affairs. She made me second resolutions on foreign affairs at AICC sessions and invited me to banquets for important foreign guests. As a member of the External Affairs Consultative Committee, I began to absorb the nuances of our foreign policy—reading, listening and interacting with officials of the External Affairs Ministry.

◆

One day, in July 1976, Om Mehta told me that he was recommending my name for the delegation of MPs to the UN General Assembly. I presumed the matter had been discussed at the highest level.

'Is this to keep me out of Sanjay's way?' I asked.

To this, Om Mehta said that my performance in the House had been so good that he felt I would be able to shine at the UN and speak for the country.

I was excited about a three-month trip to the US. Yet, I had reasons to worry. What would Baba say? How would Niru and the kids manage? What would I do all alone in a hotel in New York? The thought began to terrify me. Should I go or should I not? When I broached the subject at home, there was silence at first. Baba advised caution since no decision was final until the 'lady' had spoken.

Then came the call from the Prime Minister's Office (PMO). Indiraji told me she was sending me as part of the delegation to the UN. 'But you are not going only to the General Assembly. I want you to travel around US—speak at universities, engage with the Indian community and talk to opinion makers and the media. The Embassy is being informed. They will make all the arrangements and brief you. Remember, you are going not only as a representative of the government, but also of the party.'

I thanked Indiraji and promised to do my best. Then, hesitantly, I asked, 'Are you sending me to get me out of the way? I understand the

Guwahati AICC session will endorse the merger of the NSUI with the IYC.'

'Not at all,' the Prime Minister replied. 'Nothing will happen when you are away. So go!'

I rang up Om Mehta to tell him of my meeting. 'I told you so!' was his reply.

I then went to meet the Congress President, Dev Kant Barooah. His response was quite honest. 'Indiraji wants to protect you from her son. It is good that you are going.'

The next two weeks were hectic. Before I left, I got Geetanjali Sharma, the daughter of Shankar Dayal Sharma, appointed General Secretary, with Lalit Maken as the President of the NSUI. (Sharma and Maken were later married; a few years later, they were assassinated outside their home by terrorists.) At home, I ensured that arrangements were made for the children to be looked after and the house tended. It was decided that Manira, then five years old, would go to Bangalore to my parents; the two boys, Nikhil (seven) and Niret (eleven), would stay with my brother, John, and his wife, Meena, in Vasant Vihar, and continue to go to school. Baba, Niru and the family dog would be looked after by Mary, our cook.

With great trepidation, I left for London, where my brother, Alan, was Deputy High Commissioner. I then flew alone to New York. I was being granted true exposure to the international scene, and was being watched. I had to prove my worth.

I was driven to Beekman Tower—a fully-equipped apartment hotel on First Avenue, opposite the Indian UN mission. M.A. Vellodi, Secretary of the External Affairs Ministry, came in to brief me on the work ahead and the systems to be followed. He submitted a file of information and telephone numbers, and gave me an envelope containing my first week's daily allowance in dollars. He then informed me that there was a supermarket across the road that sold most of the things I'd need.

When he had left, I double-locked my door and stared out of the window. Suddenly, I was nervous and homesick. How would I survive here, alone, for three long months? As I grew increasingly terrified and lonely, the phone rang—it was Mohanty, the MP from Orissa, who was in a room on the floor above. I was relieved—I had a familiar face for company.

Mohanty and I gradually acquainted ourselves with life in New York—going to buy groceries, adjusting to the occasional meals at cafés (not an easy task for him, since he was a vegetarian), and making time to cook our breakfasts.

There were many voices telling me to remain cautious in New York. 'Do not get into the elevator on your own,' one woman said; 'Never get in with a stranger,' said another; 'If someone breaks into your room, let him take whatever he wants—pretend you are asleep and do not scream,' said a third. Soon I began to get scared of going anywhere or being in the room by myself! To make matters worse, Congress leader K.P. Unnikrishnan's room was totally ransacked while he was at the UN. No clues were found despite police and UN staff intervention. It turned out that the only thing missing was his liquor. Unnikrishnan remained convinced it was an intelligence job. Then came the story of an Air India hostess staying in a five-star hotel in New York. When she returned to her room late one night, a man emerged from under her bed, demanded her cash—which she gave—and departed. He was never traced.

Completely petrified now, I decided to protect myself. I got a nylon rope which I tied to the doorknob, ran it through the fridge's handle next to it, and then tied the loose end to the arm of a substantial sofa, positioned each night with great effort in front of my bedroom door. I looked into every cupboard, the bathroom, outside windows and under the bed, before securing my apartment. Undoing the knots each morning proved to be quite a task, but this was a small price to pay for security. 'What if there is a fire? You will never get out,' a friend warned me. But this was a risk I was willing to take for a good night's sleep.

Days passed, and my routine got established—undo the nylon rope, rush through breakfast, head to the mission office for the delegation meeting at 9 a.m., discuss draft statements for our committees, report the issues that emerged in the committee or outside, meet various delegations and attend receptions. Yet, each night, I missed home, the children and Niru. I kept phoning, asking Niru to come, telling him that cheap tickets were available since that was the bicentenary year of American Independence. Finally, he decided to come.

One evening, after a UN-sponsored trip out of the city, when I returned to my hotel reception to claim my room keys, I found they were missing. Who had got access to them and my room? The lady at the counter, too, appeared worried. She went to her superior, who appeared, asking, 'Were you expecting a guest?'

'No,' I replied sternly.

'There was a gentleman here an hour ago,' he said, trying to remain calm. 'He had bags, and his passport. He said he was Alva from India. He claimed to be your husband, so we gave him your keys.'

I swung from a state of panic to joy. A part of me was still angry that the hotel had let a man into my room without my permission, but I was too thrilled to drive home the point. 'Put my husband on the line,' I demanded. When I heard that 'hello', the voice I knew—I could not contain my excitement. 'I am coming up!' I said, and in a couple of minutes was in his arms. I cried with happiness. I was no longer alone, afraid or lonely in New York. I had my man with me. We went out that night, walked the streets of Manhattan, dined at a Chinese restaurant and exchanged the news of the preceding month.

It was wonderful having Niru with me, though it added to my chores in the morning. He would join me for lunch at the UN, and then, together, we'd walk the streets, window-shopping, picking up souvenirs at sales and enjoying carefree afternoons. On weekends, he would take short sightseeing tours, while I'd deliver lectures defending the Emergency at home! Given my work schedule, I could accompany him only on one trip to the West Coast.

I would have been happy to have Niru with me in New York for a while longer, but he decided to travel by Greyhound across the country. With a thirty-day ticket, he travelled by night, sightseeing by day, and staying with relations and friends where he could. With Niru on the road, I was alone in New York again. Out came the nylon rope to secure my room at night!

On his return to New York, he discovered the only Irish bar in the locality, Fannegan's. Irishmen would gather there after work every night, glugging Irish beer and singing Celtic songs. Niru often lectured them about their struggle for freedom, comparing their fight with India's own battle against the British. He told them how his father had hosted a reception for Éamon de Valera, the great Irish patriot, on his visit to India. That story was sufficient—it made Niru an 'honoured Irishman', who got a drink on the house every time he dropped in.

I was now getting worn out with the strain of running around, cooking for Niru, working at the UN and travelling on weekends. The only chore Niru did with great enthusiasm was washing clothes—leaving the bathroom wet all day. His sticky plates, cutlery and cups would be left on the table; they'd stare at me when I returned after a hard day's work, to be cleaned up. One day, in sheer desperation, I said, 'Niru, all men in this country do the dish-washing. The least you can do is scrub your own dishes after breakfast or at least soak them in hot water in the sink!' Niru's response was, 'I do not care what the Americans do. I am an Indian husband. I cannot change because I am in America!' I had to accept what could not be changed!

◆

I had been deputed to the Third Committee (Social and Humanitarian Affairs), with Nina Sibal, a young, beautiful officer, as my 'advisor'. She was a wonderful companion, but the drafts she prepared for my statements had little content and lacked political thrust. I'd work on them at night, inserting quotations of Gandhiji, Pandit Nehru, etc. Soon I started getting appreciated for my work. At a lunch hosted by our Foreign Minister for the President of the General Assembly (from Sri Lanka), when I was introduced as the 'baby of the delegation', the President commented, 'You are making a name for yourself. I understand you are the daughter of the famed Alva couple. I am honoured to meet you. *Forum* had been our Bible during the freedom struggle; Joachim and Violet are well known to us. Give my regards to Joachim.' I felt so proud on hearing this that I wrote a long letter to Baba that night, telling him of this incident.

I used to be out of New York for weekends on UN-sponsored trips or for visiting meet-groups arranged by the Embassy. Within New York, I often attended meetings and seminars on weekdays. The audiences—Indian or American, students or professionals, journalists or businessmen—were all hostile. Indira Gandhi was termed a 'dictator', the Emergency was seen as the end of the democratic system, and the Declaration of Emergency as nothing more than a thoughtless act of a rubber-stamp President.

One of my first invitations was to the State University of New York at New Paltz, through Professor Karkala, a family friend; he had come to India twice as a guest of my parents, along with his Swedish wife. He was, therefore, protective of me, and warned me about the hostile attitude in his university towards Indira Gandhi and her son. At dinner, he asked me if he could glance through my speech.

'I have no written speech,' I told him, 'only points for reference.'

The professor was shocked. 'This will not do in the US,' he told me. 'You could be misquoted. Besides, the university will ask for a copy for their records.'

I was stunned. How would I produce a written speech by the morning? Left with no option, I stayed up for hours, writing everything that I wished to say about the events at home—general facts about the Indian political system, the achievements of the past thirty years, the events that had led to the Emergency, the Constitutional provisions, Parliament's endorsement and the normal functioning of the administrative system. I then slept, with a prayer that I may be able to defend my country and my leader in a convincing way.

The next day, in the university, I was escorted to the dais. I faced a packed hall of around 600-800 students. My heart beat fast and loud. After a brief introduction, in which my closeness to Indira Gandhi and the 'turmoil in India' were emphasized, the audience was told that I was there to explain the situation and would also answer questions for an hour. I spoke for about twenty-five minutes—not reading but keeping my sheets in front of me. No one interrupted, though there were low sniggers now and again, and occasional bursts of laughter. After my speech, the questions, with self-introductions, began. Comments began to fly. I stood my ground.

'You are more of a monarchy than a democracy,' someone said. 'You have a family ruling you, don't you? First, there was Motilal Nehru, then Jawaharlal Nehru, then Indira Gandhi—and now her son will take over!'

I explained that Motilal Nehru was never Prime Minister; that Lal Bahadur Shastri had been elected after Pandit Nehru and before Indira Gandhi; and that Sanjay was only a youth leader, not even the President of the IYC! As for political families, I asked the audience about the Kennedy clan: 'How many of them led you? If Robert Kennedy had not been assassinated, he would have succeeded his brother to the White House. You all but crowned Jacqueline Kennedy your queen after her husband's assassination, didn't you? And what about Senator Edward Kennedy? It seems to me that whatever you do is right, but what the developing world does is wrong and unacceptable.

'We are a democratic country. We have had regular elections in our states and at the national level. No one can be a leader unless voted by the people and no one can reject a leader who has the common man's mandate. Indira Gandhi will be the Prime Minister until she is voted out by the electorate. She is a committed democrat, and will accept the will of the people. I assure you, the people of India are with her today.'

There was silence. I was out of breath but quite pleased with myself.

The audience was taken aback. There were a few claps. Then came more questions about the leaders in jail, media censorship, bank nationalization and the makings of a communist state. I answered every query.

Finally, to sum it all up, I said, 'India is the largest democracy in the world today. A Western democracy colonized us, plundered and divided us, and left our people poor and hungry. We fought them, threw them out and survived. Yes, we have our problems but we will find our own answers. Do not forget that our civilization goes back thousands of years; yours is only two-hundred-years old. We are used to fighting and emerging.

'You may be a rich country, but money alone cannot solve problems or buy friends and allies. As for us, we have passed the stage where we need to beg for food or funds. If we need your technology, we will buy it. India will overcome her challenges with dignity. We will solve our problems our way—not *your* way.'

The entire audience was on its feet, clapping. I had won the battle. I walked out of the hall to their ringing applause. Professor Karkala and his wife, who were waiting for me, hugged me, telling me that I had been brilliant. On my bus ride back to the hotel, past the beautifully coloured forests of autumn, I was happy that I had been able to face my first hostile audience and helped change their minds.

In the days that followed, I was on local radio. I attended a seminar at Columbia University chaired by Dean Katie Embree, at UCLA (University of California, Los Angeles), at the Asia Society and at countless meetings of the Indian community across the US.

Every meeting started on a hostile note but ended like the one at New Paltz, with thundering applause. My confidence grew. I began to get bolder and sharper with my replies, particularly to the Indians in America who were most critical of the domestic scene. I once told them: 'You have abandoned your motherland and come here to live a life of comfort and luxury. We have stayed back and are struggling to serve our people. You got the best the country could give and left. Perhaps things would have been better if you had been there. But we will succeed and overcome without you. So keep your opinions to yourselves. We can do damn well without you.'

I found myself defending my country at unexpected fora. Once, on a UN-sponsored weekend trip to Illinois in mid-September, I found myself at a huge mechanized farm. Astonished at the size of the corncobs in the fields, I asked a colleague from South America, 'Have you seen anything like this?' Before he could reply, our American guide intervened, 'In fact, we feed this to our cattle and the balance is shipped as aid to countries like yours...'

I was red with anger. 'Oh really? Thank you for the information,' I muttered and walked off. This was the arrogance of plenty. There I realized why Indiraji had told the nation, 'We will never beg for food again,' while initiating the Green Revolution.

The high-water mark of my UN days was my appearance on the podium of the UN General Assembly; I was moving a resolution on behalf of my government for the admission of Vietnam as a member of the UN. My great ambition, even as a schoolgirl, was to address the UN General Assembly one day—and there I was. It was undoubtedly one of the proudest moments of my life—a dream fulfilled at the age of thirty-four.

That session saw the Farakka Water Dispute[12] between India and Bangladesh become a focal point of discussion. We had been specially briefed about this. Accordingly, meetings were fixed for us with friendly delegations. We were doing a good job.

Then, suddenly, A.B.A. Ghani Khan Choudhury, a Minister in the West Bengal Cabinet, who was being groomed by Sanjay to replace Siddhartha Shankar Ray as Chief Minister, descended on us. He claimed to be there as 'the voice of the Bengali people' and, along with a journalist who was serving as his PA, began his round of meetings with Islamic delegations. Unknown to us, the journalist-PA kept sending dispatches to the Bengali press, reporting confidential conversations with the delegations that Choudhuryji met and the assurances that seemed to be coming, in order to build his image in Bengal. These dispatches from New York naturally reached Bangladesh, whose External Affairs Ministry began to contact their Embassies in Dhaka. India found itself in the middle of a diplomatic crisis, and our delegation began receiving SOS calls from Delhi. Soon enough, the journalist-PA was sent back to Calcutta and Choudhury's meetings drastically curtailed!

---

[12]The Indian government chose to construct a barrage (operational since 1975) at Farakka, close to the Indo-Bangladesh border, in a bid to increase the lean period headwater supply into the Bhagirathi-Hooghly branch of the Ganges and increase the navigability of the Calcutta port. With Bangladesh claiming that its rivers were drying up because of excessive drawing of water by India, and with India concerned about surplus irrigation withdrawals by Bangladesh, the water during the lean season failed to meet the assessed demands in the two countries. A dispute arose between India and Bangladesh over the sharing of the lean season flow at Farakka.

*My grandmother (Bai) and great-grandmother (Mai)
at Churchills, Mangalore*

Aged three, with my mother; 1945

Welcoming Indira Gandhi to Mount Carmel College; 1960

As a bride, ready for the Roce ceremony; 23 May 1964

*With Baba, Kamaraj Nadar and Niranjan on the eve of our wedding at
Raj Bhavan, Bangalore; May 1964*

Renowned statesman Krishna Menon raising a toast at our wedding reception;
24 May 1964

The Alva family at our wedding; 1964

Just married: Mr and Mrs Niranjan Alva; 1964

With President of India Dr S. Radhakrishnan and Maya Alva at New Delhi; 1965

With KPCC President Devaraj Urs as Convener of the State Congress Women's Front; 1972

As the President of the Delhi YWCA, escorting Prime Minister Indira Gandhi,
Sonia, Rahul and Priyanka at the annual flower show; 1975

The Indian delegation to the first UN Conference on Women in Mexico; June 1975

As Joint Secretary, AICC with AICC President Dev Kant Barooah in New Delhi; 1976

Speaking of Choudhuryji—who later became Union Railway Minister and did great service to the Bengal rail network—he was a Bengali zealot, who refused to tolerate any criticism of his compatriots, even if a critique was delivered in good humour. I remember a dinner at the residence of Saad Hashmi, the young, dynamic Deputy Permanent Representative. There were jokes flying from all sides, including a few 'sardar jokes'. Someone happened to speak of a sardar soldier in the Bangladesh war—a brave and patriotic man from the Sikh Regiment who swore to fight the enemy to the finish and struggled to remain on the battlefield even when badly wounded. Taken to hospital, he recovered and was deemed fit to return to the frontline. But he started finding excuses to remain in the hospital. A psychiatrist was called in, who pronounced his diagnosis. The young sardar wished to lead a union he had formed of hospital-workers. 'He had transfusions here,' the psychiatrist concluded, 'and all the donors were Bengali. So, his profile has changed. He wants to be a union leader not a soldier.'

There was loud laughter. Choudhuryji, however, was not amused. He stood up. 'How dare you suggest that Bengalis are not patriotic? Have you seen the roll call of honour on the walls of the central jail in Andaman? They were all Bengali patriots who languished and died for their motherland. You have insulted my people. I cannot share a meal with you!'

Out he marched, leaving us stunned. That was the end of all jokes. One of the guests wryly said, 'We knew the Bengalis were great trade unionists, but we didn't know they lacked a sense of humour!'

◆

My speeches in the Third Committee were being reported in Indian newspapers in a big way. My parents kept showing my pictures to Manira (who was now with them), telling her to be proud of me. One day, she asked my mother, 'Did you leave your daughter and go away like my mother has?' On another occasion she retorted, 'In any case, those speeches must be written by Dada!'

I kept in touch with Manira, writing to her constantly and phoning her occasionally. She seemed to be missing her parents, brothers, home and Baba, and had started expressing her unhappiness in unusual ways—hiding under beds when her teacher came, refusing to take her medicines, insisting that she be fed her meals. I was miserable every time I thought of her!

The boys, in comparison, seemed to be happy, going home from school to have lunch with Baba and returning to Vasant Vihar for the night. But I sensed that even they were longing to be back home.

News from India was not very encouraging. Congress leaders were being humiliated, getting shunted out of office, or sitting at home in sullen silence. The IYC was dictating terms, and people were growing restless. In the midst of all this, the Guwahati session of the AICC was held. It was a big show of strength. Most of the North-eastern regional groupings of the Congress merged with the Indira Congress.

One ray of light during this period came from the NSUI. With me out of the way, and the all-powerful Sanjay Gandhi in total command, the IYC had been back to its tricks, hoping to get the NSUI merger accomplished. So the IYC suggested to Indiraji that instead of the usual practice of the Prime Minister addressing each frontal organization separately, the IYC and the NSUI could have one big meeting to save time and energy. But Indiraji saw through the ploy, and conveyed a firm 'no'—I am told, she informed Dev Kant Barooah that she had given me her word that the status of the NSUI would remain unchanged during my absence, and she planned to respect that commitment. Consequently, separate conventions were held, and this provided a great boost to the NSUI. With the support of Dev Kant Barooah, students of the North-east were mobilized, and Indiraji congratulated the NSUI on its show of strength. I was thrilled.

Information trickling in from Unnikrishnan's sources suggested that the General Elections would be postponed as many Chief Ministers were demanding it. It was conveyed that the situation was not conducive to elections. The law and order situation was just returning to normal; restrictions had to be gradually lifted and the leaders released in batches. This required time and careful monitoring. So the official line was that any talk of elections at this stage was premature and dangerous. So convinced were Unnikrishnan and Virbhadra Singh about this that they decided to take a month-long break, visiting friends in the US and Europe after the session. Unlike them, Niru and I planned our return for 20 December, with stopovers in London and Paris.

As the UN session was inching to a close, the Indian Ambassador arranged for the delegation to visit Washington, where we met some friends of India, elected representatives and prominent Indians. On the last day, the Ambassador was to host a breakfast at his official residence and we were informed that we would meet the press.

The press was hostile, but by now, I was used to it. We answered all their questions calmly. Then came the loaded one: 'How long will the Emergency last? When do you expect to have your General Elections?'

'Difficult to predict anything from this distance,' came the reply from the Ambassador.

Unnikrishnan added, 'Well, it depends on the situation at home.'

Virbhadra Singh shuffled uncomfortably in his chair and said, 'I agree with them.'

'Can I say something?' I asked.

'Yes, of course,' drawled the Ambassador, patronizingly.

'I work closely with the Prime Minister,' I said. 'I know her well enough to say she is a true democrat.'

There was laughter all around. 'Then why take recourse to a draconian Emergency?' came a question.

'To save the country from the chaos created by the opposition,' I snapped back. 'As for elections, they will be held on time because Mrs Gandhi will not stay in office without the mandate of the people of India.'

There was silence and disbelief all around. The Ambassador, stunned, stood up, and said, 'On this note of hope for India, I end this press conference.'

Everyone stared at me; I was amazed at myself, but I knew I had spoken with the inner conviction that, ultimately, India and her people were more important to Indiraji than her chair or her son.

Unnikrishnan took me aside and said, 'What made you say that with such confidence? It will be headlines everywhere, here and in India. Have you been told something that I'm not aware of?'

'This is my reading of Indiraji,' I replied. 'Something tells me she will call elections, if only to free herself from the sycophants and manipulators around her.'

'I hope you are wrong,' said Unnikrishnan gravely, 'because I am starting my one-month trip tomorrow.'

After some last-minute shopping for gifts, a boat trip to the Statue of Liberty, and farewell calls, we found ourselves in London on 20 December. We spent a wonderful week in the city, bringing in Christmas with my brother and his family, attending midnight mass at the Westminster Cathedral and watching the crowds frolic in the snow at Trafalgar Square.

We spent an unforgettable New Year in Paris before flying home on 5 January 1977.

I met Indiraji when I returned, gave her a few gifts and tried to explain what I had accomplished.

'I have been receiving glowing reports. Well done! Now, there is a lot more to do, so get ready,' she smiled.

Happy as I was to be back, I remained uncertain of what the morrow would bring.

Chapter 11

DEMOCRACY PREVAILS:
THE END OF THE EMERGENCY

The life of Parliament had already been extended by one year in 1976. Now, Sanjay and his team wanted it extended further—arguing that releasing leaders and going for elections immediately thereafter would be disastrous.

But Indiraji was at heart a democrat. She may have concentrated power in her hands, but she did not want to stay without the endorsement of the people. She was beginning to sense that harsh Emergency measures, the misuse of authority by Sanjay and the suppression of fundamental rights were making her unpopular. She was not prepared to postpone elections any further. Her assessment was that if elections were held soon, the opposition leaders released from jail would have no time to unite and win; the well-organized machinery of the Congress would have a definite edge. Besides, the people, it seemed, were generally happy, as the economy was booming, food prices had been contained, and government departments, public services and industrial conglomerates were functioning smoothly.

However, Indiraji had failed to assess the seething undercurrent of anger that existed against the establishment. The press had been silenced, public opinion suppressed. And since nobody could speak frankly within the party, how could she know the truth?

After a Cabinet meeting on 18 January 1977, Indira Gandhi drove straight to AIR (All India Radio) to announce that Parliament would be dissolved, elections held, the Emergency lifted and jailed leaders released. The nation was stunned, but rejoiced. Indian democracy had survived the onslaught of the Emergency. For me, it was a moment of triumph—what I had believed in had become reality. Indira Gandhi, the democrat, had prevailed.

Indiraji's decision to hold elections, despite objections from multiple quarters, had an electrifying impact. While there was much praise for her bold initiative—one that would restore democratic rule—there was nervousness within the Congress. With the election date set for 20 March 1977, the party had to move quickly. Emergency restrictions and the fear of Sanjay had made most Congress leaders 'mauni babas'. It was difficult for the party to shed the stupor of the past two years overnight. Everywhere there were whispers: 'Who advised her? Why are we rushing into elections before things settle down?' There were no answers.

Events overtook all plans. In hindsight, while the decision to hold elections was correct, the scheduling of the process was all wrong. Lifting the Emergency, releasing jailed leaders and opposition activists, ending press censorship—they all came too fast, and descended on the country like an avalanche. Safety barriers collapsed; pent up anger surged and found expression. There were resignations and desertions, meetings and rallies of released opposition leaders, new formations and alliances, and confusion everywhere! No one seemed to know how to respond to the situation.

On 23 January 1977, leaders of the main opposition parties met at the residence of Morarji Desai and announced the formation of the Janata Party—merging Congress (O), Bharatiya Jana Sangh, Bharatiya Lok Dal (BLD) and the Socialist Party, to fight the elections unitedly with a common symbol. The new party launched its campaign with a massive rally at the Ramlila Grounds on 6 March. The election was projected as an Indira Gandhi versus JP referendum.

Soon the exodus of senior leaders began. One by one, like rats abandoning a sinking ship, they left. I returned from Bangalore to Delhi on the evening of 2 February 1977, and drove straight to 1, Safdarjung Road. There were crowds milling around the traffic circle. I got out when I spotted N.D. Tiwari with the Congress flag in his hands, raising slogans against Jagjivan Ram, and calling him a traitor and 'gaddar'; I realized that Babuji (as Jagjivan Ram was commonly referred to), who had moved the Emergency resolution in Parliament, had quit the Congress. Bahuguna, Swaran Singh, Nandini Satpathy and many others followed, to form Congress for Democracy (CFD) under his leadership.

I nervously entered the Prime Minister's house, uncertain about what to do or say. The moment she spotted me, Indiraji said, 'Babuji has resigned. He was the Chairman of the Campaign Committee. Go immediately to 14, Ashoka Road (the Campaign Committee office) with Dhawan, seal the office with a new lock, and see me in the morning.'

We did as we were told. Luckily there was no one at the office to challenge us. I visited Indiraji the next morning. She simply said, 'I have appointed you the Convener of the Campaign Committee. Go and take charge immediately.'

I was startled. How? Where? From whom? I went to my office at 5, Rajendra Prasad Road, and briefed George about our new job allocation. We stared at each other in shock and decided to await further directions.

The files stayed in the sealed office; the board went up outside my office; a formal circular regarding my appointment followed. How Sanjay could have allowed this, I have never understood. From that day on, the AICC became the hub for all publicity work for the election. Every poster, any material to be dispatched to the press, all orders for printing, had to bear my signature—'for and on behalf of AICC'. Party posters for the PCCs, which had already been designed, had to be printed, bundled and dispatched. This was more complicated than it at first appeared, given India's linguistic diversity. We finally created four regional centres—Kerala for the South, Maharashtra for the West, Delhi for the North and Calcutta for the East and North-east. Transparencies were prepared in different languages and sent to each of the centres for printing. I would make trips to these centres to follow up, check samples and give my stamp of approval for printing.

As the candidates began to be announced, material for each constituency in the North had to be sorted out, packed and dispatched. For this, I was asked to take over the Vishwa Yuvak Kendra in Chanakyapuri, Delhi—a building that V.C. Shukla and Sanjay had wrested control of despite protests. Here work would go on all night—receiving material, random checking for shortages, packing and dispatching packages before dawn. George and I worked round the clock, supervising.

Those were hectic days. Crores worth of material passed through my hands, with delivery slips and receipts prepared by George. The well-oiled wheels of the machinery worked smoothly, and there was appreciation from all.

In the midst of all this, I was called to Om Mehta's office one day and asked to sign some papers that had been prepared, asking for allotment of 2, Kushak Road, to me, as guest accommodation. It was to serve as P.C. Sethi's office for the campaign. I obliged on the assurance that advance rent was being paid by the party. Little did I know then that this one signature would cause me untold misery!

◆

I had little involvement with the campaign outside—except for a two-day trip to the North-east. Indiraji and Sanjay toured extensively. Both sought the mandate of the people, apologized for mistakes that may have been committed and promised a clean, effective government. Sanjay also expressed regret for the immoderation of the Emergency. Their speeches seemed to be having an impact, and the feedback we received at the AICC was largely positive.

While we and the government-run media projected the positive achievements of the Centre, the united opposition was intent on exposing the excesses of 'the dictator and her son'. Their slogan was: 'Vote Janata Party for freedom, Congress for dictatorship'. They projected stories of forced sterilizations and the Jama Masjid demolitions, and turned the Muslims against the Congress. To make matters worse, with Dalit leader Babuji's defection, a big chunk of the scheduled castes vote bank was also lost.

Before we could undo the damage, the elections were upon us. As results kept pouring in, we listened to the bulletins, huddled in the AICC office, in stunned silence. The results in the North were disastrous. The Congress lost all 85 seats in Uttar Pradesh, all 54 in Bihar; won 1 each in Rajasthan (out of 25) and Madhya Pradesh (out of 40). West Bengal had largely gone to the Left. In all, the Janata–CFD combine had won 298 seats, while the Congress was down to 153 (nearly 200 below the 1971 tally). Finally came the shock—Indiraji had lost, as had Sanjay. The saving grace was the South, that had voted for the Congress in large numbers—Andhra Pradesh had returned 41/42 seats to the Congress, Karnataka 26/28, Kerala 11/20 and Tamil Nadu 14/39. But this wasn't enough.[13]

As we came to terms with the numbers on the screen, we found it impossible to predict what would happen next—violence; jail; reprisal? The mood on the streets was combative. Crowds gathered, rejoicing at the defeat of the Congress. The gates of the AICC office were locked. When efforts

---

[13]See *The Election Commission*, in < http://eci.nic.in/eci_main/StatisticalReports/LS_1977/Vol_I_LS_77.pdf>, accessed on 12 October 2015.

were made to break in, the police alone could keep the premises secure.

I watched firecrackers light the midnight sky, and at dawn, walked home—cold, despondent, afraid. I sank into my bed, sobbing. The tension within me finally found release. I had one thought: What would happen to Indiraji? She had been repeatedly assured that the people were with her, that she would not confront defeat. Now things had gone terribly wrong, with her closest advisors having misjudged the silent anger of the people. If the Congress stood defeated, it was because this was the only way the common man could stop Indiraji's son.

Indiraji called the last meeting of her Cabinet at 1, Akbar Road, where a resolution was passed—thanking the voters who had stood by the party, apologizing for the mistakes of the Emergency, bowing to the will of the nation, congratulating the new government that would assume office and reiterating the party's commitment to serving the people, as it had done in the past. Indiraji then left for Rashtrapati Bhavan to submit her resignation as Prime Minister. It was 22 March 1977.

I had sought time to meet Indiraji after the results, but no one could get to her. I therefore proceeded to 1, Akbar Road, with a big bouquet of red roses and a handwritten note saying that I could not secure an appointment to meet her and would continue working with her. I added, 'The people will miss you and will bring you back soon'. I was standing under a tree, the large bouquet in hand, when Indiraji spotted me. She stopped and called me over; I ran up, gave her the flowers, and said, 'You will be back soon, ma'am.' Indiraji took the flowers and the letter with a sad smile and drove off.

The fall of the government had many repercussions. For one, Indiraji had to move out of her official residence. She shifted to 12, Wellington Crescent, with a tent pitched in the compound to serve as the office. For another, the party had to vacate its headquarters at 5, Rajendra Prasad Road, and move to Maragatham Chandrasekar's residence, then to Kamalapati Tripathi's, before finally settling into 24, Akbar Road, in January 1978, which was allotted to G. Venkataswamy, an MP from Andhra Pradesh.

Indiraji also had to release her government staff and draw on AICC personnel. One of the first ones chosen by her was V. George. 'Send me Margaret's PA. He will at least write correct English,' she is reported to have said. So out went George to the office in the tent, starting his journey with the Gandhi family, right up to the PMO in seven years. The whole AICC establishment was dismantled. Some retired, some moved to the CFD. Many were left to fend for themselves, their morale expectedly shattered. There were still others who returned to the security of their homes, or to small towns, to avoid the witch-hunt that was expected to follow.

Immediately after the debacle, we began work at the AICC under Purabidi's leadership. She called a few of us and told us that some senior leaders wanted to abandon Indiraji; they wanted her to step aside till the people's anger abated. We had to assess the mood of the party, and whip up support for our leader. We began phoning PCCs, frontal organizations and state players, asking them to call meetings and pass resolutions to endorse Indiraji's leadership. A CPP meeting was called with Y. B. Chavan in the chair. Indiraji, no longer an MP, was left out, which resulted in protests and the meeting getting disrupted. Purabidi and a few other seniors, who had insisted that she be invited, went and brought her, and she presided. That resolved matters momentarily, but the internal tussle continued.

◆

There was turmoil within the Congress, and the blame game had begun. Differences erupted over Indiraji's future role. Some, like Y.B. Chavan, who had become Leader of the Opposition in the Lok Sabha, advised her, saying, 'Sanjay and you should stay out of the public eye, at least till people forget the Emergency!' Others, eying the 'chair' in the now-truncated party, echoed Chavan's stance.

This compelled Devaraj Urs to call me up one day. 'Go to her,' he told me. 'Tell her that this is a ploy to get her out. If she stays out of the public eye, she will be forgotten. She has her governments in the South. Ask her to come to Karnataka and Andhra Pradesh on a tour. The people will welcome her.'

I conveyed Devaraj Urs' message.

Indiraji was pleased but hesitant. 'Not yet,' was her reply.

In May 1977 an opportunity arose for her to step out. Ever since the new government had taken over, the country had been witnessing widespread caste clashes. Nine Harijans had been burnt alive in Belchi, a sleepy hamlet in Bihar, by an upper-caste mob. In response, Y.B Chavan demanded an inquiry, while Indiraji, to reach out to the battered community, decided to visit Belchi. She flew to Patna, took a jeep, and then rode an elephant to cover the last leg of her journey—too slushy for any vehicle to drive through. Braving the wrath of nature to be with the families in Belchi brought her back to centre stage immediately. She hit the headlines as she attacked an indifferent and ineffective government. Once more, she became the champion of the weak and oppressed, the voice of the voiceless.

Obviously, this rattled the government. Charan Singh, then the Home Minister, decided to put an end to her re-emergence. One afternoon in October 1977, she was picked up by the police and driven to an undisclosed destination in Haryana; a convoy of vehicles, put together by Sanjay, with the speed of lightning, followed. Luckily, the level crossing gate on the way was shut. As the vehicles halted, she got out and, surrounded by her supporters, sat on a culvert, and waited for her lawyers to arrive. When they reached the spot and challenged the police, it turned out that the latter did not have a warrant to move her out of Delhi. Consequently, they were forced to drive her back. She was taken to the police headquarters guest house in Old Delhi where she spent the night. Nirmala Deshpande, the noted Gandhian, stayed with her.

The news of Indiraji's arrest spread like wild fire. The mobilization of Congress workers started, and they decided to follow her to court the next day; all of us were phoned and told to be there.

Late in the night, I had a phone call from D.P. Singh, an MP from Bihar. Rajiv (Indiraji's older son) and he were to take breakfast to Indiraji at 7 a.m. Not sure that they would be allowed to go in, they wanted me, as a woman and an MP, to come along, since I might be permitted to meet her. I gladly agreed.

We drove to Old Delhi. As expected, we were stopped at the main gates of the police headquarters. While Singh accompanied the police to get the necessary clearances, Rajiv parked his car under a tree, and both of us got busy reading the newspapers carrying headlines and pictures of the events of the previous day. And then, almost out of nowhere, the media emerged; journalists had spotted Rajiv. I slipped out, but Rajiv stayed while the cameras clicked. He only smiled, refusing to speak. Finally, the police returned. They had an entry slip only for me. I went in with the breakfast.

Indiraji and Nirmalaji were sitting in their room, waiting for news. The information I had was that she would be taken to the Tis Hazari Courts by 10 a.m. Sanjay's storm-troopers had already started gathering there, with the administration and the police watching the situation.

Breakfast done, Indiraji was ready to go. Dhirendra Brahmachari, her spiritual guru, arrived to preside over a last-minute pooja. Soon cars drove up—Indiraji entered the first car, while Nirmalaji and I got into the second vehicle. The escort car kept getting confusing signals, first moving deeper into Old Delhi, then suddenly changing route. The plan, it seemed, was to confuse the IYC crowds. Finally, we arrived at the Parliament Street Courts, only to confront a shouting mob of Janata Party supporters, and lawyers, standing on chairs, all screaming, '*Phansi do, phansi do, Indira Gandhi ko phansi do!*' ('Hang her, hang her, hang Indira Gandhi!') I managed to weave my way in and find a corner to stand. Indiraji walked into the box, refused a chair and faced the judge.

Charges were presented. Indiraji's lawyer, Frank Anthony, then stood up to rubbish each of them, with a lethal combination of facts, humour and sarcasm. The trial lasted less than half an hour. Indiraji was released, with the court rejecting all charges as unfounded and frivolous. There were cheers from supporters as Indiraji emerged, smiling.

But, in the meantime, there had been mayhem in Parliament Street. The IYC boys had reached the venue and had clashed with the sloganeering anti-Indira crowd. Police had used lathis to disperse them. The street was littered with stones and chappals. Chairs, on which the screaming lawyers had balanced themselves, were now overturned, the lawyers missing. In the midst of this wreckage, standing outside, were Rajiv and Sonia.

Indiraji got into their vehicle and was whisked away to the safety of 12, Willingdon Crescent. Here she was welcomed by enthusiastic supporters with flowers, drumrolls and sweets, with Maneka and Sanjay leading the celebrations. I watched from a distance, when Indiraji suddenly beckoned me and whispered, 'My belongings are at the police guest house. They have to be brought.' I nodded. A car was arranged, and I went with an IYC volunteer. I had my pass. We checked the room, took charge of her bag and returned, signing the register of receipt: 'For and on behalf of Smt. Indira Gandhi'.

We returned, entering through the back gate. When I walked in with the bag, I was shocked to see Sonia in the kitchen, an apron tied to her waist, cooking all alone.

'Why are you not outside celebrating?' I asked.

'I am cooking something special for my mother-in-law,' she answered.

◆

Soon after the 1977 defeat, Niru and I were invited for dinner to Sitaram Kesri's flat in South Avenue, along with 'a few party leaders', as he put it. We were busy chatting when Sanjay arrived. I was taken aback; my heart missed a beat. I kept my cool as he went around greeting everyone with folded hands. He hardly spoke, except for a few pleasantries here and there. Kesriji later mentioned that Sanjay had wanted to meet me face-to-face; he had said, '*Yeh toh ajeeb aurat hai. Unse ek baar milna hai!*' ('This is a strange woman. I need to meet her once.') But he never did.

Whatever his faults, Sanjay was a bold go-getter with an astute political mind. He was street smart and a fighter. With Maneka and his charmed (though depleted) circle of hangers-on, he faced the post-defeat challenges of his family and the party head on, going in and out of jail. Indiraji now began to depend even more on him, creating ripples in the party.

Consequently, in the months that followed the Congress' defeat, more leaders began to leave. Barooahji, insulted, humiliated and ridiculed by Sanjay and his coterie, and cold shouldered by Indiraji, started to drift away. His team at the AICC felt the chill of a frozen relationship, and quit. Pranab Mukherjee, Buta Singh, A.P. Sharma, Mir Qasim and B.P. Maurya stepped in.

I went to Indiraji and Barooahji and told them I wished to move back to Karnataka to work for the party as an MP. I was soon appointed General Secretary of the Karnataka Pradesh Congress Committee (KPCC), and became active in state politics again. This marked the end of my first stint in the AICC.

In the meantime, huge bills had piled up at 2, Kushak Road, for rent, water, electricity, etc., plus interest and penalty charges. I kept receiving repeated reminders to pay up. I went to everyone I could think of—Om Mehta, who had made me sign the papers; Pranab Mukherjee, who was Treasurer of the party; and others—but no one would help. 'There is absolutely no money with us at the moment,' was the reply. To add insult to injury, someone even suggested I take a donation box around Central Hall. I phoned Devaraj Urs. His reply was, 'Let them send you to jail, it will expose the High Command and make a martyr out of you. Then I will bail you out!'

Soon came a court order. Since I had not responded to the repeated demands for the payment of dues, an attachment of all moveables was ordered, with a twenty-four-hour deadline to deposit the dues. I did not tell

Baba anything, but carefully moved our car and valuables to my brother's residence in Vasant Vihar, with only our books and clothes in the house—I thought they'd be of little use to anyone.

Finally, the party responded to my emergency call. A draft was deposited in court to save me further embarrassment.

Chapter 12

LEGAL MILESTONES:
CHANGING INDIA, LAW BY LAW

Even as I found my way around Parliament, I had started working with
D.P. Singh, a lawyer from Bihar who lived on Canning Lane, where
he had his home office. At the Supreme Court, he shared chambers with
R.K. Garg (a communist lawyer) and K. Ramamurthy. I used to assist at
the conferences at the home office as required, and had two other juniors
for company, R.K. Jain and L.R. Singh. My drafting skills were especially
appreciated; consequently, my tray was always full with drafts for editing.
D.P. Singh once commented, 'Margaret's mind absorbs things like a blotting
paper'!

But I did not feel comfortable in the court room—I would assist but
never argue, and would earn a junior fee for each appearance. On most
occasions, I would get so concerned about the clients and their woes, that
if we happened to lose a case, I would get utterly depressed, worrying
about the client's future! D.P. Singh once told me that I could never be a
successful lawyer if I got so involved with clients. But this was how I was;
I could not change.

After the defeat of 1977, nine Congress state governments were
dismissed on the grounds that they had lost the voters' confidence in the
Lok Sabha elections. Six of them went knocking on the doors of the Supreme
Court, seeking an injunction, terming the Home Minister's action illegal
and ultra vires. Karnataka and Andhra Pradesh got themselves impleaded.
A galaxy of senior lawyers were engaged, including Siddhartha Shankar Ray,
who by then was practising law in Delhi, and R.K. Garg; I was part of the
team assisting them. I quite enjoyed the experience—wearing my bands
and black gown, walking in with renowned legal luminaries, listening to
arguments, sitting in the Supreme Court café or library, attending briefing
sessions and learning constantly. The Seven-Judge Constitution Bench heard
the matter and a landmark judgement was delivered on 6 May 1977, which

upheld the Home Ministry's action, refusing relief to the state governments. For the first time since I started practice, I received a cheque for ₹15,000 from the Government of Karnataka. While I was more than happy about the payment, I was sad that the judgement had gone against us.

◆

After the Sethi episode, Niru had serious objections to continuing in FCI. The harassment and tension of those days upset him. Besides, he felt he was living a dual life, with his position at work at variance with his status in social and political circles. He therefore decided to quit the public sector in 1978 to start law practice. It was a big decision to take, but I stood by him. He started attending D.P. Singh's office, as I once had, with L.R. Singh and R.K. Jain helping him settle in.

His first big break was an arbitration case in Goa. He was engaged by the Speaker of the Assembly, Froilan Machado, who was also the Chairman of the Goa Barge Owners' Association, to represent the association in a matter regarding the classification of workmen. The case dragged on for almost three years and was eventually won by Niru and the team, with Siddhartha Shankar Ray arguing at the final hearing.

Around this time, the air hostesses of Indian Airlines—led by Prabha Rani, a bold air hostess from Kerala—came to me seeking my support as an MP. They claimed that gender discrimination was rife in the airlines— female cabin crew could not marry without permission; if they did get the permission they needed, they could not bear children; and whether or not they married or had children, they had to retire at thirty-five years of age. Worse, they had to undergo the humiliation of an annual medical check-up by male doctors to ensure that their weight and physical measurements met the stipulated norms. The male cabin crew, on the other hand, had no such rules to follow—they could marry, have kids, go bald, develop pot-bellies, and as long as they were deemed physically fit, they could serve till fifty-five years of age. Irrespective of seniority, a male cabin crew member was always in charge of the cabin.

The air hostesses' tale of woe did not end there. I learnt that they had been knocking on the doors of those who mattered in the airlines, the ministry, the government and Parliament. If at all they secured appointments, these would be at odd hours and at odd places, and their demands would inevitably be ridiculed. The unions, too, did not support them, signing agreements to protect the rights of male employees.

I was shocked when I heard of this—not least because we had had a woman Prime Minister with a son who was an Indian Airlines pilot. I had hoped that the Mexico Declaration, which pushed for women's equality, would transform our nation. But we still seemed to have a long way to go.

I decided to help. I met A.P. Sharma, the then Minister for Civil Aviation. His response was not encouraging.

Soon after, when there was a starred question regarding this issue in Parliament, it was treated lightly with jokes and jibes. To one supplementary, the Minister, in his seventies, replied callously in Hindi, '*Hum kya karein? Public toh jawan mahilaon ko pasand karti hain. Paitees saal ke bad, cabin mein kaam karna unko mushkil hota hai.*' ('What can we do? The public likes young women. After thirty-five years of age, these women find it hard to work in the cabin.') There was laughter from all quarters.

I was livid. I raised a supplementary, 'What is the "*kaam*" [work] in the cabin? Serving food, cleaning up, attending to the aged and the children? Who can do it better—men or women? May I ask our senior Minister how old his wife is, who serves him his tea and coffee at home? If she finds it difficult, would he opt for someone younger—under thirty-five years of age—to serve him?' The House roared with laughter.

The Minister responded, '*Yeh koi sawaal hai? Alvaji toh mujhe phasana chahati hai. Meri biwi toh saath saal se jyada umar ki hai aur meri sewa bilkul theek tarah se karti hai.*' ('What kind of question is this? Alva wishes to trap me. My wife is over sixty years old and looks after me well.')

'*Toh cabin mein bhi mahilaein pachpan saal tak sewa kar sakengi na?*' ('In that case, women in flights, too, should be able to work till fifty-five years of age?') I asked. There was no answer. The next question was called. But the press did carry my question as a box-item, which gave the issue the publicity it deserved.

Prabha Rani and her team came home to thank me. We got talking. I convinced them that the courts were their only hope as what the public sector airline was doing was totally unconstitutional.

At this stage, Niru got involved. D.P. Singh, after consulting his colleagues, thought this a fit case to fight. Niru's drafting was impeccable. The matter came up when Ms Fleur Latouché, the senior-most air hostess with Indian Airlines, was to retire. Niru and I appeared before Chief Justice Chandrachud, and Niru argued. The Chief Justice intervened to say,

'Mr Alva, I appreciate the legal points, but if there were a referendum, you would lose...men overwhelmingly constitute the majority of fliers.'

Niru smiled. I nudged him under the table and passed a slip reading, 'If the men want younger air hostesses, women fliers would also like to opt for younger men in the cabin to serve them!' Niru conveyed this as the opinion of 'my lady colleague'! There was laughter all around.

'Admitted without further arguments!' said the Chief Justice.

After a protracted legal battle between the air hostesses, the unions, the airlines and the government, a judgement was delivered by Justices Syed Murtaza Fazalali and A. Varadarajan. Relying heavily on Constitutional guarantees and Justice V.R. Krishna Iyer's landmark judgement in the Muthamma case[14]—quoted extensively by us in our petition—the Judges granted the air hostesses of Indian Airlines the relief they had sought.

They upheld the four-year ban on marriage on joining service, but struck down the ban on pregnancy stating:

> The termination of the services of an air hostess under such circumstances is not only a callous and cruel act but an open insult to Indian womanhood, the most sacrosanct and cherished institution. Such a course of action is extremely detestable and abhorrent to the notions of a civilized society. Apart from being grossly unethical, it smacks of a deep rooted sense of utter selfishness at the cost of all human values.[15]

While upholding the regulation requiring them to retire at forty-five years, they struck down the discretionary power of the Managing Director to grant an annual extension of service to them beyond thirty-five years of age, saying:

> The provision does not even give any right of appeal to higher authorities

---

[14]C.B. Muthamma, India's first woman career diplomat, brought a petition against the Government of India, stating that she had been overlooked for promotion since the rules governing the employment of women in the civil services were discriminatory. Her case was upheld in 1979 in a landmark judgement by a three-member Bench headed by Justice V.R. Krishna Iyer. The court impressed upon the Government of India 'the need to overhaul all service rules to remove the stains of sex discrimination, without waiting for ad-hoc inspiration from writ petitions or gender charity'. See 'C.B. Muthamma Passes Away', *The Hindu*, in <www.thehindu.com/todays-paper/tp-national/cb-muthamma-passes-away/article162436.ece>, 15 October 2009, accessed on 15 October 2015.
[15]AIR 1981 SC 1829.

against the order passed by the managing director. Under the provision, as it stands, the extension of the retirement of an air hostess is entirely at the mercy and sweet will of the managing director. The conferment of such a wide and uncontrolled power on the managing director is clearly violative of Article 14, as the provision suffers from the vice of excessive delegation of powers.[16]

The judgement further struck down the distinction made in the rules regarding the pregnancy of a married/unmarried air hostess, stating, 'The distinction of first pregnancy of a married woman and that of an unmarried woman does not have any reasonable or rational basis and cannot be supported.'

Referring to the statement of Indian Airlines in its affidavit that 'air hostesses are recruited for providing attractive and pleasing service to passengers in a highly competitive field and consequently stress is laid on their appearance, youth, glamour and charm', the Judges stated:

Such a morbid approach is totally against our ancient culture and heritage, as a woman in our country occupies a very high and respected position in society as a mother, a wife, a companion and a social worker. It is idle to contend that young women with pleasing manners should be employed so as to act as show pieces in order to cater to the varied tastes of the passengers when in fact older women with greater experience and goodwill can look after the comforts of the passengers much better than a young woman can. Even if the corporation had been swayed or governed by these considerations, it must immediately banish or efface the same from its approach. More particularly, such observations coming from a prestigious corporation like Indian Airlines appear to be in bad taste and is proof positive of the denigration of the role of women and a demonstration of male chauvinism and verily involves nay discloses an element of unfavourable bias against the fair sex which is palpably unreasonable and smacks of pure official arbitrariness.[17]

This strongly-worded judgement led to the redrafting of the service rules of the airline, making them gender neutral. It was truly a triumph. We had won the battle. The Indian Airlines hostesses rejoiced. Soon after, Air India

---

[16]*Ibid.*
[17]*Ibid.*

hostesses started their struggle for equality, and succeeded.

Niru and I had to face many snide remarks from friends, especially men, on the disservice we had done to the fliers who had to put up with 'ungainly, ageing cabin crew on flights'. Yes, the MCPs had a reason to wail! For Niru and me, though, this case was a high-water mark in our legal careers—for it was reported, widely quoted, debated and commended as a landmark judgment that upheld women's rights.

◆

I got involved with another Constitutional issue when I was approached for help for a cobbler working on the Nungambakkam High Road in Madras. He had been denied a shelter for work under the state government scheme because he was a Christian (albeit a scheduled caste one). We decided to move the Supreme Court. Niru and I drafted the petition, and with help from Fali Nariman—who appeared without a fee—managed to get it admitted. I could not pursue the matter further, because by the time it came up for a final hearing, I was a Minister. The cobbler lost the case but the battle for SC status to Christians and other minorities has continued to be raised in Parliament and outside, and has been gathering growing support.

This subject needs to be understood more clearly. The fact is that thousands of SCs have, over the years, adopted new religions. Notwithstanding their allegiance to a new religion, since their ancestors were SCs, they should qualify as SCs. The argument that Christianity does not recognize caste is not justified, especially in India, where socially, discrimination against minority SCs continues unabated.

Moreover, STs enjoy state benefits and reservations, irrespective of their religion. Why should only the SCs be denied these benefits?

Last but not the least, the Constitution prohibits discrimination based on religion; how, then, can Sikh and Buddhist SCs enjoy state benefits, leaving out the other minorities?

This has been the plea. Many states have placed SC Christians in the OBC (other backward classes) category. However, this does not quite solve the burning issues of discrimination and poor opportunity, and the fact that many privileges, available to SC/STs, remain beyond the access of OBC Christians.

◆

Then came the matter of the son of Morarji Desai, Kanti Desai—who had been accused of financial irregularities—before a Taxation Appellate Tribunal in Goa. D.P. Singh was to handle the matter and I was to assist. We were briefed extensively by Kantibhai and his team of chartered accountants.

In Goa, during the final meeting on the eve of the hearing, D.P. Singh suddenly turned to me and said, 'You will present the matter tomorrow as I do not appear before tribunals.'

I was astounded. How could he do this to me?

Sensing my apprehension, he quickly said, 'Do not worry, there will be people in the team to assist you. You only have to present the facts and the documents. Everything is in black and white.'

Singh's reassurances did little to comfort me. I did not sleep that night—preparing for the next day, and worrying while not working. That Niru was with me, and supported me, was a consolation.

The next day, I was rather nervous. But once I was on my feet, papers in hand, I was able to present the facts so perfectly that I surprised myself! The sitting was four hours long—documents were examined, and submitted after arguments. I came out tired but quite pleased with myself, and Kantibai seemed happy as well.

The hearing continued the next day.

In a week, the final orders came, totally in our favour. I had managed to get the penalty waived and the matter closed.

I expected a big fee. But to my utter shock, D.P. Singh informed me that our client had sent a letter of appreciation but no money. 'How can we demand fees from the son of Morarjibhai?' shrugged D.P. Singh.

I was reminded of the stories my father would tell us of his early days at the bar in Udipi. Relations from surrounding areas would come with their legal work. They'd stay with him, bring vegetables and coconuts from their land as offerings, urge him to win their case, and, at the end of it all, make no payment. Unable to manage this state of affairs, he shifted to Bangalore and joined the established office of J.L. D'Silva, which changed his life completely.

One fine day, I decided that enough was enough. After assisting with a matter argued by D.P Singh in the Supreme Court, I returned home to prepare for a dinner we were hosting for over sixty guests. Suddenly, I received a call from the office. I was informed that I was needed urgently for a conference as an important matter had appeared in the supplementary list for the next day. I informed the caller that I was expecting guests, and it was impossible for me to leave. A few minutes later, there was a second call, this time from D.P. Singh himself. He urged me to drop in for the briefing, even if it was only for a while, and take the file home to prepare for the next morning.

That did it. I felt like bonded labour—available at the beck and call of a senior. I firmly but politely told Singh that I would not be able to come that evening and that I would not be able to prepare notes for the next morning either.

That night, I suddenly felt the urge to free myself from the stress and strain of the legal profession. The money I could earn was of no consequence, as I knew I'd have no time to spend it! I now saw my future more clearly. My family and my political commitments had to take priority over money.

♦

In the years to come, I'd occasionally drop in at the Supreme Court chambers for a chat or to cast my vote in the Bar Council elections, but I'd be quite happy introducing myself as 'a briefless lawyer'.

In other ways, too, I kept my association with law alive; my several interventions on the judiciary in the Rajya Sabha started creating ripples. Once, I posed the question: 'Why aren't enough women being appointed to the High Court and Supreme Court Benches?' After explaining the problems associated with finding suitable qualified women for the Benches, Shanti Bhushan, the Law Minister of the Morarji Desai government, added, 'The honourable member is a lawyer and ideally suited to be a Judge.' Then, turning to me, he said, 'I am making an offer. If you are willing, we will appoint you to the High Court right away!'

'Why should I be a Judge?' I shot back. 'I am waiting to occupy your chair, so that I can appoint more women to the Benches myself!' There was thumping of desks, and the Minister admitted that I certainly made a better Parliamentarian than a Judge!

In 1990, there was a debate in the Rajya Sabha on the state of the judiciary. We were in the opposition, and, as one of the speakers, I had researched the subject extensively. I lambasted the procedural delays in courts, the politics and the corruption assailing the judiciary, the general lack of accountability and the absence of a moral code for Judges. I mentioned cases (without names) of lawyers practising and appearing before their relations or former partners or seniors from their law offices, and of a lawyer-daughter staying with a Supreme Court Judge and meeting her clients at his residence. I received much appreciation for my speech.

The Judges, however, were furious. Some commented on my speech when I met them at social functions or meetings—which pleased me, since they had taken note of what I had conveyed. Others made threatening noises; one apparently told a lawyer-friend of mine, 'I look forward to the day she appears before me [in the Supreme Court].' Thankfully, I had put away my black robe by then!

The Allahabad High Court took note of it in a different way. I received a Notice of Contempt for my attack on the judiciary. It was only on the intervention of the Chief Justice of India, whose attention was drawn to the privileges granted to MPs for speeches delivered in Parliament, that the matter was closed.

I have since spoken across various platforms on what ails our judicial system, detailing the ills that plague both the Bench and the Bar; of judgements often tailored to serve vested interests and not the cause of justice; of the posting of matters before certain Judges/Benches manipulated through the registry; of appointments made to the Bench on considerations other than merit; and of fees charged by many senior lawyers far beyond permissible limits, with no receipts issued.

At one point, I served on the Judicial Reforms Committee of the Congress. Several suggestions were made, but as usual, very little was implemented. The transfer of High Court Judges and the appointment of external Judges as Chief Justices of High Courts were positive first-steps. There is still need for more reforms to establish judicial accountability; safeguard transparency in judicial appointments; reduce delays caused by adjournments and appeals; and create a code of conduct for lawyers. Only then will the courtroom become a chamber of justice for the average citizen.

I tried in vain to convince my party to accept Prime Minister Atal Bihari Vajpayee's Law Minister, Arun Jaitley's proposal for a judicial commission for the appointment of Judges. I am glad to see the proposal take shape under the Modi government. It will help restore the faith of the common man in the independence and sanctity of our judiciary. Despite a setback in the Supreme Court, I believe this is a reform whose time has come.

Chapter 13

THE BATTLE FOR KARNATAKA:
MY ASSOCIATION WITH DEVARAJ URS

Devaraj Urs was a towering, if low-key figure, who hailed from Hunsur in Mysore District. Pipe-smoking, pleasant, ever-smiling, he spoke beautiful Kannada, decent English, and no Hindi. His household was dominated by his short, tough wife, and three daughters.

1969—the year the Congress split—was also the year that catapulted Devaraj Urs into a position of leadership. He was appointed the KPCC President (ad hoc) of the Requisition Congress—better known as the Congress (R)—led by Indira Gandhi. He toured the state, organized the party, and strategically fought the powerful Congress (O) led by Veerendra Patil (then the Chief Minister), S. Nijalingappa, Ramakrishna Hegde and Deve Gowda.

Devaraj Urs' formula was simple—to push for the unity of the backward classes, minorities and SC/STs, who constituted 70 per cent of the state's population, yet had always been kept out of power. Instead, the upper caste Lingayats and Vokkaligas, who constituted only 28 per cent of the population, managed to rule. Devaraj Urs, with his concerted campaign, became the champion of marginalized communities, and the voice for land reform ('Land to the Tiller' was his slogan), bank nationalization and the abolition of privy purses.

We worked with Devaraj Urs—trying to generate membership in our areas and organizing meetings in the tent office outside his house. Back then, I was the only woman Block President in the state. Owing to his focused campaign, in 1971, Karnataka provided all seats when Indiraji's Congress (R) swept to power in the midterm Parliament elections.

In the meantime, the Youth Congress under Gundu Rao launched a state-wide agitation over the selection of the sons and daughters of VIPs for the contingent heading to the International Trade Fair in Japan—which, in turn, led to the resignation of the state government. In the elections that followed in 1972, the Congress (R) came to power, with Devaraj Urs as Chief Minister.

◆

On 1 January 1978—soon after the sudden dismissal of the Karnataka government under Devaraj Urs—the old guard of the Congress (O), presided over by Brahmananda Reddy, and supported by Y.B. Chavan, Vasantdada Patil and Swaran Singh, expelled Indiraji at a Congress Working Committee (CWC) meeting, to pre-empt decisions that would be taken at the AICC session called by Indiraji and her followers the next day. Leaders had been sent to various PCCs to gather support for her. Niru was sent to Goa and managed to get 4 of the 5 AICC members with him. On 2 January 1978, the Congress formally split, and Indiraji reasserted her leadership and supremacy over the party. A.R. Antulay's house served as the camp office; Devaraj Urs had become a pillar of financial support; Kemparaj Urs (Devaraj Urs' brother), Sachidanand Swami (his Political Secretary) and I (now General Secretary, KPCC) were deputed by Urs to work in Delhi to assist with preparations.

The new party was called Congress (Indira) or Congress (I) and received the overwhelming support of AICC members and MPs. Soon after, the old party symbol of the cow and calf was frozen by the Election Commission and the 'hand' allotted to us instead.

In February 1978, it was announced that Karnataka and Andhra Pradesh would go to the polls. Both governments had been dismissed despite massive majorities—the Government of Karnataka being dissolved on 31 December 1977, based on a report produced under the supervision of the Governor, Govind Narain (appointed by the new government at the Centre), which indicted Chief Minister Devaraj Urs of corruption, nepotism and the misuse of power.

I was put in charge of the KPCC campaign office. There were no funds, no vehicles, no resources. Businessmen who had been at Devaraj Urs' door regularly, seeking favours, suddenly disappeared, refusing to even take his calls. Since our cow and calf symbol was gone, the old campaign posters only served as 'raddi'; we cut out the image of Indiraji's face from those posters so that we could reuse it.

With no alternatives in sight, I phoned Devaraj Urs—who was on tour—telling him we had no way of publicizing the new symbol of the 'hand' of benediction. Devaraj Urs simply said, 'There's an easy answer. Send our workers out with buckets of coloured chuna (limestone) water, ask them to dip their hands in the solution and cover all vacant spaces on walls and buildings with their handprints.' I followed his instructions, and our workers, along with painting the city with handprints, also pasted the cut-outs of Indiraji's face alongside, writing 'Vote Congress (I)'. The strategy seemed sound—until our workers returned with blistered, burning palms! It was tragic.

To add to our woes, despite requesting the AICC to keep outside campaigners and observers (apart from Indiraji) away from the state, Giani Zail Singh and N.D. Tiwari, both seasoned leaders, landed! Even while contending with empty coffers, we had to accommodate them and their PAs, and keep them occupied. Soon after their arrival, Gianiji was taken to a public meeting organized in a busy neighbourhood, with a huge crowd in attendance to hear Devaraj Urs. When Gianiji stood up to speak in Hindi, the throngs from the freshly concluded public meeting of our rival, Raj Narain, came to join our gathering. The Assembly was swelling, growing restive, and the fact that most people could not follow the speech in Hindi did not help—it was a recipe for disaster. A small stone hit Gianiji's turban, and a few more landed on the stage. '*Hai, pathhar gire!*' ('It's raining stones!') Gianiji yelled into the mic, holding his head. That's all it took. Pandemonium broke out, with people running in all directions. Devaraj Urs grabbed the mic and thundered in Kannada, 'Do not leave! Nothing has happened! Sit down calmly!' Slowly, the crowd settled down, and then listened to Devaraj Urs for an hour.

I returned home, quite relieved. However, late at night, I received a phone call from Devaraj Urs telling me that Gianiji had been admitted to a hospital with chest pain and had suffered a mild heart attack. 'Since you speak Hindi, I am leaving him in your care. Please attend to him till his family comes.' I went to the hospital the next morning to visit Gianiji. A rather hilarious argument was raging between him and the doctors. The doctors were trying to reassure Gianiji in broken Hindi that the X-ray of his head showed no signs of injury; touching the turban where he had been hit, they said, '*Report aaya hai, saheb. Kuch nahin hai udar!*' ('The report has come, sir. There's nothing there!') Gianiji, in response, kept saying, '*Nahin, kuch hai, main janta hoon!*' ('No, there's something there, I know!') It took some subtle intervention on my part for the issue to get sorted. It was with great relief that we sent him back with his family a week later. His teammate, Tiwariji, having noted what had happened to Gianiji, decided to leave as well, saying, '*Hummein yahan to koi kaam nahin!*' ('We have nothing to do here!') We gladly agreed.

In the meantime, Indiraji extensively toured Karnataka by road. Her energy, courage and determination galvanized the party. Nirmala Deshpande, Prabha Rau and I accompanied her for the first three days. From 6 a.m. to well past midnight, we'd be on the road, with brief halts for lunch, tea, dinner, or to access toilets. Indiraji ate little—surviving on a diet of boiled groundnuts, bananas and water—and slept even less—merely covering her eyes with a black cloth and resting her head on a small pillow for a few minutes while driving on bumpy, dusty roads. It was a demanding tour, with sloganeering crowds and unscheduled halts throwing all programmes out of gear. Worse, the profusion of garlands didn't help, since Indiraji was allergic to yellow marigolds; we had to protect her from these flowers that came flying from all directions.

By the end of the third day, I was exhausted—with no sleep, dust blocking my nose, pollen in my hair, my eyes watering and throat sore. So, when we touched base in Bangalore a day later, I sheepishly told Indiraji, 'I need a break, ma'am. I must wash my hair and rest my eyes. I'm seeing double images! I don't know how you do it, but I am half-dead in just three days.'

Indiraji looked at me, rather disappointed. 'You know, you young people eat too much and sleep too much. You should cut down on both.' Then she smiled, and let me go.

I stayed back to work at the campaign office, while Indiraji (and the rest of her entourage) drove to cover the districts bordering Andhra Pradesh. She did this for twenty-three days without a break. She was a marvel!

Election-day finally dawned; soon, the results were announced. After watching Devaraj Urs' state government getting summarily dismissed, and living under President's Rule between 31 December 1977 and 28 February 1978, we had reason to be jubilant. The Congress (I) had secured a two-thirds majority. The Governor who had earlier dismissed Devaraj Urs had to swear him in with his Cabinet. Andhra Pradesh, too, returned a Congress government. It was a big blow to the government in Delhi.

This victory was followed by the first Lok Sabha by-election fought with the hand symbol in May 1978 in Azamgarh in Uttar Pradesh. Mohsina

Kidwai, despite all the odds piled against her, won this seat, defeating the former Congress MP Chandrajit Yadav who had gone with Congress (O). We were on the comeback trail!

Even as the results trickled in, Indiraji began to tour the states. She started with Karnataka. Here she received a huge welcome in most areas. However, we did have some terrible experiences as well, with Janata Party workers raising black flags at meetings and shouting hostile slogans. Some of them would stand at vantage points with Congress flags on bamboo poles, and smash the windscreens and bonnets of our cars when we stopped to greet them. To protect ourselves, we began carrying bamboo shields in the car. To keep Indiraji secure, especially if we happened to have advance information, we'd put her into a small car up front and follow in the large car behind—only to be attacked! Any number of good cars were destroyed. Mercifully, since we had a Congress government in power, the police were generally helpful and protective.

Prabha Rau, Nirmalaji and I accompanied Indiraji. We shared a room at rest houses or private homes. Since I was the host, I got to use the facilities last, which meant that I had to rush through my jobs. It was on one of these hurried mornings that Prabha Rau introduced me to the maroon sticker bindi, telling me that there were neither mirrors nor time for my elaborate powder bindi. Besides, she added, the powder bindi, which inevitably smudged across my forehead by mid-day, made me look like a 'Red Indian'.

Indiraji would be up and ready with her bag packed by 6 a.m., waiting for us for breakfast. She would often pack breakfast and fruits for us, saying, 'Hurry up! You can eat in the car.' I learnt so much from her during those days. She was warm and friendly. While her external tough persona helped her assert herself before ambitious men, with us, she was a mother.

I remember, one morning, when there was no hot water left in our geyser for a bath, I shouted in Kannada, asking the attendant to get me a bucket of water from the kitchen. A couple of minutes later there was a knock at the door. I opened it to find Indiraji with half a bucket of hot water from her geyser. 'Hurry up,' she said. 'Get ready.' I could not believe it.

On another occasion, while travelling to Delhi from Bangalore, the plane halted at Hyderabad, as per schedule. Marri Chenna Reddy, the Chief Minister, invited Indiraji for breakfast in the lounge; I stayed back. She returned with packed breakfast in her hands. 'These are for you,' she said, 'hot idlis and dosas.' I was touched. Chenna Reddy later told me, 'Indiraji is very fond of you. That day, at the Hyderabad airport, she insisted she'd pack food for you, saying, "Margaret must be hungry." She also told me you're hardworking and dedicated—but often misunderstood because you are forthright and honest with your views. She said you will learn from experience.'

There were many stories Indiraji shared with us on the road. She mentioned how difficult it was for her when she used to travel with Panditji (her father, Jawaharlal Nehru), as Sanjay was then no more than a baby. She had to carry flasks of hot water and dry Sanjay's wet nappies by the window inside the car. 'Motherhood is not an easy job,' she said, gravely.

◆

Chikmagalur (which when translated into English means 'younger daughter's place') is a small town in the Western Ghats of Karnataka. It serves as the link station for the coffee estates in the vicinity, and is well-equipped with transport services, restaurants, workshops, small hotels, medical centres and schools.

Pressure was mounting on Indiraji to seek re-election to the Lok Sabha, and Devaraj Urs convinced her that Chikmagalur was a safe constituency to contest from.

On reaching Mangalore, we drove to Chikmagalur, with crowds cheering all along the route. After filing her nomination, addressing a huge public meeting, interacting with workers and liaising with leaders for a week, she drove through Mangalore in an open jeep, on her way to the airport to take the flight to Delhi. I found myself in my hometown, standing next to her in the vehicle.

D.B. Chandre Gowda (now in the BJP [Bharatiya Janata Party]) vacated his seat to accommodate Indiraji, and became her election agent. Prabha Rau, Nirmala Deshpande and Kemparaj Urs accompanied her, while I was put in charge of the main campaign office in Bangalore with strict instructions to stop uninvited campaigners from getting to the constituency—in fact, a circular was issued to all PCCs to this effect. Mine was a terrible job: convincing the hordes who landed to return.

But there were some I could not send back—Kamalapati Tripathi being one of them. He came with his entourage—son, PA, cook, attendant, etc. When I mentioned his arrival, Indiraji was surprised, 'What will he do here? He cannot campaign. Why has he come?' She then suggested, 'Send him to Sringeri (which holds the first mutta of Adi Shankara) to conduct pujas for my success.' Kamalapati Tripathi was thrilled, as were the priests of the mutta.

Incidentally, this wasn't the last time Kamalapatiji had to be placated. I recall the many Parliamentary Party meetings held in his house. He would sit in the front room on his easy chair, his legs stretched out, his pink feet on a stool facing the door. We would wish him before venturing inside—but apparently this gesture wasn't sufficient, because Indiraji mentioned that he had complained about Najma Heptulla and me, upset that we did not touch his feet when we did our pranams!

As legions of unexpected guests poured into Karnataka, we had to devise new strategies. When two leaders of Himachal Pradesh, Ramlal and Parmar—who were not on talking terms—landed, I sent them to my brother-in-law's estate at Malandoor to be looked after by Niru. They enjoyed the climate and the hospitality, met Indiraji, toured the area for a bit and went back friends.

Then came news of the arrival of a large West Bengal contingent, headed by Pranab Mukherjee, Ghani Khan Choudhury, Priya Ranjan Dasmunsi and Subrata Mukherjee. Indiraji's immediate response was, 'Oh my god, so many of them! There will be trouble. Please separate them.' Consequently, Pranabda went to Udupi with his team, where Veerappa Moily was an MLA; this association would pay Moily rich dividends in later years. The rest went to various other segments.

When a women's contingent arrived with MPs, MLAs and Women's Front leaders—we divided them into eight teams and sent each to a different Assembly constituency. They did great work organizing women's meetings and doing door-to-door canvassing.

Despite successfully discharging my responsibilities, I found myself in the eye of a minor storm. Sanjay's team, led by F.M. Khan and Gundu Rao, began stirring trouble. They started a rumour that Devaraj Urs, Sachidanand Swami and I were secretly in touch with the opponent's Campaign Managers to defeat Indiraji; that Devaraj Urs had been promised an important assignment at the Centre for his cooperation; and that I shared a strong affinity with George Fernandes, a fellow Mangalore Catholic.

Consequently, when I accompanied Indiraji to Delhi for a break and went through the detailed campaign schedule with her and R.K. Dhawan, I had to answer a host of questions. I was asked why all meetings in

Chikmagalur ended at 6 p.m. 'Because in the hills people do not linger after sunset. They have to walk long distances to go home,' I replied. As for the places chosen for her meetings, 'They were chosen in consultation with the local leaders, to ensure maximum crowds and security,' I said. That closed the issue.

On our return to Karnataka, Indiraji decided that she wanted regular, dependable feedback. I was asked to move to Chikmagalur, with instructions to meet her every night wherever she halted. Besides, since Chandre Gowda and Devaraj Urs were on the move, the campaign office of Chikmagalur was in disarray. I was told to take charge.

Many leaders came to offer support. The AIADMK (All India Anna Dravida Munnetra Kazhagam) Chief, M.G. Ramachandran (popularly known as MGR) sent a team with a red saree, prasad, fruits and good wishes. The Left, too, lent its support. The Congress (O), led by K.P. Unnikrishnan and Singh Deo, passed a resolution to support us and even joined the campaign—much to the chagrin of A.K. Antony, the Congress (O) Chief Minister in Kerala, who resigned in protest.

Yet the campaign in Chikmagalur was not without its challenges. The Janata Party candidate was the former Congress Chief Minister of Karnataka, Veerendra Patil. His Campaign Manager, George Fernandes, was difficult to beat. He followed us to every meeting, sat at tea shops with his team of party workers and paid attention to each and every speech. When we left, he'd stand in his jeep and speak to the same crowd we had addressed, contradict everything conveyed, and abuse Indiraji and Sanjay for Emergency excesses—all this in the local languages (Kannada, Tulu and Konkani), which he was fluent in.

Then he adopted other methods of fighting back. Snehalata Reddy, George Fernandes' close associate, who had been released from jail a long time ago, died of an asthmatic attack. It became an election issue. Her mock body was carried around the constituency in processions, and Indira Gandhi blamed for arresting Snehalata Reddy during the Emergency, and for her subsequent illness and death.

This led to clashes in the temple town of Dharmasthala, where Gangadhara Gowda, the young MLA, tried to stop the procession. There was violence; the police used tear gas; curfew was imposed. Our flags, buntings and posters were pulled down by Janata workers, and burnt. These were acts of desperation. Clearly, the Janata Party sensed a pro-

Indira wave. As usual, I had to play 'Joan of Arc.' When Devaraj Urs got the police report on the tense situation in Dharmasthala, he asked me to go there immediately, encourage our leaders to come out, and urge the administration to lift curfew.

I drove to the venue at night with a police escort. The local police met me at the border and took me to the agitated local MLA's residence. He was sitting with his storm-troopers, his revolver on the table. Everyone in the room was furious with the police, saying they behaved like Janata Party agents. I calmed them down, phoned the police officer in charge and asked him to come over. There were heated exchanges. It was finally decided that curfew would be lifted by midnight. I decided to move out silently with the police and party workers. We spent the night putting up our flags and posters—which helped boost their morale. From that day, processions with Snehalata Reddy's 'body' were banned, and those attempting such demonstrations were arrested.

By the time I got back to Chikmagalur, after stopping at campaign offices on the way, there was more disturbing news. Our public meeting had been attacked, and the stage overrun by unruly Janata workers. Indiraji had to be whisked away, and Chandre Gowda rushed to the hospital in an unconscious state with head injuries and a gash on his cheek. Several others had been injured. Violent attempts were being made to postpone the election. Devaraj Urs appealed for calm. FIRs were filed and the ring leaders of the Janata attack arrested. As Chandre Gowda lay recovering in the ICU (intensive care unit), and newspaper headlines condemned George Fernandes and his team, sympathy turned to Indiraji in the last days of the electoral battle.

The results came on 7 November 1978. Indiraji had won by a margin of over 77,000 votes.[18] There were celebrations across the country, and Devaraj Urs, the architect of the victory, emerged a hero. He had slogged, and led from the front throughout the campaign. When the results were announced, he told Indiraji with tears in his eyes, 'I had staked my entire political career on your victory.' With a triumphant Indiraji, we returned to Delhi—singing, dancing and sharing sweets on the flight.

◆

---

[18]See *The Tribune*, volume 23, issues 1-26, p. 226.

Indiraji's election from Chikmagalur to the Lok Sabha was a big blow to the Janata Party government, which went into damage control mode immediately through its 'dirty tricks' department. The Privileges Committee of the Lok Sabha, packed with Janata Party members, heard a petition on the role of the former Prime Minister in Sanjay's Maruti project, with Indiraji being accused of corruption and the obstruction of information gathering. Naturally, the majority prevailed, and it was decided that Indiraji would be censured. K.S. Hegde, the Speaker of the Lok Sabha, left it to the 'wisdom of the House' to impose a suitable punishment. The House voted to send Indiraji to jail for a week, and expelled her from Parliament.

She was to be taken to Tihar Jail. While the House was adjourned, she refused to move out until all the paperwork was completed. The authorities, on their part, were extra careful not to repeat the mistakes of her earlier arrest. When Rajiv and Sonia came to Central Hall with passes, we insisted that they move into the Lok Sabha lobby with us, which they did hesitantly—only to have Lok Sabha staff-members object vociferously. We refused to budge. Even Baba and Niret joined us. Then, in an ultimate act of defiance, many of us from the Rajya Sabha entered the Lok Sabha (absolutely against the rules), raising slogans against the Speaker, the Prime Minister and the government.

After waiting and protesting for over two hours, the officials, the police and the vehicles drew up with a request to the Lok Sabha watch and ward personnel to escort Indiraji. She walked out, her head held high, amidst slogans inside and outside the House. Many teary-eyed members of Parliament followed her. She stopped, passed me a handwritten slip of paper, and asked me to read it out to the press. It started with 'to my colleagues, the women MPs', and then carried those popular lines of farewell: 'Wish me luck as you would bid goodbye/ without a tear in your eye;/ give me a smile I can keep all the while.'

Niru immediately released the contents to the French channel, AFP (Agency France Press). The BBC flashed it that night. The Indian press gave it front page coverage the next day.

Indiraji was kept in Tihar Jail, spending Christmas there. Seven days later, she was out, more popular than ever.

◆

While the Janata Party battled its inner contradictions, unrest was brewing within the Congress as well, as a rejuvenated Sanjay Gandhi, now the President of the IYC, began picking his favourites in the states to take charge. His men began to emerge from the woodwork, and posed a serious challenge to those who had stayed behind to support Indiraji. Siddhartha Shankar Ray, Dev Kant Barooah, Rajni Patel, K.C. Pant, Y.B. Chavan and many leaders of the North-east left the Congress, upset over the developing situation.

After the Chikmagalur victory, and his emergence as a national hero, Devaraj Urs expected to be rewarded and drawn into the decision-making machinery in Delhi. This did not suit the Sanjay clique—who sensed Devaraj Urs' disapproval of Sanjay's re-emergence—and they started working to marginalize him. They began feeding Indiraji's insecurity, claiming that Devaraj Urs was taking Hindi lessons, planning to tour the country and hoping to challenge the High Command. They reminded Indiraji of Devaraj Urs' many accomplishments—he had an overwhelming majority in the Assembly; he was the unanimously elected KPCC President; he had won the Assembly elections for the Congress in 1972 and 1978; he had managed the Chikmagalur election against all odds, even finding the means to fund the campaign; he had funded the AICC convention of 2 January 1978; he had several PCCs depending on him to run their offices; and he had implemented Congress programmes most efficiently, building the party from scratch after the 1969 split. Obviously—or so they claimed—Devaraj Urs was now eying Delhi.

In the summer of 1979, the brewing tension within the party led to an ugly fallout. Three events in particular brought on a clash between the High Command and Devaraj Urs: the decision to ask Devaraj Urs to step down as KPCC President; the refusal of the leadership to permit me to contest the elections for the post of the Secretary of the CPP, because I was considered a Devaraj Urs nominee; and the humiliation meted out to Urs at the AICC session in Delhi, where he was shouted down by Sanjay's youth brigade and not allowed to speak. At the same session, Indiraji had selected me to second the Foreign Affairs Resolution. A couple of Karnataka members, against Devaraj Urs, tried to disrupt my speech. But Indiraji firmly intervened and let me have my say. All the same, I sensed trouble.

After all that he had done for Indiraji and the party, Devaraj Urs' public humiliation led to an open revolt. A resolution was passed unanimously at a meeting of the KPCC at the historic Glass House (which had witnessed the 1969 split), reposing full faith and confidence in the leadership of Devaraj Urs and asking the High Command to reconsider its decision on the PCC Presidentship. I was one of the speakers.

In the meantime, the CPP elections came up. Narsingh Makwana (an SC MP from Gujarat), Charanjit Chanana (a nominee from the Sanjay Gandhi group) and I were the Rajya Sabha candidates; I had the support of the anti-Sanjay MPs. On the eve of the election, I was called by Kamalapati Tripathi and asked to withdraw my candidature 'in the interest of the party'. I refused. Voting was in progress when I was summoned once again along with the other two candidates; we were told that since Indiraji did not want to see a split in the CPP, it was best that we decided amongst ourselves who the best candidate for the post of the CPP Secretary would be. Makwana pleaded that an SC should be given an opportunity. I agreed. Voting was stayed and the compromise announced. I was told by the returning officer that thirty votes had already been cast, of which I had secured eighteen, the other two sharing the balance. My supporters were furious at my withdrawal.

The issue of the CPP election was finally out of the way, but the dispute regarding the Leader of the KPCC kept dragging. Finally, after much discussion, Devaraj Urs decided to step down, appointing K.H. Ranganath, his SC Minister, as ad-hoc President, until the election of a new President.

Soon after, Devaraj Urs fell seriously ill with 'herpes', and was confined to bed with high temperature and severe pain. Our access to him was cut off. In view of his illness, Delhi, too, did not act.

Then one morning, when he seemed to be recovering, we were called and ushered into his bedroom where a show cause notice he had received from the AICC, accusing him of indiscipline and defiance, was read out. What annoyed all of us was that the letter had been released to the press even before it could reach him. It was decided that a suitable reply should be sent at the earliest.

We were called back the next day to go through the draft. Lying in bed, Devaraj Urs seemed mighty pleased with what he termed 'the correct reply.' His admiring circle, who hardly understood English, endorsed his view wholeheartedly. When I read its contents, I was shocked—the language and tone of the missive were crude, unbecoming of a man of Devaraj Urs' stature. I objected and asked that it be redrafted. I was overruled. I came to learn that the draft had been prepared by Nirmala Sundaram, an IFS (Indian Foreign Service) officer posted in Delhi, who claimed to be

Devaraj Urs' adopted daughter. We never understood why a man with three daughters needed yet another, but what we did sense was that Sundaram seemed to have some hold over him. Despite my objections to the three-page reply with sarcastic innuendos, the letter was sent through a trusted messenger to Indiraji.

The next day, I went to Delhi for a Parliamentary Committee meeting, then to the AICC to meet Indiraji. She was walking towards her car—her glares on and an umbrella over her head—when I asked for a few moments of her time.

She stopped and asked, 'Are you also joining hands with them against me?'

'Madam,' I said, 'I have come to plead with you for a compromise. You decide who you'd like as the KPCC President and we will get him elected unanimously. But let the normal procedure—that of elections—be followed. You should know we are with you, but please respect our sentiments.'

'The KPCC cannot defy the High Command. Tell Urs he has to fall in line or go!' she answered sternly, and unwilling to listen, got into her car and drove away.

This was the first time Indiraji had spoken to me so coldly. Distraught, I returned to Bangalore to convey the message. But even there, no one was prepared to listen.

The next thing we saw was an announcement in the papers, signed by Pranab Mukherjee, expelling all of us—members of the executive, office bearers, AICC members, MPs, Ministers—for anti-party activities. We had received no show cause notice, as required by the Congress Constitution. It was clear: Indiraji had begun to toe the Sanjay line. I was reminded of V.C. Shukla's prophetic words when I had intervened to stop Chandra Shekhar's expulsion from the CPP.

In later years, Pranabda admitted to me that the whole episode was his mistake; that he had been given a list prepared by Gundu Rao and company, late at night, and he had signed it without reading the names.

Sanjay had finally succeeded. After all that I had done for Indiraji, I was out of the Congress, with nowhere to go.

Devaraj Urs promptly announced his own outfit—Congress (U).

◆

In the meantime, I had a personal shock waiting for me. I had been feeling low and weak for some time. I had gone to Willingdon Hospital (now Ram Manohar Lohia Hospital) twice, only to be told that the cause was overwork and tension. When my health took a turn for the worse, the doctors recommended tests, which I took. I proceeded to Bangalore for a crisis meeting, as some of the leaders who had pushed Devaraj Urs to challenge Indiraji had deserted him after the expulsion.

On my return, I was shocked when I was told that the reports showed pregnancy. The baby was due in November—nine years after Manira.

'How will I face Parliament?' was my question.

I was now compelled to slow down to attend to myself. But there was another problem. I had been on Eltroxin for years for my thyroid problem. I was warned that this could affect the brain development of the baby and was advised to terminate the pregnancy. Niru and I, however, decided to go ahead. Today our 'baby' is over six feet tall, absolutely fine, with two adorable kids of his own!

Generally tired, I started going to Parliament only to sign the register. After Parliament was adjourned, and Baba left for Bombay, Niru and I decided to go to Bangalore with the kids for the summer. When I returned to Delhi for a committee meeting, I saw Baba and Chittu sitting outside the house. Baba had returned earlier than planned as he had not been feeling well.

The next morning, we decided to admit him to Willingdon Hospital for medical care. I had an uneasy feeling, and asked Niru, who was still in Bangalore, to return. I also called for the children, who were in Mangalore.

But before they could reach, on the night of 29 June 1979, Baba had a massive heart attack and passed away. My greatest regret was that we had not told him that another grandchild was on the way.

We waited for Maya, the kids, Niru and family to arrive for the funeral. Friends and people from all walks of life came calling. But Indiraji—who had been most fond of Baba throughout his life—did not come, not even for the service at the Cathedral of the Sacred Heart.

A week later, at the dinner we had at home after the religious ceremonies, George Fernandes spoke movingly about his association with Baba during his early trade union days in Bombay. He recalled their first meeting—how Baba accidentally bumped into him on the footpath, and asked after him. When he heard that George had neither a roof over his head nor proper food, he insisted that he have his meals at his home whenever he wished.

'Joachim Alva was the only man who opened his doors when I started my life on the footpaths of Bombay', said an emotional George Fernandes. The children were heartbroken; Baba was their hero!

Then something rather strange happened. On 22 August 1979, while we were at dinner, there was a loud thud on the terrace, as though someone had jumped on the roof. Maya went out to look, when tiny stones fell all around her. Worried, we rang the police. They arrived, screamed warnings and walked around to find the stealthy creature on the roof—only to be greeted with more stones, one of which shattered the bulb outside. Taken aback, the police beat a hasty retreat, leaving one of their men on duty. For the next three weeks, stones continued tumbling down, smashing window panes and ventilators, or landing at our feet. Terrified, we moved to my brother, John's place, visiting our cursed residence only in the morning for clothes and essentials.

The episode of the mysterious shower of stones was splashed across the newspapers. Friends started coming to check, only to be greeted with a cascade of rubble! Acquaintances began dispensing advice and offering remarkable theories to explain this unsolved mystery. Finally I told Niru—away in Bangalore—that I wished to move back to Bangalore. Niru, who was only too happy, came back to help me shift. The day he reached, the shower of stones stopped!

After that, the general belief was that our house had been cursed—black magic or 'kallu kutti', as they called it down South, had been done, and this was clearly the act of a political opponent. There were many guesses about who this rival could be. But we continued to stay on in the house peacefully for the next five years. Maya returned to London and married a Bangladeshi Muslim barrister, settled down there, and has two children.

When the Congress withdrew support to the Charan Singh government, the government fell. I packed up, took the children, and went to Bangalore.

Back in Karnataka, Devaraj Urs, still the Chief Minister, found himself in the middle of election frenzy. He steered his outfit, the Congress (U)—as against Mrs Gandhi's Congress (I). There were a number of meetings to discuss the advisability of the party contesting the elections against Indiraji. I was totally opposed to the idea. For one, the move would divide votes and help anti-Congress forces; for another, Karnataka had been a Congress bastion, and this had to be preserved at all costs; last, but not the least, since we had masterminded the political rebirth of Indiraji, how could we, within a year, criticize her before the people? 'The masses are pro-Indiraji and anti-Janata. Let us remain neutral for now and watch the developments', I pleaded.

But Devaraj Urs had made up his mind to fight. He asked his stalwarts to contest from all the twenty-eight seats, funded them and campaigned extensively. He believed that his track record and hard work would help him sweep Karnataka. Since (luckily) I was in no condition to contest or campaign, I stayed home.

The campaign became fierce. The elections took place. The results spelt disaster for the Congress (U). The Congress (I) had secured all but one constituency in Karnataka—with Bangalore South going to the Janata Party.[19] A host of new faces, fighting (and winning) elections for the first time, appeared on the state's political horizon. I had been proven right.

In no time at all, the exodus started. MLAs switched sides from Devaraj Urs' camp to the Congress (I), and he lost his majority. He resigned on 7 January 1980, paving the way for the installation of Sanjay's nominee, Gundu Rao, as Chief Minister. A disillusioned Devaraj Urs joined hands with Maharashtra's strongman, Sharad Pawar, renaming his party Congress (S)—the 'S' standing for 'socialist'.

Drunk with success, Gundu Rao, as Chief Minister, and F.M. Khan, as his 'henchman', ran the state of Karnataka like a private jagir. Corruption and maladministration were evident in every sphere. Both claimed closeness to Sanjay and Indiraji, and used this as a passport to power in Karnataka and to importance in Delhi.

◆

Nivedith was born on 24 November 1979 at St Martha's Hospital, Bangalore. I had barely recovered, when Nivedith—only two weeks old—had to be operated for a strangulated hernia. His recovery was a miracle.

We returned to Delhi in January to confront another cold winter and an uncertain future. My term in the Rajya Sabha was to expire in April, and there was no likelihood that I'd get re-elected. The Congress (I) under Gundu Rao would ensure my defeat, while Devaraj Urs didn't have enough MLAs with him to guarantee my victory. Therefore, that winter, when Parliament met, I came to terms with the fact that it would be my last session.

I had been allotted a seat with the Congress (S), though I had not joined any party formally. I rarely attended Parliament. My women colleagues refused to believe I had had a baby; 'we haven't seen you pregnant', was their constant contention—forgetting that Parliament had been dissolved and I had left Delhi. 'It is an adopted baby', was the hush-hush rumour.

By February, I was preparing to pack up to return to Bangalore, when Devaraj Urs phoned me. 'I am told you are packing. Why?'

'Because my term is ending', I replied. 'I do not want to add to your problems'.

'You must not leave!' Devaraj Urs insisted. 'You have stood by me and I will stand by you. I am not an ungrateful Gandhi! Have faith in me. I am coming to Delhi soon. Let's meet and discuss this.'

I thanked him, still convinced that the prospects of winning were dim.

When Devaraj Urs did meet me, it turned out that he had spoken to the non-Congress opposition parties—from the Jana Sangh to the CPI—all of whom had agreed to support me as the united opposition candidate. I could not believe this turn of events!

I went to Bangalore with my baby in arms. This time, Baba was not there to guide me. Rather I was back home to a hostile Chief Minister, determined to get me defeated. When he heard of the united opposition's decision, he arrived at a counter-plan. First, he began a furtive move to woo Devaraj Urs' MLAs. Three MLAs switched sides across three days. Then he fielded Monica Das as a Congress (I) candidate; she had Gundu Rao's support because she was a Brahmin, Pranab Mukherjee's backing because she was Bengali and Indiraji's final clearance because she claimed to be a Christian (though she wasn't). Finally, Gundu Rao persuaded Sarojini Mahishi—a Brahmin like himself, a former confidante of Indiraji and a close associate of the Janata Party's National President, Chandra Shekhar—to file her nomination as a Janata Party candidate.

Not everyone within the Janata Party was pleased. Piloo Mody, a Rajya Sabha MP, who arrived as the Janata Party observer, promised to help me. This was followed by a telegram from George Fernandes to Deve Gowda, the state Janata Party President. It read: 'One Margaret Alva equals ten Sarojini Mahishis. Withdraw Mahishi immediately!' But Gundu Rao was on the war path and Mahishi stayed on.

Eventually, it was election day. After attending a breakfast hosted by Devaraj Urs at his residence, I accompanied him to the Vidhana Soudha. He asked me to stand by his side at the entrance of the voting booth. As each MLA appeared, Devaraj Urs folded his hands and said, 'Please help me; elect my candidate.' It was worth watching the faces of the Congress MLAs! Here was the man who had given them seats, funded them, campaigned for them and made them Ministers and Chairmen—asking them for assistance, despite the fact that they had abandoned him in his hour of defeat. Unable to look Devaraj Urs in the eye, they touched his feet and disappeared. After every vote had been cast, Devaraj Urs blessed me, wished me success, and left.

My campaign had been managed by Chandre Gowda, Jeevaraj Alva, Michael Fernandes and Sachidanand Swami. They were also my agents for counting. There was tension all around. When the results were announced at 5 p.m., I could barely believe the verdict. I had emerged victorious in the first round itself—and this was without spending a rupee—for even my deposit had been paid by Devaraj Urs!

Shouts of joy and crackers rent the air. '*Devaraj Urs, zindabad!*' ('Long live Devaraj Urs!') resounded across the corridors, even as Gundu Rao and company disappeared with their MPs. With Niru, I went straight to Devaraj Urs, touched his feet, garlanded him and thanked him for what he had done for me. After sharing a late lunch with him—an anxious Devaraj Urs, awaiting the results, had not had his meals—I drove to the Janata Party office to thank Deve Gowda and his team for standing by me. Finally, I went home to feed my hungry four-month-old baby, after which there were celebrations and prayers offered in thanksgiving.

As I was the only non-Congress (I) candidate to have been elected to the Rajya Sabha from the entire Southern belt, I hit the headlines.

I returned to Delhi a new person. I had regained my self-confidence. I was going to be around for the next six years. I received a huge round of applause when I took my oath in the House, and there were cheers from all sides in Central Hall when I went around with sweets.

Only one person struck a discordant note: F.M. Khan. He did not congratulate me; instead, he told me, 'If I had been there, you would never have won. Indiraji stopped me from going, you know.' I smiled and replied, 'In politics, the wheel of fortune never stands still, Khan. We may be out today but you will need my help some time. When that happens, I will, like a good Christian, help you.' Years later, my prophecy was proven true. Khan came to me for help so that he could return to the party after a six-year-long expulsion. The KPCC was not responding to his requests. Since I was a Minister (Personnel) attached to Prime Minister P.V. Narasimha Rao—who was also the Congress President—I took Khan to Rao. It was on my intervention that Khan was admitted back into the Congress. The wheel of fortune had turned indeed.

F.M. Khan's comment—that he had been stopped by Indiraji from visiting Karnataka—was true. I suspect the cause may have been a handwritten letter I had sent her a couple of days before leaving for my election. I had thanked her for having brought me to Parliament and giving me a chance to participate in national politics. 'I do not know if I will return,' I said, 'but wherever I am, I will always be with you.' With this note, I sent Indiraji a silk water-printed saree. To my surprise and delight, I received a reply from her the very next morning, thanking me for the lovely saree and wishing me success; she added, 'We were so sorry to see you go.' At the first lunch she invited me to after my election, I was thrilled to see her wearing the saree I had gifted her.

◆

After my expulsion from the Congress party in 1979, I felt lost. I had spent ten years working across party levels with Indiraji as my leader—a woman I admired and respected. Now, circumstances beyond my control had cut me off from my associates, peers, guides and friends in the Congress.

My political career could have ended right there. Had I stayed on with Gundu Rao, Sanjay—in a bid to get even with me—would have ensured that I did not get a Rajya Sabha nomination in 1980. Thanks to Devaraj Urs' intervention, I found my feet. He, too, felt that I was amongst the last five to stay on—with Sachidanand Swami, Chandre Gowda, L.G. Havanur (the Law Minister in Devaraj Urs' government) and H.R. Basavaraj (an industrialist)—and must be awarded.

I did not regret my decision to stand by Devaraj Urs. But gradually, I did sense that he was being held prisoner in the hands of astrologers—with poojas and havans being organized with alarming regularity—and being controlled by a clique headed by his adopted daughter, Nirmala Sundaram. When he visited Delhi, Niru and I were called to Nirmala's residence, where he stayed. I objected, telling him that we would be glad to meet him at Karnataka Bhavan instead. I added that whether he admitted it or not, Nirmala's impertinent letter had led to the final break with Indiraji—who, in any case, had come to resent the fact that tickets for her travel to Karnataka would be sent by him via his 'adopted daughter'. I must have caused offence with my comments because Devaraj Urs stopped inviting me to Nirmala's residence. We watched helplessly as, with time, he began to get increasingly isolated from his circle of political supporters. I only wish that Devaraj Urs had not fallen into the hands of an unscrupulous, ambitious coterie, and that he had not taken a turn towards self-destruction.

Several of my friends in the Congress were telling me to return to the party. They insisted that Indiraji still had great affection for me. In fact, Pranabda told me that she had mentioned to him her desire to have me back, saying, 'Why is Margaret still sitting out? She did so much for the party when we were out of power, and now when we are in, she isn't around...' I told him and others that I had the greatest respect and affection for Indiraji, but the way the party had treated Devaraj Urs and all of us, despite all that we had done, hurt me immensely. Besides, I did not believe in letting down a man in his hour of defeat.

Chapter 14

THE BEGINNING OF THE END:
THE JANATA PARTY'S COLLAPSE

From the outset, the loosely-knit coalition that formed the Janata Party was ridden with contradictions. If Morarji Desai was pro-West and in favour of free enterprise, George Fernandes and Madhu Dandavate were socialists, anti-multinational corporations and pro-public sector. While the Jana Sangh Ministers were largely pro-Hindutva and pro-RSS (Rashtriya Swayamsevak Sangh), Charan Singh played the farmer card and Jagjivan Ram sang the SC tune. Then, there was the North–South divide—though Neelam Sanjiva Reddy (who became the nation's President) filled this gap to some extent.

After being swept to power, the issue of leadership had surfaced. There were three main contenders—Morarji Desai, the veteran administrator; Charan Singh, the Jat leader of the farmers; and Jagjivan Ram, the acknowledged leader of the SC/ST community. The question was settled by JP and J.B. Kripalani—with Morarji Desai, the Gandhian in his eighties, becoming Prime Minister.

Morarji Desai was a strong-willed freedom fighter and a puritan. Always dressed in a spotless white khadi dhoti-kurta, with a waistcoat and Gandhi cap, he walked as erect as a pole, even at his age. He attributed such agility to 'urine therapy', propagating it quite openly. Morarji Desai refused to compromise on issues he was committed to, and as Prime Minister, was able to work out a consensus on several matters close to his heart by taking the Congress on board. He got the controversial 42nd Constitution Amendment Bill (passed during the Emergency) amended, with many offending clauses removed and former provisions restored. He ensured that henceforth, the imposition of the Emergency would be difficult—it could be enforced only in the case of war or external aggression, and even then it would require a two-third majority vote in Parliament, and a renewal by both Houses every six months, for a maximum period of three years. Indira Gandhi, with her MPs, voted for this on 7 December 1978.

As part of Morarji Desai's Cabinet, Charan Singh and Jagjivan Ram were sworn in as Home and Defence Ministers respectively. Atal Bihari Vajpayee became External Affairs Minister; George Fernandes got the Industry portfolio; H.M. Patel got Finance; L.K. Advani, Information and Broadcasting; and Madhu Dandavate, Railways. It seemed to be a formidable team, but each came with strong individual agendas and ambitions of his own.

If there was one issue regarding which they were all united, it was this—that Indira Gandhi and the Congress party had to be dealt with severely. Their swift dismissal of the state governments in the North demoralized the Congress; without funds and support, the Congress lost elections in Uttar Pradesh, Madhya Pradesh, Rajasthan and Bihar to the Janata Party; West Bengal went to the CPM under Jyoti Basu; Tamil Nadu to the AIDMK; and Jammu and Kashmir to the National Conference.

Additionally, several commissions of inquiry were set up to investigate the role of Congress Chief Ministers and bureaucrats; JP's kidney treatment in hospital; Ram Manohar Lohia's death; and Sanjay's Maruti project. The most important of these was the Shah Commission, ensconced in Patiala House, and presided over by a retired Chief Justice of the Supreme Court, J.C. Shah, to investigate Emergency excesses and uncover the role of those responsible for these indiscretions—Ministers, politicians, bureaucrats, the police, etc. A stage was set up with mics and TV cameras for the daily proceedings to be carried to the nation! While Indiraji refused to say anything before the commission, insisting that she was bound by her oath of secrecy, many of her Ministers began defending themselves, saying they were only implementing orders; H.R. Gokhale, Indiraji's Law Minister, even testified against her.

I received summons—though I wasn't called to the commission. I was grilled over and over again by the CBI regarding my role in getting V.C. Shukla's posters designed and printed. The allegation was that V.C. Shukla had enlisted AIR and DAVP staff for party-election purposes—with matters coming to a head when a DAVP producer committed suicide after transparencies and drafts of publicity material were seized in raids conducted in the DAVP offices. When asked about this, I maintained that Shukla's designs for his posters were unlike those of the AICC, and that I had designed them.

The Shah Commission fishing expedition proved counter-productive. People began turning off their TV sets when the summary of the day's proceedings were broadcast, terming the whole exercise a futile witch-hunt and a waste of public money. Even the newspaper headlines began to shift focus from the commission.

Too soon, the lustre of the Janata Party began to fade. When, in January 1978, Jimmy Carter came to India to a rousing reception in Central Hall, George Fernandes' focused attempts at sending US MNCs (Coca Cola and IBM) out of the country received serious public attention. When the Janata Party chose to send Indiraji to jail after her victory in Chikmagalur, she only gained in popularity and sympathy. In the meantime, Karpoori Thakur's tenure as Chief Minister of Bihar saw an upsurge in caste violence. Added to this, there was general disenchantment with rising prices, corruption, a breakdown of law and order, and the lack of proper administration under the Janata politicians. Those who had voted the party to power with huge expectations began to notice that their 'giants' had feet of clay.

There were demonstrations all over the country. A women's march to the Prime Minister's residence, organized by the Congress, and supported by many parties, saw slogans being raised against the rise in prices—'*Morarji tere shashan mein, aalu bikthe ration mein*' ('Morarji, in your government, even potatoes are sold in ration shops') was one of them. We carried potatoes, threw them into the Prime Minister's compound and courted arrest.

◆

In the Rajya Sabha, the Congress enjoyed a majority. So we played hell with the government. While Kamalapati Tripathi, the Leader of the Congress in the Rajya Sabha, seldom spoke, his silence was more than compensated for by Pranab Mukherjee (the Deputy Leader), N.K.P. Salve, Kalpnath Rai (the exuberant MP from Uttar Pradesh) and the women, who gradually came to be known as the 'shouting brigade'—consisting of Saroj Khaparde, Pratibha Singh, Sushila Adivarekar, Usha Malhotra and me. While Indiraji would send teams of Congress leaders to survey those areas that witnessed clashes, the 'shouting brigade', based on these reports, would keep raising issues pertaining to violence against SCs and women, and disrupt the House.

On one occasion, Saroj marched into the Well of the House and threw the bloodstained saree of a 'Harijan rape victim' on the Secretary General's table as proof of her visit to Uttar Pradesh, charging the Home Minister,

Charan Singh, with being anti-SC. He stood up to protest.

Saroj then challenged him: 'If you are truly pro-SC, as you claim, then marry me: an SC unmarried woman!'

Singh was shocked, and so was the House. He retorted, '*Yeh kya baatein hain! Main shaadi-shuda hoon!*' ('What are you saying? I'm married!')

Saroj shouted back, '*Mujhe koi parvah nahin!*' ('I don't care!')

Angry and speechless, the Home Minister sat down, while the House was adjourned.

Days after the incident, Charan Singh was admitted to AIIMS (All India Institute of Medical Sciences) with a heart attack. The joke in the lobbies was that Saroj's proposal had been too much for his heart to take.

In the meantime, angry that Saroj had humiliated his leader, one of Singh's MPs in the Rajya Sabha, Rameshwar Singh, took her on the next day, shouting, '*Agar tumari shaadi nahi huyee, toh tum rape ke barein mein kya jaanti ho?*' ('You claim to be an unmarried woman, what do you know about rape?')

Saroj told him, '*Bahar aaeeye, main aapko rape ke bare mein sikhaoonge.*' ('Come to the lobby and I will tell you.')

And true to her word, when the House adjourned, she walked up to him in the lobby, and ripped his kurta. There was commotion all around. Charan Singh phoned Indiraji when his MPs went to him with their complaint. We were all summoned by her. Saroj put on her best act, weeping, but Indiraji was really upset and insisted that we all go to Charan Singh's house to apologize. I excused myself, while the others went. Saroj justified her actions, blaming the MP for his provocation, his uncivilized behaviour, and his disparagement of an SC woman, crying bitterly throughout. Charan Singh was so confused that he ended up apologizing to Saroj for his MP's behaviour.

As for me, I spoke on several occasions in the House, and received wide appreciation from all quarters. One of my most appreciated speeches was a hard-hitting forty-minute one, made as the last speaker in the debate on the President's address. The Prime Minister was in the House to listen, and in his reply, repeatedly referred to the points I had raised. For the first time in the history of Parliament, the President's address was amended, with a paragraph added in the Rajya Sabha—one that criticized the address and the policies of the government.

Annoyed with my speeches, the Prime Minister complained to Baba, telling him he was very upset about my attacks. Baba, in a bid to make peace with a close friend, promised to bring me to him. Reluctantly, and after protesting in vain, I agreed to go with the family. As luck would have it, the day before the meeting, I tore a ligament in my foot and was bandaged. I was barely able to walk. But Baba was determined to keep the appointment. He phoned the Prime Minister's house, sought special permission to take the car into the portico, and took Niru, the kids and me along. I was in pain as I limped into Desai's office.

He looked at me and asked, 'What have you been up to?'

'I stuck my foot in the wrong place and tore a ligament, sir,' I said.

'Listening to you in Parliament, how I wish it was your tongue and not your foot!' came his reply, as he looked me straight in the eye. He was back to his normal self the next minute, having snacks and tea served to us.

Baba intervened, and tried to tell him why I was so vocal. Indiraji had brought me to Parliament, he explained, and I had to toe the party line—though I had never compromised, never done Sanjay's bidding and had stood by Niru when he had been harassed.

Morarji Desai patiently listened, then told me as we left, 'Do not trust that lady! We have all been used and kicked out.' I have never forgotten those words.

◆

Trouble continued within the Janata Party. Early 1978 saw a series of letters exchanged between the Prime Minister and his Home Minister, who objected to the growing influence and interference of the Prime Minister's son in the functioning of government, comparing his role to Sanjay Gandhi's during the Emergency. Charan Singh's vehement opposition led to him getting dropped from the Cabinet in June, along with Raj Narain, his right-hand man. This was after a heated debate on the issue in the Rajya Sabha.

Charan Singh, however, re-emerged in December, with a massive rally of farmers drawn from all over North India, dominated by the Jats. This show of strength shook the Janata Party, especially since 36 per cent of its members in the Lok Sabha were farmers. Morarji Desai was compelled to re-induct Charan Singh, granting him the posts of Finance Minister and Deputy Prime Minister. Peace was restored, but only temporarily, as each of the Ministers continued pulling in different directions.

To further muddy the pond, Maneka Gandhi's magazine, *Surya*—which had turned into a powerful tool for fighting the government and exposing its misdeeds—published erotic photographs of Jagjivan Ram's son, Suresh, taken with hidden cameras at the residence of his father. This created waves in political circles—indeed, *Surya* became the most sought-after magazine for weeks, and I still have my preserved copy! The mastermind behind the scandal was believed to be Raj Narain—who, after damaging Morarji Desai's public image, was now targeting Jagjivan Ram's family, so that Charan Singh would remain the only untarnished figure.

Complicating matters further for the Janata Party was the issue of the dual membership status of the Jana Sangh members (they were simultaneously part of the RSS). This snowballed into open confrontation between the socialists and the Jana Sangh—with the latter taking the stand that they would not quit the RSS as it was only a 'socio-cultural organization'. In protest, the socialists decided to sit separately in the House in July 1979, reducing the government to a minority.

There were desperate efforts to garner outside support for the Vote of Confidence the Prime Minister was compelled to seek. I received a message that the Prime Minister wanted to see me urgently. I went with Niru. He sought the support of Devaraj Urs' group of MPs (we had all been expelled from the Congress by then) to back the motion. 'I need his support only for the Vote of Confidence. After that, I will manage,' he said.

I flew to Bangalore. Sachidanand Swami and I had a long meeting with Devaraj Urs, urging him to support the Prime Minister. He agreed. I informed the Prime Minister accordingly. The next day, Devaraj Urs, Sachidanand Swami and I flew to Delhi together. As we entered the terminal building, a massive sloganeering crowd with flowers, garlands and shawls erupted, invoking Devaraj Urs' name. They were led by Raj Narain.

Before we knew what was happening, Devaraj Urs was lost in the sea of people. We watched dumbfounded, as he was whisked away in a motorcade; we had no way of contacting him.

We were shocked to hear in the late-night news that Devaraj Urs had committed his support to Charan Singh. I am inclined to believe that he had made the promise before he landed in Delhi. In fact, even earlier, I had noticed his growing inclination to join hands with Charan Singh, to fulfil his own dream by leading the Dalits, OBCs and minorities, while Singh mobilized the farmers. 'Between us we can sweep the next elections!' I recall him telling me. To this, I had pointed out that Charan Singh was the champion of the big farmers, while Devaraj Urs was in favour of land reforms that would grant land to the landless. We had a heated discussion. Urs lost his temper and shouted at me, 'You educated urban people do not understand rural India!'—pushing a book of Charan Singh's thoughts towards me, telling me to read it. I rejected the book and replied, 'Charan Singh can never be a national leader. He cannot look beyond Uttar Pradesh and his farmers' agenda. I cannot follow him!' I added that while I respected Urs, and would stay with him, I could not be 'carried as hand baggage' wherever he decided to go. My choice of words must have upset him, because I'm told he kept repeating the phrase to his friends, adding that despite my claims of loyalty and gratitude, I was not willing to compromise.

After the shocking turn of events at the Delhi airport, I went to the Prime Minister's house again and told him of my failed efforts. 'That is how they function. Let us see how long Charan Singh lasts and how,' was his comment. He resigned the next morning. It was 28 July 1979, just two years after he had been sworn in. The great revolution of JP seemed to be crumbling. And how!

Charan Singh, with 64 MPs of his own,[20] the support of Devaraj Urs and the socialists, and a letter of 'outside support' from the Congress, was able to muster the numbers required to fulfil his ambition. Days later, on 15 August 1979, he unfurled the national flag at the Red Fort and addressed the nation. But before he could fully savour the glory of his office, the Congress withdrew support, plunging the government into a crisis once again. Unable to work out an alternative arrangement, the President dissolved Parliament and called for fresh elections. The slogan across the country was '*Lathi goli khayenge, Indiraji ko vapas layenge!*' ('We'll suffer sticks and bullets, but we'll bring back Indiraji!')

Charan Singh continued as caretaker Prime Minister till the Congress recaptured power with 353 seats.[21] Sanjay, too, was back in the reckoning having won his constituency, and his mother was sworn in as Prime Minister once again on 14 January 1980.

The crowds gathered on the lawns of 1, Akbar Road, to greet Indiraji with slogans and flowers, before she went to Rashtrapati Bhavan to take her oath. I, too, had gone and stood with a bouquet of red roses and

---

[20]See Lok Dal, in <http:/lokdal.org.in/>, accessed on 22 October 2015.
[21]See *Statistical Report on General Elections, 1980, to the Seventh Lok Sabha Elections (Volume 1)*, in <http://eci.nic.in/eci_main/StatisticalReports/LS_1980/Vol_I_LS_80.pdf>, accessed on 22 October 2015.

a letter conveying my good wishes. Indiraji was walking around briskly, when she saw me, she stopped and waited for me. Nervous, I gave her the flowers and letter. 'Ma'am, I had told you, you would be back before long. Congratulations. I wish you every success for the future,' I blurted, my voice choked with emotion. She smiled and moved on.

Late that evening, Pranabda dropped in. 'Indiraji saw you somewhere?' he asked.

I told him of my morning meeting.

'She said you looked ill and she was worried about you. She wanted me to find out what was wrong.'

I told him that I was fine but weak after my son's birth.

Satisfied, he left.

While I was quite content staying at home, looking after the baby and attending to work only when required, I felt excited about this first occasion for direct contact with the party since my expulsion.

◆

Indiraji, in the meantime, was back in form. She had returned in her own right, even after many stalwarts had walked out on her. She promised good governance, made some important trips abroad and was hailed for her role in restoring democracy in the country.

Sanjay had sobered down with the birth of his son, Varun. He was now an MP and a General Secretary of the party, and his team was gaining control of the states. There was nothing to stop his rise as the chosen successor to his mother.

Then tragedy struck. On 23 June 1980, while flying a plane and making loops just behind his home, he lost control, struck a wire and crashed into a drain. He was killed on the spot with his trainer pilot.

Indiraji bore her loss stoically, flying out on 27 June with Rajiv to immerse his ashes. I could not get to Delhi for the funeral, but visited the house later, where the ashes were kept for public darshan. Here lay the remains of a young man who had everything going his way, whose word had become law, who could not be challenged by anyone. And now he was gone—the man who had defied every rule could not defy the will of God.

There were condolence resolutions in both Houses of Parliament. Especially touching was the speech of Bhupesh Gupta. Speaking about the crash, his voice trembling with emotion, he said:

There are occasions when many rules are waived [...] if the rules had not been waived, there would not have been the tragedy on 23 June that claimed the life of the son of the Prime Minister of the country, the General Secretary of the ruling Party and the youngest son of my friend for nearly twenty-five years, Feroze Gandhi, and if I am not charged with flattery, also of my friend, Srimati Indira Gandhi. Naturally I speak with a heavy heart.

While Indiraji bore her loss with courage and composure in public, it was clear that something within her had snapped irrevocably. She missed Sanjay, the son who had been her pillar of support and strength. Demands for Rajiv to fill the void began to grow within the party. No response from the family was forthcoming.

◆

In August 1980 I was invited to the UN Women's Conference in Copenhagen as a member of the World Peace Council delegation. It was a first in my career—I had been invited to an international conference in my personal capacity. Besides, I had to manage things for myself.

After that came the winter session of Parliament. I raised the issue of old Indian Patton tanks being surreptitiously sold to South Africa—a country we had no relations with because of its apartheid policies. In response, the Minister of State (MoS) for Defence Production, C.P.N. Singh (a protégé of Sanjay), denied any such deal.

K.P. Unnikrishnan and I got to work. He had a source in the army, and one night, after a clandestine journey that involved a change of two cars, we got to a farm and received a detailed briefing on the deal from a senior army officer; we also procured an international arms magazine with a relevant story as proof. It emerged that tanks had been loaded on a ship bound for Canada from Bombay; the ship had a layover in South Africa. The arms transfer record showed that the number of Patton tanks loaded from India matched the number offloaded in South Africa, with nothing offloaded in Canada.

With this damning information, I went to Parliament. I was told that despite several notings on the file objecting to the deal, C.P.N. Singh, on the instructions of Sanjay (who had been part of some of the negotiating meetings), had overruled all objections and approved the transfer of tanks.

Now Sanjay was gone and the Minister was in the dock.

The army, which was strongly against the deal, wanted me to expose the Minister's role. I kept getting sealed envelopes at my gate at night with copies of documents, file notings and minutes of meetings. The government was in a tizzy. How was it going to get out of this?

I got a sealed envelope one morning with a copy of a letter that had been drafted at a late night secret meeting in Singh's chamber and forwarded to Michelle, an arms dealer in London. It was claimed that I had contacted Michelle while in London, and had offered to stop pushing the matter in Parliament if I was offered a suitable commission. Michelle was to send the letter to the Minister. I was furious and shocked. I went to Bhupesh Gupta with the documents and sought his advice.

Bhupesh Gupta cautioned me, 'They will raid your house, charge you with espionage and jail you if they find these papers in your possession. Get them out of your house immediately and do not drive around in your car alone; they are capable of ramming an army truck into you and killing you...' I followed his instructions.

I then recalled a phone call I had received from someone who carried the name Michelle. D.P. Singh had been at my home at that time. Michelle claimed to have known my late father-in-law, and added that he was not a Jew but a Christian. He said he would like to meet me and explain matters. Before I could reply, D.P. Singh signalled me to end the call. I therefore told Michelle there was nothing to discuss and disconnected the line.

I went to Parliament after receiving the worrying note, and raised its contents during Zero Hour. The Treasury benches were shocked. C.P.N. Singh, in turn, said that I had tried to contact Michelle and blackmail him. I charged the Minister with misleading the House. There were loud demands for his resignation. After heated exchanges in Parliament, it was decided that the matter would be sent to the Privileges Committee.

In a letter to the Chairman of the Privileges Committee, I offered to submit, in person, all the documents I had. But the committee did not want to call me. Pranabda then asked me to cooperate with him to close the matter. I had learnt from my own sources that Indiraji was most upset about these disclosures. She had called for all the relevant files and locked them in her office.

The Chairman of the House, Justice Hidayatullah, asked for my passport for scrutiny. He saw that I had made no trip to London during the period mentioned by Michelle, who then changed his stance, stating that he was not sure of the date as my message had been left for him on his answering machine! I presumed he had recorded my voice on the phone during the conversation we had in D.P. Singh's presence, and had then doctored it. Having been a Judge, the Chairman saw through the game. He rejected the Privilege Motion, with strong words for C.P.N. Singh, who was shifted to the Ministry of Space. My exposé had claimed yet another Minister. I still recall my letter to the Chairman of the Privileges Committee on the closure issue, in which I said, 'What better credence to my charges against the Minister than his being moved from defence production to the realms of outer space!'

Another incident in the Rajya Sabha, from around that time, unfolded during Zero Hour. I wished to raise an issue, but the Chairman would not allow me. So, when he withdrew to his chamber, I followed him and told him that he was not only unreasonable but also anti-women.

He told me to calm down and sit, which I did. Then, he calmly said, 'I have been a Judge. I know how to deal with unruly lawyers!'

'And I have been a lawyer; I know how to deal with unfair Judges,' I replied.

He smiled and said, 'I wanted to say something to you in the House, which I did not. But I will say it now. I pity your husband! You drive me mad in the one hour I spend in the House. I can imagine what you do to him during your hours at home!'

I answered, 'We have an agreement, sir. He has asked me to make all the noise I want in this House, so I return, tired and silent, to *our* home. It works perfectly. We have absolute peace there.'

'You are an incorrigible devil!' Justice Hidayatullah smiled.

He never forgot this incident, and went on to recount it at a law conference where we were both on stage: me as a Minister in the government, he as the former Vice President.

◆

I was out of Delhi on a Parliamentary Committee meeting on 6 June 1982, when I received news of Devaraj Urs' death. He had passed away in Nirmala's house in Bangalore. I could not reach to join the convoy to Hunsur for his cremation. In a way, I was relieved. I could not have watched him go up in flames—this man of immense promise; this leader, known for his loyalty and commitment; this self-sacrificing friend. In my mind, Devaraj Urs will always be one of the towering political personalities of Karnataka and the Congress, the architect of a modern state.

After his death, I decided to go back. Devaraj Urs was dead, as was Sanjay. Though the state leadership kept dilly-dallying over my return, Delhi took a firm stand. I was back in the Congress.

Soon after, there was a South Zone Convention of the party at Madras. When I informed Indiraji that I would be unable to go since I had to be in the chair that afternoon, she responded, 'I leave later today, we will be able to accommodate you. Talk to Dhawan.' So it came to be—I accompanied Indiraji, drove to the convention in her motorcade, and followed her to the stage. There were many enquiring glances and raised eyebrows, especially among Karnataka Congressmen. The message was clear—I was back to centre stage again.

By 1983, it was time for the Karnataka state elections. I was asked to take charge of the distribution of election material at the KPCC office, for which I put a team together. Next, I was asked to take charge of the campaign office, as all the senior leaders were either contesting or campaigning. Gradually, we started getting reports that our chances of victory were diminishing, with the Chief Minister, Gundu Rao, in serious trouble.

The day Gundu Rao reached Bangalore, before the last lap of his campaign tour, I went to the helipad to meet him. I told him of the reports we were receiving—that the news from the field was far from encouraging and that it was best if he returned to his constituency to campaign there. Gundu Rao laughed, 'My constituency is absolutely safe. No one can defeat me! Do not panic. We are forming the government.' I returned home, while he flew off in high spirits.

Elections done, the results came in. I was proven right. Gundu Rao had lost; the Congress with 82 of 224 seats[22] was routed and the government was gone. Ramakrishna Hegde of the Janata Party became the new Chief Minister. A chapter in the Congress' history in the state of Karnataka had closed.

---

[22]See *Statistical Report on General Elections, 1983, to the Legislative Assembly of Karnataka,* in <http://eci.nic.in/eci_main/StatisticalReports/SE_1983/Statistical%20Report%201983%20 karnatkaa.pdf>, accessed on 14 April 2016.

Chapter 15

BACK TO THE ROOTS:
1981–1984

Rajiv was elected to the Lok Sabha from Amethi on 17 August 1981, and soon moved to centre stage. At every function he was the focus of attention, with people moving in, greeting him, getting introduced or introducing themselves. I used to watch Rajiv and Sonia from a distance in social gatherings, always in the company of Arun Nehru and Arun Singh, and their wives, Subhadra and Nina. They were the glamorous power set of Delhi, chased and idolized by all political and society honchos.

I was at a banquet at Rashtrapati Bhavan; I had been out of circulation for a while and was still finding my feet. I was having a quiet conversation with the diplomat, Romesh Bhandari, when suddenly, there was a hush— Indiraji and Rajiv had entered. All eyes turned to them. Within seconds, everyone moved in to greet them. Romesh quickly excused himself, saying, 'I had better pay my regards to the prince,' and as part of a swelling crowd, moved towards Rajiv. I stood with some of the guests, watching.

When the President entered, and we positioned ourselves for the usual round of introductions, Rajiv was escorted to join the Ministers. He politely refused, looked around and took his place next to me, saying, 'This is where I belong'—meaning, with the MPs. We greeted each other with a smile and I said, 'I am Margaret Alva.' 'I know that,' was his reply. Introductions done, we walked to the banquet table. I was surprised (and thrilled) to find my place next to him. Opposite us sat Mohammad Yunus, who carried on a hilarious conversation.

A few months later, on Christmas eve, 1981, I sent Manira to Indiraji's with a cake and a card. Indiraji called her in, gave her a kiss and handed her chocolates. She then phoned to wish my family and me. A day later, when Saroj Khaparde and Pratibha Singh came to greet me, they insisted I go with them to wish Indiraji personally. After some hesitation, I went along. Indiraji welcomed us warmly and personally offered us cake and sweets. The ice had broken.

◆

In mid-1981, I received an invitation from the US Department of State, through their Embassy, to visit their country for four weeks as part of the young leaders' programme. I was surprised. I met P.V. Narasimha Rao, who was External Affairs Minister, to seek his advice and permission.

'Why are they interested in you?' he asked with a mischievous smile.

'I do not know, sir. In fact, I am taken aback,' I replied.

'I can see only two reasons. Either you are being recruited into the CIA (Central Intelligence Agency) or they hope to wean you away from your Leftist inclinations. Either way, go, but be cautious,' was his razor-sharp rejoinder.

So I went. Over the first two days, I attended briefing meetings at the state department offices. The atmosphere was rather stiff, and came with the usual air of superiority—a superpower looking over the rest of the world.

The most interesting part was my tour finalization. There was a big map of the US on a board, with Washington marked with a red clip. I was asked what my interests were, where I would like to go, what institutions I wished to visit, and whom I hoped to meet. All the places I mentioned got marked with a green pin on the map; in half an hour, a red thread connected each of them and we sat down to finalize the travel itinerary—one that would cover New York, New Jersey, Boston, Cape Kennedy (now Cape Canaveral), Charlotte (in South Carolina), Los Angeles, Chicago, Seattle and Honolulu!

During my whirlwind trip, I saw the space shuttle parked at Cape Kennedy; the historic sights and museums in Boston; Kennedy's grave in Arlington; the Boeing establishment at Seattle; and the Ford factory in Chicago, where the adjoining road had huge banners by trade unions reading, 'Park your Toyotas in Tokyo', to protest against the Japanese creeping into the automobile sector. I visited the Helen Keller Centre; a battered women's home (where I was stunned to meet some Indian women); and a fundraiser for the election campaign of a woman Governor. I also had meetings with members of the League of Women Voters, went for lectures at universities; to private homes for dinners and discussions; to receptions; to sports events, school days, parades, concerts, plays and rural festivals. I interacted with officials, intellectuals, women activists, professors, businessmen, and, of course, the upbeat Indian community, which was full of praise for Indira Gandhi. They admired the resilience of Indian democracy, its capacity to sustain attacks and restore itself—a total turnaround from the scepticism of my earlier visit. Curiously, on more occasions than one, there were subtle references to how the British sought to keep the US and India apart, by insisting that India was aligned with the communist block—this while doing business in India under the garb of fostering Commonwealth ties.

I recall, most vividly, the Senate Foreign Affairs Committee meetings which were hearing evidence of the former and present heads of the CIA on operations in Asia. Each one of them spoke of the dangers of supporting corrupt and unpopular regimes, especially in Afghanistan, Pakistan and Iran. 'The arms and equipment we are giving them will ultimately be used against us, as these regimes collapse. We need to review our policies there.' How prophetic these words would prove to be!

When in Charlotte as President of the Delhi chapter of the YWCA, I had an unforgettable lunch with representatives of the YWCA at the home of an African-American member. All the invitees were African-American. My friend, Rose, a white American, and I were the only exceptions. I could not help being amazed at the opulence of the old colonial house which, our hostess proudly announced, had been inherited by her slave ancestor after the Civil War. Luxury cars were parked outside; the crockery was exquisite and the tapestry, heavy. Interestingly, when the conversation started—after a round of introductions, detailing each member's ancestry—what was evident was an undercurrent of bitterness and scorn against the establishment. The members still felt discriminated against by the dominant WASP (White Anglo-Saxon Protestant) leadership—much to the embarrassment of Rose, who was loudly overruled every time she attempted offering an excuse or an explanation. It was clear that no matter what these members may have achieved, racial prejudice was still a reality.

Therefore, during a round of debriefing and farewells, when asked to sum up my impressions, I did so with a simple sentence: 'What a great, big gap between the people and their government at Capitol Hill!' While most of those I met were friendly, open and hospitable, they were critical of the administration and the leadership. They disliked the arrogance of the military, and the American establishment's stance that it was destined to rule the world (just like the British, once upon a time).

I made a pit stop in Tokyo—where I attended a tea ceremony, participated in a pearl-finding competition, and on my way to Mount Fuji, ate an egg boiled in the sulphur spring (believed to promote youth and longevity)—before flying back to Delhi. I had been away for five weeks, doing a round-the-world trip at the cost of the US taxpayer.

◆

On 3 February 1983, Rajiv was appointed General Secretary of the AICC; he took charge of the frontal organizations of the party, began touring extensively, and started mobilizing youth, students and women. He was young, approachable and responsive to party cadres, who adored him. He had already made his mark as an organizer when he had taken charge of the Asian Games as the Convenor of the Organizing Committee.

In 1983, when Assembly elections in Nagaland were announced, a group of young MPs were summoned to Rajiv's AICC office and told they were being sent to Nagaland for the campaign; I was one among them. We were to go to the districts allotted to us and stay there till voting was done. We were briefed by the PCC office bearers, after which we were given a packet containing ₹5,000, a return air ticket, and the map, route and contact numbers of the district and the PCC.

I was deputed to a district up in the hills called Zunheboto (I hadn't heard of it until then) and my teammate was Manoranjan Bhakta, an MP from the Andaman and Nicobar Islands. We were told to leave at the earliest. My heart sank as it meant being away for two whole weeks. After the meeting, Bhakta told me he would have to go home first and would meet me directly at Zunheboto. This meant that I had to reach the destination alone.

I set out for Guwahati from where I was to be picked up by the Nagaland PCC vehicle. The airport was small. I looked around. There was no one to receive me. The Indian Airlines staff suggested I wait in the VIP lounge while they made announcements and tried locating my vehicle, without success.

I finally contacted the PCC for a car and left Kohima with an IYC escort. It was a long journey. The next day, I was driven to Zunheboto, where I received a warm welcome. The opposition camp grew uneasy with my campaign—which entailed visiting the market place, interacting with women, etc. Soon enough, I noticed on the walls huge charcoal pictures of a woman in a saree, with a huge bun and a red bindi; the caption beneath read: 'Beware, Kali has come from India!' Clearly, my presence was having an impact!

Bhakta soon joined me. We sorted out conflicts among leaders and workers, went to Bihari workers' camps to understand their concerns, and mobilized the Christian community. When the results were announced, we knew our hard work had paid off—we had managed to win five of the six seats in a district dominated by the Sema tribe, and two of the winning candidates from Zunheboto became Ministers!

The day I left, there were hugs, tears and gifts of honey, pineapples, bamboo shoots and shawls—all priceless!

◆

1983 was also the year when I went to Cuba with Professor Rasheeduddin Khan and two others as part of a friendship delegation. I spoke, without a prepared speech, at their Foreign Affairs Institute on the challenges India faced as a democratic, non-aligned, developing country. I didn't know it then, but President Fidel Castro had been listening to the proceedings in his office. We had been requesting a meeting with the President from the day we had arrived, but no clear commitment was forthcoming. Now, impressed as Fidel Castro was with my performance, he invited us for dinner to the Presidential Palace.

Finally, we were face-to-face with the icon—a man in a green military uniform, with an unkempt beard, warm eyes and an infectious grin. He only spoke Spanish but understood English well enough to correct the mistakes of his translator! He had many questions regarding India and our trips across Cuba.

Suddenly the conversation took an unusual turn. Fidel Castro had specially ordered coconut ice cream to add an Indian touch to his menu. One of his Ministers, a lady who had been in the revolution with him, was busy enjoying a large portion of the exotic dessert. Fidel Castro pointed to her and said, 'Look at her! She is fat as it is, and yet she eats and eats. Thankfully, she was not with us on the Granma[23] or we would have drowned!' He then turned to me and asked, 'How much do you weigh?'

---

[23]Granma was the yacht that carried Fidel Castro and several other rebels to Cuba's shores in 1956, thus launching the Cuban revolution.

'Why should I tell you?' I asked, adding, 'We, in India, have a saying: "Never reveal what the saree can hide." It does cover a multitude of sins!'

'Oh, yes?' he laughed. The next minute he had his large hands on my waist. 'I can pick you up and tell you how much you weigh.'

'Please don't, Your Excellency,' I begged. 'I am much heavier than you think. You will get a heart attack. Please don't—' Before I could finish my sentence, I was lifted a foot above the ground!

Fidel Castro laughed, 'Now I know how heavy you are!'

I was red in the face.

But soon enough, he put me at ease once more, regaling us with stories. He told us how the Spaniards landed in Cuba. They had set out to find India—the land of riches. But the currents brought their ships to the shores of the Caribbean. As the Spanish soldiers in their metal armour began riding on armoured horses through the waters at dawn, the rising sun shining on them, the local people mistook them for heavenly beings. They fell down on their knees in worship, only to be slaughtered and conquered. 'Do you see how different history would have been if the Spanish had landed in India instead of Cuba?' Fidel Castro asked.

'Yes, Fidel Castro would have been an Indian,' I said.

The man liked it. He thumped the table and said, 'I would have loved it! India is a great country!'

We finally left long past midnight in high spirits. I had met one of the most dynamic and charismatic leaders of the world. He was tall, handsome, charming, and he had literally swept me off my feet!

The next day saw a farewell dinner hosted by the Minister of Culture. Towards the end of the evening, he walked across and whispered in my ear that the President wished to meet me after dinner. Nervously I asked, 'Where?' 'We will let you know,' was the answer.

I spoke to our Ambassador sitting across the table, and requested him in Hindi to accompany me. He said he could not take the liberty, unless he was specifically invited by the President. 'Should I go?' I asked.

'Do you have a choice?' he smiled.

'Don't I?'

'Well, you cannot refuse an invitation from the President of Cuba. That would be considered an insult.'

My heart was pounding. Where was I going? With whom? For what? I kept running over these questions in my mind as I gulped my pudding.

When we started walking out, the Minister of Culture escorted me to a car parked at the entrance. I was then driven, the Minister by my side—destination unknown. After a long, seemingly unending journey, we drew up to the gate of a neat little home with a small garden. The front door opened, and to my great relief, there was a lady—warm and friendly—to welcome us; she had her daughter by her side. It was the home of the Minister; this was his family. I relaxed, my prayers answered. God was listening even in communist Cuba!

As we sat exchanging pleasantries, the door was flung open. There stood the President with a mischievous grin. He settled into a comfortable chair, removed his cap and got the young daughter of the Minister (who served as an interpreter too) to sit between us.

He again asked me about our visit—where we had been and what we had seen.

I listed the sites one by one.

He interrupted me to ask, 'You visited the church, and met the padre too?'

'Yes,' I said. He had obviously been keeping track of our visit, and the fact that I had entered the church alone in the middle of our tour of the old town centre.

'Any complaints?'

'No,' I replied.

'They do their job, we do ours. We do not interfere with them as long as they stick to their field,' he explained. 'What is your overall impression?'

'I went everywhere, I looked everywhere, I saw pictures of many heroes of the revolution. But there wasn't a single picture of you—except for one pointing to the US with a warning: "You may take every inch of our territory, but you will not take a single Cuban alive!" Why aren't there more posters of you?'

'Because I am here with my people. They do not need my pictures to be reminded of me.'

'How I wish leaders around the world could say the same thing!' I commented.

We had coffee and snacks as he called for a map of South Asia and spread it across a table in front of him. I sat on the carpet next to him, as he started his probing questions on Pakistan, Bangladesh, Sri Lanka, Kashmir, Punjab and Assam; communal violence; the Emergency; separatist movements; public sector enterprises; agrarian reforms, etc. He seemed to know a lot about India and her neighbours. He then told me that he adored Indira Gandhi and her courage.

'And you did something that even her husband did not dare do to her in public!' I chuckled, reminding him of the way he had thrown his arms around her and kissed her on stage at the Non-Aligned Summit in Delhi.

My capacity to explain things seemed to impress him. Our conversation went on and on. I suddenly realized it was 2 a.m.

'I must be gone, Your Excellency,' I said, my eyes burning for want of sleep.

'Why? There is so much more to talk about. I am fascinated by India and Indira!' he smiled.

'I have to leave the hotel by 8 a.m.,' I answered.

'To go where?' he asked.

'To a stud farm,' I replied.

'What? A stud farm? Are they crazy? Who fixed this?' he asked his Minister, who fumbled for a response. 'The trip should be cancelled. I don't understand. Instead of taking you to the Isle of Youth or a beach resort, they take you to a stud farm!'

After that, the questions continued until around 4 a.m. Then, Fidel Castro got up, put his large arms around me, kissed me on both my cheeks, and said, 'You did a very good job! I learnt a lot tonight. Thank you very much.'

The Minister, with his daughter, escorted me back to the hotel. I left the next day with a beautiful orange porcelain vase and two lamps shades as gifts from the President, along with his biography.

When I got home, I had a paper cutting on my table with a note from the children: 'Our apologies. Good luck!' It was an announcement appointing me National Convenor of the Congress Women's Front, with Abida Ahmed as the Chairman. I was shocked! Why had they pushed me there again?

I went to meet Indiraji with a gift and gave her my report of the visit. At the end, I asked, 'Ma'am, why have you put me in the Women's Front?'

'I do not know anything. Talk to Rajiv,' was the answer.

I met him the next day at his AICC office with the same question.

'Don't waste time asking questions. Just start working!' he smiled.

And so I did.

Chapter 16

WOMEN IN POWER:
THE MAHILA CONGRESS

I found myself the Convenor of the Women's Front, with Sudha Joshi as the new General Secretary. Rajivji, as General Secretary in charge of frontal organizations, was most supportive. In no time, we had a separate office at 1, Talkatora Road, with a three-member staff. The inauguration of this office was a big affair with both Indiraji and Rajivji present.

We got to work immediately. We set up cells for grievances and legal aid, press and publicity, training and empowerment. We decided that the state heads of the Front would stay and called a meeting in Delhi to get reports of their respective jurisdictions. Unlike the IYC, the Women's Front had no Constitution or logo, no separate budget or vehicle, no status or autonomy. We decided to correct this. A Constitution Drafting Committee of former conveners and senior women MPs was set up, district conventions were planned and a state conventions' calendar was drawn up for the year. Suddenly, Congress women were in focus.

Given the frenzy of activity within the Women's Front, the membership drive was a big success. Rajivji was, of course, the main attraction for the women—young and old—who gathered for meetings with great enthusiasm whenever he made it. In fact, there was a scramble for front rows—all of which would be occupied an hour before the meeting, mostly by young, non-political women. I attended every state convention. Rajivji came to many of them, as did the Chairman. Party leaders of the states made it a point to be seen there.

He then set about rejuvenating the frontal organizations at the district level. At a meeting of District Presidents at the Siri Fort Auditorium in the summer of 1983, he met each state unit separately and then at the plenary called upon the National Presidents to speak. Abidaji asked me to speak on behalf of our organization. My speech in Hindi was hilarious. I spoke of the problems we faced in getting Sitaram Kesri, the Treasurer, to release money to the Women's Front; how three other organizations kept offering us lifts in their vehicles, since we had none. Kesriji kept squirming in his seat as the audience roared and clapped; Rajivji, too, seemed to be having fun, as his closing speech referred to all the points I had raised. Kesriji, thoroughly embarrassed, promised with folded hands to set things right for us. Indiraji came later, and was happy that, for the first time, the frontal organizations' heads at the district level were interacting in a national forum; this would help motivate them in a big way.

◆

In the 1980s, trouble began brewing in Punjab. Rajivji visited the state himself, and asked frontal organizations to consolidate their members in the state for a campaign to counter the call for Khalistan.[24] We convened a number of women's meetings under the leadership of Amarjit Kaur, who was our head there. In each of them, mothers pleaded for a peace initiative so that security for their families could be ensured. We also had meetings behind closed doors with important Akali leaders.

Soon after, Aruna Asaf Ali, the renowned freedom fighter, decided to lead a women's delegation to the Golden Temple to meet with Jarnail Singh Bhindranwale[25] and his supporters holed up in there. It was a big delegation of women drawn from all over the country—mostly NGO representatives and women from different political parties, including me. We had a special bogey on the train to Amritsar. We sang patriotic songs and bhajans for peace and harmony late into the night. Breakfast was in the Golden Temple langar, followed by prayers at the Harmandir Sahib complex.

We then proceeded to an inner hall for the meeting, where eight of us discussed matters with Bhindranwale—a lean, tall man, with a long beard, dressed in a long, flowing, blue outfit, and turban, with a kirpan (a curved sword) in his belt and a kara (an iron bangle) around his wrist.

---

[24]The Khalistan movement, a nationalist political liberation struggle that aimed to create a separate country called Khalistan in the Punjab region, reached its high point in the 1970s and 80s.

[25]Jarnail Singh Bhindranwale, a Sikh religious authority and a political revolutionary, came to be associated with acts of violence in the early 1980s in Punjab. He supported the Anandpur Sahib Resolution—containing demands for the devolution of powers to the state and a reduction in government influence—which came to be viewed by Indira Gandhi as a secessionist document. In June 1984, Bhindranwale and his armed supporters took refuge inside the Golden Temple.

Bhindranwale had three or four aides with him. He focused his intense eyes on a frail, white-saree-clad Arunaji, who spoke of the great valour and patriotic traditions of the Sikh gurus, and the need for peace, understanding, love and unity in these critical times. 'We have come to appeal to you on behalf of Indiraji and the women of India. We want peace for our children, we want them to live. Punjab is bleeding with violence, burning with anger. Understand your people's suffering, respond to their pleas,' she begged with emotion.

Bhindranwale listened, but said little. When he did express his views, he was soft-spoken, respectful and pleasant. He insisted that he, too, wanted peace, but not at the cost of the honour and pride of the Sikh people.

A while later, as we rose to go, we repeated just one sentence, '*Hum shanti chahate hain.*' ('We want peace.') We came out with a packet of prasad and a white scarf. We could only hope that our visit had melted Bhindranwale's heart of steel.

After a meal at the langar, we marched to Jallianwala Bagh—where in 1919, scores of non-violent Indian protestors had been fired upon by the British—and with local women, shouted slogans for communal harmony. Then we paid silent homage to the martyrs. A few of us spoke about our mission for peace, after which there were prayers from all major religions and the national anthem. We returned to Delhi by the same bogey that night, hoping that our undertaking would meet with success.

But to our great disappointment, tensions continued to escalate and violence raged unabated. Police officers were targeted, as well as politicians. Harchand Singh Longowal, the Leader of the Akali Dal, came out in open support of Bhindranwale, with fresh demands for Khalistan raising national security concerns.

Indiraji addressed the nation on AIR on 2 June, asking for dialogue and unity. Repeated requests on the public communication system, urging the armed men inside the complex to come out, yielded no results. Finally, on the morning of 5 June 1984, there was news that army commandos had started shelling the building inside the Harmandir Sahib complex, which had been occupied for a while by Khalistan and Bhindranwale supporters. 'Operation Blue Star', under the command of General Krishnaswamy Sundarji, was launched to evict them from the complex.

We were in Bangalore at that time. News coverage was limited, but it seemed that a full-fledged military operation was under way. Punjab was cut off from the rest of the country. I had a sinking feeling. Was this the only way out? What would the repercussions be? Would the Sikhs take this lying down? If they reacted violently, it could lead to a civil war. How would the situation then be controlled?

Reactions were mixed. There were many who believed that military action was long overdue. Our opponents, however, said that Bhindranwale was a Frankenstein created by the Congress to fight the Akalis—so, now, it was only right that the Congress government faced the consequences! In the midst of such talk, the casualty figures emerged; they kept mounting.

Finally we had news of Bhindranwale's death and extensive damage to the temple. Sikhs all over the world now began to react—condemning the government's decision; denouncing the desecration of their holiest shrine; comparing Operation Blue Star to the massacre at Jallianwala Bagh; and vowing retaliation. While the Prime Minister had asked for limited action to flush out the militants holed in the temple, the sheer number of rebels, and their resistance and fire power compelled the army to move in tanks to dislodge them. In light of the damage, the government announced immediate repair and restoration. But this did little to appease sentiments. Indiraji became the target of Sikh anger in all parts of the country and the world.

Most of the Congress stood united with the Prime Minister. Statements of support poured in from all corners of the country. Every day groups would assemble at 1, Akbar Road, to endorse the government's decisions. Amarjit Kaur, the Rajya Sabha Sikh MP from Patiala, spoke in defence of Indiraji both inside and outside Parliament.

However, there were Congress leaders who panned the government— one of them being the Maharaja of Patiala, Amarinder Singh, who resigned from the party and took his close associates with him. He went on to join the Akali Dal, becoming a vocal and vociferous critic of the Congress and Indiraji. Some senior Sikh army officials and diplomats resigned in protest. Ironically, Operation Blue Star itself had been led by a Sikh Lieutenant General, Kuldip Singh Brar (under General Sundarji's command).

For my part, I led a Congress women's delegation drawn from several states to meet Indiraji. She seemed disturbed about the developments in Punjab. When I congratulated her on her bold stance and subsequent victory, she interrupted me: 'There is no victory or defeat in this. Let us not be happy with or proud of what has happened. We have to work to heal wounds, to hold the country together.'

We got the message. The road to recovery was long.

◆

Around this time, on the personal front, I experienced several upheavals. In October 1983, my parents came to Delhi for a holiday. The winter cold gave my father a tooth and chest infection. By the time they returned to Bangalore in mid-November, he was on antibiotics, which led to other problems.

I was in Bangalore for a day on 19 December. My father, who had been feeling giddy, was resting. When I wished him goodbye, he asked me to stay. But I couldn't as I had to host an official delegation from (what was then) Yugoslavia. I hugged him and promised to be back soon. That was my last meeting with him.

Soon after Christmas, when Niru and I were in Calcutta for an AICC session, he was admitted to St John's Hospital. By the time I reached Bangalore, he was in the ICU in a coma. My sisters, Corinne and Joan, were there with my mother. We prayed and kept vigil, hoping for a miracle. But, on the morning of 6 January 1984, on Manira's birthday, he was gone.

I have never forgiven myself for having left him when he pleaded with me to stay, nor have I excused myself for not sitting with him in the ICU, while he was in a coma. I could not bear to see him with drips and tubes, and would come out crying each time I went in.

Gentle, self-effacing and a man of God, my father had struggled all his life, and had, through sheer hard work, made his way up from a tiny village to become a Judge and then a senior lawyer, respected and admired by one and all. As a father, he was the ideal dad—he encouraged me, taught me to be honest, supported me through every crisis, loved and guided me, and had been proud of my success and achievements. Now I had lost my guiding star.

Even as I struggled to recover from this tragedy, in February 1984, Niru met with a serious car accident which almost killed him. He had successfully bid for an Ambassador at an army disposal auction in Madras, and when Joachim (his assistant) and he were driving back to Bangalore, the tyre of the newly acquired car burst; the vehicle slammed into a tree at high speed. When a passing bus observed the scene, both Niru and Joachim were presumed dead; the police were alerted. When they rushed to the spot, they noticed that the two were miraculously still alive—unconscious, bleeding, their legs broken. They shifted them to the Kolar district hospital in the vicinity, and after recovering their IDs, phoned Bangalore. Sachidanand Swami and my nephews arrived to shift them to Bangalore.

I received the first message by 10 a.m. in Delhi; I gathered that Niru and Joachim had been found in a mangled car and there was little chance of survival. The only flight out was at 4.30 p.m. I flew with Choku and reached St John's hospital by 8 p.m. Niru and Joachim were out of danger and conscious.

When he was fit to travel—his leg in a plaster, mouth sutured and wounds bandaged—we flew him to Delhi. For three months thereafter, I bathed, changed, fed and nursed Niru round the clock. He was a difficult patient—he dug holes into the plaster because it was itchy, which, in turn, had to be changed six times! I did not complain; I could live with the strain. I was grateful that he was alive. He was back on his feet in two months, able to move with crutches and help himself in some ways.

When Rajivji heard of the accident, he asked me why we had purchased an auctioned army car. 'Are you crazy? Why didn't you get a new car?' he asked. I told him we had booked a Maruti, but the waiting list was long; we had no choice but to buy the old Ambassador. The next day, I received a phone call I least expected—from the Maruti factory. A car had been released to us; 'Could we come and complete the formalities?' It was unbelievable! We had been allotted a red Maruti out of the first 200 cars that left the assembly line.

This was Rajiv Gandhi.

◆

By 1984, the political scene was getting feverish. February 1984 saw the Governor of Jammu and Kashmir replaced with Jagmohan, Sanjay's Emergency manager in Delhi. Soon after, the Farooq Abdullah government fell and Governor's Rule followed. In Andhra Pradesh, N.T. Rama Rao's government fell on account of defections (which he claimed had been engineered by the Congress Governor) and a new coalition government led by the Congress took charge. The Prime Minister was charged with preemptive action to clip opposition unity in the bud, as both these Chief Ministers had openly called for it.

In the meantime, preparations for the national convention of Congress women started in right earnest. Attendance at the state conventions was a precondition for the selection of delegates. Each delegate had to buy a badge prepared by the Organizing Committee at a fixed price of ₹50, which covered travel, stay and food.

Bangalore was chosen as the venue for the convention of 15 and 16 October. I spent time finalizing the site, accommodation and other details with the help of K.H. Patil, the PCC President. A shamiana was erected on the palace grounds, with a tented village and an exhibition area; a souvenir was to be produced with advertisements.

I went to Ramakrishna Hegde, then the Chief Minister, and told him of the convention: 'Women from all parts of India and several leaders, including the Prime Minister and Rajivji, are coming. Karnataka is playing host—not me. We need your protection, and we need support from the administration for electricity, water, toilet facilities and security. We will foot the bills, but please could you ensure that no hurdles are created?'

Hegde was most gracious. 'We will do everything to help. After all, it is the reputation of Karnataka that is at stake. Do not worry about anything.'

He kept his word. He created a team of officials to work with us and attend to all our requirements.

Just a week before the convention, some of those who had engineered my expulsion from the Congress—particularly, F.M. Khan and his cronies—became enormously upset at the importance being given to me. So they went on a fast on the lawns of the AICC. Many leaders called on Khan, ostensibly to ask him to abandon the fast, but in fact to congratulate him and support this protest by 'Indira loyalists' against the rehabilitation of those who had 'abandoned' her. I was embarrassed. I approached Rajivji and told him that I was ready to step down if this was the sentiment in the party. He asked me to ignore the protestors, and assured me that he would deal with Khan. I went to Khan before leaving for Bangalore, requesting him to call off the fast, join me and help with arrangements for the convention. He refused to budge.

Undaunted, I went on with my work. My efforts paid off. The convention drew over 50,000 delegates—far exceeding our target. Trains rolled in from all parts of India, bringing women in a range of costumes, speaking a host of languages. It was a mini-India in the tented village!

Rajiv Gandhi arrived on 14 October and visited each of the state tents; he watched dance performances, received garlands and gifts, ate with the delegates and launched 'Karuna' as the socio-economic development face of the Women's Front (Mahila Congress). The enthusiasm of the women almost knocked him off his feet. His security men were in despair! I finally took charge, making way for him to move, with women forming a ring around him. 'You are a tough woman! Even better than my men!' commented Rajiv Gandhi. I had bleeding feet at the end of it, stamped by security men and unmanageable women.

The convention was inaugurated the next morning by Indiraji. It seemed like the proceedings would be entirely disrupted by overenthusiastic women clambering on to the stage and leaders shouting slogans. I decided not to speak and requested Indiraji to begin the proceedings. 'You must speak and they must listen,' she replied, standing by my side. I spoke to an audience that now listened attentively. The new Constitution approved by the CWC was presented by Abidaji, and greeted with thunderous applause. The new name for the Women's Front flashed behind us; the 'Mahila Congress' was born. It was a moment of joy and achievement for me.

There was a procession to Sri Kanteerava Stadium in the evening, with drums, slogans, banners and dance performances. A historic public rally was addressed by Indiraji which drew over one lakh women. This was followed by a cultural programme at night at which the actress, Vyjayanthimala, danced, followed by a delegates' dinner, after which Indiraji shopped at the exhibition we had set up. Before leaving, she patted my back, with her usual 'well done'.

Rajiv Gandhi took over the next day, the convention ending with a valedictory session. Just when we thought we could congratulate ourselves for a job excellently done, Bangalore began drowning in a storm, and the rain would just not stop. Many tents collapsed. The electricity had to be switched off for fear of short circuits and fires. There was complete pandemonium. I found myself in the middle of a nightmare. I sat in the control room through the night, shifting women and their belongings to safer places—to railway platforms and to the corridors of the palace complex. Breakfast packets were prepared all night and sent to them. The trains began to depart with packed food. I sighed in relief as the last one departed in the evening. There had not been a single casualty.

I returned to Delhi, tired and exhausted, my feet swollen with the cuts and hurts I had suffered. My family was happy to have me back, and especially delighted about the positive press the event seemed to be receiving. What was most remarkable was that we had saved ₹25 lakh from the amount collected as badge fees; this was put into a fixed deposit so that the Mahila Congress could run on its interest.

Rajivji left for Delhi, telling us that he was very happy with the proceedings. The next day, along with news items detailing the convention's many successes, I was shocked to read a press release that F.M. Khan had been expelled from the Congress for six years. Rajiv Gandhi had signed the order and gone abroad with his family for a holiday.

Not long after, Gundu Rao, who had made a few sarcastic comments about Rajivji's branded sunglasses and expensive watches, came to me. He wanted an appointment with Rajivji as he wished to apologize and pledge his loyalty. He had been denied a meeting despite several attempts. I pleaded with Rajivji, who finally met him. Gundu Rao, in turn, thanked me and offered his full support to me if I wished to become the next Chief Minister of Karnataka. I smiled, knowing how hollow the promise was. I also smiled because politics in Karnataka had come a full circle![26]

Today, Gundu Rao's son is a Minister in the state. I have the satisfaction of saying that though his father did everything to finish me politically, I was instrumental in making him the IYC President of Karnataka in 1998 by taking him personally to Soniaji and pleading his case.

◆

I was called to Indiraji's residence on the evening of 22 October 1984. After congratulating me for a successful convention, she told me she was worried. It turned out that the President, Giani Zail Singh, had left on an official visit to Mauritius—which was marking 150 years of the arrival of Indian labour on the island—and then to the United Arab Emirates (UAE). The President had taken as large a delegation as his plane could accommodate—MPs, friends, family members, and cultural and business delegates from Punjab, Bihar, Gujarat, etc. Indiraji was concerned about the composition of the entourage—'It is going to be a diplomatic disaster,' she said—and expressed the desire to send an official delegation of MPs to add an intellectual spin to the celebrations. She asked me to put a delegation together—which would be sponsored by the ICCR (Indian Council for

---

[26]In the early 1990s, Gundu Rao took ill and stayed in Bombay in a public sector guest house arranged by his friend, A.R. Antulay. In 1993, he died at the age of fifty-six.

Cultural Relations)—and leave urgently for Mauritius. 'All arrangements will be made,' she assured me.

She then gave me an assignment to complete on my return: 'I have a room full of gifts presented to me from time to time. Sit with Usha Bhagat, sort them out and organize a sale. You can use the proceeds for the work of the organization you have launched.'

'Should I organize the sale on the lawns of Akbar Road or at the AICC?' I asked.

'It will be better here,' she replied (implying 1, Akbar Road).

'I will schedule this for 19 November, ma'am,' I said, and before leaving told her that upon my return, I would bring her a convention album and a file of newspaper reports covering the event.

'Get going with the delegation immediately!' were her parting words.

This was my last meeting with Indira Gandhi. She was in a dark blue house coat with a towel wrapped around her head to dry her hair.

I managed to put together a three-member delegation of MPs— Professor Rasheeduddin Khan (Delhi), Mirza Irshad Baig (Gujarat) and me. I sent Indiraji a note before we left.

All the hotels in Port Louis had been booked for Indian delegates. The only place we could find was a three-bedroom cottage facing the beach at Club Med—a somewhat shady place that seemed to offer a weekend getaway to couples, with neither phones nor room service. I took the downstairs room while Khan and Baig occupied the upstairs ones. As we moved in, I jokingly commented, 'I am sure people will think that I am Khan's second wife and that Baig is his son!' It didn't help that at Khan's wife's behest, I had been forced to keep tabs on the food he ate in the dining hall. Not surprisingly, when Khan decided to stay back one day to enjoy the beach while we went into town, guests passing by greeted him with: 'Your wife and son have left you alone today?' I was right, after all!

In Mauritius, we gave speeches, and attended cultural programmes and events. Giani Zail Singh was in his element, enjoying the fun. Ram Dulari Sinha, the ageing Minister from Bihar, spent a great deal of time singing praises of Ram Gulam, the Prime Minister of Mauritius, letting him know, *'Bihar me aapka naam gali gali mein jante hain!'* ('People know of you in all the by-lanes of Bihar!')

On the night of 30 October, we took the flight back to Delhi via Bombay, while the President left for the UAE. We landed in Bombay on the morning of 31 October. While leaving for Mauritius, I had asked the duty-free shop to keep a colour television aside for me. I went to pick this up. When I reached the counter, a grave Customs Officer came up to me and said, 'Ma'am, news has just been flashed that the Prime Minister has been shot.'

'What? Where?' I shouted, my hands trembling with the dollars I had counted.

'We have no details,' he answered.

My head spun. Leaving the money and the television with him, I rushed to the lounge. By now, everyone had gathered around the TV to hear the news; Sonia was rushing Indiraji to AIIMS. My mind went blank. All I remember is being escorted to a special flight to Delhi with scores of leaders from Maharashtra. On arrival, I saw the flag at the airport still flying at full mast. I breathed a sigh of relief. There was hope. Indiraji would survive.

I arrived home, only to be told by Manira that the BBC had announced that Indiraji was dead. Her Sikh bodyguards, Satwant Singh and Beant Singh, had shot her in her own compound. I could not believe it—she had been murdered by the very men who were to guard her and whom she had retained out of a strong commitment to secularism. Why her permission had to be sought before shifting security personnel, I have never been able to understand. This was a routine administrative matter. And when there were doubts about the activities and attitudes of personal guards, they should have been moved post-haste! Now, it was too late to undo the damage.

I sank into my pillow and sobbed. Memories of my last meeting with her, and especially of her face, flashed before my eyes. How much we had experienced together—the many years I had grown up in her shadow; the battles fought under her leadership; her humiliation in 1977, her subsequent return to power; her jail days; the joy of her victory in Chikmagalur; our parting and my return to her... I fell asleep, emotionally drained, physically exhausted, Manira clinging to me.

When I woke up, it was evening. I washed my face, changed and decided to go to AIIMS. Indiraji's body was being embalmed. Giani Zail Singh had flown back from the UAE. Rajivji was back from Calcutta, with Pranab Mukherjee and others. On my way to the hospital, I saw mobs on a rampage, attacking Sikhs in vehicles, burning their taxis at stands; several areas were up in smoke. Eshwar Das, our driver, hurriedly took us back home as crowds descended on the streets, ready to kill. That cold October night, I had cold shivers running down my spine. There were dangerous portents on the horizon. 'What are we headed for?' I wondered.

I frantically called up the Home Minister's office, the AICC, the Lieutenant Governor's office...but there was no response. I left messages asking for immediate action to quell the violence in every quarter I could think of, hoping someone, somewhere would act. But my efforts were in vain. What happened that evening and continued to happen during the following days is now a shameful chapter of our history. Innocent Sikhs were killed, their cars burnt, their homes attacked—all in response to a call for revenge—while the administration looked on, paralyzed.

We learnt later that all those who mattered had reached Rashtrapati Bhavan for the swearing-in of Rajiv Gandhi as Prime Minister. When the evening news bulletin announced that Indiraji's body was being taken to 1, Safdarjung Road, we rushed there. We watched her family carry her in, and then, when they requested to be left alone with her for the night, we left.

I spent the next two days and nights at the Teen Murti house clearing flowers and helping in whatever way I could. Religious groups came to sing and offer prayers. Diplomats, foreign dignitaries, people from every walk of life walked past the body of a leader—one of the most powerful the world will ever see—now bruised and dead.

The funeral saw millions line the roads to pay their last tributes—family, friends, followers, even critics. The country and the world stood up to salute Indira Gandhi, the woman of courage, who faced every challenge and confronted a strong, united opposition to lead the nation.

The cremation, at a site adjoining her father's samadhi, was accompanied by scenes I will never forget—Rahul burying his face in his father's chest; Priyanka and Sonia supporting each other; little Varun's hand in Priyanka's. As the sun set and the flames rose, the smoke dimmed mourners into mere silhouettes.

Later, at a massive condolence meeting on the lawns of India Gate, attended by lakhs of people, Rajiv, in a moment of emotion, made that famous statement: 'When a mighty tree falls, it is only natural that the earth around it shakes'—a statement which was taken out of context and interpreted as a justification of the attacks on the Sikhs.

That was far from the young Prime Minister's intention. For, soon after the cremation, exhausted, bereaved, he drove around the city, sacked the Lieutenant Governor, overhauled the law and order machinery, and ordered immediate relief measures for those affected. As thousands fled homes, camps were opened in different areas—some in gurdwaras, others in schools and shaadi mahals, a few in sports complexes.

In the middle of the crisis, late at night, I received a message from Rajivji's office to 'get to the camps'. By the following morning, four jeeps parked themselves outside my house, as truckloads of material were dumped. I called in women volunteers from the Mahila Congress and NGOs. Even as the rampage continued, I went into one of the camps, with Manira and a few Mahila Congress women, telling them Rajivji had sent us to help.

They collected around us, ready to throw us out, screaming that they wanted no help from us. 'You people kill us, then come to assist? Get out and leave us alone!' they shouted.

We were scared but decided to stay. 'We are your sisters; we are here to serve you,' I said.

'Did we kill her? Why punish us, because two Sikhs shot her?' they retorted.

'What happened was wrong, but the new Prime Minister did not do this to you, did he? Indiraji didn't either, did she? We did not do this to you, did we? Then why are you angry with us? Why are you throwing us out?' I told them calmly.

As tempers cooled, we started distributing buns, biscuit packets, milk cartons, blankets, dhurries, toiletries—all of which they needed. We were in these camps for over two weeks—tending to rows of people on floor-mats, mourning their dead or missing family members. Then came supplies of sarees, dhotis, salwar kameez sets and duppatas, chappals and socks. Kitchens were set up by the gurdwaras, which supplied fresh food and water. We began to work with them, and I became a friend of several Sikh leaders who appreciated the Mahila Congress' timely intervention and support. We had been the first to step in, and only later did government agencies take over. With time, many returned to their homes or families, and we withdrew.

◆

Rajivji, as Prime Minister, recast his Cabinet and dropped some old hands. I remember my first meeting with him as Prime Minister at 1, Akbar Road. I called him 'sir'.

He frowned and said, 'What did you say? *Sir*? Do not do that!'

'You are now my Prime Minister. I cannot call you by your name any more,' I replied.

'Nothing has changed, so you need not change my name,' he said, firmly.

'Yes, Prime Minister!' I said mischievously and left.

◆

General Elections were soon announced. We began campaigning right away. I did a lot of touring, touching constituencies contested by women, and then went to Mangalore and Goa with the family for Christmas.

As we drove back, the results kept pouring in. The Congress was sweeping the polls everywhere. There were celebrations all along the route; there was excitement in the air. Rajivji was now a leader in his own right, elected with an overwhelming majority of 401 seats[27]—a first in India's history. The opposition correctly remarked, 'Indira Gandhi has proven herself more powerful dead than alive!'

◆

My first decade in Parliament had been a turbulent one. I had lost four people who had shaped my life—my father, who had bequeathed his principles to me; Baba, who had taught me lessons in socialism and nation-building, and had led me to the Congress; Devaraj Urs, my guide to state politics when I had been no more than a novice; and Indiraji, who had handpicked me and brought me to Parliament, the AICC and the national stage. I had survived the onslaught of the IYC and the Emergency, and had returned to the Rajya Sabha for a second term, despite all odds.

Indiraji was a woman who was secular, a strong nationalist, at home in any part of the country and at the same time, a citizen of the world. She was a devoted daughter, a doting mother, an indulgent grandmother, a loyal friend, but a deadly opponent. Most of all, she was a woman of courage—perhaps best exemplified by the fact that she took the country to the polls in 1977. Yes, the party lost, but democracy won. While her friends and foes had written her off after that defeat, she bounced back, powered by the conviction that the people of India would return to her.

Not surprisingly, even today, men and women in distant parts of the

---

[27]See *PM India*, in <http://pmindia.gov.in/en/>, accessed on 14 April 2016.

country remember her and speak about her with awe and admiration—from the small farmers in South India, who remember the 'amma' who gave them their land; to the agitating farmers in Maharastra, who yelled when their land was acquired by the government for an SEZ (special economic zone): 'This land was given to us by Indiraji; Soniaji cannot take it away!' She was the hope of the poor, the exploited and the downtrodden; her 'garibi hatao' ('remove poverty') slogan electrified them.

Her timing was perfect, her decisions intuitive. It was said of her, 'You may agree with her, you may disagree with her, but you cannot ignore her'. India stood tall and proud under her leadership. The world stood still at the news of her death.

Upon her demise, a son had risen—young, hesitant, but sincere, Rajiv Gandhi was swept to a position of leadership at the age of forty on 31 October 1984. After two months that witnessed the assassination of a Prime Minister, the massacre of Sikhs and the Bhopal gas tragedy, the country seemed to have woken to a new dawn. There was the promise of change and rebirth.

As for me, I was now on my own, with only Niru for support. I did not know it then, but the next five years would see action and achievement, tragedy and despair. I would be tossed around, blown about in the winds, even as I'd learnt to survive in the tumultuous political setting of the nineties.

The Rajiv Gandhi Years

The Nazareth clan: My family in Bangalore; 1976

On the campaign trail with Indira Gandhi for the Chikmagalur by-election; 1978

With Bella Abzug in New York; 1979

With President Fidel Castro at Havana, Cuba; 1983

At the Mahila Congress Convention with Indira Gandhi at Bangalore; October 1984

The founding meeting of the World Women Parliamentarians for Peace at Stockholm, Sweden; 12 April 1985

*At the Indira Gandhi Canal, Rajasthan, with HM Queen Beatrix and
HRH Prince Claus of the Netherlands; 1986*

*At Rashtrapati Bhavan with Raisa Gorbacheva and
First Lady of India Janaki Venkataraman; 1986*

In Moscow, USSR, as a member of Prime Minister Rajiv Gandhi's delegation; 1987

At Rashtrapati Bhavan with President of India R. Venkataraman and President of France François Mitterrand; 1989

As Sports Minister, with Amitabh Bachchan and Madhavrao Scindia, inaugurating a cricket match between Parliamentarians and film-stars

Welcoming Prime Minister Rajiv Gandhi at the closing ceremony of the Nehru centenary year at the Jawaharlal Nehru Stadium; 14 November 1989

Being sworn in as Minister for the second time by President R. Venkataraman; June 1991

Visiting the Ajmer Dargah with President of Bangladesh Khaleda Zia; 1992

In Goa with President and Mrs Mario Soares of Portugal; 1992

Receiving Princess Diana at Tamanna School, New Delhi; February 1992

Chapter 17

IN THE GOVERNMENT:
WORKING WITH RAJIV GANDHI

It was 31 December 1984—exactly two months after the assassination of Indira Gandhi. That morning, after the massive victory in the General Elections, Rajiv Gandhi had been unanimously elected as the Leader at the CPP meeting in Central Hall. The swearing-in was scheduled for the evening. There was excitement in the air. Everyone was heading towards Rashtrapati Bhavan.

I tried getting a pass from all the sources I could tap, but in vain. No one knew where one could get a pass. When I dropped in for lunch at Central Hall, I saw Pranab Mukherjee having a meal alone. I joined him, then requested him to put me on his list of invitees, saying, 'Ministers to be sworn in will be allotted a quota of guests.'

He smiled wryly, then said, 'You put me on the list of Ministers and I will put you on my list of guests.' He continued with his lunch.

'Nice way of saying "no", Dada,' I replied, and headed home.

Meanwhile, the Mahila Congress women—unwilling to believe me when I said that I was scurrying for a pass myself—started chasing me for invitations. The phone kept ringing every minute. Disgusted, I decided to ignore them and went to sleep, planning to leave for the airport by 5 p.m. to catch the evening flight to Bombay and join my family in Mangalore for the New Year.

As has now been established, the most important events in my life happen while I sleep! The phone rang once, twice, thrice. Expecting to hear a woman's voice seeking a pass, I hesitated, but then picked up the receiver.

'Margaret?' It was a man's voice.

'Yes, who is it?' I asked.

'Rajiv *bol raha hoon*.' ('It's Rajiv.')

I thought I was dreaming. 'Who?'

'Oh, come on, it is Rajiv! What are you doing?'

I was stunned. 'To tell you the truth, I was fast asleep,' I replied, sheepishly.

'Sleeping? You have done so much to mobilize women. Get ready and come to Rashtrapati Bhavan!'

'I have no pass. I gave up after trying all morning and...'

Before I could finish, he said, 'Get there! You do not need a pass!' It was an order, and the phone went dead.

I did not know what to do. I had no driver, no pass. I rang my brother, Alan, told him to accompany me, adding, 'I do not know why, but the Prime Minister has asked me to get to Rashtrapati Bhavan. Do not mention it to anyone till we know what this is all about!' I requested.

I then phoned Niru and conveyed the same message. I told him to watch the swearing-in ceremony.

Alan and I arrived at Rashtrapati Bhavan reception, only to be refused entry without passes. I told the Protocol Officer on duty that I had been invited. He counter-checked and let me enter, but refused entry to Alan. I nervously walked in, diving into the first vacant seat I found towards the back of the Ashoka Hall, which was fast filling up.

Arun Nehru, strutting down the aisle like the king of all he surveyed, suddenly spotted me. 'What are you doing here? Your name is up there! Find your chair,' he ordered, pointing to the front row. Only then did I realize that I was actually being sworn in.

After the ceremony and the photo session, I moved towards Rajivji to thank him for the honour he had bestowed on me. He smiled and said, 'Get lost for now!' and moved to join the President and other VIP guests for tea. I was shocked, hurt and humiliated. What had I done wrong? Why this snub in my moment of glory? I slipped to the other room, had tea with a few guests and went home, where an official car was waiting for me. The only ones to greet me were my domestic staff who had gathered with a garland of small currency notes and a box of laddoos.

I rushed to the airport to catch my flight to Bombay. My brother, Don, and his wife, Meena, received me. They drove me straight to a New Year's Eve bash hosted by the city's Mangalorean community, where I received my first public recognition as a Minister in the Government of India. At the Mangalore airport, there was a big reception, and countless well-wishers thronged my sister Joan's home to receive me. We arrived in Bangalore the next day to a great, big welcome—a procession of countless cars followed me from the airport to the church (where I received blessings), and then, to 'Alandon', the family home, to be greeted with tears of joy by my mother, sister Corinne, family and friends. The only person missing was Dad; how happy and proud he would have been! The unexpected had happened to me and a new chapter of my political life had opened.

Back in Delhi, I went to meet the Prime Minister. The moment he saw me, he apologized, 'I am sorry about the other day! Vice President R. Venkataraman had phoned me, asking me to make you the Deputy Chairperson of the Rajya Sabha; he believed you were best suited for the post. But I wanted you to manage the House as Parliamentary Affairs Minister. I was afraid he would raise the issue if he saw you.'

'I am prepared to go to the chair. My mother-in-law was Deputy Chairperson for many years,' I said.

'This is the problem with you! You talk too much. I have given you a job, now do it.'

So I did.

It was time for me to 'take charge' of my ministry. All I had was a small office, next to the lift, on the first floor of Parliament House. There were no women's toilets on the floor. So I asked for an old, unused storeroom next to the office to be converted into one. When I entered my room, I found, to my utter surprise, Kalpnath Rai, the outgoing Parliamentary Affairs Minister (who had been dropped), waiting to receive me with a big bouquet of flowers. He was emotional, saying he was happy that someone he 'really loved and admired' had taken his place. Najma Heptulla was keen to become Deputy Chairperson, and came to me for help. I strongly recommended her and helped her get elected unanimously.

H.K.L. Bhagat, the Delhi MP and unquestioned boss of the Delhi Congress, was my Cabinet Minister. A short man of few words, he had his own quiet way of manipulating men and matters. He always wore dark glasses to hide an eye he had lost during Partition; one could never tell where he was looking!

I now found myself caught between Bhagat and V.P. Singh, the Leader of the House. I was not comfortable with V.P. Singh. In fact, from the very outset, I suspected him. At the most crucial times, he would go 'gayab'—just disappear—and would be found neither at home nor in the office; no one could tell where he was! When I mentioned this to the Prime Minister, he brushed aside my concerns, viewing Singh's convenient absences as a mere coincidence.

The world of Ministers is difficult to navigate, especially for a beginner. New to the game, desperate for support and advice, and intimidated by the turmoil in the House, I'd occasionally phone L.K. Advani for help, which he most often gave. I built a rapport with opposition benches and leaders, who were generally cooperative. A few, though, were always combative.

When Renuka Chowdhury, the attractive, bold and aggressive MP from the Telugu Desam Party (TDP), was sworn in, I welcomed her to the House and suggested that we close ranks and work together on women's issues; she very sweetly agreed, but did exactly the opposite!

Worse, I was caught in a battle among Congress members who wished to speak in the House—anyone left out of the list inevitably was at war with me—this despite the fact that V.P. Singh and Bhagat finalized all lists. On one occasion, in sheer desperation, I told an MP from Delhi that I was helpless as Bhagat had cut out his name. That led to a war of words between them, and I became the immediate target of Bhagat's anger. He reduced me to tears in the lobby, pulling me up for my indiscretion and thundering, 'Your job is to convey the decision to the Secretary General and not discuss it with members!'

In the midst of all this, I continued as Convener of the Mahila Congress. The role came to be quite a burden—there were constant demands from the PMO for names of Mahila Congress leaders for bank, government and PSU (public sector undertaking) Boards; to lead or receive women's delegations from a range of countries; or to attend state-level functions.

It wasn't easy, juggling my many responsibilities, at home and in office. But I was determined to prove myself. I attended several international meetings, chaired conferences, led delegations and negotiated bilateral agreements. I became a familiar face on television channels, and appeared on the front covers of a range of magazines, from *Sunday* to *Savvy*, even making it to a list of the twenty best-known women in the world. With the unstinted support of the Prime Minister, I managed to carve out a niche for myself as a champion of women's rights.

Therefore, in 1985, when I asked to go to Nairobi for the UN World Conference on Women, I was disappointed that I wasn't included in the delegation led by Maragatham Chandrasekar, who was a Minister in charge of the ministry.

◆

With Rajiv Gandhi as Prime Minister, the atmosphere in Delhi was charged with excitement and hope. We had a stable government, a young, accessible Prime Minister, a young team of Ministers bubbling with ideas for and a fresh approach to the creation of a new India—an India that focused on youth and women. With the opposition routed, the passage of bills to transform the nation was easy. 'Continuity with Change' was the new slogan. Rajivji toured extensively across the country with Sonia by his side, visiting villages, urban centres and tribal areas.

During his first year in office, he won laurels in the international community. His visit to the UN in October 1985—where he presented his proposals for nuclear disarmament—brought him much attention. He took New York by storm, stunned world leaders with his press conference, hit headlines everywhere he went and became a star. It looked like the golden era of Indian political history was in the making.

On the domestic front, the Prime Minister successfully negotiated accords with those who had long been agitating against the Centre. While these accords did not completely quell simmering sentiments or crush outbursts, they brought temporary respite to regions plagued by violence and offered a great boost to the Prime Minister's image as a statesman. At the outset came the Rajiv–Longowal Accord, which overruled the Shah Commission's suggestion that Chandigarh be given to Haryana, and stated that Chandigarh would be given to Punjab. This was followed by an accord with Subhash Ghisingh of the GNLF (Gorkha National Liberation Front), conceding an autonomous hill council for the Darjeeling hills. There was also the alliance with the National Conference in Jammu and Kashmir; the accord with the dreaded militant outfit, TNV (Tripura National Volunteers);[28] the Mizo Accord with the MNF (Mizo National Front); and the accord with AASU (All Assam Students' Union).[29]

Of these, the one with Pu Laldenga of Mizoram, who had led the underground movement of the MNF for over fifteen years, was the most

---

[28]According to this accord, TNV rebels had to surrender all arms in their possession. In turn, the Government of India would withdraw all prohibitions imposed on TNV, and the Commander-in-Chief of TNV would be made the Chairman of a tribal development council.
[29]The Assam Accord, as it came to be known, was signed to end a six-year-long mass movement demanding the detection and deportation of illegal immigrants, mostly from Bangladesh. Accordingly, all foreigners entering Assam illegally on or after 25 March 1971 would have their names deleted from electoral rolls and deported.

significant. As part of the understanding, Mizoram went to the polls (with the Congress government resigning), and Laldenga became Chief Minister. He took oath on the Constitution of India. It was a historic moment. The Prime Minister's statement on the occasion—'the party has lost but the nation has won'—was hailed by all sections.

Given how affable he was, Rajiv Gandhi managed to nurture close friendships with several state leaders. One of these trailblazers was Ramakrishna Hegde—the three-time Chief Minister of Karnataka between 1983 and 1988. When the Prime Minister visited Bangalore for the first time, party members who had lined the roads to greet him were upset that he was so engrossed in a conversation with Hegde in the front seat of his jeep—which he drove himself—that he forgot to wave to them.

Then there was Jayalalithaa—young, slim, attractive, dressed to perfection, her long hair in a plait. Jayalalithaa entered the Rajya Sabha in 1984, and became not only my close friend, but also Rajiv's, though their association went through a few twists and turns. When Tamil Nadu's Chief Minister, MGR, had a stroke, Jayalalithaa tried to get Rajivji to support her plan to become the Acting Chief Minister. During that period, her communications to the Prime Minister were sent through me in sealed envelopes, which I diligently delivered.

When MGR died in 1987, his wife assumed the Chief Minister's post, but found her government collapsing in less than a month. Jayalalithaa mobilized party cadres and won the 1989 election in alliance with the Congress, to become the Chief Minister. Rajivji, in his trademark style, managed to settle all differences during a dinner meeting in Madras, and Jayalalithaa came to have great respect and affection for him.

Charming as he was, his early years were not without controversy—and this was largely because he was frank with his views. His comments on his mother's demise, and the harsh reactions they generated, were just a prelude to what was to follow. On one occasion, when Renuka Chowdhury kept taunting him, with the government slogan, 'Mera Bharat mahaan' ('My India is great'), an irked Prime Minister shot back, 'Haan, mera Bharat mahaan, tumhara beimaan!' ('Yes, my India is great, and yours, dishonest!') This led to an uproar and the House was disrupted for days. On another occasion, he referred to Calcutta as a 'dying city', which made tempers flare not only in the House and in Calcutta, but also across the rest of the country; insulted Bengalis took to the streets for weeks!

Rajivji meant well but was dragged into controversies. I tried to caution him on a couple of occasions. I told him that his mother listened before revealing her mind, while he spoke before he heard the other side.

He smiled and retorted, 'Look who is talking! The pot calling the kettle black!'

'True,' I said, 'but you are in a position where everything you say is analyzed and often misunderstood.'

He never changed. We had quite a job on our hands, doing damage-control in the House.

But, with all that, the people adored him, especially the women! As Prime Minister, he used to regularly invite MPs with their spouses for dinner; on one occasion, P.A. Sangma, the MoS for Commerce, arrived halfway through dinner. Apologizing to the host, he said jokingly, 'What can I do? You are so loved that my three wives were quarrelling over who should go with me. Unable to settle the issue, I finally left them all behind!'

28 December 1985 saw a big celebration in Bombay to mark the centenary of the Indian National Congress. The man behind the show was the great organizer and fundraiser of the party, Murli Deora, also the Chief of the Mumbai Pradesh Congress. Everyone who was anyone was there. Party cadres from all over the country rubbed shoulders, long lost colleagues were locked in bear hugs, and Ministers and AICC bosses trooped in with special passes. I had gone with the family because Niru felt that the children should be reminded of their family's association with the party and the freedom struggle in Mumbai.

It was a memorable event, the highlight of which was the address of the Congress President, who was at his eloquent best, with a remarkable speech, beautifully delivered. One passage that I still recall is:

> Millions of ordinary Congress workers throughout the country are full of enthusiasm for the Congress policies and programmes. But they are handicapped, for on their backs ride the brokers of power and influence, who dispense patronage to convert a mass movement into a feudal oligarchy. They are self-perpetuating cliques, who thrive by invoking the slogans of caste and religion and by enmeshing the living body of the Congress in their net of avarice.[30]

---

[30]See J.C. Johari, *Indian National Congress since Independence* (New Delhi: Lotus Press, 2006).

Truer words have never been said, but could we hope for change? I was also apprehensive about the reaction that the term 'power brokers' would generate; would those who had entrenched themselves around Indiraji, and now Rajivji, take the jibe lying down?

Subsequent events proved that these power brokers would get together and conspire to defame him.

◆

Rajiv Gandhi's dreams were ambitious, but a few early experiments were ahead of their time. In an attempt to modernize government functioning and make the bureaucracy respond to the needs of common citizens, brainstorming sessions over weekends were introduced to bring together select groups of senior bureaucrats, young Ministers, bankers, NGOs, corporate honchos and intellectuals, to discuss public policy issues. It was hailed as the right step at the right time. But soon there were problems, with charges and counter-charges of conflicting interests. This ended the novel experiment.

Then there was the introduction of a five-day week with longer hours in Central government departments. The logic behind this move was that this would give government employees more time with their families; government servants, who seldom worked full-time, would now be forced to clock in longer hours on work days; and the money saved on electricity, petrol and tea in offices would more than compensate for the lost day of work. Whether government servants actually worked extra hours during the five-day work week, or spent time with their families on weekends, remains a subject of debate. What we do know is that many state governments have followed suit.

Next came the big government initiative to encourage the use of computers. Incentives were offered to stenographers and typists to shift to computers, with training offered at government cost. But the move failed. So government offices ended up with the old secretarial staff at typewriters and new recruits at computers. To complicate matters, the unions would not allow the old cadre of typists, who were unwilling to adopt new technology, to be eased out. The opposition, in true style, mocked the venture and joked about 'the fascination of a young man for a new toy'.

The same problem confronted us when the PMO gave instructions to get rid of old, brown, ugly files tied in string and introduce neat, modern files with Velcro bands. Given the general lack of enthusiasm from those lower down, all that followed was this—order sheets were presented in Velcro files to the PMO, and then sent back to the department in the old, brown, ugly files.

Notwithstanding these early hiccups, a few innovative measures met with definite success—among these, the review and removal of many outdated British laws from statute books. The most striking of these were the amendments to the prison manual—which, until then, declared the king's birthday a holiday; prescribed the old British uniform of khaki short-pants and white shirts for prison staff; and imposed a ban on Gandhi caps and khadi clothes for prisoners.

Rajivji's commitment to decentralized decision-making and faith in the panchayati model were genuine. While most opposition parties were quick to dismiss panchayati raj as a failed experiment, Rajivji was determined to nurture it with his slogan, 'Power to the People'. Consultations were held with state governments, district level officers, NGOs, anganwadi workers and women's organizations, with the Prime Minister listening to each view.

I was closely involved with the campaign since 33 per cent reservation for women in panchayats was part of the proposed legislation. At a special AICC session held at Talkatora Indoor Stadium in Delhi in May 1985, I was asked to move the resolution for reservation in elected bodies, as well as within the party organization. G.K. Moopanar, who was General Secretary of the AICC, told me that he did not believe in the proposal and would walk out (which he did) rather than vote for it. Nobody else uttered a word against the resolution, and in a bid to please Rajiv Gandhi, voted in favour with both hands raised!

However, the bill—known as the 64th Constitution Amendment Bill—did not have a smooth passage. When it was introduced in Parliament, it got the two-thirds majority vote it needed in the Lok Sabha, but was defeated by two votes in the Rajya Sabha in 1989. General Elections came soon after. While panchayati raj became part of the Congress' manifesto and campaign, we could not take the idea to fruition since we were defeated in the elections. The bills were shelved, and Rajivji's dream of 'power to the people' was shattered. Nonetheless, the model proposed by him was accepted in later years and has come to stay.

Besides pushing for Constitutional status for panchayati raj and seeking reservation for women, Rajivji was instrumental in lowering the voting age to eighteen years despite stiff opposition from political parties, including his own. His rejoinder to each of their arguments was, 'The youth must have a say in shaping their future and choosing their representatives.'

The new government was also committed to overhauling the educational system. A new education policy was drafted which aimed to, among other things, help school dropouts re-enter the system; provide special residential schools (Navodaya Schools) in rural areas to help bright students catch up with their urban counterparts; offer the option of an Open University to those who wished to pursue academics while working, or for those who found themselves without a seat in a local college; set up mobile schools for migrant children; and encourage school medical cards, compulsory sports activities, mid-day meals and crèches (which would be attached to primary and secondary schools to help girls study, secure in the knowledge that their siblings were being cared for).

After consultations all over the country, piloted by the Human Resource Development (HRD) Minister, P.V. Narasimha Rao, and his proactive Education Secretary, Anil Bordia, the Prime Minister called a meeting at his house to finalize the draft. P.V. Narasimha Rao, Anil Bordia, Krishna Sahi (the MoS for Education), Gopi Arora, Sarla Grewal (from the PMO) and I were present. Discussions started at 10 a.m., and continued over a working lunch, tea and dinner. We went through it page after page, looking at every word, comma and full stop, with all changes copied to the computer file by P.V. Narasimha Rao himself. I repeatedly objected to the male-oriented vocabulary in the draft—such as, 'posts will be manned by women'—and finally commented, 'Who the hell drafted this? He certainly has a patriarchal mind-set!' A mischievous smile played on Rajivji's face as he looked at his Minister, who with his characteristic pout retorted, 'Why don't you do the drafting yourself since you are so good with the new UN vocabulary for women's empowerment?' It was a slap on my face, but each of my suggestions was carried through. It was finally 3 a.m., the next morning, when we broke up. This was the way the Prime Minister worked when he wanted a job done. Soon the NEP (New Education Policy) was adopted with every effort made for its proper implementation.

Soon after I came to the Women and Child Development Ministry, I was asked to host the first meeting of the SAARC (South Asian Association for Regional Cooperation) Technical Committee on Women, of which I became Chairperson by virtue of the fact that India was the Chairman of SAARC. The Prime Minister wanted the meeting to be organized in a location that wasn't conventional—so we chose Shillong in the North-east. It was quite a job getting things going, but finally arrangements fell in place—the SAARC Ministers would assemble in Calcutta for dinner and a cultural programme, they'd fly the next morning to Shillong, and the Prime Minister would inaugurate the event.

We reached Shillong to a warm welcome. The next afternoon, we were at the airport at Umroi to receive the Prime Minister. The helicopter that was bringing him from Guwahati was sighted; the assembled crowd cheered. But before the helicopter could descend, the clouds closed in. After several attempts, it returned to Guwahati. I was in despair. What would we do? Then came a message: 'Keep the meeting going. The Prime Minister will come by road'. True to his word, in an hour-and-a-half, accompanied by A.K. Antony and a few other dignitaries, the Prime Minister was at the venue and on the dais of the Legislative Assembly Hall. I could not believe it; neither could the audience, which kept cheering and clapping! My welcome speech introducing the theme of the conference, too, was a hit. One statement of mine was especially remembered and quoted ever after:

If a man does not marry even at thirty, we call him an eligible bachelor. But when a woman does not marry by then, she is called an old maid. In middle age, a man is said to be in the prime of life, whereas at the same age a woman is 'no spring chicken'. Grey hair gives a man 'a distinguished look' but makes a woman 'an old hag'.

Sheila Dikshit, the Congress MP from Kannauj in Uttar Pradesh, had met me at my residence one day and asked to be involved with any worthwhile work in the party or on a government committee. So, when we finalized the delegation for Shillong, I included her name, and she attended the event. When Rajivji was leaving, she asked to return with him as she had to attend to some urgent personal work. She flew with him, and the next thing we heard was that she had been appointed MoS in the PMO.

Shortly after my speech at Shillong, the Prime Minister said to me, 'You know, Margaret, you have a terrible reputation.'

'What have I done?' I asked, amazed.

'Most men are afraid of you. They think you are anti-male!'

'That is a good reputation to have in politics,' I answered, adding, 'though, I must say, I am very fond of some men.'

His ears went red and he never repeated that complaint again.

The next conference, which we hosted jointly with UNICEF (United Nations Children's Emergency Fund), was on the 'status of the girl child in South Asia'. Over 500 delegates—Ministers, legislators, officials, NGOs, journalists from SAARC, besides UN representatives—participated. I was elected Chairperson. The document we produced went to the meeting of the heads of government of SAARC countries and resulted in the next year, and the decade that followed, being dedicated to the girl child.

◆

It was January 1986. My family and I were at the airport for a formal reception of Pope John Paul II. Suddenly, I was summoned by the Prime Minister.

He took me aside and asked, 'When does your term finish?'

'In April,' I replied.

'What are you doing about it?' was the next question.

'What can I do? You have to decide,' I smiled.

'Don't take this lightly. I'm not joking! You had better spend more time in the state. You have many "friends" there who will try to defeat you. Get serious and start working.'

'Yes,' I replied, though I was puzzled by the sudden urgency in his tone.

Later, I discovered that at a dinner hosted by the Prime Minister at his residence the previous night, Monica Das, the Rajya Sabha member from Karnataka, pleaded with him for her re-nomination.

Confused, he asked her what prevented her from getting re-nominated.

To this, her response, with tears in her eyes, was, 'Margaret Alva!'

'How can I ignore my Minister?' he asked.

Das, refusing to let go, said, 'Margaret can come from Goa or Maharashtra! You have to help me.' Then she clung to his arm and those around had a hard time getting him out of her grip.

That explained the alert at the airport!

In February that year, my name was announced as nominee for our only seat. The Prime Minister asked me to meet Ramakrishna Hegde, saying, 'He will help.' Luckily, I bumped into Hegdeji at a wedding in Bangalore, where he told me, 'Rajivji has spoken to me. Don't worry. File your nomination and leave it to me.'

Gundu Rao and company had made elaborate plans to defeat me. They were to field an independent candidate to divert votes. In the meantime, the Chief Minister announced that his Janata Party would be contesting all four seats. I thus became the fifth candidate for the four seats to be filled.

I was stunned but thrilled. My opponents sat back to watch the fun. I did not know how things would proceed. There was tension all around, even as each of the nominations was cleared.

Soon after, there was a phone call from the Prime Minister. 'How are things going? Do you need any help? Should I send anyone from here? Are you in touch with the Chief Minister?' He seemed really concerned, and was reaching out despite the fact that he was leaving for Sweden the following day to attend the funeral of Olof Palme, the assassinated Swedish Prime Minister.

I assured him that I would get through, since I seemed to have a fair amount of support from all leaders—though a few Congressmen were hoping for the worst.

To my delight, an hour before withdrawals closed, one of the four Janata Party candidates withdrew. The election consequently was unanimous. Ramakrishna Hegde had kept his word. I was back in the Rajya Sabha for my third term without spending a paisa. There was jubilation all around. I went home and called the Prime Minister.

'I have got through!' I said, excitedly.

'Already? How did you manage that?' he asked.

'A trade secret!' I laughed.

We both knew the truth.

'The first visit I paid on the morning after the election, with the family, was to Hegdeji, to thank him. He hosted us to a sumptuous breakfast and shared wonderful stories about his early days in Karwar as part of Baba's election campaign team. It is a memory I hold close.

◆

I toured extensively during my years in the ministry, often reaching out to women in distant and remote areas. One such trip almost ended in tragedy. After a visit to the tribal villages on the Pakistan border (where we were received with great love and enthusiasm), while we were travelling by road from Jaisalmer to Jodhpur, our state government Ambassador, hurtling at high speed, began to swerve, even as the driver lost control. The brake cable had snapped. At a bend, the car went off the road, rolled a couple of times and landed upside down in the desert sands.

Sudha Raina, the Chairperson of the State Social Welfare Board, S.C. Sharma, my PA and Nivedith (barely nine), who were with me, were all trapped inside. The glass had smashed, and the doors were jammed. The police escort team managed to get us out even as our belongings lay scattered all around. Shaken, we sat by the roadside, waiting for a relief car, which finally brought us to our destination three hours behind schedule. Ashok Gehlot, in the meantime, undeterred by the mishap, waited anxiously to escort me straight to the stage for the first of the three public functions which had been arranged. Sharma and Nivedith had their minor bruises attended to, while Sudha was taken in an ambulance due to sharp spasms of pain in her back. My body was full of blue patches due to the impact, but I carried on till I arrived home by the late evening flight. Then I collapsed, crying and shivering. The shock and pain kept me in bed for a week. This is the price one pays for public life, I told myself.

◆

Despite all my official work, the family found time for holidays together—by train or road—every summer. I managed to combine official visits with some of these vacations. The children saw the country and learnt a lot while travelling. In fact, we manage to accommodate an annual holiday together even today.

To mark Niret's twenty-first birthday, we decided to fly to Ladakh in the third week of August 1986. But fate had other plans. Shortly before we were to leave, I had a few visitors. Suddenly, there were voices outside screaming, '*Roko, roko!*' ('Stop, stop!') The security men promptly shut my office doors, assuming there had been an attack. A few waiting visitors, in the meantime, jumped up and rushed outside. There they saw that my official car—which had been reversed by the driver—had run straight into Nivedith (Babu), who had dashed out with money to buy kites. When I came out, I saw Babu bleeding—his mouth smashed, his chest and right arm skinned, carrying tyre marks. We rushed him in the same car to AIIMS.

Babu was just six. He was still conscious when Niru began shouting at the driver for his carelessness. The boy intervened to say, 'It is not his fault. I ran out. He did not see me.' The doctors were surprised that he was cogent and also that his ribs had not been broken. 'You have done something good, madam. The child would have been dead on the spot if even a single broken rib had pierced his lungs or heart,' they said.

Babu was placed bare-bodied under a tent. For the next ten days, we watched over him, even as the paediatrician, Dr (Mrs) Rohatgi, gently removed the stones embedded in his muscles.

The following days were among the most challenging ones. Amendments to the women's bills had to be moved and piloted. I found myself living between the hospital and Parliament. Every night, I'd sit in the hospital bathroom, preparing for debates and answers in the House. However, all this could be endured, as long as my family was safe. I thanked God for having saved our child.

That was also the week Chittaranjan was engaged to Padma—a charming Hindu Konkani journalist. They were married a few months later and have two children.

Chapter 18

THE WORLD, AN OYSTER:
ON AN INTERNATIONAL PLATFORM

India was the first country to recognize the anti-apartheid movement of South Africa as the official freedom movement of the country. The Congress worked closely with the African National Congress (ANC). I was deputed by the Prime Minister to liaise with their office in Delhi for the supply of the material required for their freedom fighters. The lists were to be cleared by the Prime Minister and items supplied by the AICC.

Madam Msima—the podgy, jolly lady we called 'Mama' (whose husband was an underground fighter)—and her children had been stationed in Delhi for over two decades and became part of our family. She came to me with all her problems. Years later, in recognition of my help and support to their freedom movement, South African President Thabo Mbeki, on a visit to India, honoured me at a public function.

One of the first initiatives launched by the Prime Minister was the summit of six nations—Greece, Mexico, Sweden, Tanzania, Argentina and India—to mobilize support for a move calling on the superpowers to reduce weapons and eliminate nuclear armaments. I was nominated Minister-in-waiting to the Mexican President. At this historic meeting in January 1985, a plan of action for nuclear disarmament—called the Delhi Declaration—was announced. The Prime Minister wanted the mobilization of further support for this initiative through women Parliamentarians and women's organizations. At the suggestion of Swedish Prime Minister Olof Palme, a meeting of prominent women Parliamentarians from important countries was called in Sweden in 1985 to discuss the matter. I was nominated as India's representative.

I was new to the topic of disarmament, though I had attended several conferences on the subject. The Ministry of External Affairs produced a background paper for me, and also arranged a halt in Vienna on my way to Sweden, so I could be briefed by the Ambassador of India, Muchkund Dubey, for the United Nations Conference on Disarmament.

The Swedish conference was inaugurated by Olof Palme, with a message from Rajiv Gandhi. The two-day brainstorming session saw women Parliamentarians from across the globe making a commitment to peace and disarmament. A plan for the mobilization of support was worked out and the World Women Parliamentarians for Peace (WWPP) was launched. On the team were Maj Britt Theorin (Sweden), Silvia Hernández Enriguez (Mexico), Patricia Giles (Australia), Valentina Tereshkova (USSR), Gertrude Mongella (Tanzania), Barbara Boxer (USA) and me. Maj. Britt Theorin of Sweden became its first President.

In 1986, I succeeded Theorin as President at a big international conference organized at the Vigyan Bhavan, Delhi, inaugurated by the Prime Minister and presided over by the Speaker, Balram Jakhar. Our women MPs and MLAs stole the show with their numbers and active participation. Foreign delegates were hosted by women's organizations, taken to visit their projects and homes, and briefed on our programmes for women. WWPP hit the headlines.

Margaret Papandreou—tall, stately, full of fire and ideas, and the First Lady of Greece—was the founder of the Women's Union of Greece, an independent feminist organization. She also launched an international coalition of women called 'Women for a Meaningful Summit' to mobilize and represent women's views at the Reagan–Gorbachev Summit, for easing tensions between the two military power blocs. To this end, a preparatory meeting was held in Greece in November 1986. Feminist writer, Devaki Jain, and I were among the invitees.

In Greece, Mrs Papandreou, in her address, said:

> I believe this [session] is historic because of the coming together of women from the women's movement, and women from the peace movement; women from the superpowers, from other nuclear powers, from the countries of the Five Continents' Peace Initiative, from the Third World. [...] We will ally ourselves with others working for the same aims. So we hail the Five Continents' Peace Initiative and applaud their serious efforts to halt the arms race. These are leaders of non-nuclear countries who felt compelled to speak up and put their political power behind this cause.

This was a strong endorsement of the Delhi initiative! As a follow up, it was decided that we'd get an international team of women to participate in the 'women's chain' between the White House and the Russian Embassy during the Reagan–Gorbachev meeting in Washington in the winter of 1987. It was freezing cold in Washington, but this did not stop women representing a range of nations from joining hands in a symbol of unity—singing and dancing, raising slogans for an agreement on disarmament, pushing for a nuclear-free world and asking for peace. At the end of it, we presented an appeal signed by hundreds of women, which was received at the gates of the White House and the USSR Embassy. It was a soul-stirring experience.

◆

In 1986, Queen Beatrix of the Netherlands, accompanied by Prince Claus, paid an official visit to India. I was appointed Minister-in-waiting. I was nervous; I had never been in close proximity to a reigning monarch before. But when I met them, they were both so warm, friendly and informal that my assignment became a pleasure trip. They had come with a large delegation of political leaders, artists, businessmen and journalists, with whom we travelled to Agra, Varanasi, Jaipur, Jaisalmer, Udaipur, Anand and Bombay. Our schedule was hectic. Besides sightseeing and entertainment, I had a clear brief regarding the topics I had to pursue with our royal visitors—namely, the cleaning of the Ganga; the technical support required to plug seepages and attend to falling slabs along the walls of the Indira Gandhi canal; the need for continued assistance for Anand's Operation Flood Phase II;[31] and support for the construction of the new Mumbai port. This I did, with positive results.

At the final farewell at the airport at Mumbai, the red carpet had been rolled out and the press was in full strength. The royal couple walked up to the plane, wishing and thanking everyone. Queen Beatrix gave me a warm embrace as I told her how much I enjoyed looking after her. Next came Prince Claus, known for his wry sense of humour. He said, 'I am going to wish you goodbye the way I want to!' I sensed what was coming and pleaded, 'Your Highness, the press is here...' But before I could complete my sentence, he clasped my outstretched hand and kissed me on both my cheeks. Luckily, it all happened too fast for the press to click!

---

[31]Launched in 1970, Operation Flood, a dairy development programme of the National Dairy Development Board (NDDB), made India—till then a milk-deficient nation—the largest milk producer in the world. While at Anand, I asked why the symbol of NDDB was a bull, when milk came from the cow. 'No bull–no calf–no calf–no milk', was the Chairman, Dr Kurien's answer.

This trip built a lasting bond between the royal couple and me. We exchanged gifts and greetings, and kept in touch. Soon after the couple's visit, Niru and I received an invitation to visit the Netherlands as guests of Queen Beatrix and Prince Claus—the highlight of which was dinner at the palace. We presumed it would be an official affair and phoned the Ambassador for guidance regarding protocol. The Ambassador was surprised, claiming he had no invitation. Upon enquiry, he was told that it was a private affair.

Niru and I nervously drove to the palace and arrived exactly on time. We were escorted upstairs to a cosy private apartment and received by the royal couple. It was an informal affair. The Prince took Niru to the bar, poured him a drink, and brought me a glass of white wine. Then we sat at a table for four, had our meal, and shared stories—with Queen Beatrix telling us that she often rode her bicycle across town! At 10 p.m., as advised by the Ambassador, we rose to say goodbye, but were kept back, and asked, 'What's the hurry?' The Queen took me around a gallery that held their sons' stone carvings, while Prince Claus promised Niru that he would come to India with his sons on a private trip. We finally left past 11 p.m., with Prince Claus escorting us to our car. It was a storybook evening for us.

Over the course of our conversation I had mentioned visiting fascinating confectionery stores with sweets of myriad shapes and colours—it was impossible to make a choice! The next morning a big box arrived, with a handwritten note from Her Majesty, and a selection of sweets for the kids.

On our way home, we went to Paris by train—it was a beautiful journey through Europe's countryside—and we were hosted by Ambassador Sonu Kochar. She arranged a visit to the Paris Air Show—an unforgettable experience.

Prince Claus is no more—he passed away after a prolonged illness. But every time Queen Beatrix passed through India, I'd get a message from the Embassy, and we'd meet to chat, exchange news and trade views. She has abdicated the throne, but our friendship continues.

◆

In 1987, there was a surprise request from the Government of Sri Lanka, which had been battling the Liberation Tigers of Tamil Eelam (LTTE)—the separatist Tamil group led by V. Prabhakaran. The LTTE claimed that its demands for equal status in the administration had been consistently resisted by the government, while the government was outraged by the violent attacks of the LTTE.

Within India, the LTTE had received open support from the Tamil population, and parties in Tamil Nadu and parts of the South which endorsed the militant group's demands for a Tamil state covering the Tamil-dominated Northern and Eastern areas of the island-nation. LTTE leaders visited Delhi regularly as government guests, and called on MPs and Ministers. It was also widely believed that their cadres had received training and equipment from India.

Therefore, when the Sri Lankan President asked for help to deal with the problem and negotiate a settlement—their reason being that the Sri Lankan army had no access to the LTTE-dominated areas, and they needed India to restore peace—we were taken aback. The Council of Ministers was called for an emergency meeting at Vigyan Bhavan, where the Prime Minister and several senior Ministers were attending a conference. After a briefing on the situation, the request and its implications, there was a brief discussion. Most of the Ministers wanted India to volunteer help, calling this a 'moment of destiny'.

I was apprehensive but too junior to intervene. I listened, rather bewildered, as there was talk of Indian soldiers going to Sri Lanka, and of the Indian Peace Keeping Force (IPKF) venturing into areas dominated by Tamils fighting for their legitimate rights. I saw in the Sri Lankan government's request a sinister ploy to make Indians fight Indian settlers. I finally mustered the courage to express my concerns. I asked, 'Would this not result in Indian soldiers fighting the Tamils on behalf of the Sri Lankan government? What would be the reaction there and in Tamil Nadu?'

P.V. Narasimha Rao said, 'Yes, Indian soldiers fighting the Tamils is a distinct possibility, and we will have to be prepared for the consequences.'

The decision was taken and the IPKF began flying into Sri Lanka. The rest is history.

During that period, very little information came to us on the developments in Northern and Eastern Sri Lanka. In 1987, when Rajiv Gandhi, on an official visit to Sri Lanka, was hit on his head and neck with a gun by a soldier in uniform, a sense of disquiet set in. What were we doing in that country and for whose benefit? The Prime Minister received a hero's welcome when he returned home safely, but a sense of nervousness lingered.

◆

Having graduated, Niret had to choose a career. I was keen that he join the services. But Niru wanted him to venture into the media—TV at that. There was only one government-run channel and no one had visualized what was to come. But Niru, a voracious reader, was clear that things would change. 'TV will open up—there is a whole world before you. You have the makings of a journalist. Do not miss the opportunity,' he advised. He also told him he was an Alva who would never be able to submit to the discipline of the civil services, to the whims and fancies of politicians. And so, Niret decided to be the third generation of journalists in the Alva family. He did a one-year course at the Indian Institute of Mass Communication (IIMC) and joined the PTI as a trainee reporter-cum-TV scriptwriter in 1988. The salary was low, but he got the exposure he needed.

In the summer of 1989, Niret came home quite excited, announcing that he was to go to Sri Lanka to be dropped behind IPKF lines (without a visa or identity), to secretly film their operations there. I tried to stop him, but he said I was not even supposed to know of his mission, and so should not intervene.

He came back (I thanked God for it) with films and stories of horror. The people were angry, abusing us, calling us traitors and agents of Sri Lankan President J.R. Jayewardene. The IPKF was demoralized—they were 'enemies' for the Tamils, who referred to their LTTE cadres as 'our boys' fighting to 'defend us'. The Sinhala population called the IPKF the 'occupation force'. 'Why are you here?' was repeatedly asked of the IPKF.

Jungles were being cleared and roads being built for IPKF vehicles to move, making these areas accessible to Sri Lankan forces as well. The IPKF forces were facing heavy causalities and injuries as land mines went off. They were under attack by an unknown and unseen enemy. They had no clear orders regarding how to deal with the LTTE fighters—protect, kill or disarm? When they'd come within close range of LTTE leaders, whom they could pick up or eliminate, they would be ordered by their commanders to 'lay off'. There was frustration in their ranks.

24 May 1989 was our silver wedding anniversary. We had a big reception at home. Rajivji came alone to spend an hour with the family. During dinner, he began speaking to the kids. Choku proudly spoke of his Sri Lanka adventure. Rajivji forgot everything else, and started questioning him

on his visit. Niret began to sing like a lark. At the end of it, Rajivji said, 'I have not been told anything of this! I want those tapes; get them for me urgently!'—it was almost an order! Choku was in a fix. His bosses insisted that this was secret footage and had to be cleared by the IB before it could be handed over to anyone, while the PMO kept phoning repeatedly for the promised tapes. I finally told the PMO that they would have to deal with the IB directly. It became quite evident to me then that the Prime Minister was not being told the truth about the IPKF operations. Why? I've never understood.

◆

Indo-Soviet relations—and especially the links between the two countries at a people-to-people level—were a high priority for the new government. Consequently, the first country the Prime Minister visited in May 1985 was the Soviet Union, where two long-term economic agreements were signed.

In turn, Mikhail Gorbachev's first visit to a 'third world' state brought him to New Delhi in late 1986. I was made Minister-in-waiting to Raisa Gorbacheva, the President's wife—small-built, simple but smartly dressed; warm, friendly and quite open—who shared with me her country's concerns, while asking countless questions about our development programmes. Based on the probing questions she asked me about our loss-making public sector units and our move away from cooperative farming, I sensed that the Soviet Union was planning to gradually dismantle state-controlled enterprises.

Along the way, Raisa Gorbacheva spoke to me about the trauma of the war in Afghanistan: 'We made a mistake there,' she admitted. 'When our young men started coming home maimed, in wheelchairs or on stretchers, there was public outrage. Everywhere we went, we were asked, "Why? Why are you doing this?" We had no answers. You see, when soldiers die and the body bags come back, they are buried with due ceremony and life goes on. But when they return with their spirits broken and their bodies crippled, their tragedies come to be lived by each of their loved ones every day. It is sad, it is difficult. We had to get out.'

Sharp and intelligent, Raisa Gorbacheva seemed to be the power behind her husband. At Rashtrapati Bhavan, when the couple called on the Indian President, sitting between the First Lady and me, she was more interested in the discussions between the two leaders, and wanted the mics on their table to be turned up; she would cut short local visits to get back to her husband before he departed for official talks or engagements. 'I like to go through his papers and speeches before he leaves, because I do not trust those around him,' she explained.

In July 1987, the Indian Prime Minister, accompanied by Sonia Gandhi, led a high-level delegation—which included P.V. Narasimha Rao, Arjun Singh, P. Shiv Shankar, and a host of bureaucrats—to launch a year-long Festival of India in the USSR. I was surprised and thrilled when my name was announced as the only MoS included.

I flew in from Mexico, where I had gone for a convention of the WWPP, and reached Moscow before the Indian contingent arrived, just in time to participate in the International Convention of Women on Peace and Development organized by the Committee of Soviet Women. President Gorbachev and Raisa Gorbacheva were to be the star participants, with women leaders from the socialist world and friendly countries attending. I had received an invitation but had no card, badge or car. On arrival, I rang Ambassador T.N. Kaul for help, who informed me that I had landed a bit too late. 'This is not India, my dear. Things are handled differently here. But I will try to do my best. Get ready. I will be in your hotel in twenty minutes,' he said.

Before I could get organized, Ambassador Kaul arrived with the news that he had managed to get through to the 'top brass' and that I had to rush to the venue. When we reached, I was amazed to see someone waiting to escort me straight to the stage, to a seat next to Raisa Gorbacheva. I was also slated to speak! This not only revealed the clout that Ambassador Kaul wielded in Moscow, but also highlighted the importance that India was given by the Soviet leadership.

I spoke extempore. As a former President of WWPP, I made an emotional appeal for non-violence, quoting from the Mexico Declaration, and asked women to unite and lead the 'battle for peace'. I received a standing ovation, warm hugs from VIPs on stage, and special mention in the speeches of President Gorbachev and the others who followed.

Soon after, the Indian delegation arrived. I spent the next day with the Indian and Russian officials, looking into arrangements for the inaugural function. The sky was overcast and a downpour in the evening, during the opening ceremony, seemed likely.

I jokingly told my Soviet counterpart, 'At such times, we pray that the rain clouds disappear. But here you do not believe in God. So what do we do?'

He laughed, 'Madam, we do not need God for this. We have technology to make the clouds over Moscow disappear! We will give you clear skies this evening.'

I smiled, unconvinced.

To my astonishment, when we arrived for the programme at 6 p.m., we had blue skies above us. The opening ceremony in the massive stadium was stunning; the Indian performers kept the jam-packed stands enthralled.

Rajivji and Sonia stayed at the Kremlin, and the rest of us were housed in different dachas (cottages) within its walls. Narasimha Rao, Arjun Singh and I were in one such dacha. I was like a 'maid in waiting', looking after them and keeping them updated on the daily itinerary, which included a host of events. Among these was a ceremony for signing the joint protocols. We were lined up in order of seniority, and I found myself at a spot towards the end of the official row. By a strange coincidence, Rajiv Gandhi's and Gorbachev's seats for the ceremony got exchanged, and I found myself right behind India's Prime Minister. Naturally, I appeared in all the press photographs. A senior Minister cattily remarked, 'Some people know exactly where to position themselves!'—little realizing that I had no say in the matter.

Aside from these minor brushes, I got to be part of a series of unforgettable events in the Soviet Union, including a banquet hosted by the Prime Minister and Sonia for Gorbachev and his wife at the Indian Ambassador's residence. The guest list was stunning, with the entire Soviet politburo in attendance, along with the Indian delegation. I found myself sitting next to Eduard Shevardnadze—the Soviet Foreign Minister, who later became the President of Georgia—with whom I discussed an earlier visit to Kiev. During the course of the evening, I saw President Gorbachev mischievously look at a blushing Sonia, and point to the coloured rice decorations on the table, saying, 'Don't you do this with spaghetti as well?' He was politely informed about the significance of coloured rice. Then President Gorbachev pointed to me and said, 'This Minister took Moscow by storm with her brilliant speech at the women's convention!' I could not have been more flattered. When the delegation left, I stayed back for the launch of the youth festival.

I further strengthened my relationship with Raisa Gorbacheva during the opening of the women's exhibition. When the Embassy approached her to inaugurate the event, she said she would gladly do it, adding, 'I hope Margaret will be there with me!' So came an SOS for me to go with a delegation. Raisa Gorbacheva and I spent over two hours going around the venue of a painstakingly put-together exhibition to reflect our women's lives and celebrate their achievements. There were live demonstrations and food counters. Raisa Gorbacheva tasted Indian food and chai, watched the weavers and potters, and greatly enjoyed the cultural programme.

◆

I was Minister-in-waiting to another interesting couple visiting India—the President of France, François Mitterrand, and his wife, Danielle. François Mitterrand was tall and stately, a man of few words, while his wife Danielle was short, informal and very active. After a round of meetings in Delhi, we flew to Calcutta, where Satyajit Ray was to be presented the highest honour of the French government—the Légion d'Honneur. The function was to be held on the steps of the Victoria Museum in the presence of dignitaries from the worlds of art, culture, cinema and politics. The Indian Ambassador to France, Sonu Kochar, and I were ready in the hotel lobby half an hour ahead of time. As the time of departure approached, there was frantic activity within the French delegation—with whispers, phone calls, and security personnel going up and down in lifts. We waited patiently, but the President and his party were not to be seen. Sonu went to her French counterpart, whose face showed serious concern. There were no answers. We imagined the President had taken ill, until our Protocol Officer came up to me and whispered, 'The First Lady is missing. No one knows where she is!'

There was panic. Could she have been kidnapped? Could she have gone out incognito and lost her way? What would we do?

Then the President appeared, smiled and got into the car with me. The motorcade went straight to the function, thirty minutes behind schedule. The ceremony completed, we moved into the foyer for tea. Suddenly, out of nowhere, Danielle Mitterrand emerged, accompanied by Dominique Lapierre, the famous author of *City of Joy*. She was cool and composed, smiling as if nothing had happened.

We later learnt that Danielle Mitterrand had wanted to visit the old corners of Calcutta, where she had spent a few months in the 1970s, backpacking. Officially, it was explained as a visit to Mother Teresa's home. While there was no doubt that she had enjoyed her outing, she had sent the Government of West Bengal into a tizzy for well over two hours! Luckily for all of us, the local press did not get a whiff of the story.

In the meantime, the French Ambassador kept trying to impress on us the need to let France's survey ship venture into the protected waters around the Andaman and Nicobar islands for scientific study. Permission had been refused and the ship was forced to move out. The Ambassador's efforts to reverse that decision fell on deaf ears, despite long and loud arguments over it during our flight out of Calcutta.

We then got to Mumbai, where the Prime Minister and Sonia joined the Mitterrands for the Governor's lunch at Raj Bhavan, after which we drove them to the airport for the ceremonial departure. This was one of the most taxing assignments I handled—always behind schedule and worse, with no idea what was being whispered, as all conversations were in French!

Chapter 19

HUMAN RESOURCES:
WOMEN AND CHILD DEVELOPMENT

The Prime Minister's desire to convert India's growing population from a constraint to a positive development asset led to the creation of the new Ministry of HRD in September 1985—with P.V. Narasimha Rao as Cabinet Minister—merging the Ministries of Education, Culture, Women, Children, Youth Affairs and Sports. For a short time, Health and Family Welfare was also brought under its purview.

I now became MoS Women and Children, Youth Affairs and Sports. Krishna Sahi became MoS Education and Culture, with Saroj Khaparde becoming MoS Health and Family Welfare. Saroj and Krishna would always sit on either side of our boss in Parliament, while I'd be relegated to the seat behind. I once complained that I felt like the neglected step-child. Every time Krishna, Saroj and I would walk into Parliament for Question Hour, there'd be comments like: 'Here comes P.V. and his harem.' There was once an exchange in the Lok Sabha between him and A.B. Vajpayee on the matter. Vajpayee commented, 'P.V. saheb, there should be more equitable distribution. How have you managed to corner all the three young ladies? This is not fair!' Pat came the reply, 'Do not be jealous. Only the foot knows where the shoe pinches!' The House roared with laughter.

My first day of questions in the Lok Sabha, after I moved to this ministry, frightened me. There were five starred questions. At the briefing meeting in the morning, I pleaded with P.V. Narasimha Rao, 'I am very nervous, sir. This is the first time I am facing the Lok Sabha. Please help me out.'

'Certainly not!' came the reply. 'You have been terrorising Ministers with your questions for ten years. The officers used to warn us when your starred questions were listed. Today I will sit back and enjoy the fun when you are harassed!'

But I managed quite well and received all round appreciation for my maiden performance! One of the most encouraging compliments I received was from Nitish Kumar (now the Chief Minister of Bihar), who said, '*Ye mantri to tayyari kar ke aathi hai aur kuch chhupane ki koshish nahi karti.*' ('This Minister comes prepared and does not try to conceal facts!')

The Department of Women and Children had been known as the Department of Women's Welfare; it was part of the Ministry of Welfare, and women's issues were clubbed with those of SC/STs, the differently-abled, senior citizens, etc. It was at my behest that the division was rechristened Department of Women and Child Development (WCD)—thus shifting the focus from welfare to development. In my first interview as MoS WCD, I said: 'At last, women have been recognized as human resource [as part of the HRD Ministry] and capable of development!'

I had a wonderful team of women officers in the Ministry of WCD—with Roma Mazumdar as the Secretary of the ministry. Roma was a low-key, committed bureaucrat, who believed in doing what was expected of an honest officer; she'd offer her views and advice, even critique ideas when the occasion called for it, but once a decision was taken, she'd implement it to the best of her ability. Not surprisingly, working with her was always a pleasure, and she became my pillar of strength and stability. When the Cabinet Secretary, B.G. Deshmukh, was to retire in March 1989, Roma, the senior-most officer, was expected to succeed him. But to everyone's surprise and Roma's anger, she was overlooked and T.N. Seshan became Cabinet Secretary. Roma decided to resign. I held her back, went to the Prime Minister and told him that the decision had upset everyone, especially women, who had not expected this from his government. The Prime Minister said that he had his reasons, but promised to do something for Roma. True to his word, he offered Roma the post of Ambassador to the Netherlands. I forced her to accept it. Roma left and, sadly for me, took my excellent cook with her as well!

Together, my team and I worked on many new projects for women. In the years that followed, as part of the WCD Ministry, we mobilized women at the grassroots and in NGOs, and won their support for the government's initiative of enforcing 33 per cent reservation for women in the panchayati raj system. We also created strong, meaningful linkages with women in the SAARC countries, and focussed on women in the unorganized sector. The government set up two important committees to study the condition of women—the first considered women in the unorganized sector (with Ela Bhatt of the Self Employed Women's Association [SEWA] as Chairperson) and the second studied women in detention (with Justice Krishna Iyer as Chairman). Both committees produced very good reports with path-breaking recommendations, many of which have been implemented over the years.

Special cells were created in all relevant ministries to look into rules and programmes that were in opposition to women's interests. I was made an ex-officio member of all of them, with instructions to report to the PMO directly.

The Indecent Representation of Women (Prohibition) Act was piloted.[32] The department also drafted amendments to laws such as the Dowry Prohibition Act, marriage laws and SITA (Suppression of Immoral Traffic Act). There had been longstanding demands for changes in the law for immoral trafficking. I still recall the debate on SITA in the House. As I stood up to move the amendment bill, several male members started walking out, saying, 'Today is your day. Let the women members speak.'

I was shocked and annoyed. 'Sit down and listen to us if you do not wish to speak,' I said. 'But let me say, there would be no need for this act if it were not for men.' The gentlemen of the House were stunned. Many of them apologized and actually participated in the debate.

Even as we analyzed SITA threadbare, there were demands to bring boys and men under the purview of this law. Women's organizations, in the meantime, asked for the legalization of prostitution, which they claimed was the only solution if one hoped to prevent women's exploitation by pimps and law-enforcing authorities. Though this was not accepted, many amendments were made and the name of the law changed to ITPA (Immoral Traffic [Prevention] Act). Whereas SITA only acknowledged the trafficking of women, ITPA replaced all references to 'women' and 'girls' with 'persons'; consequently, trafficking in *human beings*, as against only women, was now prohibited.

I had served as a member of the Joint Select Committee for amendments to the Dowry Prohibition Act. That the 1961 Act was ineffective was clear from official figures of cases registered and those that had secured convictions. Apart from the fact that dowry deaths mostly happened behind

---

[32]There was a fallout to this. I declined to attend an award function as Chief Guest for the film *Ram Teri Ganga Maili* as the actress' appearance in a wet, white see-through saree was quite indecent and caused a furore.

the closed doors of the in-laws' house, since the giver of dowry and the taker were equated in the eyes of the old law, it became doubly hard for the bride's family to file an FIR. There was an urgent need for change. The most important amendment we pushed through was the 'presumption of dowry murder' if the bride died within seven years of marriage in the husband's or in-laws' home under suspicious circumstances. The crime was made a non-bailable offence. We also extended the definition of dowry beyond marriage negotiation demands, and viewed it as more than a one-time offence. The results of these amendments have been astounding. The crimes registered against dowry offenders have multiplied, the conviction rate has shown a dramatic increase and whole families have been jailed for the heinous crime. No doubt there has been some misuse of the provisions in the amended law, but by and large, it has served as a deterrent and also as a means of securing justice for dowry victims.

Even as we made positive legislative changes, we were confronted with the Shah Bano case. A divorced Muslim woman, Shah Bano, was granted maintenance from her husband by the Supreme Court under Section 125 of the Code of Criminal Procedure (CrPC).[33] The conservative sections of the Muslim community saw this as an attack on their religion and their right to their own religious personal law. They rallied with the Muslim Personal Law Board, marched down Rajpath with black bands and demanded Parliamentary intervention to overturn the judgement. Even senior leaders like Najma Heptulla and Z.R. Ansari joined the campaign. The Prime Minister was determined to resist these pressures and contain communal elements.

On 23 August 1985, Arif Mohammad Khan, a young Minister, spoke in Parliament, defending the judgement and pointing out that Section 125

---

[33]Section 125 of the Code of Criminal Procedure orders for the maintenance of wives, children and parents. If any person having sufficient means neglects or refuses to maintain:

(a) his wife, unable to maintain herself, or

(b) his legitimate or illegitimate minor child, whether married or not, unable to maintain itself, or

(c) his legitimate or illegitimate child (not being a married daughter) who has attained majority, where such child is, by reason of any physical or mental abnormality or injury, unable to maintain itself, or

(d) his father and mother, unable to maintain himself or herself,

a Magistrate of the first class may, upon proof of such neglect or refusal, order such person to make a monthly allowance for the maintenance of his wife or such child, father or mother [...]

of the CrPC applied to all people in India and offered financial support to those needing help after divorce; he asserted that the law had nothing to do with religion. His speech was welcomed by most sections of the House, except for a few uncompromising Muslim MPs. Khan claimed that he had made his speech with the Prime Minister's clearance.

Now events snowballed. There were shrill demands for an act of Parliament to overturn the judgement, and threats that a failure to do so would see the Congress facing decimation in the polls ahead. Rajivji found himself torn between his commitment to secular politics and the need for minority mobilization. Many meetings and discussions were held, many compromise formulae drafted, but nothing seemed to work.

As Minister for Women, I pleaded with the Prime Minister to stand firm. But I began to sense a note of disquiet in his responses. I persisted. 'Your grandfather had the courage to stand up to Hindu right-wing groups and bring in the Hindu Code Bill despite their opposition. Today everyone has accepted it. Please do not tarnish your image,' I begged.

Rajivji was upset. 'Yes, my grandfather was a Hindu dealing with Hindu law. Here I am a Hindu dealing with Muslim law. Do you see the difference?' Then he added, 'Anyway, how many of your women are supporting us?'

I suggested that he have a meeting with women representatives—NGOs, activists, lawyers, journalists, etc.—to mobilize support.

A few days later, I was called to a meeting at the Prime Minister's house. There were approximately thirty women around the table. Rajendra Kumari Bajpai and I were the only Ministers. Most opposed the government's move to nullify the Supreme Court judgement.

The Prime Minister and a couple of his officers tried to present the arguments of the Muslim clergy.

I intervened and opposed the clergy's arguments. Light-heartedly, I asked, 'Why this proposed amendment only for Muslim women? What about Christian women? We are also minorities. Who will provide for us?'

'Get divorced and come to me. I will tell you where to go!' the Prime Minister shot back rather curtly.

When the meeting adjourned, Rajivji turned to me, red in the face, and said, 'A fine Minister I have—contradicting me in an open meeting. You were called in to help. If you could not support me, the least you could have done was shut up!'

I came out stunned. I was under the impression that we were there to garner support for the opposition of any legislation denying divorced Muslim women the right to maintenance.

That's when I realized that things had begun to change…

I met the Prime Minister again a couple of days later to plead against this legislation. 'Do not take away the rights of Muslim women. You know their condition,' I requested.

The Prime Minister replied, 'Do you know that educated Muslim women like Najma Heptulla and Mohsina Kidwai are pleading for this law? Get me 50,000 Muslim women to oppose this move at Rajpath, like you did at Bangalore, and I will concede your demand.'

'Where will I get these women from? Muslim women are afraid of their clergy; many have no voice,' I replied.

'Okay, get me a few hundred of them at least,' he said.

'I will try,' I responded, but knew it was a challenge I would never win.

As a last resort, I went to Sonia and pleaded with her to stop the move. 'It will destroy his image. The silent majority is with him. Please do something!' She agreed with me, but said, 'I do not interfere with his official work.' There the matter ended.

The bill came to Parliament in 1986, piloted by the Prime Minister himself, and the Muslim Women (Protection of Rights on Divorce) Bill was passed. Arif Mohammad Khan resigned; others, who had placed their faith in a forward-looking, secular leader, were devastated. Rumblings within the party began.

I came home shattered after a heated argument with Najma. 'I thought you were a secular leader who would defend the rights of your women. Instead, you join those fundamentalist clerics? Wait till they insist that you wear a burka in the chair!' I told her, beside myself with rage.

But more than angry, I was distraught. 'Now the slide will begin,' I told myself. I was proven right.

◆

In May 1987, I received an invitation from the Chairman of the Kennedy School of Government—the former Ambassador to India, John Kenneth Galbraith—to deliver the annual Rama S. Mehta lecture at Redcliffe College, Harvard University. Nervous, I kept putting off a decision, until Galbraith lost patience and called Rajivji for help.

I was asked what my problem was.

'To tell you the truth, I am scared. What will I say to an audience of intellectuals at Harvard? *Mere bas ka nahi hai,*' ('It's more than I can handle') I told him truthfully.

'Don't be stupid,' Rajivji replied. 'They know so little about India. Whatever you say, will go! So please respond to Galbraith immediately and give him a date!'

And that is what I did.

My department helped with facts and figures on women's development issues and prepared a draft. I worked on this for days before flying to Cambridge. My brother, Alan, Consul General in Chicago, was there with me. After attending a lunch hosted by Galbraith at his home, I delivered my lecture in the evening at Redcliffe and answered questions with a kind of confidence that surprised me! At the end of the two-hour session, Galbraith, a towering six-foot-plus man, with a long, hooked nose and a warm smile, threw his arms around me and gave me a real tight hug, saying, 'You were brilliant! That was one of the best speeches I have heard on the challenges confronting Indian women.' Needless to say, I was thrilled.

◆

As Minister for Women, I was invited by the UN women's division to chair three important expert groups. The first, in New York, assessed the impact of the UN Decade for Women, and the second, in Vienna, analyzed violence against women. Both the groups drew outstanding women from different continents. Later, I was invited to chair the UNESCO (United Nations Educational, Scientific and Cultural Organization)-sponsored conference on 'Women and the Culture of Peace' in Vietnam, which declared Hanoi the 'City of Peace'. These were just three of the many UN-sponsored meetings I was involved with.

◆

In September 1987, the sati of Roop Kanwar in Sikar, Rajasthan, caused outrage not only amongst women activists, but also among all sections of people across the country. There was loud criticism over the lack of action by the Rajasthan government, and heated comments in Parliament, holding the state squarely responsible.

Several of our leaders at the Centre felt that since the Rajasthan government was led by the Congress, the matter had to be handled carefully so as not to embarrass the Chief Minister and the party. Therefore, within Parliament, I defended the Government of Rajasthan, even while making it clear that the issue was linked to crime and violence against women, and that while sati might be sanctioned by religious or cultural beliefs, it could not be tolerated. I assured the House that stringent action would be taken against the culprits.

The Chief Minister, on his part, assured us that the site where sati had been committed was being cordoned off and no customary ceremonies would be allowed. But to everyone's dismay, lakhs of people collected at the location for the thirteenth-day ceremony; fairs and dances were organized and shown on TV. I was furious.

I went to the Prime Minister and submitted my resignation. 'I cannot defend this anymore!' I said.

His reply was, 'Why are you resigning? You are not responsible. Let the man responsible resign.' He then picked up the phone, got through to the Chief Minister—Hari Deo Joshi—and simply said in Hindi, 'You have let me down. Go to the Governor and submit your resignation!'

And so Joshi resigned.

We then launched a campaign to create awareness about the social evil that sati was, and also to sensitize people to the ills of child marriage. This became a massive movement, with many conventions and seminars held in the state by the party and NGOs, much to the discomfiture of powerful Congressmen there.

Then came the demand for legislation to ban sati, as also all forms of Sati worship. A meeting was called by the Prime Minister to discuss the matter, and he, in turn, authorized P.V. Narasimha Rao to take the final decision. Several senior Congress leaders felt that bringing a special legislation to ban sati would alienate the Rajputs from the Congress. I, however, pointed out that lack of action in the matter would go against the values that the Congress was committed to. The HRD Minister agreed with me and stated, 'To defend the principles that the party has always stood for, if we are to lose some votes—so be it. The party should be prepared to even lose an election for its principles.'

In the meantime, Rajput MPs, cutting across party lines, went to the Prime Minister, protesting against the proposed bill, claiming that it was an insult to the community and an assault on Rajput traditions. He listened and sent them to meet me, with a hurried call on the RAX (secure telephone lines) warning me of what was to come.

I sat nervously as Rajput MPs from different parties marched into my office. They were agitated and said, 'You, as a Christian, do not understand how sensitive this issue is for us.'

When they were done with their protests, I asked a couple of those I knew well about a widowed sister and a widowed mother in their own families. 'Why have you not followed the tradition if it is so sacrosanct? Is there one rule for the rich and another for the poor?' I asked.

They had no reply, and soon the meeting ended.

The Commission of Sati (Prevention) Act prepared by the WCD was enacted by Parliament in 1987 to become law. But it was preceded by a conflict between the Home Ministry and the WCD over who should pilot the bill. C.G. Somiah, the Home Secretary, insisted that it was a matter of women's survival, while I asserted that it was a crime of murder, and so the Home Ministry ought to pilot it. In fact, I was in favour of a simple amendment in the CrPC to include sati in the definition of murder.

After the file moved up and down between the two ministries—with me refusing to pilot the bill—I was summoned to the PMO. The Home Secretary was there.

Rajivji tried to convince me that it was my job to pilot the bill.

I resisted. 'If your Home Secretary is tied to a pillar in Connaught Place and burned, with people watching, what would you term it? Murder? If it happens to a helpless woman, why does it become women's welfare?'

'Why do you want to burn this poor harmless man?' the Prime Minister asked, jocularly. But then he became serious and insisted that I do the job.

I had no choice; I piloted the bill.

I should add here that C.G. Somiah ended up as my 'samdhi' a few years later, when my son, Nikhil, married his only daughter, Pria.

◆

I ran into a public controversy while supporting an initiative of Champa behn, the well-known Gandhian of Madhya Pradesh.

The Bedia community of Sagar district had seen no marriages for four hundred years. They trained their children as street performers and it was said that their girls were sold into the flesh trade by the time they were twelve years old. With Champa behn's efforts, a mass marriage for them was announced with government support. It was a real festival. The grooms received land and cash from the government, while the brides received household articles and their bridal clothes. Chief Minister Motilal Vora and I, along with a large team of women from Delhi, which included Mohini Giri and Padma Seth, attended. Instead of applauding the event, a Privilege Motion was moved against all of us in the State Assembly, accusing us of presiding over child marriages. I was told that the lobbies which earned huge money from the trafficking of girls were upset and wanted to corner us for our intervention. But Champa behn carried on with her work, undeterred by threats and abuses, even as Voraji dealt with the political fallout.

◆

During my years in the WCD Ministry, I found myself dealing with a number of thorny matters—from the rights of anganwadi workers, to maternity benefits, spousal transfer issues and the entitlement of women IFS officers—and, in each case, the aim was to do right by women.

There were demands and dharnas, supported by opposition parties, NGOs and state governments, to make anganwadi workers government servants and raise their allowances. At first I rejected the petition, since the Integrated Child Development Services (ICDS) Programme had been launched as a voluntary movement for local women to deliver specific services. Making them government servants would destroy the character of the initiative, besides making them liable for transfers that would interfere with local commitment. Finally, as a compromise, we decided to raise their emoluments, provide them with promotional avenues and, with the panchayati raj reservations expected to be initiated, encourage them to get involved with local bodies as well. Matters settled down, but over the years the demand has been voiced persistently.

The other issue that got women in government service agitated was maternity leave—which we restricted to two deliveries alone. To voice their opposition to this ceiling, they went on a hunger strike outside Shastri Bhavan. When I spoke to their representatives, I was told that women had no control over their husbands and were being penalized for a decision that wasn't necessarily theirs. In response I explained that, unlike China, Indian women could have any number of children, but not at the taxpayers' cost. Their husbands would have to foot the bill if they wanted more children. I emphasized that, in the long run, this would be in the interest of their health and their family's welfare. The women finally called off their agitation, and the rule stayed. This was later extended to medical leave for miscarriages as well.

But the matter resurfaced in another avatar. I saw a news item that read: 'Government denies maternity leave on moral grounds'. Apparently, an unmarried woman officer had been denied maternity benefits. I phoned the concerned Minister who strongly defended the action, claiming it was in keeping with India's cultural traditions. I decided to fight the Minister. I wrote to him pointing out that the Maternity Benefits Act did not mention 'a married woman' anywhere. It simply spoke of women employees. 'How can you add words and impose your moral interpretations on the law?' I asked. The Minister had no answer, and the lady got her benefits. (Incidentally, it turned out that the lady in question had actually been married to a serving officer in the government, but since she had neither reported her marriage to the department nor changed her name, it had been presumed that she was unmarried!)

A rule for posting working wives where their husbands were employed was introduced to help women keep their jobs after marriage. However, this rule came with its own set of problems, with men without working wives protesting that the rule was doubly unfair to them. Besides running a family without a second salary, they were getting shunted out to accommodate the working wives of transferred husbands, they claimed. We, therefore, decided that the rule had to be made less lopsided— husbands also had to be prepared to move where their wives were if both partners wished to be posted in the same place. Interestingly, with this, requests for same-city postings began to decline considerably.

Then came the matter of discrimination against women IFS officers. An IFS couple posted together was entitled to only one allowance, as against two, besides braving cuts in their quota of servants. This was brought to my notice during my transit through Beijing, en route to North Korea, when I was at Deepa Wadhwa's for dinner. She and her husband were IFS officers, posted together. She explained how they, and couples like them, were affected financially when they opted for same-city postings—all this while she struggled in the kitchen with a baby in arms. The irony was that if a spouse worked in any other organization, there were no cuts imposed. On my return, I took the matter up with the External Affairs Ministry. The ministry resisted any suggestion for change. A few years later, when

I became Minister for Personnel in the Narasimha Rao government, I reopened the matter. I managed to have the unfair rules changed, and was felicitated at a meeting of the Foreign Service Wives' Association for being their voice.

◆

Changing mindsets in a male-oriented society required careful intervention. While replicating the Anand milk cooperative story in other states, we had varied problems. In Punjab, for instance, the society (dominated by men) opted for bi-monthly payments for supplied milk instead of a daily release through women's passbooks. The result—the women supplied milk, but the men queued up to receive payments. We quickly restored the original system of daily payments to women.

◆

In 1988, when the Prime Minister, Gopi Arora (his key aide), Sarla Grewal (his Principal Secretary), Mani Shankar Aiyar (Joint Secretary in the PMO) and I were on a flight, the Prime Minister suddenly came out of his cabin and started asking questions about why the huge allocations made for women's development programmes failed to impact women's lives in a meaningful way. 'Why don't we see results?' he asked.

We tried explaining why. First, these allocations went to different ministries, and not all of them were serious about targeting women in their programmes. Second, different departments had different priorities and target groups, often working at cross purposes and even in competition. Third, since funds were allocated on an annual basis, no long-term planning was possible. And fourth, funds were allocated in the last quarter to states or released to 'chosen' NGOs and groups to avoid lapsing, and were most often diverted or misused.

The Prime Minister then directed me to set up a group to work on a ten-year perspective plan for women—to cover the last decade of the century—with a vision document for Indian women for the twenty-first century. 'They must catch up with the men by the turn of the millennium. Work on a long-term plan, and begin immediately!' he ordered.

So I got going. I put together a team—representatives of NGOs, women activists, academicians, officials, etc.—for consultations and suggestions. It was unanimously agreed that a structured committee would be time-consuming, since it would come with demands for tours, staff, offices, vehicles and budgets. We decided to study earlier reports on the status of women, identify those sectors that needed a shift in focus to enable women to emerge in the next decade, recommend measures to remove hurdles impeding their progress, and initiate follow-up action.

We identified eight sectors crucial to women's lives—rural development and agriculture, employment and training, supportive services, education, health and family welfare, legislation, political participation and decision-making, and media and communication. We then set up small groups of experts to work on each of these areas. They sought inputs from experts, grassroots-level organizations, and Central and state governments, and collected data. They organized consultations—all hosted by well-known institutions in different parts of the country, like SNDT (Shreemati Nathibai Damodar Thackersey Women's University) in Maharashtra, Avinashilingam University in Tamil Nadu, Panjab University in Chandigarh, the Institute of Rural Management–Anand (IRMA) in Gujarat, Indian Council of Agricultural Research (ICAR) in Andhra Pradesh, SEWA in Uttar Pradesh and the All India Women's Conference (AIWC) in Delhi.

Dr Nandini Azad was roped in as a Consultant to coordinate and guide these meetings. The Joint Secretary in the WCD Ministry, C.P. Sujaya, was made Secretary of the core group, while I was the Chairperson, and Roma Mazumdar the Convener. Things ought to have functioned with clockwork efficiency. However, we soon confronted difficulties we least anticipated. For reasons that baffled me, C.P. Sujaya refused to cooperate. Then there was opposition from some women's groups, who called the Perspective Plan a gimmick of the government to win over women's votes in the forthcoming elections. Press statements followed, accusing me of hijacking the agenda of NGOs and encroaching on their space. Allegations were made that we were neither experts nor activists.

But we carried on even as the idea of a long-term plan for the empowerment of women began to garner support. I used to sit up at night, going through, editing and improving the drafts, processing data and giving shape to the final report. In six months, our draft report was ready for circulation, discussion, inputs and of course, criticism and correction. Seminars were organized in different states and the women's agenda took shape.

The report—called the National Perspective Plan for the Empowerment of Women (1990–2000)—was presented to the Prime Minister. It received wide publicity.

I was asked to prepare a summary document for the Cabinet. That's when I hit a stone wall! A male-dominated Cabinet stiffly opposed the recommendations with the kind of vehemence I had not anticipated. I still remember the remark of Abdul Ghafoor, the former Chief Minister of Bihar, at the meeting: '*Saab, yeh kya baat hai! Aapki mantri UN se naye-naye idea leke aa rahi hai, aur hum mardon ko sata rahi hai! Shaadi mein kuchh milta tha, woh band kar liya. Biwi ko kabhi-kabhi daante the, woh crime ban gaya. Kabhi kahin pasand ki picture dekhte the, woh bhi ban karwa diya.*' ('Your Minister returns from the UN with new-fangled ideas and wants to trouble us men! Where once we could hope to get something upon marriage, now the practice has been stopped. Where once it was okay for a wife to get scolded, now the custom is illegal! Some exciting films we used to watch on occasion have been banned!') Then, turning to me with folded hands, he said, '*Hum mard jayenge kahaan? Isko band kijeeye!*' ('Where do we, the men, go? Stop this please!')

Following his lead, everyone else chimed in; they said the ideas were premature and dangerous. The real point of worry for the men was a recommendation for the reservation of 33 per cent of all seats for women, from panchayats to Parliament. Their remonstrations compelled the Prime Minister to set the recommendations aside at least for the time being. He told me, 'We have to stoop to conquer. We will find a way to implement the plan through administrative action.' And this we did.

I presented the plan at a meeting of State Ministers, who agreed to find a way of implementing the suggested programmes. Many years later, when I was a Minister in Narasimha Rao's government, I received a request from Atal Bihari Vajpayee, then the Chairman of the Standing Committee for HRD, to appear before the committee for a discussion on the National Perspective Plan. I was surprised and flattered, and though there was no such precedent, I did go. In his introduction, Vajpayeeji congratulated me for the document. He said that he had studied it and found it to be a well-presented blueprint for women's development. I made a presentation and answered questions for over two hours. The committee was most appreciative of the plan.

Over the years, the plan has been reviewed and updated by the NCW (National Commission for Women). Most of its suggestions have found a place in Central and state government initiatives for women's development. The Manmohan Singh-appointed High-Level Committee (HLC) for Women's Empowerment—of which Manira was a member—was asked to review the steps taken in the direction of women's empowerment since 1989, clearly bringing the National Perspective Plan back in focus.[34]

---

[34]Recently, I was surprised when I was told that the Department of WCD did not have a copy of the National Perspective Plan, nor did NIPCCD (National Institute of Public Cooperation and Child Development) or the Parliament House library. I produced my only copy and had it reprinted for circulation.

Chapter 20

ON THE RUN:
YOUTH AFFAIRS AND SPORTS

With the government placing a special emphasis on involving youth in nation-building, our work in the Ministry of Youth Affairs gathered pace and our endeavours met with success. A National Youth Policy was adopted, a National Youth Day announced (12 January) and a National Youth Award instituted. Youth hostels were constructed all over the country, university festivals revived and regional youth fests (leading to one large national fest) launched. The youth were truly occupying centre stage.

In 1986, I became the Chairperson of the Nehru Yuva Kendra Sangathan—an autonomous organization launched to mobilize the young for community work and nation-building. It especially targeted rural youth—covering non-formal education and training, awareness generation, skill development and self-employment, besides sports—all to be fine-tuned through sustained exposure to new ideas and development strategies. The goals were to be executed through a network of District Coordinators, appointed on contract for a period of three years, after undergoing special training. We worked hard to make the Nehru Yuva Kendra Sangathan a success. Rajivji himself handpicked the first team. Thanks to everyone's efforts, the programme started with a bang.[35]

I spoke at countless events for youth across the country. One of the surprise invitations was to the University of Guwahati, where no Congress leader had been allowed to enter by the AGP (Assam Gana Parishad)-controlled student union.

◆

---

[35]Unfortunately, after the Rajiv Gandhi era, the Nehru Yuva Kendra Sangathan became an almost non-existent organization, and most of the Coordinators became corrupt power-brokers in their local fiefdoms. Efforts to revive and recast the organization were made, but the vision was lost—the Coordinators had been politicized, and under the NDA (National Democratic Alliance, led by the BJP), its goals acquired a saffron tinge, particularly in the Hindi heartland.

In August 1989, we set off for North Korea for the Non-Aligned Youth Festival at Pyongyang. Ours was a large group consisting of Indian youth, and Culture Ministry representatives, led by Minister Ghulam Nabi Azad. Nikhil was a member of the youth band, which had been selected through open competition. Besides watching an extraordinarily evocative and instructive opening ceremony, we exchanged pleasantries with President Kim Il-sung (through an interpreter). The President posed for a group photograph.

Before he could leave, I asked for an opportunity to make a request.

There was stunned silence all around, but the President smiled and stopped to listen.

I explained that as Minister for Youth Affairs and Sports, I found the display by the students during the opening ceremony stunning. I asked if he would consider sending three or four trainers to India, since we wanted to project India's history—much like they had done—to mark the end of the Nehru centenary year.

Kim II-sung smiled and said that he could not send his trainers to India, but could train our people if we sent them to North Korea.

'Thank you!' I said, and accepted that offer.

Unfortunately, our coaches returned rather disappointed.

Thankfully, we had also roped in trainers from many other countries for the show. Under their guidance, on 14 November 1989, 50,000 school children from all over the country showcased India's success story with a synchronized placard display. It was an unbelievable sight and an unforgettable achievement. The Prime Minister presided over the event.

14 November 1989 also witnessed the opening of Jawahar Bhawan— built with the contributions of well-wishers; all Congress MPs and legislators gave a month's salary. Jawahar Bhawan was to house the AICC headquarters. As the function at the Nehru Stadium was ending, I mentioned to Rajivji that I would not be able to make it to Jawahar Bhawan as the roads would be closed once he left. 'Get into my car,' he said. 'You must attend that function!' Thus I was present at this historic event as well.

But these are sad memories of all the last public functions of a Prime Minister of promise.

◆

Apart from being Minister of Women, Children and Youth Affairs, I was also in charge of sports. Sports was not really my forte. I had been a cricket buff in college, skipping lectures to attend matches with friends; I played basketball regularly and badminton occasionally—but that was the extent of my expertise. So, when I landed in the Sports Ministry, I was a novice! It didn't help that the sports federations were a law unto themselves. And it certainly was added pressure that the Prime Minister was keenly following our achievements in the sports arena.

Thanks to his close association with the Asian Games of 1982, the first year saw the budget for the ministry jump from ₹100 crore to ₹300 crore. The SAI (Sports Authority of India) South Zone training centre at Bangalore procured the latest equipment and state-of-the-art infrastructure. The National Institute of Sports at Patiala was upgraded. Foreign coaches were brought in and sports administrators recruited for the regional centres at Gandhinagar, Trivandrum and Calcutta. An academy for contact sports in the North-east, rowing academies in the Andaman Islands and Alleppey (now Alappuzha), and a gymnastics academy at Thalassery were set up, and local talent was identified for specialized training by foreign coaches. Prize money for medals across competition-levels and job quotas for sportspersons were announced. Specially selected and well-equipped sports schools trained talented students on scholarships. In each state, with SAI funding, sports hostels were set up, coaches posted and equipment procured for university students.

Pro-sports agendas were adopted. The new education policy introduced the concept of 'sports for all'—making it a part of the curriculum. Besides, to keep the sports facilities that had been created for the Asian Games in good shape, earn revenue for their maintenance and also make them available to the public, a 'pay and play' scheme was introduced; this not only raised funds but also helped popularize sports.

The fact that the Prime Minister knew Delhi's sports infrastructure—stadia, halls, hostels and all—created problems for us. Every time he came for an event, he would point out fused bulbs, a broken railing, faded flags or a malfunctioning score board. And so, days before his slated visit, we would start making the rounds to put things in place. Replacing fused bulbs in the stadia proved difficult as they had been imported in bulk for the Asian Games, and were not available locally. When I mentioned this, pat came his response: 'We got them from Germany. Ask the Embassy to trace the company, place an order with them and stock sufficient bulbs!'

The bulbs came in six weeks flat.

To better our prospects in international sports, the Arun Singh Committee was set up to study all aspects of sports development and make recommendations for improving our performance. The report, captioned 'Operation Excellence', was comprehensive. It selected eleven disciplines, with medal-winning prospects, for intensive training and support from the government. The other disciplines could compete if they reached qualifying standards, but their respective federations would have to raise funds themselves.

Besides this, the report set guidelines for elections in the federations, specifying the number of terms for officials, the age limit, etc. There was a clear stipulation that those who refused to follow the guidelines would receive no government support for training, travel to federation meetings abroad, equipment, etc. The report went on to specify the composition of selection committees for international competitions, with strict qualifications and procedures for the appointment of national coaches, who were to be paid by the government—thus making them independent of the pressures of the federations.

Naturally, when the Ministry of Sports accepted the report and the guidelines, the federations were up in arms and refused to fall in line. A meeting of the federations, which had some serving bureaucrats of the Central and state governments and a few military personnel, under the Chairmanship of V.C. Shukla—the President of the Indian Olympic Association (IOA)—passed a resolution rejecting the guidelines as a violation of the Olympic Charter. The Prime Minister was livid. He asked me to call a meeting of the federations at SAI, which he would attend.

We had a packed hall; everyone was there, but no one knew what the agenda was. P.V. Narasimha Rao, the Chairman of SAI, was presiding. Arun Singh, too, was present. After the usual round of introductions, I opened the discussion saying that the Prime Minster, as President of SAI, was concerned about the differences publicly expressed by the IOA and the federations over 'Operation Excellence'; he had therefore decided to listen to the IOA's views himself.

One by one, members began listing their objections, till everyone had been heard. Arun Singh, in turn, clarified many issues, but the old argument kept getting repeated: 'These guidelines take away the autonomy of the IOA and the federations. The International Olympic Committee (IOC) will de-recognize the IOA and we will be out of all international events!'

The Prime Minister listened patiently and finally spoke: 'These guidelines must be followed. If we are de-recognized, so much the better! In any case, we go to competitions and win nothing. For thirty years, China did not participate in international competitions. But when they finally did, they swept every event. We need to stay home for twenty years and train. The government, on its part, is happy to provide the best infrastructure and support if the IOA and federations follow these guidelines. Otherwise, they will have to fend for themselves and we will put the SAI in charge of training our athletes! As for the IOC, your Minister will deal with that issue. Thank you all.'

The meeting ended. There was stunned silence all around. The Prime Minister had endorsed the guidelines in no uncertain terms. It was now time for the federations and the IOA to decide their course of action.

Later that week, I got a phone call from General Sundarji, who wished to drop in with his colleagues from the Air Force and Navy. Sundarji was our neighbour and a close friend. But what happened was something I had least anticipated. I received a message that the three Chiefs were on their way, and in minutes, sirens blazing, three motorcades, one after the other, entered my 23, Safdarjung Road premises. The Chiefs walked in, escorted by Aide-de-camps (ADCs) and security personnel. The sight drew a crowd on the road outside. To onlookers, it must have seemed like a full-scale raid.

The Chiefs got straight to the point. They apologized for the irresponsible manner in which their officers had behaved at the IOA meeting and promised to support any initiative the Sports Ministry took to improve the image of the country. They also offered their support to train specified squads for competitions. I learnt that the Prime Minister had given them a piece of his mind on the issue.

While we managed to get the military and many federations on board, there was an uncompromising group, led by Suresh Kalmadi, V.C. Shukla, P.K. Malhotra and Pawanjit S. Bindra, which carried on a campaign in the press against the Sports Ministry and me personally. They blamed us for destroying sports in the country.

I now had to fight on two fronts. I had to not only deal with Shukla and team, but also manage the President of the IOC. We decided to deal with the IOA first by getting V.C. Shukla out of his post. After a lot of maneuvering, the required number of members signed a requisition for an extraordinary meeting—one that went on well past midnight, and saw Shukla voted out. It was a huge victory, and those who had been part of the coup came straight to my house to celebrate, led by the doyen of the sports fraternity, Sardar Bhalinder Singh, also a member of the IOC. The IOA office was sealed that night.

Then came the second challenge—managing the President of the IOC, Juan Antonio Samaranch. Sardar Bhalinder Singh came forward to help, and thanks to him, I received an invitation from Samaranch for a meeting in Lausanne at the Olympic headquarters. I made the trip alone. Samaranch treated me as his personal guest, taking me round the Olympic museum, presenting me with prized memorabilia, and listening patiently to what I had to say over lunch. He was convinced that Indian sports needed a total overhaul.

'Tell your Prime Minister,' he said, 'that I will do everything possible to help!' He added with a smile, 'You are a tough woman. There are very few like you in sports ministries. I wish I could get you onto the IOC. You would be an asset.'

It was quite a compliment coming from him. I did not get to the IOC, but I got a letter from Samaranch endorsing the government's stand! This was a triumph. I came back like a conquering heroine, reported the outcome to P.V. Narasimha Rao, and then to the Prime Minister, who was thrilled. I hosted a lunch for the sports media and released the letter from Samaranch, which came as a shock to the federations.

Now the federations had no option but to submit. The guidelines were notified and enforced. Those who did not fall in line lost their offices in SAI and funding from government. The only sport we could not rope in was cricket—the BCCI (Board of Control for Cricket in India) refused to submit to government interference. I am glad that the Supreme Court has now stepped in to make the BCCI more accountable.

Over time, the hostility of the IOA began to thaw. Suresh Kalmadi, as President of the Athletics Federation, chose to cooperate with SAI and the Sports Ministry. We became good friends and went to sports events abroad together on many occasions.

◆

Sports is a state subject; federations are registered under state laws and regulations. To bring a central uniform sports legislation, it became necessary to shift the subject to the concurrent list by a Constitution amendment.

This was my next mission—to get states to agree to move sports to the concurrent list. Several states saw merit in the idea. The amendment was approved by the Cabinet and listed for discussion and passage in the Rajya Sabha in the winter session of 1989.

But the day the amendment was to be discussed, a determined group of MPs and sports representatives met the Prime Minister and pleaded that the bill be deferred for further consultations with stakeholders. The Prime Minister gave in, and conveyed the news to me. I was shocked, but had no choice. The amendment was buried for good. Sadly, the problem of dealing with the federations continues to plague Indian sports even today.

◆

Within the Sports Ministry itself, I faced a number of unusual situations.

Early one morning, I received a phone call from the Prime Minister. He was posting an officer from Uttar Pradesh to the Sports Ministry as Joint Secretary. He wanted me to be 'patient and understanding' with him. The officer came to meet me the next day. He introduced himself as Mata Prasad.

'Are you interested in sports?' I asked, to open the conversation.

'I know nothing about this subject, madam, but I will learn,' he replied, adding, 'I come from a poor scheduled caste family. As a child, the only games I played were gilli-danda and kabaddi in my village school.'

I welcomed Mata Prasad and told him to come to me if he faced problems.

I later learnt that Prasad had been the Home Secretary of Uttar Pradesh and had been unceremoniously shunted out after being blamed for mishandling some communal clashes. A deeply upset Prasad, on his part, claimed that the entire episode was a conspiracy of upper-caste officers who could not come to terms with an SC officer being their boss.

The Prime Minister often enquired about Prasad, and I could understand his concern. Happily for all of us, Prasad learnt very fast, getting totally involved with his assignment. I came to respect him for his sincerity and honesty, and we got on very well.

While the Mata Prasad episode ended on a happy note, there were other situations I confronted that were quite awkward. One day, a file with a letter from the External Affairs Ministry reached my desk. The letter requested the use of the Indira Gandhi Stadium for a public function—the visit of Pope John Paul II to India. There was to be a religious ceremony followed by a reception by the Christian community.

The Sports Ministry guidelines clearly stated that stadia/sports facilities would not be made available or hired out for religious or political functions. How, then, could I permit the use of the Indira Gandhi Stadium for the visit of a religious leader? I faced pressure from all sides. As a Catholic, I knew I would be in trouble whether or not I cleared the request. After some thought, I decided to stick to the guidelines and recorded my note on the file, rejecting the request.

Surprised at my response, the External Affairs Ministry contacted P.V. Narasimha Rao, who summoned me to ask, 'Do you want to create a diplomatic crisis for us? The Pope may be a religious leader, but he is our guest as a Head of State. We cannot refuse permission.'

'That is your decision, sir,' I responded. 'You may clear the request. I have done what I believe is my duty, as I fear that any decision to the contrary might set a dangerous precedent.'

He dismissed my apprehensions. The stadium was made available for the function, and I was among the thousands who filled it.

A third event I distinctly recall involved my Sports Secretary, R. Gopalaswamy, who had been the Secretary of Civil Supplies in Kerala. Gopalaswamy was honest and sincere, but a stickler for the rule book. When we wanted to introduce certain changes, for which we had the budget, he went through the proposals, and along with the Financial Advisor, shot them down on one account or another.

I tried talking to him. I told him that I respected his age and experience, but I also had to get things done. 'Sports cannot be run like civil supplies,' I told him, adding, 'you sit on that side of the table to advise and I sit on this side of the table to decide!' But my talk had no impact.

I finally went to the Prime Minister for help. He asked Gopi Arora to assist. Arora sat with us in the Sports Ministry on a Saturday morning to sort out the issues. Every concern was analyzed and Arora suggested a way out for each of them. At the end of the meeting, I was happy. I gave the file to the Sports Secretary, assuming that matters had been settled.

But on Monday I received the file back with a detailed note about why the proposals discussed could not be approved. I was dismayed. I spoke to Gopi Arora and, at his behest, sent the file to him.

The next morning, I was shocked to see a boxed item in the newspapers announcing Gopalaswamy's appointment as Advisor in the Planning Commission. This was the Prime Minister's decision-making pattern—swift and firm.

◆

As a former Sports Minister, there are two events I fondly remember—the Asian Games (1986) and the Olympic Games (1988) in Seoul. On both occasions, I witnessed and shared the highs and lows of our teams on the field. The saddest moment at the Asian Games was when Shiny Abraham was stripped of her silver medal on technical grounds even after winning the race convincingly; she had accidently changed lanes too early and was disqualified! Shiny was inconsolable. We spent the evening at the village with all our athletes trying to lighten the blow.

The Asian Games turned out to be memorable for another reason. Several of our officials disappeared in the evenings, leaving me all alone to attend official receptions. When I asked where they went, I was told that they were at 'Church Street', in the heart of town.

One day I asked our Ambassador Sudhir Devare to take me to the street our officials seemed to frequent. He seemed surprised and warned me, 'It will not be your cup of tea. But I will take you if you insist!' I did insist, and we went. As our car was spotted, I saw many of our people stare in dismay and slink away. It was only then that I was told that it was the most popular 'night life' street of the city. 'If we hit the headlines in India tomorrow, I will say I was only doing my duty, as part of protocol—accompanying the Minister!' the Ambassador commented, smiling mischievously. 'And I will say, I went where the Ambassador took me for dinner!' I replied. We walked the streets and returned; we had certainly spoilt the evening for many.

At the Arjuna awards ceremony soon after, President Giani Zail Singh, in an impromptu speech, and in his inimical style, said, '*Yeh mantri bechari bahut kaam kar rahi hain, par sab uske pichche pade hain! Unke daftar mein jo lift-waala hai, uski naukri pucci hain. Par yeh bichari temporary hain. Unko PM [Prime Minister] kabhi bhi nikaal sakte hain.*' ('This poor Minister is slogging, yet everyone seems to be out to get her! While the person who mans the elevator to her office is permanent, our poor Minister is temporary. The Prime Minister can remove her any time!') The Ashoka Hall resounded with laughter, as he added, '*Par mein unko support karta hoon!*' ('Nonetheless, I support her!') That was Gianiji at his best.

The Olympics in Seoul were exciting. I enjoyed the event immensely. Our country's sports performance, however, remained poor, and I had to face a hostile press and Parliament on my return.

Then there were the Commonwealth Games. After a great deal of lobbying, we got the go-ahead from the government to bid for them. The Sports Ministry and the IOA joined hands to prepare all the material for our presentation. Around this time, I also went to Western Samoa, a dot in the South Pacific, for a Commonwealth Youth Affairs Ministers' conference. The event was to be inaugurated by the King, and was unlike any other I had been to. There were no chairs and we had to squat on the floor in a circle, much to the discomfiture of those in Western formal clothes. The King arrived bare-chested, in a half-skirt that looked like a rolled up lungi. A cup of a local brew was offered, first to him, then to all the guests, who had to drink from the same goblet—a token of the King's warm welcome.

We liaised with the Youth Affairs Ministers, received a lot of support and were hopeful of victory, especially because the Commonwealth Games had never been held in the Afro-Asian region of the Commonwealth. But we lost to Cardiff—a loss attributed to our boycott of the previous Commonwealth Games because South African all-white teams had been permitted to participate.

In response, the Afro-Asian Games Council took shape, with Saudi Arabia and India taking the lead. We hosted the first meeting in India, which was attended by over ninety countries. After several postponements, the first Afro-Asian Games were held at Hyderabad in 2003; ninety-six countries participated. The next round of games was set to take place in Algeria in 2007. However, the event got indefinitely postponed, and eventually, politics and conflicting pressures led to the natural death of the initiative. But we won the bid for the XIX Commonwealth Games—though it got mired in controversy right from the start.

◆

We had sought and received help from several countries for our sports development programmes. I led delegations to many of them to sign protocols or negotiate new agreements. My Cuban experience in this regard was most interesting.

On the last day of my visit to Mexico for a WWPP meeting, I received a strange message from the PMO through the Embassy, which said, 'PM has directed MoS to visit Cuba for a couple of days, as the President of Cuba has made this request.'

I was confused. What was I going to do there? I had no official itinerary or gifts and no briefing for the trip. But the Embassy intervened, took care of all the arrangements, and I landed in Cuba.

I had a two-hour meeting with President Fidel Castro, who received me in an office outside the hall where the Communist Party politburo was in session. As usual, he was in great form, asking many questions about the Prime Minister, the government and the country.

Towards the end of our discussion, he became serious, bent across the table, held my hand and said, 'Tell two things to Rajiv on my behalf. I have been a friend of his mother; I have admired her. She was a great leader, a great woman. He must follow in her footsteps—not depart from her policies and programmes. Otherwise, he will have problems. And second, tell him not to trust his Finance Minister. He is conspiring against him. He will stab him in the back. He is a dangerous man. Rajiv must be careful.'

I told the Cuban President that the Finance Minister, V.P. Singh, was a Gandhi friend and supporter, and Rajiv depended on him for help and advice.

He shook his head gravely and said, 'That is not good, not good.'

I remained worried about the Cuban President's second message, recalling the many times that V.P. Singh had let us down in the House. But I decided to focus on the tasks at hand first. In order to make my visit official, the ministry advised me, through the Embassy in Cuba, to sign a protocol that had been finalized for training our boxers there on a long-term basis. So, the next morning, I went to the Ministry of Sports to work out the details. Despite repeated requests for more training seats for our boxers, the Cubans would not budge; they said that they had limited training capacity and had to accommodate boxers from other countries too. I had to finally accept the two slots they were giving.

I was invited to tea by the President before we signed the protocol, and he asked me if everything had been worked out.

I said, 'Yes, but you could have been more generous to us.'

'What is the problem?' he asked his Sports Minister, who explained the issues at hand.

Fidel Castro was furious. He did not mince words as he threw up his hands and gave the Minister a dressing down. Then he laughed and said, 'My officers think India is like Nicaragua—a friendly country. They are crazy!' Fidel Castro then asked for the copy of the protocol, which the Minister proudly presented. He pulled out his pen and changed the number as per my request.

The Minister was stunned and so was I. But that was Cuba.

The signing was delayed by an hour as the document had to be redone. When I arrived at the ceremony that followed, the cold glares I received could have frozen me to ice! But here began the story of India's training in the boxing ring under Cuban coaches.

When I returned to India and repeated to the Prime Minister the message from the Cuban President, he brushed it aside saying, 'What does he know of India?'

As events unfolded, I reminded him of the message from Fidel Castro. He remained silent. He knew he had made a mistake.

◆

The domestic scene changed drastically when I joined the government in 1984. My new assignment and responsibilities took me out of home frequently. But Sunday was observed as family day—church together in the morning, and lunch at home or at the club, with occasional picnics on weekends. We shifted to a sprawling ministerial bunglow at 23, Safdarjung Road, in May 1985, with large lawns, an office block and a staff-quarters complex. It was like an empire with its own politics and intrigues. Luckily, I had an efficient and well-trained team to run the establishment—Sarojamma in the kitchen and for Babu's care; Judy, Jack of all jobs, to run the household; and S.C. Sharma in the home office.

Niru had become Director of the SBI (State Bank of India)—South Zone (at Bangalore) by the kind courtesy of Pranab Mukherjee, going on to become the Vice President of the Board. He and the children missed me, no doubt, but, in retrospect, I feel they enjoyed the freedom and 'space'—as they now term it—that they got.

Chapter 21

AN OLD SAGA:
BACK TO THE NORTH-EAST

M y involvement with the North-east continued during the Rajiv Gandhi years. In 1986, I was sent to Nagaland to prepare a factual report on the state government's functioning. This was after a series of complaints were received against the Chief Minister, S.C. Jamir—a man who had been Parliamentary Secretary in Pandit Nehru's government and had gone on to become the Chief Minister of Nagaland. He had always been viewed as a respected (though controversial) tribal leader and a committed nationalist. His opinions were valued in Delhi. However, in the mid-1980s, he ran into trouble with the party, the MLAs and the public. The gifts received for his son's wedding became a public issue.

I reached Kohima, and met the Chief Minister and his MLAs in a state government guest house. The party functionaries and workers were to meet me the next day, as also journalists. Late in the night, I was told that a different guest house had been arranged for me to meet party workers. So, early the next morning, I was shifted out. No one knew where I was. Naturally, no one turned up. By the time news of my whereabouts became public, I was shifted again! Finally, I abandoned guest houses and met those I had to, at the home of a party leader. Here I received reports and memoranda.

After going through all the material I had gathered, my report confirmed the complaints the Centre had received about serious malfunctioning in the state government. The Chief Minister was asked to step down. Hokishe Sema[36]—a low-key, pleasant gentleman, liked by both Indiraji and Rajiv—succeeded Jamir.

---

[36]Frustrated with the manipulations of the rival groups in the Congress, Hokishe Sema eventually left the Congress to join the BJP, and then retired to his farm—a disappointed man. The last time I visited him, he was out in the sun working with his hands, with a large hat on his head and gumboots on his feet. His son, after retiring from the army, joined the Congress, and was made an office bearer when I was in charge of the state. Jamir's son, Apok, became an MP, and then returned to state politics to become an MLA.

◆

In 1988, on the eve of the Assembly elections in Meghalaya, the Congress High Command decided that a change in leadership was the need of the hour and wanted P.A. Sangma, who was an MoS in Delhi, to go as Chief Minister. Captain Williamson Sangma, the incumbent Chief Minister, was a nationalist; the unchallenged leader of Meghalaya since its creation in 1972; the architect of a progressive, integrated state; and a leader accepted by all factions and tribes of Meghalaya, despite being a Garo himself. But age was catching up.

When Sangma was told of the Prime Minister's proposal to make him Chief Minister, he seemed hesitant. So M.M. Jacob, who had been Deputy Chairman of the Rajya Sabha, and I were asked to persuade him. We succeeded in our mission.

In the countdown to the Assembly elections, Rajesh Pilot (Minister for Surface Transport) and I were deputed to oversee the campaign. I noticed that P.R. Kyndiah, the astute Khasi leader and Home Minister, was a strong supporter of the Khasi Students' Union (KSU) agitation. He hoped to emerge as either the kingmaker or the Chief Minister after the elections. I kept track of his activities, and grew increasingly concerned.

The Prime Minister's visit to the state to address a public rally at the stadium was announced. Sangma and Pilot went to Guwahati to fly him by helicopter to Shillong. I was left to coordinate the rally.

That morning, there came the news of a KSU call for a 'Shillong bandh' to ensure that the Congress rally was boycotted. I rang up the Chief Secretary, whose wife kept answering the phone, telling me that her husband was in the bathroom. After three attempts, I told her, 'Ask him to be ready in ten minutes because I am coming there!'

The Chief Secretary was prepared for my arrival. I came straight to the point. 'What arrangements have you made to ensure that the people come out?' I asked.

'I can do nothing,' he replied. 'This is a people's movement.'

'Why has the road transport stopped?' I shouted.

'I do not know. I will have to check. Perhaps the drivers have not reported.'

'Get me the Home Minister on telephone,' I demanded.

The Chief Secretary kept dialling his number. 'No reply,' he finally said.

I left the Chief Secretary's house. Nobody could trace the Home Minister. It was now 8 a.m., and not a volunteer had reached the venue to put up flags and buntings. The roads were deserted, all transport had stopped and Shillong looked like a ghost town. I returned to the guest house where, thankfully, a few office bearers and Youth Congress boys had arrived. 'We have to cancel the function!' they clamoured. 'People will not come. Even Congress workers and supporters are afraid to break a KSU-imposed people's curfew. Besides, buses are not being allowed to enter Shillong, the police and the administration refuse to cooperate, even the Home Minister is missing! What can we do?'

I had to do some quick thinking. I noticed that the campaign jeeps and vans were parked in the compound. I told the IYC boys to pull out all the flags from the vehicles and take them across the city, announcing that negotiations with the KSU at the highest level had succeeded, the curfew was lifted, and everyone was invited to participate in the rally to welcome Rajiv Gandhi.

The strategy worked. Streams of people appeared on the roads as IYC boys carried flags and shouted slogans. By 10 a.m., the police had taken their positions. Soon, buses started coming in with Congress workers from surrounding villages. Then the leaders appeared in their white, ironed khadi outfits, each wanting to know how the KSU had been handled. Since no one knew who had 'negotiated' the settlement, the KSU leaders began suspecting one another, and there was disarray within the union.

By the time the helicopter landed, the stadium was teeming with people and the dais was packed with leaders, including the Home Minister, who had appeared out of nowhere! Pilot and Sangma were shocked to see the turnout, since police reports had told them that Shillong was under curfew. When I told them what had transpired, they could not believe their ears. Everyone congratulated me. Kyndiah, seated next to me, acknowledged, 'Yes, it is really a big turnout.'

'Yes, despite you, Mr Kyndiah,' I responded, grinding my teeth.

I was proud of my achievement. I had singlehandedly beaten the KSU, the administration and the opposition parties. As for the Home Minister, he soon lost his job. My relationship with Kyndiah should have ended right there, but fortunately, despite a host of petty differences with him in the early years, we became good friends. In fact, Kyndiah came to jokingly refer to me as his 'girlfriend'.

In February 1993, P.R. Kyndiah became Governor of Mizoram—a post he would hold until January 1998. As for P.A. Sangma, he became the Chief Minister of Meghalaya in 1988—a post he held till March 1990, while M.M. Jacob became the Governor of Meghalaya in 1995—a post he held for twelve long years.

Chapter 22

THE WHEEL TURNS: A NATIONAL ELECTORAL DEFEAT, A STATE VICTORY AND AFTER

Rajiv Gandhi became Prime Minister riding a popularity-cum-sympathy wave, and did a lot to spur change in the country. But somewhere along the line, he and his team began to stumble—buffeted by conflicting pressures inside and outside the government. Worse, those closest to him began to pull the rug from under his feet.

Arun Nehru and Arun Singh were his friends and advisors—the former a close relation who quit his job as a private sector executive, at Indiraji's behest, to come to Parliament from Rae Bareli in Uttar Pradesh; the latter, a Doon School and Cambridge friend who, like Arun Nehru, quit his job to become a politician. Both became Ministers and Rajiv had implicit trust in them.

But each of these relationships began to sour halfway through his term. We heard rumours that Arun Nehru, the all-powerful Internal Security Minister who reported directly to the Prime Minister, had begun to drift away. Then, in April 1986, when Arun Nehru was in Kashmir recovering from a heart attack, there came news that he was stripped of his charge, making him MoS without portfolio. The reason given was the delicate state of his health. Arun Nehru returned to Delhi soon after and is said to have stormed into the Home Secretary's office and then into the Home Minister, Buta Singh's, abusing them in the worst possible language. After this, he resigned. As though this were not bad enough, he left the Congress to begin a strident campaign against the Prime Minister, claiming that huge corruption existed within the government. While he had been party to every decision of the government— from Kashmir and the Golden Temple, to the Czech pistol deal[37] and the

---

[37]A CBI inquiry was instituted into the purchase of 55,000 CZ95 pistols in 1986 from erstwhile Czechoslovakia, and specifically from the firm, Merkuria Foreign Trade Corp; it was alleged that Arun Nehru had entered into a criminal conspiracy, causing loss to the exchequer. While

Bofors gun deal[38]—he now conveniently distanced himself from everything.

When the Indian government signed the US$1.4 billion arms contract with the Swedish company, AB Bofors, in March 1986, competitors who had lost out began a campaign of slander. In April 1987, Swedish Radio claimed in a broadcast that Bofors had offered kickbacks to top Indian politicians and key defence officials to clinch the deal. Soon after, the Prime Minister made a statement in the Lok Sabha clarifying that no middlemen were involved in the deal, nor were there any 'kickbacks'. Later, he was to make a statement in the Rajya Sabha in response to a discussion on the subject. At lunch time, I sent him a note asking him not to personally intervene and let the Defence Ministry handle the matter. But he insisted, 'I have to clear my name and that of my family. I must go on record on the issue!'

Arun Singh, who was MoS Defence, should have stood up to defend the Prime Minister. But after a statement denying the receipt of commissions, he chose to remain silent. Even as the controversy raged, I bumped into him in the PMO. We both had appointments with the Prime Minister. Arun Singh went in first, while I sat sipping coffee with George. I waited for an hour-and-a-half, but Arun remained inside. I shrugged my shoulders and looked at George with an enquiring glance. He smiled and shrugged his shoulders in reply. Sensing another crisis coming, I left. And the crisis did come. Arun Singh resigned from the government in July 1987 and left for the hills of Almora. While he asserted that he had resigned for undisclosed personal reasons, the damage was done. The news devastated all of us.

The Bofors controversy snowballed, compelling the government in August 1987 to agree to a JPC inquiry into the entire issue. B. Shankaranand, a Congress politician from Karnataka, went on to become its Chairman.

Despite a formal inquiry being underway, the opposition campaign went on relentlessly. Journalist Chitra Subramaniam, on her part, kept feeding stories and interviews from so called 'investigating agencies' in Sweden and

---

the CBI's closure report contended that nothing incriminating could be found against Arun Nehru, the Trial Court rejected the CBI's closure report. Finally, in 2013, the Supreme Court stayed, till further order, the proceedings pending in the Trial Court. See 'SC Stays Trial in Rajiv-era Czech Pistol Purchase Scam', *The Times of India*, 23 March 2013.

[38]In a bid to replace old field guns and artillery, the Indian government decided to go ahead with the induction of bigger calibre 155 mm howitzers, and signed a deal in 1986 with the Swedish metals and armaments major, AB Bofors. *The Independent* of Bombay published documents that clearly pointed to Arun Nehru's role as a prime negotiator in the gun deal. See Prabhu Chawla, 'New Suspicions', *India Today*, 30 September 1990.

Switzerland that claimed that there had been pay-offs—indirectly targeting the Prime Minister.

Distraught, I once asked Rajivji what the facts really were. 'Why are they going on like this? Who got the commissions? Why don't we expose them?'

'Margaret, I tell you the truth,' he said. 'Neither any member of my family nor I has received a pie from this deal.'

I believed him.

Most people held that V.P. Singh, who had been shifted from the Finance to the Defence Ministry, and then dropped, had instigated the Bofors charges with selective leaks. He resigned from the Congress and Parliament to form the Jan Morcha party in October 1987, which Arun Nehru joined. Singh became the focal point of an anti-Rajiv campaign, fighting and winning a by-election from Allahabad in 1988 with support from opposition parties.

The JPC, in the meantime, gave a clean chit to Rajivji and his family in its report submitted in July 1989. Furthermore, while the Swedish police kept coming out with selective leaks, no one could furnish any substantial proof. The death of Swedish Prime Minister Olof Palme—who allegedly had been involved with the arms agreement—made it even more difficult to establish anything conclusively.[39] The government on its part denied every charge most vehemently.

Despite the obvious absence of any concrete evidence, Singh kept making statements such as, 'I have all the names and details in my pocket diary! Defeat this government and I will produce the facts.' To add to the clamour, the opposition coined the slogan, '*Galli galli mein shor hai, Rajiv Gandhi chor hai!*' ('The streets echo that Rajiv Gandhi is a thief.') Rajivji was deeply hurt when he heard this refrain, for his image of a clean young leader was getting tarnished.

He wasn't wrong. Public perception changed drastically—a shift fuelled by unremitting speculative discussions about the so-called kickbacks, and an opposition campaign that aimed to keep the issue alive for the 1989 elections. The situation was reminiscent of the pre-Emergency period of the 1970s, when a united opposition had accused his mother and brother of corruption.

---

[39]Several governments have come and gone since then, but not one of them has been able to link Rajiv Gandhi directly to the kickbacks. Ottavio Quattrocchi, the Italian businessman, known to be close to the family, was presumed to be the link in the deal, but even he is dead now.

To stem the tide, the Prime Minister campaigned endlessly, addressing over 170 rallies and meetings, driving himself to the point of exhaustion. I was with him in some constituencies of Karnataka—where Assembly elections were also on. Whenever possible, I'd prepare hot food at home and take it in the car so he could eat as we drove. The first time I served this to him, he commented, 'This is the first hot meal I've had in this entire leg of the campaign!'

Everywhere he went, he was very well received. In spite of the opposition's smear campaign, the crowds remained responsive. We hoped that this would bring us the votes we needed.

But it was a tough battle. After launching the Jan Morcha, Singh, in October 1988, formed the Janata Dal—merging a part of the old Janata Party, two factions of the Lok Dal and his own Jan Morcha. The Janata Dal in turn joined forces with three regional parties—the Telugu Desam of Andhra Pradesh, the DMK of Tamil Nadu and Asom Gana Parishad of Assam—and the Congress (S), to form the National Front. Together, they made Bofors the main election issue. Besides, the sacking of the Foreign Secretary, A.P. Venkateswaran, at a press conference;[40] the open conflict with the President;[41] the failed attempt to control the press through legislation;[42] and operation Brasstacks on the Indo-Pak border[43] were cited as proof of

---

[40]Venkateswaran made a public statement that the IPKF operations in Sri Lanka were a mistake. Weeks later, when a journalist asked the Prime Minister about Venkateswaran's announcement of his impending visit to Pakistan for the SAARC Summit, he famously said, 'Soon, you will be talking to a new Foreign Secretary.' Venkateswaran immediately resigned.

[41]The President was allegedly peeved that the Prime Minister had not called on him to brief him about foreign visits, while the Prime Minister held him responsible for the Punjab problem. The rift between them became public knowledge, doing damage to the position of both the President and the Prime Minister.

[42]When the press was pursuing the Bofors 'scandal', the Prime Minister was concerned that journalists were, in his words, 'trying to stage a coup against the elected government of the country'. To contain the spread of misinformation, he tried passing the Indian Postal (Amendment) Bill, 1988, which would give powers to the Central and state governments to intercept, detain or dispose of postal articles. President Giani Zail Singh refused to sign the bill. The government also tried passing the Press Regulation Bill, which would have allowed the Registrar of newspapers to collect information from the press; this, too, did not see the light of day.

[43]Operation Brasstacks was the code name of a major military exercise of the Indian Army in Rajasthan that took place between 1986 and 1987. The magnitude of the exercise put Pakistan on the defensive—worried as it was that India, by displaying its prowess, was planning to invade the country.

the Prime Minister's 'immaturity'.

It didn't help that the Congress made a few strategic blunders, too. Already, the Shah Bano judgement reversal through legislation and the banning of renowned author Salman Rushdie's *Satanic Verses* had damaged the party's secular credentials. But when the Prime Minister launched his election campaign from the disputed site of the Ram temple in Ayodhya, and promised 'Ram Rajya' to the nation if elected back to power, all secular forces were shocked. The Congress' fate was sealed. We lost the election—though we emerged as the single largest party with 197 seats.[44]

There were two decisions taken by Rajivji after the defeat which highlighted his statesmanship. When the Congress emerged as the single largest party, he was invited by the President, R. Venkataraman (who had succeeded Zail Singh), to form the government. But he declined. 'The people have voted us out. We will play the role of a responsible opposition,' he stated, thus allowing V.P. Singh, with only 143 MPs of the Janata Dal, to become the seventh Prime Minister of India on 2 December 1989. This minority government received outside support of the BJP (85 seats) and the Communists (45 seats).[45] I believe this was a mistake.

When the outgoing Cabinet received an invitation for the swearing-in ceremony, a few senior former Ministers reached 7, Race Course Road, to proudly announce that instead of watching the 'traitor' being sworn in, they had come to be with Rajivji, who smiled and calmly told them that he was attending the swearing-in ceremony of the Prime Minister of India—this was his duty. The former Ministers were stunned and quietly followed him to the ceremony.

Yet, in return, one of the first actions of the new government was to withdraw Rajivji's SPG (special protection group) security, despite being entirely aware of the threat to him and his family.

Soon after the defeat, all of us had to look for alternative houses. Rajivji chose 10, Janpath—the house that Lal Bahadur Shastri had lived in as Prime Minister. It has two entrances—one from Janpath, and the other opening into the AICC through a side lane from Akbar Road. There was a huge elephant's grave outside the gate leading to the AICC, which many

---

[44]*Statistical Report on General Elections, 1989*, in <http://eci.nic.in/eci_main/statisticalreports/LS_1989/Vol_I_LS_89.pdf>, accessed on 9 November 2015.
[45]*Ibid.*

felt was inauspicious. But he laughed at these suggestions and ignored these superstitious concerns. I remember the last days of the shifting, when Rajivji was sorting out papers and carrying boxes to his car himself, helped only by George and a couple of attendants. Dressed in blue jeans and a T-shirt, he seemed to enjoy what he was doing, just like any other householder shifting home.

After the defeat, the crowds that came to the gates to meet him multiplied. People travelled from near and far, and waited despite the winter cold. There was an outpouring of sympathy and also a growing fear of harassment by the new regime, especially in North India. The people, most of whom were Congress workers, needed a patient hearing.

One morning in December, while coming out of a meeting, I saw the security staff push the crowds away rather harshly. Many of those gathered recognized me and called out for help. I stopped to listen. They were agitated and angry. 'We have not come for favours,' they yelled. 'We are here to tell Rajivji that we are with him and will make him the Prime Minister again. His security staff defeated him by keeping him away from his people, his workers. Send these men away! Open the gates and let us meet him!' I promised to convey their anguish and urged the security personnel to be more understanding.

On reaching home, I phoned Rajivji and narrated what I had heard and seen. 'Do not lecture me!' he said. 'If you feel so concerned, come and manage the darshans in the mornings!'

I accepted the challenge and started work the very next day. People would queue up for a security check from 7.30 a.m.—men and women in separate lines. Once in, I got them to arrange themselves state-wise on the dhurries on the lawns. The Seva Dal volunteers ensured orderliness. For an hour each morning, between 8.30 and 9.30 a.m., Rajivji would go from group to group, posing for photographs, receiving requests (which would be passed on to me). Between 9.30 and 10 a.m., party leaders would meet him separately.

I carried on with this work for over a year—arranging people into manageable groups; sorting petitions; getting these acknowledged; and ensuring that requests were followed up—till an old hand at the AICC decided to ask two other people to assist. Tired of their interference, I quietly withdrew.

◆

While we were preparing for the elections in Karnataka, which (as mentioned earlier) had been clubbed with the 1989 national polls, there were serious divisions among the state's leaders. Unable to finalize the candidate list, the entire Election Committee came to Delhi to meet Ghulam Nabi Azad, the General Secretary in charge of Karnataka. Even after several meetings, the leaders failed to arrive at a consensus. They were finally summoned to Azad's residence like school kids and warned that if they did not produce a list, the High Command would have to do it! *'Ye Karnatak ke natak ko hum khatam karenge!'* ('We will end Karnataka's tantrums!') is what Azad is supposed to have said.

Humiliated and angry, many Karnataka leaders drove to my house. I calmed them down and then got talking. I told them that the fault was ours as we had failed to sit together and choose our candidates. At my suggestion, ten of us—including leaders like K.H. Patil, B. Basavalingappa, S. Bangarappa, K.S. Nagarathnamma, as well as the heads of frontal organizations—arranged ourselves around my large dining table. I chaired the discussion, and, to everyone's surprise, we proceeded with the decision-making process without a problem. Many names emerged by consensus, and where differences arose, we put down panels. By 9 p.m. we had completed half the list. As news of this exercise spread, more and more leaders began to arrive. Post-dinner, we completed the first round—the core group now expanding to fifteen members—and met again the next day to put final touches to the list.

A few notable leaders were missing—among them Jaffer Sharief, Veerappa Moily, S.M. Krishna and Veerendra Patil. I believe they complained to Azad that an unauthorized exercise was going on at my residence. Azad rang me up. I told him we were preparing our list for the consideration of the Election Committee, and if fifteen of twenty-one members were ready to submit a unanimous list, why should anyone object?

Consequently, our list, signed by fifteen members, went to Rajivji (as Congress President), with my covering letter. The Election Committee met thereafter, added names to this list and sent it to the Central Election Committee. When I visited 7, Race Course Road, I found the final list as approved by the Central Election Committee being typed and noticed that two of my closest supporters (both SCs) had been replaced. I was furious, particularly when I learnt that false charges had been made against them. A very angry Sharief is said to have complained about us. But I could do nothing.

With this list, I was asked to accompany Veerendra Patil by chartered plane that night. Patil was dropped at Hyderabad and I proceeded to Bangalore to release the names. Of the 140 names we had submitted to the Central Election Committee, 110 had been approved.

In the fortnight that followed, I toured Karnataka extensively, covering a large number of constituencies with Nage Gowda—a powerful leader from Mandya and a great organizer—and a few other leaders. Thanks to the efforts of everyone involved, the Congress returned with a massive majority in the Assembly, winning 178 seats out of 224.[46] We had lost at the Centre, but we had done well in this Southern state. Veerendra Patil became the Chief Minister. Ironically, the night we had made a tentative list, all the leaders sitting round my dining table were committed to making me the Chief Minister; when the results were announced, many of them were in the running themselves!

When the Ministers were to be announced, the Chief Minister refused to have Bangarappa in the Cabinet. On learning of this, Bangarappa and Shivamurthy—a leader from Chitradurga and a Bangarappa protégé—rushed to my house for help. I went to Rajivji, who said he could do little to help since the Chief Minister was adamant that Bangarappa was to be kept out.

'Shall I go and request Patil?' I asked.

'If you think you can manage Patil better than me, try it!' he said, curtly.

So I drove to Karnataka Bhavan. The Chief Minister was reading his newspapers. He returned my 'Good morning' greeting without looking up. Hesitantly, I told him I had come to seek a ministerial berth for Bangarappa. At first, Patil refused to reconsider his decision, but after some pleading, said, 'Rajivji has to decide.'

'If Rajivji includes Bangarappa, will you accept the decision?' I asked.

The Chief Minister hesitated, then said, 'Bangarappa only wrecks governments and parties! I cannot trust him.'

'It will be safer to have him in, where you can control him, sir, rather than leave him out, disgruntled,' I replied.

Patil seemed to agree. 'Okay, I will discuss this again with Rajivji before I leave this evening,' he said.

I went back to Rajivji and told him what had transpired.

He was amused. 'How do you manage these old men?' he asked.

---

[46]See Parvathi Menon, 'Silent Shift', *Frontline*, Volume 16, Issue 22, 5 November 1999.

I only smiled.

Patil's final list had Bangarappa's name, but his portfolio was Horticulture! Bangarappa was back again at my door, pleading, 'This is humiliating; please do something!' On my intervention, 'Horticulture' was changed to 'Agriculture' when Rajivji signed the list. That is how Bangarappa's prestige was restored.

A few days later, Bangarappa welcomed me to his new ministerial bungalow in Bangalore with flowers and sweets. He said, 'You looked after me in Delhi; I will look after you in Karnataka!' Soon after, he got Shivamurthy to organize a massive Banjara Conference in Davangere with me as chief guest. He praised me to the skies. But the promises and accolades were only temporary, as subsequent developments showed.

In October 1990, even as severe communal riots rocked areas between Bangalore and Mysore, the Chief Minister suffered a stroke. No one was told of the illness. Rajivji flew to Bangalore to take stock of the situation. A meeting was held at Kumara Krupa to plan his visit to the affected areas the next day. Veerappa Moily was asked to take charge of the arrangements—organizing a helicopter, coordinating local security, etc. But the next morning, Rajivji drove there, fuming, as the helicopter had not been fuelled. This was seen as a deliberate ploy to scuttle the visit and avoid getting government inaction exposed by the victims. Not surprisingly, after a harrowing day—which saw us listening to victims, promising them financial assistance and arranging security—we were all at the receiving end.

After this rather gruelling schedule, we went to see the indisposed Chief Minister. Rajivji was shocked when he saw Patil's condition—partially paralyzed by a stroke. No one had informed him. This infuriated him further. He told Patil's family that the Chief Minister needed immediate medical attention and could not possibly continue with his taxing job. He asked them to decide where they would like to shift him for treatment and promised help.

On the way back, Rajivji said that Karnataka confronted a crisis which had to be sorted out immediately. On reaching the guest house, he called me inside and said, 'What do we do ? Who can succeed Veerendra Patil?'

'Think about matters for a day or two. After all, changing a senior leader because he is ill may not be perceived kindly by the public,' I cautioned.

Soon after, K.H. Patil (a senior Minister) and I drove with him to the airport. 'Stay back and keep me informed about developments,' I was told.

Then he casually turned to K.H. Patil and said, 'Put the MLAs together!' I was confused about this comment, but an exuberant K.H. Patil construed the statement to mean that he would be Chief Minister. He was excited as we drove back!

The next morning, statements reached the press; rumours spread; pressure groups promptly got working. Then came the announcement that two observers from Delhi were to arrive. A Congress Legislature Party meeting was called. There was praise for the work that the Chief Minister had done, and good wishes for his health. Then an unexpected announcement was made. The Congress had nominated Bangarappa as Chief Minister! There was disbelief all around. I thought K.H. Patil would have a stroke, as his face turned a deep red! Clearly, he felt cheated, more so as his supporters had assembled to felicitate him. The majority of the MLAs, both from the Veerendra Patil and K.H. Patil camps, were unhappy as Bangarappa, besides being arrogant, was a maverick who had changed or split parties several times!

Why Bangarappa was selected over everyone else was a mystery—though, to me, it was obvious that his 'backward class' tag was being showcased to counter V.P. Singh's espousal of the Mandal Commission report.[47]

Unfortunately, once he came to power, Bangarappa got involved in a series of controversies. Charges of corruption and nepotism began mounting, even as his arrogance ballooned—he had made Shivamurthy his Revenue Minister, but sacked him in no time! Then came a computer deal, which his loyal Chief Secretary, J. Alexander, got approved, without listing the matter in the Cabinet agenda. This landed both of them in trouble and they had to face a CBI inquiry later.[48] Karnataka was plunged into a wave of dissidence.

◆

---

[47]On 1 January 1979, the Morarji Desai government chose Bindeshwari Prasad Mandal, a former Chief Minister of Bihar, to head the Second Backward Class Commission. Mandal submitted his report two years later, but by then, the Morarji Desai government had fallen. On 7 August 1990, V.P. Singh, in a bid to gather the support of the backward classes and emerge as a champion for social justice, announced in Parliament that his government had accepted the Mandal Commission Report, which recommended 27 per cent reservation for OBC candidates across Central government jobs.

[48]In 1994, the CBI charge-sheeted Bangarappa and others on the grounds that the accused had entered into a 'criminal conspiracy' to cause a loss to the state government by purchasing 100 Apple Macintosh computers from Classik Computers at high rates—a case that is now referred to as the 'Classik Computer' scam.

From the outset, trouble began brewing for Prime Minister V.P. Singh. Chandra Shekhar—who had walked from Kanyakumari to Delhi, addressing meetings and creating a niche for himself as an all-India leader—had walked out in protest when V.P. Singh was selected Prime Minister.

Then there was trouble from the BJP—which, from 2 Lok Sabha seats in 1984, had secured 85 seats in 1989, thanks to its strident Ayodhya campaign and calls for building a Ram temple. When V.P. Singh came to power, the BJP, in a bid to further cash in on Hindu sentiment, decided to organize a 'rath yatra' (a chariot procession) from Somnath in Gujarat to the Babri Masjid in Ayodhya, with L.K. Advani (the BJP President) and Pramod Mahajan (a key aide) leading the brigade. The plan was to force the government to hand over the disputed site at Ayodhya to Hindutva forces, demolish the mosque that was there and lay the foundation stone (shilanyas) for the construction of the Ram temple on 30 October 1990. As expected, there was a communal backlash. Riots broke out in Gujarat, Karnataka, Uttar Pradesh and Andhra Pradesh. The rath yatra turned into a 'rakt yatra' ('a trip of blood'). In light of the law and order situation, the then Chief Minister of Bihar, Lalu Prasad Yadav, arrested Advani in Samastipur on 23 October, before he could reach the disputed site at Ayodhya. Advani—who had already threatened to revoke his party's support to the V.P. Singh government if his campaign was stalled—now withdrew BJP support. V.P. Singh, in an attempt to present a brave façade, proudly claimed to be a believer in a secular India—an ideal for which he was prepared to sacrifice power.

To further complicate matters, V.P. Singh's decision to implement the recommendations of the Mandal Commission led to widespread protests by the upper castes. In many universities, the protests turned violent. V.P. Singh, who had hoped to position himself as a champion of the OBCs and secular forces, now found himself losing support everywhere.

On 7 November 1990, the eleven-month-old government of V. P. Singh collapsed after losing a confidence vote by a wide margin. Chandra Shekhar, thus far seething with resentment, seized the opportunity. He left the Janata Dal with several of his supporters to form the Janata Dal (Socialist). He won a Confidence Motion with the support of his 64 MPs, and the outside support of the Congress' 197 MPs, along with a few others. He was sworn in as Prime Minister on 10 November 1990. It was a quirk of fate—that the man who had challenged Indiraji during the pre-Emergency years, only to be jailed by her, became Prime Minister a decade later with the support of her son!

Expectedly, the Janata Dal (S)–Congress relationship was uneasy. Rajivji, as Leader of the Opposition, dictated terms which the Prime Minister was less than happy with. The final straw was the posting of two Haryana policemen at 10, Janpath—construed as an attempt to spy on Rajivji's activities. The Congress decided to boycott Parliament in retaliation. Unable to face these pressures from the outside, and with the Congress' withdrawal of support, Chandra Shekhar resigned on 6 March 1991. He remained in office as a caretaker until fresh elections could be held in May and June that year.

Chapter 23

AN ICON DIES:
THE END OF THE RAJIV GANDHI ERA

In 1991, the elections were upon us again! They were to be held in three phases—on 20 May, 12 June and 15 June 1991. My third term in the Rajya Sabha was to end in 1992, and the convention was that the party did not offer more than three consecutive terms in the House. I was therefore keen to contest the Lok Sabha elections, and asked for the seat from Karwar—in Uttara Kannada (also spelt as Canara) in Karnataka. My father-in-law had represented it for three terms, I had been working there since I was married, and after 1974, I had adopted the region as my own. I knew I had the support of the local leaders, with whom I had worked during every election.

When the Lok Sabha seats for Karnataka were being discussed, I was called for the meeting and asked for my views on many of them. But Karwar wasn't mentioned. At the end of the meeting, I was asked to leave, as a decision had to be made regarding Karwar. I sat with George in the anteroom. Dinesh Singh, the MP from Pratapgarh, Uttar Pradesh, came out halfway through and whispered to me, 'Rajivji is inclined to give Karwar to you. Meet him separately.' The meeting ended. Bangarappa emerged, and without a hint of regret on his face, said, 'Sorry madam, I could not help you!'

I was livid. 'Why?' I asked. 'Have you forgotten all your promises? And so soon?'

'It is not possible,' was Bangarappa's brusque reply.

I burst out in anger, 'Now expect a battle! I will fight you to the finish.' And this I did.

As I sat waiting for a decision to be taken, there were repeated calls to George from Sheila Dikshit, whose seat had not yet been announced. 'I have to catch the train tonight, please tell Rajivji I am waiting,' she said. George suggested I send a slip in, which I did. 'She can continue waiting,' was Rajivji's reply on the slip. I left it to George to convey the message and went home in tears.

I went to 10, Janpath, early the next morning and was called in immediately. P. Chidambaram, the Congress MP from Sivaganga, Tamil Nadu, was about to leave. Rajivji kept him back. I could not contain my dismay. I asked, tears streaming down my cheeks, 'You consulted me regarding all the Lok Sabha seats, but when it came to a seat for me, you let me down. Why?'

'You are being most unfair,' Rajivji said, and passed me the paper napkins he always kept in his drawer. Then he added, 'First, stop crying. And now, let me tell you, your Chief Minister would not agree when I suggested keeping Karwar for you. I could have forced him to reconsider, but I did not. I do not trust the man; he will defeat you and finish your career. I will bring you back to the Rajya Sabha next year. So why are you worried?'

Then, turning to Chidambaram, he said, 'Look how weak and miserable she looks! She is just out of surgery. Can she fight a hostile Chief Minister and win?'

Chidambaram agreed with him. So I lost out.

I was then appointed Joint Spokesperson for the campaign with Pranab Mukherjee. He also put me in charge of his campaign tours, with Jairam Ramesh to assist me—which had to be frozen in consultation with the Election Management Committee, which included P.V. Narasimha Rao, R.K. Dhawan and M.L. Fotedar.

Finalizing his itineraries was never easy, since there were contesting demands for his meetings. We did our best to include every legitimate request, but there were limitations to our capacity to monitor arrangements and check on crowds. I recall pulling up Murli Deora for taking Rajivji around Bombay in an open jeep until 5 a.m. When the question of his campaign in South India was discussed, we advised him to limit his meetings, as the Congress was well-positioned; at other times, we recommended specific constituencies.

On one occasion, Rajivji was scheduled to visit Mohsina Kidwai's constituency in Uttar Pradesh, where a huge crowd was waiting. For some strange reason, he overflew the venue. Mohsinaji was desperate, and asked that he halt in her constituency after his two other meetings in the state. I conveyed the request, but, for reasons I was not privy to, he did not go. I had to face the flak, as Mohsinaji accused me of misguiding Rajivji and messing up the programme!

This was just one of several occasions in 1991 when I was in the eye of a storm. But I had no time to pause and ponder, since there were press notes to be prepared, press briefings to be done and dinners for select journalists to be organized—planned by me but hosted by senior leaders.

I recall two such dinners. One was at the residence of P.V. Narasimha Rao, who readily agreed to play host, provided no non-vegetarian food was served inside the house. So we arranged the dinner on the lawns. Everything was beautifully set, when suddenly, an hour before the guests were to arrive, there was a dust storm and arrangements went for a toss. We were compelled to shift inside, non-vegetarian food, et al. The host was visibly upset but philosophically muttered, 'What cannot be cured must be endured.' While Rao's Brahmin household had been polluted, the journalists had no reason to complain; they enjoyed the food.

The second memorable dinner was hosted at my home at 23, Ashoka Road. Rajivji attended and was in great form, mingling with journalists and party leaders of the Campaign Committee. This was his last interaction with the Delhi press.

◆

1991 was a do-or-die battle for everyone. Rajivji toured endlessly by helicopters, small planes and cars in the scorching heat of summer. His itinerary was packed with meetings from morn to night. He would return late at night, dusty, tanned and tired; his hands swollen, even bleeding; his arms scratched by the enthusiastic crowds pulling at him. He would sometimes come back, extremely worked up—either because the meetings had been small and at short-notice, for which the candidates blamed us; or because the required material had not reached the venue, or speakers hadn't been dispatched!

Once, while showing us his inflamed fingers, he said he had taken out his wedding ring and given it to Sonia for safekeeping. As for Soniaji, she was in Amethi with their daughter, Priyanka, looking after his constituency. Whenever they had an opportunity, they came to spend time with him during his halts in Delhi.

On the road, Rajivji would send countless messages, asking for particular leaders to be dispatched to precise areas that confronted problems—be it to Mysore, where Congress candidate Chandraprabha Urs kept threatening to withdraw if refused more money and speakers; or to Mangalore, where the temple towns of Udupi and Dharmasthala were seething after a visit by senior Congress leader Janardhan Poojary. To deal with the Mysore imbroglio, I was told to go, while asking for Rao to be sent to pacify the religious heads. I conveyed the message but received an unexpected response: 'I am too old and tired to run about like Rajiv!' And that's where matters stood.

There is a hilarious incident involving his campaign in Karnataka. He was to address a meeting in Belgaum (the constituency of Congress leader B. Shankaranand) at the local stadium. He was flying in by helicopter, accompanied by Suman Dubey, his friend. But the helicopter, caught in bad weather, had to land in a field outside the city! Rajivji walked to the highway to find local transport to get to town. He hailed speeding vehicles— one of which stopped and agreed to drive him to his destination. Rajivji sat in the front seat beside the driver, while the family sat behind. After a while, the driver, a doctor, suspected that the man next to him was, in fact, a well-known figure. Nervously, he asked him, 'Are you, by any chance, Rajiv Gandhi?' When Rajiv answered in the affirmative, he went on to ask, 'What exactly are you doing here alone and without a vehicle?' The family was shocked to hear his story and brought him safely to the guest house, where we—unaware of what had happened—were getting ready to proceed to the stadium to receive him. Due to heavy rain, there was no crowd in the stadium. Sportingly, Rajivji decided to spend time at the Mahatma Gandhi Medical College hostel, meeting students over tea.

I had flown alone to Belgaum from Bangalore in the small aircraft which was to take Rajivji to his next meetings. The small plane, caught in a storm, rattled and sent cans of Coca Cola (which he loved) flying all around me. I clung to my seat, praying desperately, but preparing for the worst. Luckily we survived and landed at the Belgaum airport. We flew to Bidar that evening for a massive meeting.

After the meeting, we moved towards the aircraft to get to Hyderabad for a late night meeting and a halt. The security men got in while I stood at the foot of the steps. Rajivji turned around and asked, 'Why are you there? Are you not coming along?'

'There is no seat for me, I am told,' I replied.

'Nonsense, get in!' he said and got one of his security men to alight to make room for me.

Hyderabad was a madhouse—milling crowds and no security—with Rajivji deciding to walk through narrow streets to the house of P. Shiv Shankar, a former Minister, to see his son who had met with an accident that day. We formed a ring around him to keep the crowds at bay. After the visit and a public meeting, we came to the guest house for a briefing meeting with the local leaders. The next day, Rajivji carried on with his tour while I took the morning flight back to Delhi.

On the night of 19 May, he returned to Delhi. On the morning of 20 May, he voted with Sonia and Priyanka before flying out to Uttar Pradesh. In the evening he was to change from the helicopter to his plane and proceed to Orissa. We received a message that we were to meet him at the airport. But, suddenly, he changed his plans and returned home. I was asked to meet him at 10, Janpath.

When I arrived, he asked George why he had called me. George produced a handwritten sheet of paper with Rajivji's programme for Tamil Nadu, which Rajivji himself had prepared and signed. It mentioned five constituencies—those of Mani Shankar Aiyar (Mayiladuthurai), Maragatham Chandrasekar (Sriperumbudur), PCC President V.K. Ramamurthy (Krishnagiri) and P. Chidambaram (Sivaganga), ending with a joint rally with Jayalalithaa at Hosur on 22 May. Hosur was to be the last programme of the campaign.

I asked him why he was going to so many meetings in a state we were in any case winning—Jayalalithaa was a strong partner, and in alliance with us.

'If I do not campaign there, she will say she won the state for us. I must go!' he replied, adding, 'Do not get bullied by anyone, especially by my security. Do what I have told you. Finalize and announce this programme. And go to Mysore—that woman (Chandraprabha Urs) is driving me nuts! And meet me in Bangalore. The plane will come there for me, and we will fly back to Delhi.'

It was a long list of instructions, and I was ordered to follow every one of them.

Rajivji left for Orissa the next morning. I saw him off and then flew to Bangalore to make the trip to Mysore and join him on the trip back to Delhi on 22 May.

On the night of 21 May, I was with my mother in her sitting room, when a constable came to the window with a message for me.

'Saab is gone,' he said in Kannada.

I jumped up, thinking it was Niru. 'Where? What happened?' I demanded.

'A bomb blast at the meeting near Madras,' he replied.

Now I was confused. 'Which "saab"?' I demanded, my voice trembling. 'Rajiv Gandhi!'

'Where is he now?' I asked, still confused, still shocked.

'He died, ma!' he replied through the window.

My head spun, my heart began pounding, as I slumped into my mother's arms and wept like a child. My mother forced a cup of milk down my throat as I fell asleep. I woke up past midnight to answer phone calls from home and elsewhere; everyone expressed disbelief and grief. Niru and Manira had received the news from Padma Alva in the Press Trust of India, and were among the first to reach 10, Janpath. At that point, there was no confirmation of his death—only garbled messages. Then Niru and Manira called me, and confirmed the tragedy.

I do not know how anything was arranged for me, but I was on the first flight to Delhi on the morning of 22 May. My world had suddenly collapsed. The person I had worked so closely with was gone. The nation stood still—friends and foes shaken.

Priyanka and Sonia flew back with Rajivji's body. He lay at the same place his mother had, seven years earlier, at Teen Murti House. Manira and I sat there together through the night of 22 May, and I continued to hold vigil for the days and nights that followed. I could hardly believe it—his handsome, smiling face, and his entire body were bandaged in white; there was nothing to see. Sitting there, I recalled how often Rajivji had shown implicit faith in me, and had granted me the opportunity to prove my worth. We differed at times, but he respected my opinion and accepted my advice. With his passing away, I felt like a political orphan—tossed about in turbulent waters, with an uncertain future. I was heartbroken.

As I sat there, I also recalled the many times I had warned Rajivji about the risks he was taking—I reminded him about the failed attempts on his life at Rajghat[49] and in Colombo—but each time, he brushed away

---

[49]Karamjit Singh from Punjab attempted to assassinate Rajiv Gandhi on 2 October 1986, when the latter went to offer prayers at Rajghat on the Mahatma's birth anniversary. Singh fired three shots, but fortunately, the bullets were out of range.

my fears, and proceeded to join the waiting crowds, or drive off in open jeeps to shake hands with his people. 'You have to be right a hundred times out of a hundred; they need to be right only once,' I used to tell him. 'You are paranoid; I have to reach out to the public,' was his reply.

I wasn't the only one who had warned him. A young Rahul, too, is said to have railed against his father's poor security during a visit from the UK that March. The Congress, on its part, kept petitioning the government for better arrangements. With SPG cover withdrawn by V.P. Singh, the journalist, Mark Tully, had warned Rajivji about the danger he was putting himself in by campaigning non-stop. To that, Rajivji's characteristic reply was, 'All these years, you people wrote about us having too much security. And now you complain that we have too little!' Why Chandra Shekhar as Prime Minister, in government with our support, did not restore his SPG cover, is something I still do not understand.

Early on 23 May, Rahul arrived with Priyanka (who received him at the airport) and went into a room with their mother. Then they sat with close family and friends in silence, as the clock ticked and leaders from across the world walked past to pay homage. 'Why did this have to happen to him?' is what everyone asked. There were no answers, only silent tears.

On 24 May, the cremation took place at Vir Bhoomi, close to where his mother had been cremated at Shakti Sthal. It was my wedding anniversary. I recalled that only two years earlier, Rajivji had spent a couple of hours with us, while we were celebrating our silver jubilee. I watched as Rahul, Priyanka and Sonia performed the final ceremonies together. At Indiraji's funeral, Rahul had clung to his father for support and solace; today, he was the pillar supporting his mother and sister. As the flames rose against the evening sky, there were loud sobs. The son, who had risen from his mother's ashes to lead the party and the nation, was gone. Only memories stayed.

There was a terrible thunderstorm that night, unusual for May. It seemed that nature had joined the nation in mourning. Later, the ashes collected in urns were kept at Teen Murti House and handed over to state leaders to immerse in regional rivers. Three urns were to go to the Triveni Sangam in Allahabad for the main immersion ceremonies.

I was among those who made the trip to Allahabad by train. There were crowds all along the route, attempting to catch a last glimpse of what remained of their leader; flower petals rained on the coaches, and there were unending shouts of '*Rajiv Gandhi amar rahe!*' ('May Rajiv Gandhi remain immortal!') After a halt at the historic Anand Bhavan, for prayers and for a last public viewing, we boarded three launches—one for the family, and two others for the team that accompanied them. We watched as Sonia and the children gradually emptied the contents of the urns, to be carried away in the swirling currents of the Ganga.

On our way back, Madhavrao Scindia, the Congress leader, came to me and asked 'Why did you do that?'

'Do what?' I asked.

'You actually drank the waters of the Sangam! Do you know that it's a most polluted spot carrying every kind of debris? As a Hindu, I would not think of doing it. And you are a Christian—what prompted you to take that decision?'

'I just had an urge,' I said. 'After all, it is said to be a holy spot. When will I make another visit? So I went ahead.'

'You will be lucky if you are alive in the morning!' he cautioned, as we boarded the sleeper coach.

I was taken aback. Sharing the cabin with P.V. saheb and two others, I repeated what Scindia had said in panic. He sagely said, 'Nothing is going to happen to you. Sleep peacefully. You will be fine!'

So, I relaxed, but could not sleep, thinking of the events that had overtaken us.

◆

After the assasination, I attended an unending series of condolence meetings and read postmortem reports of the tragedy. How did it happen? Who was behind it? And why did Rajiv have to make a trip to Tamil Nadu? Many claimed it was part of an international conspiracy, others talked of the LTTE. A few newspapers ran stories about the warnings that had come from the Palestine Liberation Organization Chief, Yasser Arafat, during his visit to Delhi. Apparently, Arafat had cautioned India about plans being hatched to eliminate him during the campaign. Then there were questions regarding his security cover and why it had not been upgraded by the government, despite repeated requests by Congress leaders. There was a lot of noise, but no answers.

Soon the Justice J.S. Verma Commission of Inquiry was set up. Additionally, a Special Investigation Team (SIT) under D.R. Karthikeyan, an Indian Police Service (IPS) officer, was constituted.

Before I could come to terms with the assassination, there began a spate of attacks on me. My loyalty was questioned, the programme covering the five constituencies in Tamil Nadu was criticized, and the choice of venue at Sriperumbudur was condemned. PCC President V.K. Ramamurthy went to the press asking that my role in the events be investigated, while BJP leader, Subramanian Swamy, claimed that the details of Rajiv Gandhi's visit had been leaked in advance by me!

I was horrified. How could I have leaked the programme, when the itinerary had been given to me by Rajiv Gandhi himself only on 20 May? And how could I be blamed for the selected constituencies, when the list had been drawn up by Rajivji himself? I had merely followed procedure by informing the candidates on phone about his visits; the venue, as always, had been selected by the candidate and the local leaders. As for the logistics of his trip, security personnel had been involved from the outset. In fact, he wanted to halt at Sriperumbudur for the night, but the local security rejected this as being unacceptable, as there was no proper accommodation available. Maragatham Chandrasekar offered the ground floor of the house of a businessman—which the businessman was prepared to vacate. But the security officers and the rest of us ruled that out. So it was decided that he would return to the Airports Authority guest house for the night.

Moreover, before the visit to Tamil Nadu, I had been in constant touch with Governor B. Narain Singh as the state was under President's Rule. He had assured me that every detail of the trip was being looked after by him. 'Rajiv is like my son! Do not worry. Leave things to me,' he kept repeating every time I phoned. When I asked him if I ought to fly down to monitor the details, he said an emphatic 'no'! 'You must trust me, Margaretji! I know my responsibilities,' he declared when I phoned him at around 2 p.m. on that fateful day. After the catastrophe, one had to ask the Governor—where were his intelligence officers? What were their inputs? Where were the local security personnel? But the Governor chose silence when confronted.

In the meantime, all sorts of far-fetched theories were concocted to drive home *my* purported guilt. One story doing the rounds was that a team of Catholic leaders had been planted around Rajiv Gandhi by the Vatican to eliminate him and make Sonia Gandhi the Prime Minister— aiming to incriminate not just me, but also George, P.C. Alexander and Oscar Fernandes, among others.

Then there emerged a theory about Sivarasan—the one-eyed LTTE mastermind behind the assassination plot—who had been found in a house in Konanakunte, Karnataka. The house was rented by LTTE-sympathizer Ranganath, and was owned by Puttenahalli Anjanappa, a friend of Bangarappa's. Since Anjanappa's younger brother, Ashwathnarayana, an SC youth Congress leader, had been built up in the party by me, some claimed that the circuitous chain of associations highlighted my role in the plot!

If I was out of harm's way, it was because I still had Rajivji's handwritten programme itinerary with his signature on it; by this one act, he had saved me.

Soon after our return from Allahabad, I went to see Sonia. 'I owe you and the children an explanation,' I said and produced Rajivji's handwritten paper. She saw it, read it carefully and returned it, saying, 'This is definitely his.'

I also explained to her the sequence of events on the fateful day of the assassination and prior, and told her I was prepared to appear before any commission of inquiry or court of law to place the facts on record. In fact, I insisted on filing an affidavit before the Justice J.S. Verma Commission of Inquiry, explaining my role and duties under Rajiv Gandhi. I said that my conscience was clear but events seemed to have conspired against me. Today, in hindsight, I am convinced that if I faced this most traumatic phase of my life with courage, it was because of my innate faith in God.

Until then, I had not been very close to Sonia. But in her grief, I felt drawn to her as never before. She appeared lonely and shattered, yet composed and dignified in her new role as a widowed mother. One day, I went to her and said, 'I do not mean to impose. But now, I wish to stand by you; you do not walk alone. If there's anything I can do at any time to help, I will do it. Also, know that there are many like me who wish to reach out. After all, you are the link to our past, a symbol of the memories we cherish.' In the days that followed, I met her regularly just to keep in touch.

After the 1991 elections, a minority Congress-led government came to power on 20 June. The results were a disappointment, even though the Congress emerged as the single largest party with 232 seats. We seemed to have fared poorly in constituencies that voted before the tragedy and swept the polls in those that voted after. As for the BJP, it secured 120 seats, and the Left, 49.[50] In this new government, as MoS Personnel, the

---

[50] See *Statistical Report of General Elections, 1991 to the Tenth Lok Sabha*, in <http://eci.nic.in/eci_main/StatisticalReports/LS_1991/VOL_I_91.pdf>, accessed on 17 November 2015.

CBI functioned under me. I went to Madras, inspected the SIT office there and insisted on having three copies of all records made. I asked for each copy to be kept in a different site for safety. All the requirements of the investigating team were sanctioned, and special security was provided by the state government. I personally kept abreast of all developments as inquiries proceeded, and answered those questions that emerged in Parliament.

But even today there are many lingering doubts, multiple question marks. The assassination of Rajiv Gandhi remains steeped in mystery.

The P.V. Narasimha Rao Years

Chapter 24

BACK IN THE GOVERNMENT:
TAKING CHARGE OF NEW DEPARTMENTS

Even as Rajivji's body lay in state, the CWC met, passed a condolence resolution and decided to request Soniaji to take over. Despite tremendous pressure on her to accept the mantle of leadership as Congress President, she flatly refused.

Thus began P.V. Narasimha Rao's ascent to power. He had been appointed Chairman of the Election Management Committee by Rajivji (even though he had announced his retirement from active politics). Following a number of behind-the-scenes consultations and confabulations, all lead contenders for the top post—including Arjun Singh, Sharad Pawar and N.D. Tiwari—dropped out of the race, leaving P.V. Narasimha Rao to fill the vacuum by consensus.

As the new Congress President, he decided to tour the constituencies which were yet to go to the polls. I was asked to join Jairam Ramesh, once again, to work out the itinerary. I refused to get involved. After putting my heart and soul into this work and facing disaster, I had no desire to venture out again. Jairam took over, and started accompanying Rao on his tours. The man who had told Rajiv Gandhi a few weeks earlier that he was 'too old to run around like him' was now hopping around the country, spurred by his ambitions.

Even as the elections reinstated the Congress in power, there was a great deal of suspense over who the Prime Minister would be. There were five names in the reckoning—N.D. Tiwari, Arjun Singh, Sharad Pawar, S.D. Sharma (who was Sonia's first choice) and P.V. Narasimha Rao. There were several rounds of negotiations, with many promises made, before Rao, with Sonia's blessings, became the choice. The formal meeting of the CPP endorsed the decision of the CWC.

P.V. Narasimha Rao came with a profile that, at once, provoked adulation and reproach. In 1980, Indira Gandhi had appointed him her

Foreign Minister, overruling Sanjay's objections. Perhaps, to prove his loyalty to her, he did nothing to stop the anti-Sikh riots of November 1984, during which time he was Home Minister. While both commissions set up to look into the riots absolved him, questions lingered. Then he was put in charge of the HRD Ministry by Rajiv Gandhi, who greatly respected his age and experience, though Rao remained critical of Rajivji's way of functioning and was suspicious of those who shared a rapport with him, including me.

When he was selected by the party as the Prime Minister, I went to his house to congratulate him. While waiting, I noticed the mess in the sitting room. I quickly got the place rearranged, dusted and cleaned, to make it presentable for the VIPs who were beginning to pour in.

There were pulls and pressures from all quarters over the choice of Ministers. I decided that I would not beg or lobby for anything. I sat at home listening to rumours from those who dropped in—mostly young hopefuls seeking my help. It was around lunch-time that I received a call for the swearing-in at Rashtrapati Bhavan.

I later learnt that my name was among the last to be included. Bangarappa, as Chief Minister of Karnataka, insisted on having D.K. Taradevi Siddhartha as the woman from his state, while strongly opposing my inclusion. The Prime Minister is supposed to have told him, 'You can give me your list, but you cannot dictate mine.' And so I was in as MoS with independent charge.

The next morning, I met the Prime Minister. He asked me what I would like by way of a ministry. I said, 'I would like to work with you, sir, as I have done in the past.' He nodded and I left.

What I had meant to indicate was that I wished to be MoS PMO. But when the allocation of portfolios was announced, I was shocked to see my name against MoS for Personnel, Pensions and Public Grievances (PPP) under the Prime Minister. This not only meant that my dreams of being part of the PMO were shattered, but also that I had been downgraded from 'independent charge' to MoS! I went straight to him, and told him that I felt let down. He dealt with the matter diplomatically. 'Do you wish to be independent of the Prime Minister? You realize, don't you, that you will report to me like every Cabinet Minister does? Work with this portfolio for some time. I want someone I can trust, and I know you will like it and do well. If you do not like the nature of your work, come to me later and I will shift you out.' This was his promise before I took charge of my ministry. My predecessor was P. Chidambaram.

◆

Having accepted the post of MoS PPP, I decided to make the best of it. I worked hard. Senior bureaucrats initially seemed pleased to have an inexperienced woman Minister, but soon started commenting: 'This is a hard nut to crack!' Not surprisingly, the usual practice of putting summary slips on files to guide the Minister petered out—officers learnt that I actually went through the files, especially when I sensed a 'management' of facts, and called a meeting with the Secretary of the ministry and my own Personal Secretary to clarify issues!

I strove to bring a human touch to the administrative machinery. I introduced a system of direct access to officials of all ranks. Every Wednesday afternoon became an 'open house'. Thus reports regarding the functioning of various departments and offices reached me. While senior officials raised objections to this change in protocol—which gave junior officials access to the Minister—I stuck to my decision to keep information channels open.

Additionally, I asked every ministry to set a 'meetingless day' each week to meet the public and redress their grievances. The day was prominently displayed at the reception of each ministry, with the name of the designated nodal officer mentioned. Of course, this was before the age of RTI (Right to Information), at a time when contacting any official for any information or redressal was a Herculean task.

A subject I remained committed to during my term as MoS PPP was women's issues. I lectured at most of our advanced training institutes and, to sensitize staff to women's concerns, got special programmes introduced and manuals prepared. Every ministry and department was required to set up a cell to deal with sexual harassment of women at the workplace.

The Pension Department got fully computerized. This ensured that the pension book with the sanction order was made available to officials on the day of retirement, thus cutting red tape and protecting them from harassment. While this change was proudly announced, when I visited the department offices, I was amazed to find bundles and bundles of pension papers piled up. I was told that the original papers had to be preserved for audit purposes!

◆

When I took charge of the department, there were several ongoing issues. The rivalry between the services was well-known, with the IAS (Indian Administrative Service) seeking to corner all important posts—those of Ambassadors, and of heads of various commissions, PSUs and international organizations. In an age of specialization—when there was urgent need for officers trained and experienced in a field to head relevant ministries and departments—this was a peculiar trend that hinged on political patronage.

Further complicating the situation was the fact that administrative tribunals—established to serve as Special Courts for resolving disputes—had begun to interfere in matters beyond their mandate, like cadre postings of AIS officers. The roster system was being disturbed and favours to the children of serving or former colleagues began to surface. In some cases, High Courts began to issue orders regarding the cadre change of officers. As a clear pattern of collusion between government law officers and senior officials began to emerge, I brought the matter to the notice of the Prime Minister. He advised me to meet the Chief Justice for guidance, which I did. Chief Justice M.N. Venkatachaliah appreciated the problem and asked me to have the matter formally mentioned before him. On the advice of my colleagues—who urged me to get a private senior counsel to appear for the department—the eminent Constitutional lawyer, K.K. Venugopal, was engaged to argue the matter. The Chief Justice, in turn, passed a strong judgement, upholding the government's prerogative to make rules regarding cadre allotments and management. It was a great victory for DoPT (Department of Personnel and Training), but the establishment was unhappy. K.K. Venugopal's bill was not settled till the PMO intervened.

I was disturbed by cases of civil servants—those who stuck to principles—being victimized and shunted around, with their seniors seldom speaking up for them, and only suggesting that they seek legal redress. In my own way, I tried to attend to this. I paid special attention to appeals against adverse remarks in confidential reports (CRs). While going through them, I discovered cases of caste bias, unfair interpretation of actions taken in good faith, and even vendetta. I made detailed notes and placed the facts in perspective before the Prime Minister—who generally endorsed my opinion—leading to the expunging of those remarks that would have ruined careers. In fact, on more than one occasion, he commended my painstaking efforts to ensure justice to aggrieved officials.

◆

In the months that followed, there were many battles I successfully fought against the 'iron frame' I had been cast into. When I started work as MoS PPP, I noticed that the Civil Services Board (CSB), chaired by the Cabinet Secretary, would screen all files meant for the PMO, and even make recommendations that were at variance with my recommendations. I objected, and convinced the Prime Minister that it was a humiliating procedure. He saw my point and, for the length of my tenure, files came to be seen by the CSB and then routed through me to the Prime Minister for orders.

There were two particular instances when I had to fight the CSB–PMO nexus singlehandedly. The first pertained to an appointment to the UPSC (Union Public Service Commission). I found that the name I had recorded on a file, after a discussion with the Prime Minister, was sought to be changed rather cleverly—by dividing the file and getting another name approved by him. When the file came back to me, I was both shocked and furious. I met the Prime Minister with the papers and said that unless he endorsed the name he had earlier accepted, I would be compelled to quit on moral grounds. I had my way, and the person the CSB had been rooting for got appointed in the next round of vacancies. I had the distinction of seeing the first tribal woman chair the UPSC and the first SC woman become its member, besides appointing the first SC Establishment Officer of the Ministry of Personnel.

The second occasion I fought the CSB–PMO nexus was when the deputation of the IAS officer, K.P. Krishnan, to the World Bank was being sabotaged. I pleaded on behalf of Krishnan—a brilliant, hardworking and honest officer serving as my Personal Secretary. The Prime Minister, who was sitting on the file, confided that there were serious objections to the posting as the feeling was that those working with the MoS PPP always managed to land plum deputations. Finally, though, he agreed to have Krishnan go to the World Bank. The CSB, after much dilly-dallying, cleared his appointment.

◆

There were other issues I confronted which involved the UPSC. There were agitations and severe political pressure to raise the age of recruitment by the UPSC and increase the number of attempts permitted. The training academies, on their part, held that it was impossible to sensitize and train recruits after the age of twenty-five, by which time they were, in any case, likely to be committed to other careers. Ultimately, we worked out a compromise. We increased the number of attempts, provided SC/ST recruits were not beyond thirty years of age, and the general category ones were not over twenty-eight years.

In addition, I attempted making the exams paperless and computerized by issuing identity cards to registered candidates, who could access notified computerized exam centres thrice in the specified year. The central data bank would release the question paper on computer screens (changing each time), and the marks would go directly to the UPSC data centre while getting recorded on the identity card of the candidate as well. The cut-off marks for selection would be announced in advance so that each candidate would know if she/he had made the grade. I argued that this system would save crores of rupees, besides being leak-proof. We made detailed presentations to the Prime Minister, a team of senior officers and UPSC members. But the proposal got caught in red tape—typical of our decision-making processes. Besides, many intermediaries made big money through the system, resulting in the usual resistance. I imagine mine was an idea ahead of its time, for today, the system I had proposed has been adopted for banking and some other examinations, with great success.

◆

When I assumed office I knew that the CBI was a law unto itself. The institution was being exploited by business competitors, politicians, and even bureaucrats, to settle scores.

Therefore, I called a meeting of all senior officers from across the country at the CBI headquarters—the first Minister to do so—and decided to review pendencies as a first step. We found cases that had been in limbo for up to twenty years, and had just been kept open—like swords dangling over the heads of citizens. We classified these cases into definite slabs—15- to 20-year pendencies, and 10- to 15-year pendencies. These were to be reviewed and a status report on each of them was to be prepared within three months. When the reports came in, it was shocking to see 'no evidence available' against most of them. In such cases, seized books were photocopied and returned, and closure reports filed for most of them. We then moved to the 5- to 10-year slab. I'm happy to say that through a systematic review procedure, the department managed to bring down pendencies drastically.

We also ensured that procedures were streamlined to ensure relatively quicker investigations. Vacancies at all levels were gradually reduced; allowances for field officials raised; and 'dead wood' on deputation repatriated.

High-profile cases—the Rajiv Gandhi assassination case, the Bofors investigation, the Jain Hawala scandal and some others—were placed under SITs and handled by specially selected competent officials. Complaints of harassment and the misuse of CBI powers were looked into at my level in an attempt to end such abuse.

It pains me to watch the fall in the CBI's reputation, and the perception of its role and functioning. The Supreme Court has had to intervene more than once to ensure its independent functioning, and punish erring officials.

◆

Given the economic crisis the country was confronting, it was important for the government to curtail public expenditure. On my part, I tried trimming all superfluous spending in my department. I began personally overseeing the appointment of consultants—whether they were retiring officials, or those on contract. This was an important measure, as consultants used government staff and facilities, made regular field trips, and got remunerated handsomely for reports which could (and should) in the normal course be produced by officials on duty in government!

The Prime Minister announced a 10 per cent reduction in government appointments as an austerity measure. I decided to set an example in the DoPT by doing away with one post of an Additional Secretary and one of a Joint Secretary, both of which were in any case lying vacant. The Secretary of the DoPT and several department heads objected. But I refused to give in. Besides, I saw the chain of posts that came with each Joint Secretary and Additional Secretary—under secretaries and deputy secretaries, desk officers, section officers, lower-division and upper-division clerks, PAs, typists, stenographers, attendants, drivers, etc.—almost a whole army contingent. I realized that my decision would save the government big money. The movement of files was recognized and, in no time, the department was running smoothly—showing how over-staffed our ministries were.

When the next cadre review exercise began, it was decided to implement the 10 per cent cut for IAS, IPS and IFS cadres at the recruitment stage.

This wasn't easy since there was stiff resistance from many lobbies. But we did it. Biju Patnaik (Orissa) and Chimanbhai Patel (Gujarat) complained about the poor representation of their state AIS officers at the Central level. 'We will stop accepting future allotments if you do not move our senior officers to the Centre!' the Chief Ministers had threatened at a National Development Council meeting. To broker peace, I was asked to meet them and sort out their problems. I showed them the actual position on the ground, and proved that we had already filled all available quotas of their states at the Centre. The fact was that Chief Ministers preferred to have state-cadre officers as the heads of important departments rather than AIS officers, since the former would be more pliable. But, since this fact could not be articulated, the matter was laid to rest.

Then came the issue of foreign trips and appointments. I noticed that the three-year limit for officials on deputation to international organizations or on study leave had been ignored—too many vested interests benefitted from lax procedures. Officials were happy getting plum deputations, with high tax-free salaries abroad, while continually extending their tenures by exerting pressure, often without even seeking clearances from the DoPT. We decided to review all such extended deputations, and issued notices, asking the officials to make a choice—return or resign—failing which they would face compulsory retirement. Many returned, some resigned, while, in a couple of cases, orders of termination were issued.

Training programmes abroad—short and long—were another big racket. Rural development, drinking water and sanitation, education, children and healthcare services, small-scale industries—any and every area of study took officials to Western countries, often with their spouses. In truth, these trips were all-paid-for joy-rides. I decided this had to stop. We signed a Memorandum of Understanding (MoU) with Northwestern University, specifically with the Kellogg School of Management, for upgrading the Management Development Institute at Gurgaon; it was decided that we would exchange faculty and introduce local training programmes that matched international standards.[51]

---

[51]Interestingly, we also signed an MoU with China, at the end of a bilateral visit, on training Chinese bureaucrats in India. They were keen to study our selection and training processes, and the rotation system between the Centre and the states (which ensured national unity, while giving autonomy to the states). This was an important MoU—one of the early protocols signed with China after our relations had thawed.

We were literally funding the Kennedy School of Public Administration at Harvard University with taxpayers' money! The one-year programme (with family) offered to senior officers was being grabbed for all the wrong reasons. Moreover, when I lectured there, I was startled by the manner in which these officers spoke about their country and its political leadership at a question-and-answer session. When Harvard increased its fee structure, I decided we had to cut down on this programme. A less-than-pleased John Kenneth Galbraith, the father of the Harvard programme, spoke to the Prime Minister, who intervened. It was ultimately agreed that the amount earmarked for the programme would stay at the same level for now, while the number of officials being sent would be reduced.

In the case of other programmes, I insisted that women and SC/STs get adequate representation; that a careful selection of candidates, purely on merit, be done; and that Asian countries, which had shown success in certain fields, be included for training. A clause was introduced that officials, on their return, would serve as trainers in our training institutions for at least two years; this was to ensure that the knowledge and skills gained abroad were transmitted to others in the country.

Along with wasteful expenditure came the problem of nepotism. On a visit to the World Bank I had heard of the brazen way in which officers on delegations for negotiations lobbied for posts for themselves or their children. I therefore decided to look into the issue of the children of serving senior government officials securing jobs in multinational companies and foreign-funded organizations. I had a questionnaire circulated to get clarity on the issue. Expectedly, there were protests, with long notes on why it was impossible to collect such data. While the process of reviewing the matter was set in motion, it was never completed; I guess there were too many skeletons in the closet and no one wished to let them out. For the future, I hope this questionnaire will be part of CRs to be filled by every official. The issue of the two-year cooling period for officials wishing to go to the private sector or to an organization based abroad on retirement or resignation has been repeatedly relaxed—which needs attention.

Last, but not the least, I was very firm on enforcing rules when it came to proven acts of corruption. While corruption is rampant at all levels and has come to be accepted as part of the system, I could not endorse it or look away. During my tenure, consequently, three Chief Secretaries (of Karnataka, Nagaland and Sikkim) resigned or received dismissal orders from the DoPT on grave charges or convictions, while two of my Personal Secretaries, Kushal Singh and Giji Thomson, ended their careers as Chief Secretaries of their states, and two others went on foreign assignments.

◆

For a year, I held additional 'charge' of the Science and Technology portfolio. While the portfolio was being handled by the Prime Minister, I had to deal with all Parliamentary work, including questions.

This was a real test for me. The job involved hours of preparation and briefing sessions by secretaries and officers of the ministries for replies to questions in both Houses of Parliament. Among the officers who used to come for briefing sessions was Dr A.P.J. Abdul Kalam, then the Secretary for Space (later, our President). He used to draw diagrams, showing important space launch processes, and train me for the supplementaries. He always praised the hot home-made snacks I served at these sessions, even when he reached the Rashtrapati Bhavan.

As Minister for Science and Technology, I travelled to a number of significant places, including Sriharikota; visited atomic plants; flew over the silent volcano of Barren Island (which was a real learning experience); and flew by helicopter to the ONGC (Oil and Natural Gas Corporation) platform out at sea. But I was never happy with our decisions to expand nuclear power production. Small, locally manageable, environment-friendly alternatives should have been our choice. They would have been safer and cheaper substitutes.

Here I must mention my visit to an undisclosed place in the country where nuclear waste is buried after being embedded in small containers in huge concrete blocks. I was terrified at the thought of some nuclear activity igniting just one of them—the repercussions would be a human and ecological disaster. I once raised the issue of human security vis-à-vis our nuclear programme in a Consultative Committee meeting, when Dr Raja Ramanna (nominated member) flew into a rage, and told me I was misinformed and causing panic, which he termed as 'anti-national'.

When the US and some Western countries imposed an embargo on the supply of crucial material to India after our nuclear test, our space and super computer development programmes were hit. There was a 'Calling Attention Motion' in the House on the subject, to which I replied, as briefed by Dr Abdul Kalam. I told the House that nothing would stop our programmes.

'We may be slowed down a bit, but no one can stop Indian scientists; there is no match to Indian brains. We will overcome.' There was thumping of desks from all sides. India went on to prove Dr Kalam right.

While there's no doubt that I had good briefing sessions, after a point, the strain of looking after these eight additional ministries began to tell on me. I mentioned this to the Prime Minister during a briefing meeting, 'Sir, I spend all my time understanding the intricacies of these portfolios and preparing for Question Hour. Last night, I didn't even sleep for four hours!'

The Prime Minister was unmoved. 'Think of the nights you slept more than you should have,' was his caustic reply.

Nonetheless, he got the point. He soon appointed three Ministers to deal with these ministries.

◆

In April 1992, my term in the Rajya Sabha was due to end. Rajivji had promised to get me back, but he was gone, leaving behind only one witness, P. Chidambaram. Oscar Fernandes, as the PCC President, was cryptic (it was impossible to gauge his mind), while Bangarappa remained totally opposed to having me around. In fact, it was common knowledge that on the night of 21 May 1991, when news of Rajivji's assassination came, Bangarappa dined with his friends in his suite at Karnataka Bhavan, Delhi, declaring, 'The patron is gone; now let's see how long she survives!'—referring to me, of course.

I knew I was in a hapless situation. Sachidanand Swami's name had already been announced for one seat. The second was pending. My sole hope was the Prime Minister. I spoke to him hesitantly.

His response was, 'Yes, I know. Let me see.'

Since the Congress was against giving a representative four consecutive terms in the Rajya Sabha, I explained to him that I had only two terms from the party—the third having been won when I had been out of the Congress with Devaraj Urs.

'I am glad you have clarified this point,' he said, quite relieved.

Matters should have ended there, but Manira, who was working for *The Observer*, came home one night with news she had picked up from a senior journalist close to the Congress. Apparently, V. George was getting a Rajya Sabha seat from Karnataka. I was stunned. I then got to know from Bangalore that he had got himself enrolled on the voters' list there. To add to the chaos, there was also a rumour that Soniaji wanted him accommodated.

The situation looked grim again, and time was running out. The Prime Minister was to leave on a foreign trip the next day, and there were only two days left for nominations to close. I was at Hyderabad House, with Ministers and senior party functionaries, to see him off. I spotted Bangarappa walking with the Prime Minister, having a long conversation with him. 'There goes my seat,' I whispered to Saroj Khaparde, standing next to me. 'Speak to him now,' she advised.

As the Prime Minister walked up, I offered him my good wishes.

'Why are you still here and not in Bangalore?' he asked.

'How can I go without an announcement?' I replied.

'You go!' was his order.

But I was not going to make a fool of myself, especially with George's name doing the rounds.

A couple of hours after the Prime Minister left, there was a message to the AICC, announcing my name as the party's second candidate. I rushed by the last flight to Bangalore.

The first thing I did in the morning was to collect the nomination papers and go to the Chief Minister's residence with Swamiji. My supporters and I thanked Bangarappa for his 'kind support' (which he accepted with a little discomfort) and requested him to sign our nomination papers, which he 'willingly' did, directing the Legislature Party office to keep everything ready for us to file the papers.

It was the last day for nominations. We prepared four sets of papers and waited for the PCC President to arrive with the required B Form. But he was nowhere to be found. We were told he was in a function far away and would return only by lunch-time. There was tension all around. Finally, at around 2 p.m., the documents we needed arrived in a sealed envelope. Papers filed, I returned to Delhi.

Here I met party colleagues who told me of the background manipulations that had been underway. In order to keep me out, Bangarappa and his coterie had recommended V. George, and convinced him to contest, with the help of the Karnataka Youth Congress leader, K.J. George. They got V. George's name onto the voters' list and told the Prime Minister that Sonia wanted him in the Rajya Sabha. But he was too shrewd a politician to be fooled. He is supposed to have said, 'If Soniaji wants V. George in the Rajya Sabha, let her talk to me directly and I will get it done.' But the call did not come. Rao waited till his plane left the country and then made his decision. Bangarappa's bluff had been called.

Winning this Rajya Sabha seat was a huge challenge. There were many who hoped that I would not make it. I met Sharad Pawar, who was Defence Minister, by chance, at a dinner. He told me to meet him the next day. Swamiji and I went to his office. He informed us that plans were being hatched to defeat me and that I should be very careful. He offered to go to Bangalore as an observer, to manage the elections, if the Prime Minister sent him. I was thrilled.

Swamiji and I went to the Prime Minister—who was back—and made the request. He looked surprised. 'Will Pawar really go?' he asked.

'Yes, he will. He has offered his services,' I replied.

So Pawarji was sent to Karnataka. He stayed at the army guest house for the week, played golf and kept himself informed about political developments, while we made our rounds, meeting the MLAs of various parties. Wherever we went, there was only one comment: 'We wish you success, but please be careful about your Chief Minister!'

A day before the elections, Pawarji asked us to submit lists of forty-five MLAs of our choice, to be allotted to us for voting, which we did. He then had a meeting with Bangarappa, Oscar Fernandes and a couple of senior leaders, and worked out the strategy for the next day. When I went through the final lists, I found that four names had been changed. I was upset. Pawarji advised me not to say anything about my chosen voters as those left out would get upset.

On D-day, in the morning, I had a phone call from Jayalalithaa. She said she had directed the lone AIADMK MLA to vote for me. I also managed to get the support of a couple of other voters. Unlike my earlier elections, I was on my own this time, with only Niru beside me.

My heart began pounding as counting began. As expected, four of my votes had been diverted. I entered the second round, and got through with preferential votes. If I had not secured those three last-minute votes, I would have been out of the race.

Over a dinner I hosted, I thanked Pawarji, the MLAs and the leaders, some of whom were clearly very unhappy. Back in Delhi, I thanked the Prime Minister, and then went to Soniaji with sweets and flowers. She was warm and friendly. I told her that while I had wanted to come to her before leaving for Karnataka for her blessings, I was nervous since I feared she would be upset about George not getting the seat. Suddenly, she turned serious. 'I neither suggested nor asked for it. George came to me for permission to accept the Rajya Sabha seat from Karnataka that had been offered to him. I told him he was free to do so. I do not know why my name has been dragged into this. I am glad you have won. You have worked hard for the party and in the government. I wish you luck,' she said. I was so relieved to hear that.

This would be my fourth consecutive term in the Rajya Sabha. For my family it was a record of sorts—an Alva in Parliament from 1952 to 1998, without a break. No other family could claim this distinction. Fate and God had been on our side. I kept asking myself, over the next few days, what I had done to be blessed in this manner. I came from humble origins and a non-political background. Niru was my cornerstone—he should have been here and not me.

I often felt guilty about being in Parliament while Niru was out. He had the political acumen, was a brilliant speaker, and had suffered with his parents the travails of the freedom movement. He should have inherited the political mantle. There was no justification for him being out and for me being in. I did not want to get involved full-time in the party and had firmly declined the party post offered in Bangalore. It was he who forced me into it, saying, 'My mother went to jail with a five-month baby in arms—you have to keep up the family tradition.' In fact, when my name was announced for the Rajya Sabha, in 1974, I requested Baba to have it changed to Niru, but was asked to fall in line and file my nomination. Niru stood by me and helped me at every stage, working to keep the family comfortable. I had once requested Indiraji to consider Niru as my replacement when my term ended in 1980. 'You are doing well—we will look after him,' she had assured me. But fate and unforeseen events overtook us and I was out of the party in 1980 (when my term ended), to be re-elected as a united opposition candidate.

We had seen ups and downs, faced many difficulties and challenges, but had survived and succeeded, even against very powerful persons like Sanjay Gandhi (at the height of his power), Gundu Rao and F.M. Khan, and now the all-powerful Chief Minister, Bangarappa.

◆

In Karnataka, in the meantime, things were spinning out of control. The anti-Bangarappa wave kept growing, with MLAs camping in Delhi demanding a change in leadership. I became a rallying point; meetings took place in my house, with all appointments fixed by me.

Throughout this period, the Prime Minister patiently listened but never responded. One day, when I was alone with him, I asked in desperation, 'Why don't you do something? The Karnataka government does not function and the state is going to wrack and ruin!'

'When Bangarappa is capable of hanging himself, why should I sully my hands hanging him? I am giving him a long rope to hang himself with!' he replied.

And this is what happened. After the Classik Computer scandal, the failure of his state government to curb the Kaveri riots cost him his 'gaddi'.[52] I was relieved to see him go. Bangarappa left the Congress soon after to form the Karnataka Congress Party (KCP) with his followers.

The Speaker, S.M. Krishna, who had supported the anti-Bangarappa campaign every step of the way, was beaten by Veerappa Moily to the post of a Chief Minister. The reason offered by the High Command was that an OBC had to be replaced by an OBC. A disappointed Krishna was persuaded to become the Deputy Chief Minister—a post he accepted with great reluctance, since Moily had been his Deputy Minister when he had been the Finance Minister. I felt he ought to have refused the post, and stayed on as Speaker. But once he accepted it, he should have played his role with dignity. Instead, in no time, his supporters were back in Delhi with a litany of charges against Moily and his style of functioning. We were back to square one. This time, I refused to get involved because I had promised the Prime Minister—when he agreed to replace Bangarappa—that there would be no further trouble. My unresponsiveness to Krishna's coterie was held against me for a long time.

Even while I tried distancing myself, I got caught in an unexpected controversy involving Bangarappa. Replying to a debate after he was sworn in as Chief Minister, Veerappa Moily committed on the floor of the House to handing over the Classik Computer case to the CBI. I received a letter from the state government, with the copy of the speech, requesting follow-up action.

---

[52]After the Kaveri Water Tribunal's award—which directed the Government of Karnataka to release water to Tamil Nadu within a year—was gazetted by the Government of India on 11 December 1991, the cities of Bangalore and Mysore erupted in violence, with mobs targeting the Tamilians in the state between 11 and 12 December. The violence terrified the Tamilian populace, forcing several to flee.

I refused to comply and kept the file with me. Then, one day, Home Minister S.B. Chavan called me 'for a cup of tea' to his office, which was down the corridor. When I walked in, I was surprised to see Moily sitting there. The Home Minister came straight to the point. 'Why are you not helping your Chief Minister?' he asked.

'In what way?' I enquired.

'The CBI must take up the case, as requested. Otherwise, how will Moily face the Assembly?'

'Bangarappa was our Chief Minister! How do I order a CBI inquiry against him? Moily should not have given such assurances in the House.' I replied.

'Now that the deed is done, we have to see the commitment through. Please do whatever is required by him,' he advised.

'I will have to do as you say, but I will record that I am clearing the file as per your directions,' I told him.

And that's what I did. I then called Bangarappa's Chief Secretary, J. Alexander, to Delhi, and explained why I had to proceed with the inquiry. The CBI launched its investigation against Bangarappa and Alexander.[53] Despite being aware of my compulsions, Bangarappa held me responsible for all that followed and began a strident campaign against me.[54]

◆

The Legislator's Cooperative Society at Bangalore had allotted BDA (Bangalore Development Authority) plots to its members. I purchased a 4,000 square foot plot in RMV II Stage. We started building there in 1994 and completed the construction in 1995. Suddenly, M. Rajasekhara Murthy, a senior Congress leader (who had six BDA plots in his family), went to the press, claiming that I had got the plot on a false affidavit, as I had a house in Bangalore already. The controversy raged for some time, but the

---

[53]In 2003, the Special Court for CBI cases acquitted Bangarappa and J. Alexander of all charges, including corruption and the receipt of kickbacks in the Classik Computer scam. In 2011, the Karnataka High Court upheld the order of the Special Court.

[54]Interestingly, in 2009, Bangarappa, back in the Congress fold, addressed three big rallies with me in my constituency. His popularity had clearly faded on account of his 'turncoat' politics and his willingness to abandon his socialist commitment in a bid to win favours for himself and his sons. As for J. Alexander, he quit his post, to join the party later and become the President of the Bangalore DCC (District Congress Committee), with the help of powerful 'patrons' elsewhere.

documents I submitted to the society and to the Prime Minister showed that we had no title to the other house. I explained the facts to the Prime Minister as I was a Minister, and wrote to him with the documents, offering to step down if I was found guilty. He said nothing when he took the papers, but I heard later that he sent them to the Law Minister (H.R. Bhardwaj) for an opinion, who gave me a clean chit. This was the way he operated.

The house is a tribute to Niru's determination and hard work. He sat there with his assistant, Srinivas, supervising the work, day after day. It was meant to be our retirement home.

◆

Niret had met Anuja Chauhan—still in college—at Stage Door (a theatre group). After a course in advertising in Australia, she returned for a career at Hindustan Thomson/JWT. I was getting titbits of information on the blossoming romance. Then, one day, out of the blue, before his departure for the Royal Netherlands Institute of Journalism for a course in TV journalism at Rotterdam, Niret came to say that he wished to get engaged. It came as a shock—our eldest son had decided to get engaged without seeking our consent or advice. We had so many girls in mind for him. Now we were to end up with a Hindu Rajput girl, about whom we knew nothing, except that she was the daughter of Pushpa and Lt Col. Raman, who had immigrated to Australia. We decided not to stand in his way. 'You have made your choice. You lie on the bed you make; if anything goes wrong you have only yourself to blame,' Niru told him firmly the next morning. The engagement ceremony took place before he left. It was during his absence that Anuja grew close to us, joining us for lunch on Sundays, etc.

They were married on 8 January 1994. We had both ceremonies—Hindu and Christian—with the late Dr Wilfred D'Souza, the then Chief Minister of Goa, proposing the toast. The reception on our lawns was attended by the who's who of Delhi. Friends and relations, from all over the country and abroad, came to celebrate the event. They stayed with us after the wedding. Anuja fit into the family in no time (though her clothes were often out of sync with family tradition)—climbing the ladder at JWT to become its youngest Vice President and Executive Creative Director.

On 7 September 1995, our first grandchild, Niharika, was born. Manira and I were in China attending the World Conference on Women. Nikka, as we called her, was a doll, a delight and the joy of the family, pampered by everyone. I organized a big tea for over a hundred women to celebrate her arrival and to raise a toast to the 'Alva girl child.' There have been two additions since then—Nayantara (Tara, as we call her) in June 1998 and Daivik John in March 2001.

◆

Along with Karnataka, the North-east was also a part of my life, and even as a Minister, I supervised many election campaigns in these states. I served on the Prime Minister's special team for the North-east. We were divided into three groups, each led by a Cabinet Minister, to visit and interact with local leaders, workers and the rural population.

I remember, on one occasion, our group arrived in Arunachal Pradesh to a rousing reception and also a rather strange demonstration outside Chief Minister Gegong Apang's house (which we were visiting for dinner). A group of women were protesting against Apang's recent marriage to a young girl, against the wishes of his devoted wife. Apang had a hard time extricating himself from the mess—explaining that the protests were politically motivated, since local tribal custom did not place a limit on the number of wives a man could have. And all this while his senior wife served as the hostess of the Chief Minister!

Incidentally, this wasn't the only occasion when we found ourselves in the middle of a storm whipped up by Apang. When P.A. Sangma and I paid a visit to the Don Bosco School and Orphanage, Apang complained to the Union HRD Minister, Arjun Singh, that we had clandestinely fixed a meeting with Christian anti-national elements in a secret place. An irate Sangma abused Apang, accusing him of trying to sully his reputation because he wished to usurp the position of the Chairman of the NEC (North Eastern Council) despite not having the support of the leaders of the region. Both were finally pacified, and Apang apologized. The fact was that Apang had been harassing Christian groups—accusing them of conversions, claiming that they were involved in anti-national activities, and threatening to close down their institutions. But after a trip to the West, he changed his mind and publicly declared that he had witnessed the progress made by Christian countries and wanted to follow them.[55]

---

[55]Gegong Apang, over the years, had several problems with the Centre and the Congress High Command, which resulted in his forming the Arunachal Congress in 1996. He took almost

In 1993, I was put in charge of the Assembly election campaign in Mizoram. The assignment began with a controversy—with the Chief Election Commissioner, T.N. Seshan, issuing a show cause notice to Assam Chief Minister Hiteswar Saikia and me for travelling by an army helicopter from Guwahati to Aizawl. Saikia insisted he was entitled to use the helicopter after paying for it and was free to travel with anyone he chose. Since he had followed the rule book, the matter was closed. I stayed in the Raj Bhavan complex for security and my host was Kyndiah.

As part of my assignment in Mizoram, I was to handle election funds. I also had to manage the church, youth fora and women's organizations—who formed the most powerful opinion-makers in the state, and controlled community responses to parties and candidates. This election campaign proved to be rather unique, because the youth groups announced a five-point code of conduct to be followed by all parties, voters and candidates, copies of which were distributed to all and displayed at important sites. The five-point code of conduct prohibited public meetings by parties, loudspeakers and posters, feasting and drinking at the candidates' cost and disbursing money or vehicles to voters. It allowed candidates to organize meetings only on 'common platforms', to be chaired by the youth leader in charge of the village. Any candidate violating the code would be boycotted.

Therefore, when meetings had to be organized, the youth leader announced the date, made all arrangements and invited candidates to speak for ten minutes each, after giving firm instructions to the audience: 'No cheering or jeering. All questions must be asked through the chair.' Once the meeting ended, the community members sat, heads bowed, to seek God's help and guidance to choose the best candidate.

It was with great difficulty that I got two public meetings cleared for the Prime Minister—the first at Aizawl, and the second in Lunglei. At the last minute, however, the Prime Minister changed his programme, deciding to go to Lunglei first. So I had to get to Lunglei. With a convoy of four

---

the entire Legislature Party with him and continued as Chief Minister. In 2003, he merged his party with the BJP, to give the latter its first government in the North-east. But this was short-lived as he deserted the BJP in 2004, ahead of Assembly elections in the state, and joined the Congress. He remained Chief Minister till 2007, when he had to resign due to a split among the MLAs. Dorjee Khandu succeeded him as Leader of the Congress Legislature Party. In 2010, Apang was arrested and sent to jail for financial fraud, after he had dominated the politics of the region for roughly three decades.

vehicles, we left at 1 p.m. instead of the planned 7 a.m.—the departure delayed by the number of travel formalities to be completed in the region. The Governor's wife kept pleading with me not to leave as it was late, the journey was long and treacherous, and the roads bumpy and unsafe. But we had no choice in the matter, and set off, receiving warm welcomes along the way from the villagers who spotted the Congress flag on our cars. Many youngsters, when they saw me, shouted, 'Sports mantri, sports mantri!' ('Sports Minister!')—recalling my earlier avatar, when I had become extremely popular while distributing footballs to village clubs.

As night descended, human habitations disappeared, and our vehicle found itself manipulating hairpin bends and waterfalls on a landslide-hit narrow road, gunners in the front and at the back keeping watch in open jeeps. I looked on, terrified. In contrast, in the front seat, the PCC President of Assam, Nakul Das, went off to sleep, while next to me, D.D. Lapang, the Chief Minister of Meghalaya, nodded off, swerving with every bend in the road and landing on my shoulder. This only added to the discomfort of an already difficult journey. If I had a moment of relief, it was when we approached a border check post, which I mistakenly assumed was Lunglei.

Next to this post was a small tea stall, dimly lit; on venturing inside, it proved to be a veritable Aladdin's cave! There were rubies, clothes, bags, shoes, perfumes, watches, pens, cosmetics, spices on display—unbelievable Chinese products, smuggled through Burma—clearly, a flourishing trade outlet. 'This is the only way we get some stuff; India is far away, Burma is next door,' the shopkeepers said, nonchalantly.

We had a three-hour drive ahead of us, as our car zipped down bumpy gullies. Suddenly, on a sharp bend, the lights fell on a European couple standing at the edge of the road—the man in short khaki pants, a white shirt and a Tommy hat of a bygone era, and a short-haired woman in a red dress that stretched below her knees. Assuming that they were stranded in the wilderness and in need of help, I asked the driver to stop. But he refused. I shouted at him—which finally woke up my companions—but the driver drove on. By now, the couple wasn't to be seen; we had whizzed past them. Finally, the driver very calmly explained, 'We see many like them on these roads. They are not real, they are dangerous.' He pointed to the flower beds all along this road; they marked accident sites of the past—vehicles that had gone into the abyss, with bodies never recovered.

In the front seat, Nakul Das quietly added, 'Madam, in fact it is just past midnight. These things happen in these areas.'

My hair stood on edge. 'You mean they are ghosts?'

'That is what they say in these areas,' he answered, gravely.

If true, I had seen my first ghosts on the lonely road by the Burmese border!

We finally arrived in Lunglei past 1.00 a.m. I was shaken and exhausted. The SPG advance team, fearing the worst, was in the middle of arranging a vehicle and calling the local police to look for us; they were most relieved to see us.

The Prime Minister had a well-attended rally in Lunglei, and we flew with him to Aizawl for the next meeting. After this, I briefed him about the campaign and told him I was sending a suitcase back with him. 'What suitcase?' he asked.

'I have saved forty lakh rupees, as expenditure is strictly controlled under the youth code. I have dispersed only one lakh per candidate instead of the two sent.'

The Prime Minister seemed puzzled but pleased. He later told me to give another five lakh rupees to the Chief Minister and the PCC for last-minute requirements, which I did. The rest of the money was sent back to Sitaram Kesri, the party's Treasurer.

When I returned to Delhi, and met Kesriji, he said, 'Jai ho, Margaret! You are the first person in the history of the AICC to have brought money back. The rest only give me pending bills. I congratulate you.'

For the campaign, I had only been given an allowance of ₹5,000 for personal expenses. The bonus I got was the empty suitcase that was left after the return of party funds.

◆

In the course of his work, Niret made some dangerous trips to troubled spots like Kashmir, where he managed secret meetings with Mujahideen Chief Abdul Majid Dar and his group. His next assignment was in Assam, to cover 'Operation Rhino'. He spent days in the jungles with ULFA (United Liberation Front of Asom) cadres, who he said were friendly and hospitable. While he was there, I had a phone call from the Prime Minister asking if my son was in Assam. When I said he was, the angry response was, 'I have enough trouble on my hands. All I need is to have your son kidnapped. What kind of a mother are you?' He directed Chief Minister Saikia to trace Niret and send him back immediately. These trips, at the height of conflicts, though dangerous for him and agonizing for the family, gave him insights into why the other side was angry and demanding freedom.

◆

I was sent to Bihar as AICC observer in 1995 for the Assembly elections. This was when Lalu Prasad Yadav, the Chief Minister, was facing heat from the CBI in the fodder scam. It was a crazy campaign with everyone in the party working against everyone, and leaders involved in caste squabbles. Within each election office, there were stocks of country-made weapons. As I moved around the state—despite being cautioned about the dangers that loomed in the countryside after sunset—I got to see poverty, makeshift clinics in tin sheds and children asleep on bare mud-paths in the height of summer. It was shocking. There was corruption everywhere, and disdain for the law, as the common citizen suffered in silence.

As MoS in charge of the CBI, I received special attention from Lalu Prasad Yadav, with references, all in Hindi, like: 'An important Minister has landed from Delhi and is making speeches. Does anyone win elections in Bihar with speeches? Let her speak and go. Lalu knows how to win and he will win!' And this is exactly what happened!

◆

Nikhil, our second son, born ten days before my mother-in-law died, had been a quiet introvert. He always complained about being neglected as Manira came just thirteen months after him. 'My place in the family is the worst to be in—Niret is the eldest and Manira the youngest—I have no special place. I only get my brother's hand-me-downs', he wrote in his class essay on 'My Family'. Passing out of St Columba's, he graduated from St Stephen's in 1991 with a Maths Honours degree. His interests were many and his talents impressive. He was Sports Secretary of the college and captained college teams in athletics and cross country. He was in the Delhi State Junior Shooting team with Rahul Gandhi, Jaspal Rana and others, winning many laurels for the state, including the National Junior Gold Cup and the Delhi State Gold Cup. He was made Special Police Officer by the Commissioner of Police to enable him to join the Delhi Police shooting team.

Music was in his blood. He played five instruments. His teacher at the Delhi School of Music—a Russian lady—told us, 'Nikhil is brilliant, so very brilliant, he could be a concert pianist. But he will not cooperate. Why don't you come to check on his progress?' I had to tell her the truth. Nikhil had forbidden us from interfering with his music training. 'If you come to meet my teacher, I will stop going there. She is trying to push me into her mould of a musician, which I am not prepared to accept...' So that was it.

Mukul Wasnik, who was then the MoS Youth Affairs and Sports, included Nikhil in the Indian contingent of the Japanese Youth Friendship ship in September 1993, which went from Japan to the Mediterranean and back. He came back a changed person. He was part of the Indian contingent for the World Youth Festival in Moscow in 1985 and the Non-Aligned Youth Festival in Pyongyang in 1989—chosen through open competitions.

Niru walked into his room one day, while he was busy with his music mixer, and asked him what he was up to. 'I am putting together a band with my friends. We are also producing jingles for advertisements,' he replied. Niru was furious—'What nonsense is this? You want me to be known as the father of a band master? Stop this and get to your classes. I have always hoped to see you become a brilliant mathematician,' he shouted. Nikhil listened calmly and replied, red-faced with anger, 'The trouble with you and Mamma is that you are too full of yourselves...you will live to be known as Nikhil Alva's parents one day.'

He had applied to Jamia Millia Islamia for a Master's degree in Mass Communication, but the Board decided that with an Alva background he could go anywhere, and so left him out. Many of his friends got in. I offered to speak to Aruna Asaf Ali to help. Nikhil would have none of this. 'They do not want me; I do not want them...I will set up my own company and employ their graduates before long,' he said. And he did do it.

Miditech was born in 1992, and many young people from Jamia and other institutes joined, to make it one of the top production houses in the country. They started with a bank loan for unemployed graduates, for which I stood guarantee. Niret joined him soon after, as did Pria, Manira and Nivedith in later years. Together they have done us proud. We are indeed known as the parents of the Alva boys today.

◆

I juggled multiple commitments during those years—international assignments among them. I was Minister-in-waiting to Khaleda Zia, the

Prime Minister of Bangladesh, when she visited India in 1992. Smartly attired with her hair in a bouffant, she exhibited all the trappings of an army wife. At the end of her trip, at a private luncheon hosted by the Prime Minister, the latter announced with a smile, 'In response to my Minister, Mrs Alva's desire for Dhaka sarees, we have decided to permit their import!' Zia was mighty pleased and promised to send me a Dhaka saree—which she did.

I was also Minister-in-waiting to the First Lady of the US, Hillary Clinton, who was visiting with her daughter, Chelsea, in 1995; together, we flew by Air Force Two to SEWA in Gujarat and Agra, after a packed programme in Delhi. Mrs Clinton—warm, informal and friendly—was curious about Indian politics. We had interesting discussions and struck a rapport.

When I visited New York later that year for a meeting at the UN, I received a special invitation to tea with the First Lady at the White House (through Ambassador Frank Wisner). We had a memorable evening with Nancy Powell, Melanne Verveer and Maya Ray, the wife of our Ambassador.

The question of the First Lady attending the UN World Conference on Women in Beijing later that year came up. It was obvious that the administration did not want her to go. She asked me what I thought of the idea. I told her she must attend. 'You are getting a platform to address the women of the world at the official and the NGO conferences. Do not miss the opportunity! You will be misunderstood and criticized if you do not go.' She did come to Beijing and made a lasting impression.

I have admired Hillary Clinton for her courage and self-confidence through all the ups and downs of her life. Years later, Vital Voices, a women's NGO she co-founded with Senator Nancy Kassebaum Baker, selected me for the Global Leadership Award, which was presented at a glittering ceremony at the Kennedy Centre in Washington DC. Niru and Manira accompanied me. There were several lunches, receptions and meetings I attended, speaking on a variety of subjects, besides giving television and radio interviews. I was really upset when in 2008 she lost the race to the Presidency. I hope she will make it this time.

I made some other fascinating international trips during this period: to Rome as an elected member of the Executive of the Society for International Development; to the scenic Rockefeller Foundation Bellagio Center as a member of the expert team to reorient population policies as a follow-up to the International Conference on Population and Development in

Cairo (for which I was nominated by its Secretary General, Nafis Sadik, of UNFPA [United Nations Population Fund])[56]; to Cameroon as part of an international team of the Commonwealth Observer Group, where I saw the ingenious ways in which elections were manipulated, be it by halting public transport or by allotting voter lists to the wrong booths in opposition-dominated areas; to Australia where I was the keynote speaker on human trafficking at a CPA conference (incidentally, it was here that I won my first and only lottery at the casino—a princely sum of $200!); and to Austria on an international panel to work out strategies to fight child trafficking.

At international meetings, I made it a point to endorse the causes I cherished. For instance, at Davos, as part of the PGA (Parliamentarians for Global Action) team to the World Economic Forum Consultation, I voiced my views, along with Parliamentarians from Africa, Asia and Latin America, who spoke out strongly against the policies of the International Monetary Fund and the World Bank—both of which exerted a great deal of pressure on the developing world. I made one of my strongest speeches on economic policies that hurt already impoverished populations, curtailing their full recovery from colonial exploitation. I raised the issue of our markets being opened for the free flow of goods, capital and technology, while the most important arm of production—labour—was blocked from free movement to developed countries in need of productive manpower. I received a standing ovation from the delegates, but never received another invitation to the forum.

One more important confrontation I had was in the chambers of the Security Council, where a meeting had been fixed by the PGA to discuss the threat of international terrorism in the wake of the 9/11 attack. I listened to speeches on the need for nations to unite to fight the menace of violence. I intervened towards the end, and endorsed the concerns of all the nations and the need for united action. I then pointed out that for decades, we, in the subcontinent, had been drawing attention to the threats we faced on account of hostile acts from our border-states—whether in

---

[56]The United Nations coordinated an International Conference on Population and Development in Cairo in September 1994, and its programme of action became the steering document for the UNFPA. The conference delegates arrived at four qualitative and quantitative goals— universal education; reduction in infant and child mortality; reduction in maternal mortality; and access to reproductive and sexual health services.

Kashmir or the North-east. Countless innocent lives had been lost. But what response had we received? Lectures on restraint, sermons on the right to self-determination and global support for so-called democratic movements within our territory. One attack on US soil, and the world was expected to sit up and join forces to fight the 'menace of terrorism'. While I did mourn the deaths in the twin towers, I had to ask—were the lives of these people more precious than those of our people, who had been under attack for years? I wanted every action of the recent past to be analyzed, not just this one event. There was stunned silence when I was done, and the meeting came to an abrupt end. The Secretary General of the PGA, Shazia Rafi, who hails from Pakistan, hugged me and said she wished there were more Parliamentarians like me, bold enough to take on the West and its stooges.

International assignments sometimes had their moments of friction. In 1995, the women MPs of both Houses, with a large contingent of NGO workers, were to proceed to Beijing to attend the World Conference on Women. Both Najma Heptulla and I made it known that we wished to lead the delegation. Obviously, I was upset when Madhavrao Scindia, the HRD Minister, chose Najma (who was Deputy Chairperson of the Rajya Sabha) as the Leader of the government delegation when he left after making the country statement. A direct consequence was that two camps emerged— invitations for events were distributed to favourites, with the rest of us left out. Therefore, when we received an invitation for a reception hosted by her, those of us on the 'outside' boycotted it, and got together in my suite for an evening of fun—with Renuka Chowdhury, the star performer, imitating a range of personalities from N.T. Rama Rao to P.V. Narasimha Rao, and Louise Khurshid (an active member of the Congress), Mercy Ravi (a politician from Kerala) and Vasundhara Raje Scindia (an MP of the BJP) contributing their bit. This day remains unforgettable, also because I received news that evening about the birth of my first grandchild.

There was never a dull day on the trip. But the most shocking news was of Mrs Basavarajeshwari, the MoS WCD, being dropped from the Council of Ministers while she was at the conference. Could the Prime Minister not have waited till she returned? There were no explanations or answers.

At the NGO venue, which we visited, there were groups from every part of the world, presenting their own agendas. As we assembled to leave, Fathima Beevi, the Judge of the Supreme Court, went missing. Mercy Ravi finally found her dancing with women of the 'Gay Rights tent' singing, 'We shall overcome...'

Though we saw signs of development and modern infrastructure in the urban areas, especially Beijing, the rural areas were still very much like any Asian village—small houses, barefeet children with unkempt hair and runny noses, pigs and chickens running in and out, and toilets in a disastrous state.

◆

When the President of Portugal, Mario Soares, visited India, I was Minister-in-waiting once again. On a visit to Goa, he insisted that I dance with him—despite my harried pleas that I did not dance. *The Observer* printed a photo of us. I sent the picture clipping to the Prime Minister with my report, adding, 'The travails of a woman Minister on duty!' He acknowledged the note and added a postscript, 'It takes two to tango; I am glad you did it'. Most do not know that he did have a sense of humour! Incidentally, Mario Soares, who had been incarcerated by the Portuguese for his support to Goa's freedom struggle, received a hero's welcome in the state, with crowds on the streets shouting 'Viva Mario!' wherever we went.

◆

The Interpol General Assembly in Beijing in October 1995 took me on an official visit to China again with the Director of the CBI, the Secretary Personnel and a couple of other officers. I learnt a lot from the presentations, especially on the crime syndicates involved with human trafficking, drug peddling, money laundering and terrorism. I spoke on the problems associated with corruption, black money, the investigation of international crimes and terrorism. Niru and I drove around Tiananmen Square that evening, but photography was prohibited. After Beijing, the Indian delegation was invited to Shanghai as guests of the Mayor, who gave us a great welcome and extended warm hospitality. We had a stopover at Hong Kong, where we went to the famous island of Macau, to witness our Indian host gamble for shockingly high stakes and win.

◆

Manira had passed out of Jesus & Mary Convent in 1988 and graduated from St Stephen's College. She was sent to boarding school in Bangalore for two years, which she openly resented—viewing it as discrimination—thus compelling us to bring her back. She was bold and self-confident, with a will of her own. She travelled through Europe on her own at eighteen and joined *The Observer* in 1991 as a trainee, reporting to Chandan Mitra. She made several trips with me in India and abroad, attending meetings and conferences, which provided her early international exposure. After two years in the print media, she decided to shift to the electronic media, joined Miditech and plunged into production.

In April 1995, Manira married Joe Pinto—the son of Bertie and Juliet Pinto, a well-known family of Mangalore—an environmental engineer who was back from the US to launch his own business. She is the only one of our children to marry within the community. The wedding reception, on the lawns of 23, Ashoka Road, was a beautiful affair, with violet as the theme colour because of her name—Manira Violet. When she moved to Bangalore we felt as if the family had broken up—we missed her. The only consolation was that I could see her often on my trips there. Manira and Joe soon moved to the US. When their first child was to be born in June 1999, Niru and I went to be with her and spent a month looking after her and the baby—Tavish. But I found the going tough and was glad to return home at the end of it. They moved back to India in early 2000. Their second child, Zoya, was born in 2003, the week Mother Teresa was beatified, and so got the second name—Theresa. I declined the invitation to join President Kalam's delegation to Spain and Portugal to be with Manira for the event.

Politically conscious and outspoken, Manira has been active in social and NGO circles, besides making a mark in television documentary production. She became a member of the High-Level Committee for Women's Empowerment appointed by the UPA government, playing an important role in the drafting of its report. She also serves as the Treasurer of the Alva Foundation.

◆

In March 1995, after attending the World Summit for Social Development at Copenhagen with the Prime Minister, we travelled to the airport by bus. There was an interesting discussion on the agenda of the summit and the new areas that the developing world was being urged to 'open up', besides the many commitments we had made for social development.

'Such "opening up" is inevitable,' said the Prime Minister. 'We have to be prepared for it.'

'But there will be strong reactions to such moves at home, sir, and elections are not far away. We have to be cautious,' I warned.

A.N. Verma, the Principal Secretary to the Prime Minister—as if he were the government's conscience-keeper—said, 'We must be prepared for defeat, if it comes to that. But there is no way liberalization as a policy can be reversed!'

The Prime Minister listened with a grave expression, and pouted.

Later, on the flight, I raised the issue. 'Are we to accept Verma's formula and prepare for defeat? You said nothing to him in reply! Why?' I asked.

'Win or lose,' he said gravely, 'I am not bothered. After all, I will go down in history as the only non-Nehru–Gandhi Prime Minister to last a full term, despite them.' I fell silent.

I had several arguments with him over various issues. 'Why don't you take decisions, sir? You let matters drag on—why?' I once, asked.

'Not taking a decision is also a decision,' he answered, unperturbed.

◆

In August 1995, the family decided on a holiday in the Andaman & Nicobar Islands. The Lt. Governor, an old friend from Kerala, offered his residence as he was on holiday in his home state. A trip to Barren Island by the Governor's yacht was arranged. We arrived in the morning, spent a relaxed day on the beach and headed back in high spirits. Then, mid-way, the sky turned black, and we were stuck in a raging storm—the deck lashed by angry waves and the small vessel tossed in the high seas. We prayed for almost two hours—the whole family seemed to be on the verge of drowning. And then the sky cleared and the stars became visible; the sea calmed. We were saved, even as I swore never to venture out to sea again. Then we touched land.

We were to fly back that evening, but bad weather resulted in the cancellation of the bi-weekly flight back. The next day was my Question Hour in Parliament. I phoned the Prime Minister and told him that I was stranded far away. 'Nice excuse to extend your holiday. I will have you flown back—don't worry,' he assured me. And he did fly us back in the Air Force cargo plane which was returning empty after unloading supplies. It was an unforgettable journey, but we reached Calcutta in time for our evening flight to Delhi—and my briefing sessions for Question Hour in Parliament.

Chapter 25

SUCCESSES AND SCANDALS:
THE GOVERNMENT UNDER P.V. NARASIMHA RAO

P.V. Narasimha Rao led a minority government. He had to plan his strategy carefully. Soon after taking charge, he called a meeting of a small group of us. He listed the challenges we faced, then asked for our suggestions on how to manage them. After detailed discussions, it was decided that we'd divide the commitments made in our manifesto into five lists:

1. Subjects which can be dealt with administratively, without going to Parliament;
2. Legislation that can go through by consensus without difficulty;
3. Legislation that can go through by negotiating with friendly parties;
4. Legislation for which careful floor management will have to be planned;
5. Subjects which are almost impossible to legislate—to be kept for the final year.

Following this, each of the ministries was given a task-list for the first year and asked to start work on legislation for the second year. This process worked beautifully, and by the time we reached the middle of the second year, the government seemed well-settled, with the Prime Minister in control.

This was his style of functioning—he spoke little, but his actions, when taken, were decisive. He was quick to grasp that his was a minority government that had to rule by consensus, taking the opposition on board. Significantly, he realized that the most effective of Prime Ministers granted their Council of Ministers responsibility. Consequently, the Cabinet was given the status envisaged by the Constitution, and most important decisions were taken there and not in the PMO.

His expertise came to the fore when the country struggled with an economic crisis it had inherited. Along with his Finance Minister,

Manmohan Singh, he took bold steps that came with far-reaching, positive consequences—industrial licensing was made simpler; several areas reserved for public enterprises were opened up; export subsidies were slashed; and gradually, measures were introduced for private and financial institutions to buy public sector shares. Not surprisingly, investments rose from US$100 million to US$3.5 billion during his five-year tenure, and economic growth leapt from a mere 1.5 per cent in 1991 to 7.5 per cent in 1996.[57] Thanks to his encouragement, Manmohan Singh—who, along with his team in the Planning Commission, had been referred to as 'a bunch of jokers' by Rajiv Gandhi—left a definite mark on India's economic history.

Besides being resolute, the Prime Minister was also a strategic player. At the Tirupati plenary session of the AICC in April 1992, an open contest for half the seats in the CWC were announced, instead of the party's traditional and time-tested nomination approach. Out of the blue, Arjun Singh and Sharad Pawar formed an axis to win the crucial polls; a list of ten names, drawn up by them, came to be circulated, from which nine members were elected. The Prime Minister spotted trouble—the rise of a rival centre of authority in the party's top-most body. Therefore, when the results were announced, agitated, he stood up to state that it was a sad day for him—for the party had failed to elect a single woman or SC candidate to the CWC. In fact, the only SC member on the panel, N.Y. Hanumanthappa of Karnataka, had been defeated by Jitendra Prasada, his Political Secretary. With this speech, he cleverly discredited the elections. Then came the final blow—he said that if he had been so elected, he would have resigned—thus making a covert appeal to his supporters to quit. Promptly, Jitendra Prasada resigned; this was followed by a spate of resignations of other elected members. As President, he now used his powers under the Congress Constitution to nominate all of them back to the CWC. He then went on to nominate ten members of his choice—including the podgy, ever-smiling Omem Deori, an unknown woman leader from Arunachal Pradesh, as the women's representative. He had cleverly and carefully cut his opponents down to size.

Perhaps because of his purposeful, yet silent manner of functioning, P.V. Narasimha Rao found himself growing increasingly isolated. This came to a head during the Harshad Mehta scandal. Mehta is said to have

---

[57] *World Trade Organization, Dispute Settlement Reports, 1999*, Volume 5 (UK: Cambridge University Press, 2002).

exploited loopholes in the banking system and siphoned off funds through inter-bank transactions. When the scam was exposed, expectedly, banks demanded their money back. Under pressure, Mehta, in 1993, sought to divert attention by claiming that he had delivered a suitcase containing ₹1 crore to the Prime Minister's residence in November 1991 to get off the hook. How much money and the precise denomination of the notes that could fit into a suitcase of the size mentioned by Mehta became a subject of public debate and jokes. While Mehta's allegation could never be proved, the Prime Minister was bailed out by the admission of the party Treasurer that the amount which had been sent to him was a donation for the Punjab election. None of the senior Ministers or other party functionaries came forward to defend the Prime Minister.

His sense of isolation compelled him to create a team of his own. Gradually, a group of advisors emerged, which included V.C. Shukla, Jitendra Prasada, Devendra Dwivedi, Bhuvanesh Chaturvedi (who became MoS PMO) and the IYC President, M.S. Bitta.

◆

Several attempts to revive, strengthen and empower traditional village panchayats had been made after Independence. But the idea gained real momentum under Rajiv Gandhi as Prime Minister, with the 64th Constitution Amendment Bill getting introduced and passed in the Lok Sabha in 1989, but defeated in the Rajya Sabha.

It was the Congress government under P.V. Narasimha Rao that finally got the two bills passed in 1992 as the 73rd and 74th Constitution Amendments with the required number of states endorsing them. This heralded a new phase in our democracy—taking it to the grassroots and providing representation through reservations for women, SC/STs and minorities. It was undoubtedly the largest silent, peaceful, democratic revolution in the world. The endorsement of the amendments in Parliament was a tribute to the memory of Rajiv Gandhi, whose dream and commitment this was.

The passage of these Constitution amendments has led to the establishment of gram panchayats, taluk panchayats and zilla panchayats, with almost six million representatives elected by popular ballot, one-third of them women.

◆

1993 saw impeachment proceedings initiated against a Supreme Court Judge for the first time in our history. Justice V. Ramaswami of Tamil Nadu—formerly a Chief Justice of the Punjab and Haryana High Courts, and at the height of his career, a Supreme Court Judge—found himself embroiled in a controversy when the ostentatious expenditure on his official residence and his daughter's marriage came to be reported. On 1 February 1991, the Supreme Court Bar Association had passed a resolution calling for his impeachment on charges of corruption. The BJP and the Left submitted a 'Motion of Impeachment', seeking his removal from office. Accepting the motion on 12 March 1991, Speaker Rabi Ray had constituted a committee composed of Justice P.B. Sawant of the Supreme Court, Chief Justice P.D. Desai of the Bombay High Court and Justice O. Chinnappa Reddy, a retired Judge of the Supreme Court, to investigate the matter. The committee found Ramaswami guilty on eleven out of fourteen charges.

The Impeachment Motion was brought to the Lok Sabha for debate and voting on 10 May 1993. The Lok Sabha served as a courtroom, with a special podium erected at the main entrance to the House to act as the 'bar'. Charges were presented by CPM leader, Somnath Chatterjee, while Kapil Sibal defended the Judge from the podium.

Sibal's was a brilliant defence—be it in terms of language and tenor, or the legal arguments presented and the issues raised. He systematically demolished the entire charge sheet. The debate continued all day and spilt over to the next, when the MPs were to have the final say through a recorded vote.

Emotions were running high; there was an obvious North-South, upper caste-SC divide. Many claimed that the impeachment proceedings were a conspiracy to defame the SCs, and a backlash against their rise to positions of power. The matter was hotly debated in Central Hall, the lobbies and corridors, and of course, the press galleries.

Given the divided opinions on the matter, a few seniors kept pushing for the whip. I joined the ranks of those who demanded a free conscience vote, as a whip would not allow us the right to decide for ourselves; besides, this was not a policy issue. The Prime Minister, who had so far been silent on the matter, called me aside and asked, 'So, you are lobbying for a free vote? You are a Minister and must be more discreet. Please wait till the party takes a decision.'

'Sir, I feel very strongly about this issue,' I responded, given that I was vehemently opposed to the motion. 'You have heard Kapil Sibal. The majority wants a free vote. Please do not issue a whip. It will be unethical.'

After long consultations, the Congress and its allies decided to abstain from voting. Of the 401 members in the Lok Sabha, 196 voted for the Motion of Impeachment, with 205 abstentions. The motion—which required not less than a two-third majority of the total number of members present and voting, and an absolute majority of the total membership—thus failed to pass.[58] A historic chapter in India's Parliamentary history was closed.

◆

During his term (and even after), the Prime Minister found himself battling a number of corruption allegations—the Harshad Mehta scam being the first. Then came the Jain Hawala exposé.

In February 1991, two Kashmiri students—Shahabuddin Ghauri and Ashfaq Lone—were arrested under TADA (Terrorist and Disruptive Activities [Prevention] Act). The investigating officers suspected that the two were acting as a conduit for passing hawala money to terrorists. The investigations pointed to the Jain brothers—industrialists B.R., N.K. and S.K. Jain. What emerged was a scam of unimaginable proportions, with journalist Vineet Narain's *Kalachakra* revealing the extent.

It emerged that between 1989 and 1991, the Jain brothers had illegally transferred funds amounting to US$33 million from all parts of the world to a range of Indian leaders across political parties in return for various favours. Even more damaging was the fact that the Jains, protected by powerful political entities, had also channelled hawala money to Kashmiri militants.

In the diary entries of the Jains, the names of 115 politicians and officials cropped up. The list shook the establishment. Among those mentioned were L.K. Advani, Arjun Singh, Sharad Yadav and Devi Lal, besides Ministers from the Cabinet and several others.

Suddenly, a ticking bomb landed on my lap. The CBI was under my charge. The then Director of the CBI, K. Vijaya Rama Rao, called on me one evening to inform me that the Home Minister, on instructions from the PMO, had directed him to submit the names under investigation to the Supreme Court—this was in response to a notice from the court which

---

[58]'Impeachment that Wasn't', *The Indian Express*, 9 September 2008.

was hearing a PIL (Public Interest Litigation) filed by Vineet Narain. I was left speechless. Many of those under the scanner were my colleagues. I asked Rama Rao to wait and went to meet the Prime Minister to ask, 'How can we do this to your Ministers? They are a part of your team. Call them, explain the circumstances, and let them resign, if they so wish, or sack them. But what we are doing is wrong, sir. Please think of the fallout.'

He was unresponsive. Then, he asked, 'Are you convinced they are all innocent?'

'How can I say, sir?' I argued.

'Then keep quiet and do not interfere!' was his stern reply.

'In that case, I will keep quiet in Parliament, too. I cannot defend this.' I got up.

'Don't worry, I will defend my decision,' he shot back as I left.

And so it was—the CBI filed the list in the Supreme Court. All hell broke loose. There were whispers and discussions everywhere, with tempers running high. The CBI began investigating together with the Enforcement Directorate. I was caught in the crossfire. I got nasty phone calls from MPs and party leaders. No one would believe me when I said I had no role to play in this. 'Then why are you sitting in this ministry like a dumb doll?' a senior Minister asked. I had no answers. All I knew was that decisions were being taken at the 'highest level'.

As the drama unfolded, the Cabinet and the party were vertically divided. To justify his position before the party, the Prime Minister claimed, 'This is a question of national security; the same source is funding Ministers, politicians, bureaucrats and terrorist outfits. Can I ignore the issue?' But leaders were not appeased by such rhetoric.

Within Parliament, after a lot of furore and several disruptions, the government agreed to a discussion. Atal Bihari Vajpayee opened the debate and spoke with a mix of anger, humour and sarcasm. I took notes for the Prime Minister; the government was to respond that evening.

At around 5 p.m. that day, I was called to the Prime Minister's Parliament House office. Rama Rao, A.N. Verma and a couple of PMO officials were there with him. I was given a sheaf of typed sheets and asked to go through them, which I did.

'You can suggest changes before it is finalized,' said a grave Prime Minister.

'Why me? You have the experts you need around you, sir,' I replied.

'Because you will have to respond to the debate tonight,' he answered, calmly.

'Me? But you had said you were doing it!' I said in shock.

'You are the Minister in charge of the CBI. I will intervene at the end, if necessary. You will do a good job, don't worry,' he assured me.

My heart pounded. How could he do this to me? And what choice did I have? Finally, I said, 'Let me go through the papers carefully once again.' I made a few language changes and added at the end: 'The matter is in court. The law will take its course. I am confident and hopeful that my colleagues will come out clean.'

The Prime Minister read the additions and cut out the last sentence, saying, 'This is not necessary!'

I stood in Parliament with the papers in my trembling hands. '*Arey! Kiya sab kaam aapne, our khada kiya us bichari mantri ko*' ('You are responsible for all this, and you make that poor Minister stand up here'), shouted Atal Bihari Vajpayee, as the whole House thumped the desks. I collected myself, and went through my written reply calmly, placing the facts in sequence and telling the House that we had to submit to the directions of the Supreme Court in response to a PIL. There were nasty snide remarks from both sides of the House. It was obvious that everyone, whether named or unnamed, saw this as a clever ploy to fix or finish political opponents and critics.

Many of those charge-sheeted were denied tickets in the 1996 elections. The Hawala case dragged on—despite a change of governments. On 8 April 1997, the Delhi High Court Judge, Mohammad Shamim, acquitted L.K. Advani and V.C. Shukla, saying that there was no clinching evidence— only coded entries in private dairies that proved no trail of payments.

After this, there was one common intent and resolve across all parties— to bury the Jain Hawala case.

◆

As though the Harshad Mehta and Hawala scandal weren't bad enough, the Prime Minister found himself embroiled in the Lakhubhai Pathak case. Pathak, a UK-based pickle tycoon, claimed that during his visit to New York in 1983, he had been introduced to Narasimha Rao (then the Foreign Minister) by the controversial godman, Chandraswami, and his associate, K.N. Agarwal (aka Mamaji), in a hotel room. Here, P.V. Narasimha Rao, it was claimed, had promised Pathak a contract for the supply of newsprint and paper pulp in India. Pathak claimed that in January 1984, on this assurance, he had paid Chandraswami US$1,00,000 by two cheques, but the contract did not fructify. Upset, he filed a complaint of cheating in September 1987. In February 1988, the CBI registered an FIR.

This case came to haunt P.V. Narasimha Rao as his tenure as Prime Minister ended—for, on 9 July 1996, the Chief Metropolitan Magistrate proceeded against him as an accused in the case. The Delhi High Court upheld the Chief Metropolitan Magistrate's order. However, Rao (with Chandraswami and Mamaji) was finally acquitted in December 2003. Pathak, in the meantime, had died.

Out of loyalty to my former boss, I was among the few who attended a couple of hearings and was present when the final judgement was pronounced, which came as a huge relief to him and his well-wishers. Sadly, the real culprits got away with the money.

◆

Despite multiple pulls and pressures, we were running a minority government as efficiently as possible. But, on 26 July 1993, a No-confidence Motion was tabled against us in the Lok Sabha.

We were short of a simple majority by fourteen votes. Every possible vote had to be secured; there was hectic activity and lobbying round the clock. The trusted core team of the Prime Minister took charge. Members who were out of Delhi or the country were summoned, and negotiations with parties launched.

Ultimately, the Jharkhand Mukti Morcha (JMM) members and the Janata Dal's Ajit Singh group voted against the motion—though Ajit Singh himself abstained. We thus managed to defeat the motion on 28 July. There were slogans and rejoicing both inside and outside the House.

But matters did not end there. Shortly thereafter, the President of the Rashtriya Mukti Morcha (RMM), Ravinder Kumar, filed a complaint with the CBI, alleging that Prime Minister Narasimha Rao, along with some of his party colleagues, had bribed four MPs of the JMM (Shibu Soren, Simon Marandi, Shailendra Mahato and Suraj Mandal) to vote in favour of the Congress in the motion. Kumar alleged that once the four MPs voted as directed, they were paid ₹30 lakh each. Further, he claimed that the Prime Minister had received money from Hawala operator, S.K. Jain, to win over these voters.

The Special Judge, Delhi, took cognizance of the alleged offence, and prosecution proceedings were launched against the purported givers and recipients of the bribes—who, in turn, filed petitions in the High Court, seeking to quash charges. But their petitions were dismissed. The appeals were then heard by a Bench of three Judges who referred them to a Five-Judge Constitution Bench. These Judges, by a 3:2 majority, held that the alleged bribe-takers, who voted on the No-confidence Motion, were entitled to immunity from prosecution for the offences of bribery and criminal conspiracy, in view of Article 105(2) of the Constitution.[59] They also ruled that MPs are 'public servants', and therefore, a prosecuting agency, before filing a charge sheet in a Criminal Court against an MP, has to obtain the permission of the Chairman of the Rajya Sabha or the Speaker of the Lok Sabha, as the case may be.

So, the JMM bribery saga, too, reached a conclusion.

◆

Even as the government battled multiple corruption charges, a huge calamity unfolded. After L.K. Advani's rath yatra, and the BJP's subsequent victory across the four state assemblies of Uttar Pradesh, Himachal Pradesh, Rajasthan and Madhya Pradesh—largely by mobilizing the Hindu vote bank—the VHP (Vishva Hindu Parishad)–RSS combine acquired land around the disputed mosque at Ayodhya in October 1991. They began levelling it to construct a temple. Worried by these developments, in July 1992, a team from the Central government visited the area and found a 'large concrete platform'[60] being built—in clear contravention of court orders. It demanded that status quo be maintained. Clearly, Kalyan Singh, the BJP Chief Minister, with an RSS grounding, had allowed all this to happen. To make matters worse, besides focusing on Ayodhya, Mathura and Kashi, kar-sevaks began adding to the list of disputed structures all over the country.

The Prime Minister kept negotiations going, hoping to find an acceptable solution. Arjun Singh, in the meantime, met Kalyan Singh in Lucknow and

---

[59]The article states: 'No Member of Parliament shall be liable to any proceedings in any court in respect of anything said or any vote given by him in Parliament or any committee thereof, and no person shall be so liable in respect of the publication by or under the authority of either House of Parliament of any report, paper, votes or proceedings.'
[60]See Madhav Godbole, *Unfinished Innings* (New Delhi: Orient Longman, 1996).

publicly declared that he had received an assurance that all would be fine.

Suddenly, after August 1992, the talks through emissaries with apolitical sadhus, which had been proceeding smoothly, were called off without explanation. Obviously the political forces behind the dispute did not want a peaceful solution. The Prime Minister's advisors suggested that the Prime Minister meet Advani. Despite having doubts about Advani's intentions, he is said to have had a secret meeting with him. But nothing useful materialized.

I am not surprised by this. Gauri Advani, L.K. Advani's daughter-in-law at that time (now divorced), circulated a letter citing plans for the destruction of the Babri Masjid, discussed in a train compartment that carried her, her father-in-law and others to Ayodhya on the eve of the demolition.

In the meantime, the VHP announced 6 December 1992 as the date for the commencement of temple construction. From mid-November, volunteers began pouring into Ayodhya, carrying bricks; they were fed and housed by the Uttar Pradesh government. The Centre sent 20,000 troops into the state, and they were stationed close to the Babri Masjid, with instructions to move in if required. But on 6 December 1992, the over one-lakh strong force of RSS, VHP, BJP volunteers pushed past the cordon of the police and climbed the mosque, brandishing saffron flags and attacking the structure with axes and hammers. The police ran away; the closely-stationed central forces, who kept waiting for orders, failed to act; and the Babri Masjid came down as thousands of kar-sevaks and leaders—including L.K. Advani, Uma Bharati and Murli Manohar Joshi—cheered.

It was a lazy Sunday afternoon when staff living in my quarters suddenly rushed in, fear writ large on their faces: 'Bahut bura hua hai, Ayodhya ko nuksaan pahuncha hai. Ab gadbad shuru ho jayegi. Danga hoga desh mein. Hamein bachaye.' ('Something terrible has happened, there has been destruction in Ayodhya. Now there will be trouble. There will be riots in the country. Save us.') I could not understand what they were saying till the children switched on the television, which carried live news of the events in Ayodhya. We gaped in disbelief. How could this have happened?

I rushed to the Prime Minister's house; the gates were shut. I was told that he was resting and could not be disturbed. I was furious! 'Desh jalnewala hai. PM so rahe hain? Uthaaeeye unhein, mein milna chahati hoon.' ('The country is going to burn. The Prime Minister is sleeping?

Wake him up, I need to meet him!') The otherwise friendly SPG at the gates refused to let me in. I went home, angry and disappointed, and got back to watching television coverage of one of the most tragic events in the history of independent India—all this while the Prime Minister rested.

The Babri Masjid episode was a disaster for the government, the Congress and the nation. After the demolition, the Prime Minister found himself totally isolated. The undercurrent of anger and distrust was fuelled by the general belief that he had colluded with the RSS to let the masjid fall. A number of questions, all valid, were raised: Why did the Prime Minister not see the writing on the wall? Why did he not suspect Advani's intentions? Why was Article 356 (President's Rule) not imposed? And why were central forces not moved into the area to deal with any and all eventualities? These questions persist.

◆

Soniaji and the Prime Minister had never really appeared comfortable with each other. She seemed unable to trust him, not least because of his proximity to Chandraswami, who was being investigated for his role in Rajivji's assassination. The Prime Minister, on his part, had always been unnerved by her aloofness. But after the Babri Masjid episode, the undercurrent of coldness and suspicion increased.

I used to meet Soniaji regularly, trying, in my own way, to broker peace and also persuade her to lead the party. Before my efforts could yield results, the decision of the government (the PMO to be precise) to appeal against the Delhi High Court decision[61] to quash complaints in the Bofors case was announced. Soniaji was doubly upset with him. I clarified to her that while I was in charge of the CBI, I had neither been asked nor told about this development, and all instructions had gone directly through A.N. Verma when the Prime Minister was abroad.

At this, she snapped, 'What does the Prime Minister want to do? Send me to jail?'

I protested, 'You misunderstand.'

---

[61]In September 1992, the High Court quashed the FIR in the Bofors case. It also quashed the Letter Rogatory (a formal request made to a foreign court for judicial assistance, which also includes the recording of evidence on foreign soil) issued to the Swiss Court. In December that year, the Supreme Court reversed the Delhi High Court's judgement.

She shot back, 'What has the Congress government done for me? This house was allotted to me by the Chandra Shekhar government. I am not seeking any favours for myself and my children from him.' She was really angry.

I conveyed her response to the Prime Minister. Like Soniaji, he snapped at me, 'What does she want from me? I cannot close the Bofors case which is before the courts. It will go on.'

Consequently, I found myself playing an (unwilling) intercessor. While Soniaji remained angry, the Prime Minister would call me over now and then on Sunday evenings to know the 'mood' at 10, Janpath. He seemed keen to avoid confrontation, but was unable to break the ice. My sincere efforts to help made me a suspect in both 'camps'.

◆

In Karnataka, in the meantime, Veerappa Moily proved to be as unpopular as Bangarappa had been controversial. Party workers were unhappy, the bureaucracy uneasy, and a large section of legislators were in revolt. Given that Moily rarely kept his promises, he soon earned the title of 'Oily Moily'.

Once more, the party in Karnataka was in disarray. One day the Prime Minister decided to respond to the crisis by telling me, 'Get ready! Pack up and prepare to move to Bangalore. I am appointing you as KPCC President.'

I was stunned! How could I move? I spoke to him calmly and said that I did not want to be an imposition upon warring leaders, who would use, then reject me. 'Please speak to them first and get them to agree,' I pleaded.

So he called the quarrelling factions to Delhi. There was a meeting at his residence. Instead of telling them that he planned to send me as President, he asked them to hold a discussion amongst themselves and give him a panel of names for a new PCC President. The meeting room turned into the proverbial Tower of Babel. Each person had a point of view, dictated by caste, community and religion, and no consensus seemed to emerge. I was secretly happy and relieved. When they left, he told me philosophically, 'I understand your point. They can agree about nothing.'

After all that debate and discussion, the Prime Minister characteristically shocked everybody by choosing an old, obscure Brahmin MP from Kolar, V. Krishna Rao. He was neither respected nor listened to, and the party became more rudderless than ever before.

When the Assembly elections of 1994 came, the Chief Minister—who had boasted that he would win a two-thirds majority in the 224-member House—gave the party the worst drubbing it had ever received, winning only 34 seats![62] He then went into hibernation.[63]

◆

In early 1996, the Prime Minister decided to bow down in the face of growing demands for his withdrawal as the party's President. There was again a race for the post. This time the two main contenders were Pranab Mukherjee and Sitaram Kesri, still the seasoned and wily Treasurer of the party. I attended a couple of meetings of the Mukherjee camp. But when I visited Central Hall and the AICC, I felt that the undercurrent of support for Kesri was growing, clearly with the blessings of 10, Janpath. The argument put forth was that Kesri was an old Nehru–Gandhi loyalist and so would be the ideal stop-gap arrangement till such time as Sonia decided to accept the top position.

I reported my observations to Pranabda and his assembled supporters. But my comments annoyed him. He asked me how my insights helped, then shouted, 'You are supposed to be working for me, not listening to *their* arguments!' I was taken aback, especially since I had strongly pleaded Pranabda's case with the Prime Minister earlier, who had said, 'I do not want to upset the lady!' Kesriji became Vice President while Pranabda was appointed as the Deputy Chairman of the Planning Commission, and subsequently, as a Union Cabinet Minister—which he was happy with.

Relations between Arjun Singh and Narasimha Rao had always remained hostile. The resentment grew after the latter beat Singh in the race for the Prime Minister's post. During negotiations, Rao is supposed to have agreed to step down as the AICC President after becoming the Prime Minister—a post that Arjun Singh presumed he would get. But once in the saddle, he refused to budge and clung on to both positions. This angered Singh and his supporters. The demolition of the Babri Masjid and the riots that followed only increased the antagonism. Unlike M.L. Fotedar, who

---

[62]See *Statistical Report on General Elections, 1994, to the Legislative Assembly of Karnataka*, in <http://eci.nic.in/eci_main/statisticalreports/SE_1994/StatisticalReport-KT94.pdf>, accessed on 22 November 2015.

[63]While in 'hibernation', Veerappa Moily started translating Indian mythological texts. He resurfaced in 2000 as the Chairman of the Tax Reforms Commission set up by the BJP government.

openly attacked the Prime Minister and resigned, Arjun Singh continued attacking him while still in the Cabinet.

Along with Singh, other voices of discontent emerged—several criticizing the economic reforms of the government, claiming that they were in conflict with the stated policies of the party. Gradually, an anti-P.V. group surfaced. This faction—comprising N.D. Tiwari, Arjun Singh, Sheila Dikshit, Shiv Charan Mathur, M.L. Fotedar, P. Shiv Shankar and K.N. Singh—received tacit support from 10, Janpath.

In March 1993, the anti-P.V. group sat in dharna outside the venue of the AICC session at Surajkund. In 1994, Arjun Singh resigned. Efforts at a compromise failed and the Congress (Tiwari) took formal shape. Besides the Congress (Tiwari), a number of other dissident, breakaway factions emerged—the Karnataka Congress, headed by Bangarappa; the Tamil Maanila Congress, led by G.K. Moopanar; and the Madhya Pradesh Vikas Congress, floated by Madhavrao Scindia. In the midst of this, the Congress denied P.V. Narasimha Rao a ticket to contest the 1996 elections to Parliament on grounds that he had to atone for not doing enough to prevent the demolition of the Babri Masjid. He faded out, unsung.

In this General Election, the Indian National Congress won only 140 seats. In the concurrent state elections in Assam, Haryana, Kerala, Tamil Nadu, West Bengal and the union territory of Pondicherry, the Congress (which controlled each of these states, except for Tamil Nadu and West Bengal) fared badly.

The Congress (Tiwari) fared even worse, securing four seats, while the Karnataka Congress and Madhya Pradesh Vikas Congress won one seat each. If any splinter-party performed well, it was the Tamil Maanila Congress.[64]

A number of reasons were attributed to the Congress' defeat, from the trail of scandals to the Babri Masjid demolition, which lost the party its Muslim votes. Moreover, the crude manner in which Congress President Sitaram Kesri, at the manifesto release ceremony at the AICC, announced that Rao would be denied a party ticket, was condemned by Congressmen and opposition parties alike—thus denting the party's image. It must also be admitted that each split weakened the Congress, dividing its secular

[64]*Statistical Report on General Elections, 1996*, in <http://eci.nic.in/eci_main/StatisticalReports/ LS_1996/Vol_I_LS_96.pdf>, accessed on 20 November 2015.

vote bank. 1996 brought the first BJP-led government to power under Atal Bihari Vajpayee.

While P.V. Narasimha Rao led the party and the government through grave challenges for a full five-year term, he wasn't working alone. Many of us slogged for him, helped him through emergencies and managed members in both Houses during the most tumultuous sessions. But he did not reward me for my work. While he may have had his compulsions—forced to accommodate his favourites, or curtailed by his conjecture that I was a Sonia loyalist—I will never fully understand his reasons. Halfway through his term, he gave Cabinet berths to several Ministers, but left me out. He did not bring me into the CWC either. Despite it all, I refused to go with the Congress (Tiwari) in 1995.

◆

Despite heading a minority government that was riddled with scams and scheming leaders, P.V. Narasimha Rao was the first non-Nehru–Gandhi Prime Minister who had lasted a full five-year term. He had taken the first steps towards economic reforms. But for the fall of the Babri Masjid, his was a remarkable tenure. Yet he was denied a ticket to contest. The Congress sidelined and humiliated him. But I had learnt many lessons from him. I had great respect and admiration for his leadership. I am sure history will judge him likewise.

With the defeat of the Congress, another chapter of my political career had closed. I was still a member of the Rajya Sabha, but suddenly felt all alone. P.V. Narasimha Rao, with whom I had worked closely for over twelve years in the party and the government, had moved out. Though I was friendly with Soniaji, the rapport I had with 10, Janpath during Rajivji's days was missing. Karnataka had bosses who were not very supportive either. The party was divided and in a shambles, both at the Centre and in the states, as Sitaram Kesri lacked the image or the capacity to lead. Non-political backroom boys became active and were viewed with suspicion. Each frustrated leader was positioning himself to capture the seat of power when the occasion arose. All in all, the future appeared uncertain and bleak for me as the end of my fourth term approached.

While in the opposition, we fought our battles against the Vajpayee government—on minority rights, communal tensions, foreign policy reversals and Centre–state relations. I remember a debate on the communal situation, during which I made a hard-hitting speech. Advaniji, the Home Minister, intervened to say—'Margaretji, why are you so angry? I am a product of a Christian education. I was educated by the Jesuits in Karachi.'

'Then how did you go astray?' I asked to the loud thumping of desks from opposition benches.

Soon the Vajpayee government began to flounder and was gone in thirteen days, taking the country back to the polls.

As a CPA observer for elections in Cameroon

*As Minister-in-waiting to First Lady of
USA Hillary Clinton, on her
visit to India; 1995*

*Secretary-general Kofi Annan (second from right) meeting
with the delegation of Parliamentarians for Global Action; 1997*

On the campaign trail in Uttara Kannada for the Parliamentary elections; 1999

Thanking voters after a Lok Sabha victory; October 1999

With His Holiness Pope John Paul II, as India's representative for the celebrations at Vatican City to mark 2000 years of the birth of Christ; November 2000

With President Bill Clinton and Benazir Bhutto at the President's breakfast meeting at Washington, USA; 2000

At Nikhil's wedding, serving P.V. Narasimha Rao and
Atal Bihari Vajpayee; 27 December 1997

With Leader of the Opposition Sonia Gandhi leading a protest march
against the NDA government; 2003

As a member of the first goodwill delegation of journalists and Parliamentarians to Pakistan, presenting a khadi angavastra to President Pervez Musharraf; August 2003

Resting after the Dandi March II with Congress President Sonia Gandhi at Ahmedabad; 2005

Paying tribute to Joachim and Violet Alva at the unveiling ceremony of their portrait in the Central Hall of Parliament; 5 December 2007

With President Pratibha Patil and Speaker Somnath Chatterjee at Joachim and Violet Alva's stamp release at Rashtrapati Bhavan; 2009

Presenting an Honorary Doctorate to Prime Minister Manmohan Singh at the G.B. Pant University, Uttarakhand; 2010

With Niranjan and Aung San Suu Kyi at Bangalore; November 2012

With Niranjan and President Pranab Mukherjee at Raj Bhavan, Jaipur; 2013

*As Governor, greeting BJP leaders at the swearing-in of
Chief Minister Vasundhara Raje; 2013*

The family at our golden wedding celebrations at Raj Bhavan, Jaipur; 24 May 2014

In the Lok Sabha

Chapter 26

FORGING FORWARD: IN THE LOWER HOUSE

After the collapse of the thirteen-day Vajpayee government on 1 June 1996, the Congress, as the second largest party, declined to form a government. Instead, it chose to support a government headed by the Janata Dal, with Karnataka Chief Minister H.D. Deve Gowda assuming the position of Prime Minister. It was a United Front coalition. But it was far from stable, troubled by internal strife, accommodating, as it did, parties with drastically different ideologies.

In the middle of all this there emerged the rumour that Deve Gowda was planning to begin inquiries into Sitaram Kesri's role in an old murder case—the killing of government physician Dr Surendra Tanwar. Kesriji claimed this was a conspiracy to frame him, and as the party's President, threatened withdrawal of Congress support—plunging the country into a Constitutional crisis.

Out of the blue, I.K. Gujral, the Foreign Minister under Deve Gowda, came to see me. He asked me to help sort out the issue between the Prime Minister and the Congress President by arranging a meeting for him with the latter. I had known Gujralji from the Indira Gandhi era, when he had been part of the Congress. With some difficulty, I persuaded Kesriji to meet him. The meeting took place in my house—23, Ashoka Road. After a two-hour discussion, they decided to consult their own leaders and meet again at my house. This they did, resulting in Gujralji emerging as the compromise Prime Minister. Both thanked me for my intervention and help. But for my response, the United Front government would have fallen, Gujralji would not have become Prime Minister, and the country would have been confronting yet another election.

As it happened, the Congress withdrew support to the Deve Gowda government, and on 11 April, the United Front lost the Vote of Confidence. In order to avoid elections, the United Front elected I.K. Gujral as its new Leader. He was sworn in as Prime Minister on 21 April 1997, with

Congress support.

Yet, when the issue of selecting the next Vice President of India cropped up, neither of them responded to my request for support—though Kesriji did make a commitment that, 'If it is to be a woman, it will be you!' However, they chose I.K. Gujral's long-time friend—Krishan Kant.

Gujral's government began to flounder after he rejected the demand of Arjun Singh (who had returned to the Congress) that the United Front eject the DMK from its ranks, on grounds of the DMK's suspected involvement in the assassination of Rajiv Gandhi. The Congress withdrew support. General Elections followed.

After the elections, the BJP's Atal Bihari Vajpayee put together a coalition of parties to become the Prime Minister. But when the AIADMK withdrew support, his thirteen-month government collapsed. Vajpayeeji remained caretaker Prime Minister even as fresh elections were called.

In the elections of September–October 1999, the NDA, headed by the BJP, secured a majority and Atal Bihari Vajpayee took the oath of office as Prime Minister once again. After a long period of instability, India had a government that would last the full five-year term.

◆

The Congress, in the meantime, was dealing with internal turmoil. This had been the story ever since Sitaram Kesri had become its President, with almost every election we contested being lost. There were increasingly loud demands for Soniaji to step out and take over the leadership of the party. At the Calcutta session of the AICC in December 1997, when she entered the venue, everyone stood up with slogans demanding that she go up to the stage. She firmly refused. Later, in response to repeated demands for her to speak, she called for unity within the party and a commitment from all members to safeguard the ideology of the Congress. She appeared calm, clear and in total control of the situation and herself.

Earlier, in Delhi, Mamata Banerjee—who was planning a massive rally of her supporters in West Bengal during the AICC session in Calcutta—met Soniaji and invited her to address it. She was expected to announce her new party, the Trinamool Congress (TMC), at the rally. Soniaji declined and, at her suggestion, I went to Calcutta and met Mamata. I requested her not to precipitate matters and told her it was not possible for Soniaji to attend her 'show of strength'. She invited me to attend the rally instead, which I declined, suggesting she invite Kesriji. 'Never!' was her angry reply.

What followed is now history. On 14 March 1998, Kesriji resigned. The CWC met and passed a resolution for Soniaji's ascent as Congress President. With this, the sagging spirits of the party revived and the workers suddenly seemed to come to life. In her new avatar as Congress President, Soniaji made a whirlwind tour of the Southern states, addressing massive rallies in Madras, Cochin, Bangalore, Goa and Hyderabad. She requested me to go through and clean up her speeches during her stopover in Bangalore, which I gladly did at night at the Raj Bhavan.

As Head of the Grievances Cell of the Congress—with Archana Dalmia assisting me—I would leave home at 8 a.m. and return past 3 p.m., with piles of papers to be sorted out, and replies to be drafted by hand.

Around this time, R.D. Pradhan persuaded me to join the Congress President's office as Coordinator. But there were many hurdles placed in my way by those around Soniaji, making it impossible for me to function effectively. My job was never defined, nor were my duties specified.

In 1999, just when the party seemed to be uniting under Soniaji's leadership, she faced unexpected opposition from a trio—Sharad Pawar, Tariq Anwar and P.A. Sangma (in true Amar-Akbar-Anthony style). A letter was circulated to the CWC, raising the issue of her foreign origins and suggesting that she step down as Congress President. There was disbelief and anger in party circles, while Soniaji reacted by submitting her resignation. After much difficulty, she was persuaded to stay on, and Pawar and company were expelled, leading to the formation of the NCP (Nationalist Congress Party). Another chunk of the party was gone.

Soniaji contested the 1999 Lok Sabha elections from Bellary in Karnataka and Amethi in Uttar Pradesh. She won both seats but chose to retain Amethi, and became the Leader of the Opposition. She took keen interest in the proceedings and guided the party, meeting senior leaders every morning when the House was in session. Manmohan Singh was appointed Leader of the Opposition in the Rajya Sabha.

◆

Nikhil had met Pria Somiah, the only daughter of C.G. Somiah and Indira (who had been in college with me), at the age of fourteen. The children used to cycle to Moti Bagh every evening for badminton and other games. I heard of the friendship and met her at a couple of parties at our home.

Graduating from Hindu College, she went to Sophia's, Bombay, for a diploma in Media and Communications, and returned to join Miditech. They were married on 27 December 1997, the Coorg-style ceremony held earlier at Bangalore, and ours at Delhi. Around the dining table that evening sat five Prime Ministers—past, present and future—Atal Bihari Vajpayee, Narasimha Rao, I.K. Gujral, H.D. Deve Gowda and V.P. Singh. The toast was proposed by the famous journalist Mark Tully. They stayed on with us. Rian Niranjan, their firstborn, arrived on 8 September 2000, with Laila Indira coming in July 2003.

But we had problems soon after. Niru was noticed gasping for breath while climbing the stairs on an evening out with the family. Dr Reddy, the cardiologist at AIIMS, found four blockages in his arteries and directed us to Dr Baba Das at Apollo, where he was operated. We went through traumatic days, but he recovered well. In the midst of all this, our locked house in Bangalore was ransacked. Luckily, there was nothing to take away. I have always suspected that it was the job of one of our intelligence outfits.

◆

I did not get a ticket for the Lok Sabha elections in 1996, despite my best efforts, as I still had two years left in the Rajya Sabha. In 1998, as my fourth term in the Rajya Sabha was drawing to a close, I was keen to contest a Lok Sabha seat. I became the Congress candidate from Uttara Kannada. This was aided by the fact that the four-time Congress MP from there, Devaraya Naik, had returned to the Congress after switching parties.

R.V. Deshpande, a small-town lawyer from Haliyal, who had started his politics in the Congress, joined the Congress (O) with Ramakrishna Hegde. He became a powerful Janata Party Minister. He would praise me on public platforms and recall his close association with the senior Alvas during his college days. As the Janata Party government in the state began to flounder, he expressed his desire to join the Congress. Despite strong reservations from district Congress leaders, it was on my strong recommendation that he was inducted into the Congress in the presence of the AICC General Secretary, Ghulam Nabi Azad, at a big rally on the eve of the 1998 Parliamentary elections. I believed that this would strengthen our party.

This was my first election. Inexperienced and short of funds, I lost, despite a spirited campaign, by 62,000 votes, exposing the overrated clout of R.V. Deshpande. After the defeat, I toured the constituency, thanking the voters and workers who had stood by me, which was much appreciated.

I then began to experience first-hand the hold of the Brahmin lobby in the district—who controlled the Congress and secured plum positions at all levels even though they formed only 10 per cent of the population, with the OBCs, minorities and SC/STs constituting over 80 per cent. I clearly saw the need for uniting the backward communities and fighting back. I toured the constituency regularly, covered every panchayat and interacted with local leaders. I had used my Rajya Sabha MP-fund to finance key projects in the area. This helped me connect first-hand with the local people.

Therefore, when the 1999 elections were announced thirteen months later, I contested again, and won by a margin of 16,000 votes. I had finally achieved my ambition of being elected directly by the people.

◆

We had moved to 23, Ashoka Road in 1990, after the fall of Rajivji's government, with help from Santosh Hegde who had become Additional Solicitor General. We had done it up beautifully and stayed there till 1998, when my Rajya Sabha term ended. I had three months to vacate. When you are a nobody in Delhi, all doors shut on you. I was refused an extension, with no guest accommodation made available. We were under tremendous pressure from the new allottee of the house—Shabana Azmi, who had been nominated to the Rajya Sabha. The House Committee staff was in awe of her, as she kept phoning them to get the place vacated. So began the hunt for private accommodation, which took us to the National Media Centre in Gurgaon with Nikhil and Pria. Niret decided to move with his family to a flat in Nizamuddin. It broke my heart to see him go. He was the eldest, on whom we depended a lot. But, in a few months, they also shifted to the National Media Centre. It was lovely—three houses close to each other, providing plenty of scope to meet and share resources.

The first committee I was nominated to by the party was the House Committee. The real advantage of my membership to this 'club' was being allotted 12, Safdarjung Lane. I moved there after battling important leaders for its allotment and spent ten years there with Nivedith, Nikhil, Pria and the children till August 2009.

◆

I stepped into the Lok Sabha after twenty-four years in the Rajya Sabha, and after serving as a minister for ten years. I was more senior than most of my colleagues. I was, therefore, quite upset to see that I had been relegated to the fifth row. I protested, and was moved to the second row and placed directly behind Soniaji. This pleased me, despite the many snide remarks that came my way.

During my Lok Sabha years, one of the big battles we fought in the House was for the passage of the Women's Reservation Bill—for 33 per cent of all seats to be allotted to women in Parliament and in the State Legislative Assemblies. After being introduced in 1996, the bill had gone to a Joint Select Committee—headed by senior CPI MP, Geeta Mukherjee—of which I was a member. It lapsed when the United Front government fell.

Then, in 1999, after most of the objections had been ironed out, Law Minister Ram Jethmalani sought to introduce the bill. Before he could do so, the bill was snatched out of his hands by a member of the Samajwadi Party (SP), and torn. We were furious. We organized marches to Parliament, with huge demonstrations on Parliament Street, and dharnas and sit-ins by the statue of Mahatma Gandhi.

Against a backdrop of shouts and counter-shouts, slogans and jeering, the bill was listed again. The Visitors' Gallery was packed with women. Women MPs supporting the bill got into the Well of the House and formed a chain to prevent members of the SP, RJD (Rashtriya Janata Dal), the Lok Jan Shakti Party and the Janata Dal (United)—who opposed the proposed legislation—from getting to Ram Jethmalani. Renuka Chowdhury and I stood in front of Mulayam Singh Yadav (SP) and Lalu Prasad Yadav (RJD). Both the Yadavs hotly objected, saying, '*Arre, aap kya kar rahey hain? Hum kuchch nahin dekh sak rahe hai!*' ('What are you doing? We can see nothing!') Renuka was quick to retort, 'That is the idea. We will block you here and the women of India will throw you out in the elections.' Soon SP and RJD women started shouting slogans against the bill. When we challenged them, they apologized, saying they had to follow the orders of their leaders who would deny them seats if they did not obey. One day, Mulayam Singh stopped me on the steps of Parliament and told me to work out a consensus for a lower percentage of reserved seats. But the NGOs and women activities shouted me down when I proposed it at a meeting.

Despite our best efforts, nothing happened. The bill was introduced, but it died a natural death with the dissolution of the Lok Sabha.

The bill was passed in the Rajya Sabha under the UPA government, so it cannot lapse. But it still needs to be passed by the Lok Sabha. Most parties are committed to it. I hope they have the courage to support it when it comes up for voting.

◆

I was nominated to the Panel of Vice Chairmen by the Speaker. However, Madhavrao Scindia, the Deputy Leader, and Priya Ranjan Dasmunsi, the Chief Whip, expected us to rush to the Well of the House whenever we had to register our protests, without doing so themselves, in view of their 'position'. One day, when I was compelled to go to the Well, Speaker G.M.C. Balayogi admonished me: 'You are a Presiding Officer. You cannot do this. Go back to your seat!' From that day, I refused to join the shouting brigade, which annoyed the leadership. But I stood my ground.

When the issue of the Parliamentary Committee on the Empowerment of Women—which had members of both Houses—came up, there was tension. Najma Heptulla, the Deputy Chairperson of the Rajya Sabha, was keen to continue as its Chairperson, even though the committee had now been transferred to the Lok Sabha. Soniaji had sent my name for the post of Chairperson, and the Speaker assured me that he would do what was necessary. However, the process was blocked as the Rajya Sabha failed to send the names of its members to the Speaker's office, despite several requests and reminders. It became a real tug-of-war. As 8 March—International Women's Day—was approaching, the issue was raised on the floor of the Lok Sabha. The Speaker assured the House that he would announce the committee by 8 March. He also informed the Chairman of the Rajya Sabha, Bhairon Singh Shekhawat, that he would make the announcement without including Rajya Sabha members if the required names were not received before that.

On witnessing these developments, I went to Soniaji and requested her to withdraw my name. She told me to leave it to the discretion of the Speaker, who had his way. On 8 March 2000, the names of members of both Houses were announced. I was named the Chairperson.

For five years, I chaired the Parliamentary Committee on the Empowerment of Women. We did a lot of work—touring states; visiting remote areas, jails and rehabilitation centres; and interacting with Central and state government officials, NGO representatives, elected members of local bodies, the administration, etc. We produced fourteen reports, covering various subjects affecting women. Each of them was well-received.

I recall two important meetings—one with the Chairmen of public sector banks and officers of the Banking Department of the Ministry of Finance; and the second, with the Inspectors General (IGs) of state prisons, and Home and Law Ministry officials.

The first meeting aimed at understanding the role of banks in empowering women. I raised two pointed questions: why were banks paying 4–4.5 per cent interest on SHG (self-help group) deposits while charging them 12–14 per cent on the advances they sought for their activities? And what would be the impact on the banks' profits if SHGs decided to withdraw their deposits, manage their own banking activities and set up a women's bank? There was consternation on their faces. To begin with, they said they were unable to give us precise figures detailing SHG deposits with them. As for the big gap between the interest paid to and charged from SHGs, we were given vague answers like 'risk factor', 'costs of handling small deposits', etc. As for the women's bank, they said it was an impractical and unworkable proposition. 'In that case, we accept the challenge. A "women's bank" will materialize before long!' I said. I launched a campaign for a women's bank right away. I wrote to the Prime Minister, the Finance Minister and Soniaji as Chairperson of the National Advisory Council, and got the idea included in the Congress' manifesto and in our report to Parliament, detailing strategies for economic empowerment. I started speaking about the concept on public platforms and in Parliament. The idea began to gradually gain attention. I am proud that it has become a reality today, though its outreach is still limited to urban middle-class women. I have therefore suggested to the government that post offices be used as extension counters for the bank. Despite pressures and efforts to sabotage its functioning, I hope this bank will survive and serve our women.

The second meeting was on the issue of women in detention. When I was the Minister in charge of Women and Child Development, I had (as mentioned earlier) persuaded Justice Krishna Iyer to head a committee on the subject. After visiting jails across states and interacting with women inmates, his committee produced a report detailing the appalling conditions the women inmates faced—those given bail or parole would continue languishing behind bars (because their families would not come to take them—a pre-condition for release); halfway homes were in a shambles; they had no idea of what they were being paid for their work (all entries of deposits and expenses were being made by unscrupulous wardens). Within prison departments, there were a large number of vacancies and very few women, and there were no Boards of Visitors with the mandatory women representatives. After detailing the dismal lives of women inmates, Justice Iyer went on to provide excellent suggestions for change. I had tried incorporating his ideas in the ministry's plans. But once we lost power at the Centre in 1989, the focus was lost.

I decided to bring this report on the table. We summoned the Home Secretary and his officials dealing with the subject. The Home Secretary did not turn up, claiming that he was busy elsewhere, and instead sent a subordinate. I recorded our displeasure and adjourned the meeting, urging his team to 'give us a date at his convenience'. This did the trick! The Home Secretary summoned the IGs of prisons from across the states and appeared before the committee with his top team. The all-day meeting was very effective, most of Justice Iyer's suggestions were accepted, and an allocation of ₹1,800 crore followed to improve the condition of women prisoners and launch open jails for them. Our work received wide publicity and was welcomed at all levels.

◆

Between 2000 and 2004, I also became a member of the Standing Committee on Environment, Forests and Tourism, which took us to many parts of the country on tours that were truly educational and revealing. I engaged with a range of issues—the cleaning of the Dal Lake, the Bamboo Mission,[65] illegal sand mining, coastal erosion, forest laws, the problems of tribals, encroachments on the rights of forest-dwellers, and the human–animal conflict in national parks. The committee also took us to exotic tourist spots and luxurious locations.

◆

During my Lok Sabha years, I started getting Soniaji to Central Hall for dosa-coffee sessions. Members of both Houses, and of all parties, began to sit around her for informal exchanges. MPs and journalists began looking

---

[65]Keeping in view the vast untapped potential of the bamboo plant, the Bamboo Mission, a Centrally-sponsored scheme, hoped to promote the growth of the bamboo sector and facilitate the marketing of bamboo-based handicrafts.

forward to these tête-à-têtes. It was at one of these sessions that a journalist asked her why there were such few women in her team in the AICC.

She refuted this charge by offering the names of those who were there.

Then, someone asked, 'Why not Margaretji? She is so senior and experienced!'

As Soniaji looked at me, all I could say was, 'I am always out!'

To this, she said, 'You are always in my heart, Margaret.'

I was taken aback. 'I will be happy staying there!' I said.

There was stunned silence for a second and then there were peals of laughter as we dispersed.

◆

The Speaker, G.M.C. Balayogi, was a pleasant low-key person from the TDP, and a first-time MP. He had great confidence in me, sending me to the chair whenever the going got tough. When he was elected, my former PA, K.S. Raju (who also hailed from Andhra Pradesh), requested me to get him into his office, which I did, as his Officer on Special Duty. He, along with the Speaker, met with a tragic end in March 2002 when the helicopter in which they were travelling to Delhi crashed into a pond. Inquiries later showed that the pilot had attempted an emergency landing as he had run out of fuel. His family was devastated. I helped his sons get jobs through the Lok Sabha Secretariat.

It was G.M.C. Balayogi who included me in the delegation to the Inter-Parliamentary Union (IPU) meeting in Marrakesh in March 2002, where l was elected to the Women's Coordination Committee for a three-year term as a representative of the Asian region. I had neither planned for nor expected it. When nominations were called for from the floor, the SAARC women proposed my name and it went through unanimously, to be confirmed by the Executive Committee. I now came to be invited to every meeting of the IPU. Before I left for Marrakesh, Soniaji told me to make sure I made a trip to Petra—the ancient city carved out of rock in the desert—which I did. It was an exhausting all-day trip, but worth the sweat and toil. Petra is a tribute to human ingenuity.

◆

I participated in some important debates, though, most often, my name stayed on the list of speakers, with party time consumed by members like

Priya Ranjan Dasmunsi, Mani Shankar Aiyar and Shivraj Patil. I walked out in protest on one occasion against the injustice. I was in the chair every afternoon, becoming popular with backbenchers across parties, whose names rarely appeared as speakers on their party's official lists. They would send me slips and I used to call them for brief interventions whenever possible, for which they were most grateful.

I also served as the party's Parliamentary Party Spokesperson for some time, which was resented by some senior persons (whose names I will not mention) who viewed this as a case of 'too many posts to one person.' This resulted in my being eased out.

I had the rare honour of chairing the Joint Session of Parliament in the Central Hall in 2002 on the Prevention of Terrorism Bill, since I was on the Panel of Presiding Officers selected by the Speaker. It was obvious that some senior party members resented this as well, because they disrupted the proceedings soon after I took the chair, on the lame excuse that George Fernandes (who was being boycotted by the party) had taken the floor to speak.

◆

Soniaji nominated me to attend a meeting called in Rome by the Italian Parliament to mark two thousand years of the birth of Christ in November 2000. I was thrilled. It was a select group of religious, political, intellectual and civil society leaders from all over the world. The meetings were held in the Vatican, within its inner precincts, with lawns thrown open for lunches and banquets. It was truly a royal atmosphere—but warm, relaxed and friendly. The participants came from all continents; belonged to different races, tribes and colours; spoke in countless languages; but were united by a single bond—the Catholic Church. There were discussions and dialogues on the challenges it faced and the way forward. Listening was an education and a source of inspiration and enlightenment.

His Holiness Pope John Paul II was our host. He sat through every session, his back bent, listening attentively. At the last session, I was among the ten people from different regions of the world selected to speak for five minutes. I spoke of the cry for justice for humanity, from the womb to the tomb, in every society and nation, and concluded with the words of Christ: 'Do unto others as you would have them do unto you', referring, in particular, to the duty of developed nations to reach out to the poor and developing ones. I added, 'It is no longer a cry for charity, but for justice.' I received a thunderous applause, with many getting on their feet to cheer me. Then, as I knelt before His Holiness, he held my hands, and placing his hand on my head, blessed me and India. It is a moment I will never forget. I was honoured and humbled.

The concluding ceremony was on the raised platform outside St Peter's Basilica, the seat of the Catholic Church. The Mass was said by His Holiness, with thousands of pilgrims from all over the world assembled in St Peter's Square and beyond. It was here that I felt the power of the Church, with kings and queens, heads of state and government, writers, thinkers, poets, trade unionists, bureaucrats and diplomats, youth, men and women, religious and lay people, all down on their knees, as His Holiness ascended the steps to the altar.

Then there was a big surprise—Mikhail Gorbachev walked to the podium to deliver the jubilee address on behalf of the nations of the world. He spoke of the world yearning for the liberation of Christ promised two thousand years ago. It was a moving address by a former hardcore atheist—a communist, who had found solace in the teachings of Christ. The three-hour ceremony brought the curtains down on a historic event, at a historic venue, to mark a truly historic milestone in human history. I will remain ever grateful to Soniaji for offering me the special opportunity to participate in these celebrations. I was back at the Vatican later for other events, including the funeral of Pope John Paul II—but there was no function to match this one.

That year also saw me join the delegation of women Parliamentarians for the special session of the UN General Assembly on 'Women 2000: Gender, Equity, Development and Peace for the Twenty-first Century'. There were the usual discussions, statements and reports, with a plan of action for the future. The trip brought me into close contact with Phoolan Devi (later gunned down), who related to me her tale of childhood suppression, violence by the upper castes, and her fight-back.

In July, I was in Nepal as a speaker for the training programme for Parliamentarians on 'Mainstreaming Gender Equality' organized by UNDP (United Nations Development Programme). Mohini Giri and I used this opportunity to visit a rehabilitation centre for girls rescued from brothels in India and to discuss the issue of tightening border controls to prevent this tragedy. Here I saw the misery of a beautiful ten-year-old girl, seven-months pregnant, unable to move.

I was also a member of the first goodwill delegation of journalists, Parliamentarians and social activists to Pakistan, organized by SAFMA (South Asian Free Media Association) in August 2003. We crossed the Wagah border after a train journey from Delhi, and reached Lahore by the evening. We had warm receptions everywhere we went. Lahore was so much like India—red stone structures, old buildings, parks, and markets of the British and Mughal eras. In Islamabad, we had interesting exchanges in a seminar where I made four suggestions—for more people-to-people contact, especially among the youth and students; for opening the media on both sides; for increasing business and commerce between the two countries; and for sports exchanges.

We went to the weekly open market on Sunday where Lalu Prasad Yadav offered one of his famous couplets: '*Hindustan se aya Lalu, pasand kiya Pakistan ka aalu*' ('Lalu comes from India and appreciates Pakistan's potatoes'), while biting a large boiled potato—which made headlines. The reception we got in the markets and shops, with lassi, tea and snacks being offered to '*hamare bhai-behen*' ('our brothers and sisters'), was heartwarming; many shops refused to charge us for the small items we bought.

There were dinners hosted by the Governor in Lahore, and the Prime Minister in Islamabad. But the high point was the reception at the Presidential Palace by General Pervez Musharraf, who told Laluji that he was so popular in Pakistan that he could win any election from anywhere in the country. I presented him with a white khadi angavastra and, at his request, put it around his neck. He kept it on for the rest of the morning.

My dominant impression was the vast gap between the warmth of the common people and the hostile response of the administration to matters concerning Indo-Pak relations. I made three more visits to that country, and always emphasized our common history and our fight against colonial rulers.

I was nominated to the Indo-British Roundtable by the government and played an important role at its meetings held alternately in India and the UK. Education and trade, besides the problems of Indians settled in the UK, dominated the agenda.

There were two meetings of great significance to which I was invited in my own capacity—one was the seminar in 2003 on 'South Asia: Bridging the Great Divides' at Harvard University. It was an initiative of Professor Sugata Bose, the grand-nephew of Subhas Chandra Bose, drawing well-known personalities and intellectuals from India, Pakistan, Sri Lanka, Bangladesh and Nepal, besides students and professors of the university. I spoke on the panel on 'Religion in South Asian Politics'. Niru was with me. We made a brief trip to Buffalo, and then to the Niagara Falls and Toronto after the seminar.

The other event was at Cambridge University, UK, in 1999. It was a brainstorming session of writers for a book—*The Planetary Interest*, edited by Kennedy Graham. My chapter offered India's perspective on population growth.

◆

Even while fulfilling my responsibilities in the Lok Sabha and in the Congress, I began to spend a lot of time in my constituency, working on various development projects; to fund these, I brought in ₹10,000 crore from the World Bank, Asian Development Bank (ADB), and the Central and state governments. As my commitments within my constituency grew, I opted out of my post in the Congress President's office, where I had served as a Coordinator for over a year.

I ensured that the Karwar beach was lit, a children's park with a toy train opened, an old ship from the navy installed as a prime attraction, and walking tracks created with a grant from the Ministry of Tourism. I also ensured that several state highways got converted into national highways—thanks to Major General B.C. Khanduri, the BJP Minister for Surface Transport. Many villages were linked by roads. Through my MP fund, anganwadis, kitchens for mid-day meals in schools, shaadi ghars, ranga mandirs and mahila mandals were built; computers were donated to schools; and contributions were made to the Swatchh Gram Programme, which aimed to clean villages. The *Alva Patrika* was launched to inform party cadres about the projects initiated.

But my work did not end here. The Uttara Kannada district was plagued with problems. It had suffered severe damage due to multiple power projects, including a nuclear power station at Kaiga. Besides, the Seabird Naval Base at Karwar had taken away massive chunks of the coastal belt and caused large-scale erosion. Then there was the Konkan Railway that acquired fertile agricultural land, leading to the displacement of populations and the destruction of farms, fields and fishermen's villages.

Over time, many promises had been made—rebuilding villages in new locations; providing land for land or compensation; offering jobs to displaced families; securing the coastline; and safeguarding the livelihoods of fishermen by constructing new fishing harbours, markets and cold storages. But they had all been forgotten. There had been both peaceful agitations and angry protests by displaced families—all in vain.

The Government of Karnataka, under Chief Minister S.R. Bommai, had signed an MoU with the Defence Ministry, closing the issue of further compensation for the Seabird evacuees. As a result, those who refused to move out of their homes and lands, demanding higher compensation, were forcibly picked up, bundled into trucks and dumped in makeshift tin shelters in sandy lands allotted for their rehabilitation. This happened despite the fact that the evacuees had appealed against their removal to the courts.

When I visited the area, I was shocked to see the condition of displaced communities. In the height of summer, the sand burnt and the tin sheds turned into ovens. The families sat, dehydrated and hungry, under casuarina trees that barely protected them. There was no regular water supply.

I spoke to the press, expressed my anger, issued warnings to the administration and flew back to Delhi to raise the issue in Parliament. I compared the condition of these people in my constituency to that of Jews in Nazi concentration camps, and demanded immediate action from the Defence Ministry to prevent the death of innocent citizens. In response, a special team from Delhi visited the area and submitted a critical report to the Centre—though the comparison with Nazi concentration camps was rejected.

I met George Fernandes, who was Defence Minister, and demanded his immediate intervention. I challenged him to visit my constituency and make his own assessment as a socialist leader. He said that he was prepared if Karnataka's Chief Minister, S.M. Krishna, attended a meeting in Delhi, equipped with facts and figures. I made the Chief Minister accept the invitation. Our meeting was successful. Shortly after that, George Fernandes visited Karwar for an official function and announced that 'in response to my friend and colleague's demands', he would be releasing ₹17 crore for the rehabilitation of the Seabird evacuees—and this despite the MoU that had already been signed by a former Karnataka government. Fernandes' announcement was a great victory for me.

I now focused on the nuclear plant at Kaiga, which saw regular mishaps like gas leaks and fire bursts, besides hushed-up internal accidents. The power plant also contributed to a rise in water-pollution levels. The populations around this power station suffered all kinds of deformities and ailments. But they would not move for want of sufficient compensation and proper rehabilitation. All efforts at getting the Kaiga authorities to respond had failed. I raised the issue in Parliament, and wrote to the Science and Technology Minister, but my plea for assistance was rejected.

Then came the opportunity for me to take up the matter with Prime Minister Atal Bihari Vajpayee directly. When the second reactor at Kaiga was to go critical, as the local MP, I was invited to speak. I placed a request for a seat in one of the Prime Minister's helicopters to travel from Goa to the project site. I received a prompt response from the PMO, inviting me to fly with him from Delhi itself. I made full use of the opportunity to brief Vajpayeeji about the situation in Kaiga. I showed him a file detailing my correspondence on the matter and read out the relevant paragraphs of various reports on the subject. The Prime Minister smiled and said 'Dekhenge!' ('We'll see!'), even as Brajesh Mishra objected to this off-the-record request.

I flew with him to the public meeting, surprising all the VIPs waiting on the tarmac. At the meeting, I made an emotional appeal on behalf of 'my suffering people of Kaiga' and received a heart-warming response from the crowd. I also extracted a public promise from the Chief Minister, S.M. Krishna, that the Uttara Kannada district, which was already burdened with five hydro-power projects and one nuclear power plant, would not have any more such ventures. This was hailed by not only the audience but also by all political parties.

Then, Vajpayeeji, in his inimical style, thanked the people of the district for their sacrifices and added in Hindi, 'Your MP, Alvaji, has been pleading for increased compensation for those living around this plant, so that they can be moved to a safer location. In response to her pressing request on our flight from Delhi, I am releasing ₹2 crore.'

This was an unexpected triumph. The state government, in turn, had to match the amount and provide land. At long last, the Kaiga rehabilitation issue had been solved.

Finally, there was the issue of forest encroachments, which rocked the constituency. The district administration received orders from the Centre to evict 44,000 'encroachers' as a follow-up to a Supreme Court order. Notices were promptly issued to these 'encroaching' families. They were told that they had only limited time to move, failing which they would be forcibly evicted. There was a hue and cry. All the district organizations fighting to protect the rights of forest-dwellers organized an impressive rally which drew over 30,000 people. At the very end, I was called upon to strike a huge traditional war-drum as a challenge and a warning to the authorities. 'Not a dwelling will be touched as long as I am here to represent you!' I declared, and the crowds applauded.

But the battle had just begun. I wrote to the Prime Minister asking:

> Where should we shift these families? Huge chunks of our forest and fertile lands have been acquired or drowned for Central Government projects. Should we dump them in the sea or send them up in hot air balloons? [...] Let the Supreme Court ensure the demolition of the houses of the rich and mighty in the encroached Sainik Farms, standing right under its nose, before touching these poor families in the remote areas of the Western Ghats.

After this, with some successful lobbying, a unanimous resolution was passed in the Assembly to stop the demolitions, conduct a survey to identify true forest-dwellers and deal appropriately with encroachers. Committees were set up in each taluka to examine documents, with provisions for appeals. This diffused the situation.

To this day, a battle continues between the state and the forest-dwellers, despite the fact that the Forest Rights Act[66] gives land rights to the traditional inhabitants of the forests.

I should add that I lobbied for this law in Parliament and in the Standing Committee for Forests and Environment. In Parliament, I raised the issue of the harassment of poor and helpless forest-dwellers and condemned the fact that they were being denied the right to forest produce and livelihoods.

◆

Ramakrishna Hegde was a colourful personality, seen in a suit and bow-tie at New Year eve dances at the Bangalore Club. He was, in many ways, a new-age politician, popular in social circles as also with leaders across political parties. He was the one Karnataka politician I knew who was

---

[66]The Scheduled Tribes and Other Traditional Forest Dwellers (Recognition of Forest Rights) Act, 2006 (also called the Forest Rights Act) was passed in India on 18 December 2006. The law concerns the rights of forest-dwelling communities to land and other resources, denied to them over decades as a result of the continuance of colonial forest laws in India.

gracious in victory and defeat—never vindictive. Rajiv Gandhi especially liked and respected him.

The last meeting I had with Ramakrishna Hegde was on 30 August 2003, the day after his seventy-seventh birthday. He was ill and tired after the previous day's celebrations, but insisted that I come upstairs and spend some time with him.

He recalled his early days with my parents-in-law in North Canara. Though he parted ways with the Congress after the split in 1969, to become the Janata Party's Karanataka Chief Minister later, he had been extremely kind to Niru and me.

Gundu Rao, as Chief Minister, had tried to acquire our two-acre plot by the sea in Karwar for a bus stand, when I was out of the party with Devaraj Urs. But he failed to complete the process. When Hegde took over as Chief Minister and the file came to him (processed by none other than Francis Lynn, whom I had known since my college days), he recorded: 'This is the only land Joachim Alva purchased in his constituency. He is a freedom fighter and has served the state as an MP for many years. His land shall not be touched.' This is the respect he had for Baba. He had also helped me with my 1986 Rajya Sabha election.

Hegde talked for over an hour and asked me a couple of searching questions. 'Why did you decide to go to Karwar when you had so many options for a seat?'

'It was sentiment,' I answered.

'You have made a mistake. This is the district that I belong to and that I worked for. But they stabbed me in the back and defeated me. Never trust these leaders. They will not let you survive.'

It was stunning advice which I received with a smile. Then came the next question: 'Why did you admit [R.V.] Deshpande to the Congress? Do not depend on him or trust him. I built him, helped him, but he betrayed me.'

Over the years, these words have come to haunt me, as Deshpande made every attempt to defeat me, despite all I did to get him into the party, secure him a ticket and support his bid for a ministerial post after he joined. Sadly, Deshpande's money-power could not be matched by us in the elections.

I attended Hegde's funeral in January 2004 and was given a place with the family. It was ironical to see Deshpande move around and take charge of arrangements, perhaps to make amends for what he had done to him.

Years later, Hegde's daughter, Mamta Nichani, contested the Lok Sabha election on the Congress ticket; she lost.

◆

Pranab Mukherjee warned me by way of friendly advice: 'The more time you spend in your constituency, the more difficult it will be to win the next election!' Back then I had laughed at the suggestion, but with time he was proven right. No matter what I did, it caused offence to one section or another.

Thanks to the twenty-five-year battle I fought for the Siddis from my district—from the time I presented a petition on the their behalf as a backbencher in the Rajya Sabha—in the 2003 bill in Parliament, only the Siddis of Uttara Kannada were declared STs, despite the fact that there are Siddis in Gujarat, Telangana, Goa and also in multiple districts in Karnataka. While I brought the Siddis justice, it came to be resented by some other communities that had not been included in the ST list, as also by the upper castes that had treated the Siddis as bonded labour on their araca plantations and farms.

I was also the target of the unhappiness of SC leaders when I gave my support to the Moger community, which was seeking SC status and the benefits that the status enjoyed in South Canara. In 2011, the Karnataka High Court upheld the Moger community's demands in the district as legitimate. But the Dakshina Kannada District Scheduled Caste and Scheduled Tribes Organisations' Federation decided to move the Supreme Court, challenging the High Court ruling. The state government—under pressure from powerful SC leaders—withdrew its order to issue caste certificates to the Moger community of North Canara.

Spearheading the protests of the local people, I appeared before the Parliamentary Standing Committee on Power which visited our area and endorsed our objections to two coal-based power plants coming up in total contravention of environmental norms.

I was thus able to stop the power plants from coming up as per the public assurance of Chief Minister S.M. Krishna that the district would not be burdened with more such initiatives. But powerful people who had lost money were unhappy and connived to get me out of the district.

Finally, I upset a number of leaders when—after receiving funding from UNICEF through my NGO, Karuna—I introduced a training programme for women elected to local bodies, pushed for SHGs, and established a twenty-four-hour helpline for women in distress, providing them free legal aid. These initiatives helped women grow increasingly aware of their roles and rights. Women began to contest from their constituencies as general candidates (when reservations ended due to rotation) and win, taking their numbers far beyond 33 per cent. Naturally, many men began to feel threatened. 'If Margaret Alva continues as an MP here, we will soon be out of the reckoning!' they began to murmur. Moreover, when the ADB project—which aimed to modernize the drainage system, roads, public utilities and buildings—led to increased cess and charges, these irate men were up in arms. 'Who asked for this?' they shouted. 'Why should we pay more?'

Therefore, despite all the good work that I had done, the 2004 elections saw the anti-Margaret forces uniting. Before I could stem the tide, I was out, and the BJP's Ananth Kumar Hegde was in.

After my defeat, I was hurt by the ingratitude of the voters; the women I had done so much for had been won over with small nose rings, which they were told were of gold. But, equally, I was frustrated that religion had become a huge factor, with the BJP–RSS combine launching a vicious campaign against me through local temples. Postcards were distributed which read, 'A vote for Alva is a vote for Rome; a vote for the BJP is a vote for Ram!' To make matters worse, the Siddis, who were divided along religious lines, were incorrectly told that only Christian Siddis had been included in the ST list by me. The fact that the General and Assembly elections were held concurrently served as the final blow, with the failures of the Congress in the state impacting the number of seats we won to Parliament—we secured only 8 out of 28 seats.[67]

I enjoyed my five years in the Lok Sabha, working night and day to nurture my constituency, and fighting battles inside and outside Parliament. But, at the end of it, I lost and was back to square one. I swore never to talk of 'development' in my district again.

---

[67]See *Statistical Report on General Elections, 2004,* in <http://eci.nic.in/eci_main/statisticalreports/ls_2004/vol_i_ls_2004.pdf>, accessed on 27 April 2016.

The AICC Days

Chapter 27

QUE SERA SERA: IN THE AICC

After I lost my election in 2004, I was bitter because, among other things, I sensed that our own leaders had connived to defeat me. I was especially angry with the Karnataka Congress Chief, R.V. Deshpande, who had masterminded my defeat, in a bid to win a party nomination for his son for the Uttara Kannada seat in the next election.

At home, I grumbled about the many let-downs I had faced, even as reports of sabotage kept appearing in newspapers. Finally, one day, Niret said to me, 'How long are you going to be angry? Forget about what happened and look ahead. Unless you forgive Deshpande and his men, you will never have peace.'

I realized he was right. So I said a prayer before the altar at home: 'Lord, help me truly forgive.' I felt a wave of peace within me as my eyes went dim. I had cleansed my mind of bitter thoughts.

Later that day, I had a call from the Congress President's office confirming my appointment with her. When I met her, she told me that she had decided to appoint me as the General Secretary of the AICC. She asked me not to talk about it till a formal announcement was made. I was shocked at the unexpected news, as much as I was thrilled. I thanked her and then confided in her that I would have a problem with my accommodation as I had to move out of government premises. I had no place of my own in Delhi. She quickly responded, 'We will find a place, do not worry. I'll speak to Ghulam Nabi.' (He was the new Urban Development Minister.)

Guarding the secret, I left for Bangkok to participate in an international conference on AIDS, where I was on a panel as a speaker with the actor Richard Gere.

There was an exhibition at the venue with all the major multinationals presenting their drugs to fight AIDS. The conference had obviously been funded by them to create an environment of anxiety so that they could sell their wares. What especially astounded me were the cleverly displayed notices for the attention of NGOs, urging them to submit applications for human trials in their countries. I picked up a couple of these forms and pamphlets, and raised the issue on my return home.

At the meeting, I made four points. I asked why India was shown in red on the global map when we were far below the danger zone of 5 per cent of the population being diagnosed with AIDS. I then asked how authentic the collected statistics were, when the reach of health services was far from universal in India, and AIDS testing kits and centres were limited. In a country where there were more deaths from malnutrition, dehydration and childbirth than from AIDS—and where healthcare budgets were limited and stretched to the maximum—I questioned the decision to make the HIV virus a priority. Finally, I asked why everyone was talking about the 'pandemic' of AIDS, specifically in Asia and Africa—the suggestion being that the US and Europe were so clean and pure that these continents were free of AIDS. If this was, in fact, the case, I asked the esteemed speakers on the panel from the West if they could share their experiences and tell us how they had achieved such spectacular results.

There were loud cheers from the audience—mostly from the Asian and African attendees. Richard Gere, in response, started his speech with: 'The lady who spoke, spoke from her head, not from her heart...'

'That is very necessary!' I retorted.

Needless to say, I never got invited to another international conference on AIDS. I had made too many people uncomfortable!

The closing session of the conference had a galaxy of leaders, including Nelson Mandela and Sonia Gandhi. Both received standing ovations after their speeches. I was so proud to see Soniaji speak with confidence and feeling. There was an aura around her, with every speaker heaping praise on her for having opted out of the Prime Minister's post. As she moved out of the venue, I followed her to offer my congratulations. 'Get back soon!' she said, as she left.

I was back the next evening to be received with the announcement of the new team at the AICC, which included me. When I reached home, I was greeted by friends, followers and well-wishers. And so started my new innings at the AICC.

I met Ghulam Nabi Azad, as directed by the Congress President, who asked me what I would like to do to get a house. I told him that the post of Advisor, BPST (Bureau of Parliamentary Studies and Training) was vacant, and if the Speaker agreed, I would like it. The job would give me a residence, a PA and a telephone, with an office in the Parliament House complex. The Speaker, Somnath Chatterjee, was happy to oblige, and so I got to stay on at 12, Safdarjung Lane. The Speaker was keen to rejuvenate the BPST. Together we introduced weekly lectures by eminent people on subjects of current relevance. The training programmes which I chaired for new MPs were a great hit. The number of programmes for MPs and officials from the newly independent countries of the erstwhile USSR, Africa and South Asia increased enormously, even as we introduced new speakers.

Simultaneously, I fulfilled my duties at the AICC. My first challenge was Maharashtra, where Assembly elections were due in October 2004. Everyone had written off another term for the Congress, which was in power in the state. Prabha Rau, the Maharashtra PCC President, whom I had known for years; Sushilkumar Shinde, the Chief Minister, who had replaced Vilasrao Deshmukh a little earlier; and I made a good team, even as we decided to fight the anti-incumbency factor. It was a do-or-die battle.

I received a big welcome when I reached Mumbai, with a motorcade that stretched for over a mile, and posters, banners, music and slogans all along the route. I met key state leaders over two days and, with Shinde and Rau, drew up a plan of action for mobilizing the cadres. We sent out teams of senior leaders to each district to collect feedback. Acting on these reports, we covered every district in Maharashtra—travelling by air, rail, road and even bullock cart. While meeting leaders, sorting out differences and addressing conventions, we brought warring factions together. We thrashed out all concerns with the NCP—with whom we had a pre-poll alliance—and the Republican Party of India (RPI), and neutralized a hostile press to a large extent. All this rattled the Shiv Sena supremo, Bal Thackeray, who at a rally in Shivaji Park told his followers to 'drown the two women [Rau and me, instead of Ganpati] in the sea to save the state from destruction'. I replied the next day with the comment, 'We are too fat to drown. We will only float!'

Once I had done my homework for each seat, the State Election Committee met to finalize names. At the end of this exercise, we moved to Delhi for the Central Election Committee meeting where the Chief Minister, PCC President and I argued for each candidate with winning prospects. When the meeting concluded, M.L. Fotedar congratulated me; 'I have not seen any General Secretary as well prepared as you,' he said.

There was a last-minute hitch, however, before we could announce names. The NCP, all of a sudden, demanded five extra seats. Efforts to bring them around failed. I finally sought Soniaji's permission to meet Sharad Pawar. At his office, with Ahmed Patel, I told Pawarji that the press had been called at 4 p.m. to release the list. The five seats in question had to be finalized before that, and only he could break the deadlock.

'There is nothing I can do,' Pawarji said.

'Pawarji, we have tried everything. Now I have come to touch your feet and beg for this favour,' I said, and rose.

He stood up. 'You are like my sister! Do not touch my feet please,' he pleaded, as he put his arm round my shoulders.

'If I am your sister, you cannot say "no" to me,' I said, smiling.

He smiled, conceded four of the five seats, and Patel and I left. I came back walking on air, even as Patel declared that he was more than surprised at the turn of events. That day the list was announced, with all issues settled.

The campaign was carefully planned. The Bombay Regional Congress Committee (BRCC) Chief was Gurudas Kamat—a dynamic, young Congressman, popular with workers as well as the public, and a great asset. He effortlessly slipped into the shoes of the doyens of the Mumbai Congress, Rajni Patel and Murli Deora. Five Secretaries—Ajay Maken, B.K. Hariprasad, Bharatsinh Solanki, Ved Prakash and Siddharth Patel— were put in charge of five divisions, with full autonomy vis-à-vis the distribution of funds, the handling of the press and the preparation of the lists of campaigners in consultation with local leaders. The system worked beautifully. When the election results came, we had won.

Then came the first hiccup. The NCP had three seats more than us—it had contested 124 seats and won 71, while the Congress had contested 157 and won 68.[68] Promptly, the NCP began to demand the Chief Minister's post, which had until then been conceded to us. Even as we tried keeping our MLAs in Maharashtra together, we heard that our negotiators in Delhi were on the verge of giving in to the NCP demand. We rushed back and joined the meeting, where there were heated exchanges and divided opinions. I met Soniaji separately and told her we had to remain firm. The tussle between the NCP and the Congress went on for thirteen days. Finally, Ahmed Patel and I were deputed to the residence of Sharad Pawar. After closed-door

---

[68]Kalpana Sharma, 'Congress–NCP Retains Maharashtra', *The Hindu*, 16 October 2004.

negotiations, he agreed to continue with the 1999 formula—with a Congress Chief Minister and an NCP Deputy Chief Minister. In exchange, the NCP would have two more Ministers of Cabinet rank and one Minister of State from the Congress quota. We made the announcement to the press waiting outside Pawarji's house.

Now the scene shifted back to Mumbai, where Ghulam Nabi Azad and Ashok Gehlot came as observers to 'consult' MLAs regarding their choice of leader. We had assumed that Sushilkumar Shinde—a Dalit leader who had led the campaign, funded candidates and garnered a lot of support—would be the natural choice. But, to our shock and dismay, the name of Vilasrao Deshmukh was announced. Shinde, Rau, Kamat and I had not been consulted or even informed! While we had slogged in the state, others in Delhi thought it fit to choose the Chief Minister. This had happened in true-Congress style—a style that I just could not understand.

After the swearing-in, we returned to Delhi. While we were having tea at my house, Shinde received a call from Soniaji, who told him that he was to be appointed Governor of Andhra Pradesh. He had not been asked, but informed!

I had many more shocks to endure as I settled down to my new job. When we began discussing Cabinet formation, Soniaji wanted a particular MLA from Mumbai to be made a Minister. But Vilasrao Deshmukh would not have him. We tried to convince Deshmukh but failed. I could not help but wonder why the Congress President had brought this man back as Chief Minister after he had been unceremoniously removed earlier!

Vilasrao Deshmukh, on his part, knew that Rau and I had backed Shinde. As a result, he was hostile to us from the outset. He did everything he could to get me out of Maharashtra. The eternal complaint was that as the General Secretary, I spent all my time in the PCC and toured the state with the PCC President. I had to ask: what else was I expected to do? My job was to attend every meeting I was invited to in the districts and interact with grassroots workers—which I did as efficiently as I could. But Deshmukh was worried that reports of maladministration and corruption would go to Delhi through me.

Worse, when Vilasrao Deshmukh came to Delhi and the AICC, he would not meet me. I once reported this to Soniaji at a meeting in her office, in the presence of Deshmukh and Ahmed Patel, and also referred to a comment he had made in Maharashtra Sadan the previous day—'I do not need the General Secretary; I know whom to keep happy in Delhi, and how!' Soniaji was visibly upset despite Deshmukh's unconvincing denials, and told him firmly, 'You will meet me only with the General Secretary in the future.'

In the meantime, the Chief Minister was fast losing popularity. There had been an open revolt and angry demonstrations against him over the indiscriminate demolition of slums in Mumbai for infrastructure development; livid MLAs came knocking at the doors of the Congress President with photographs to prove their point. There was also anger over the development of Mumbai's mill lands, as mill owners were being allowed to sell off their surplus land without paying the mill workers their long-standing dues. Corruption charges, too, began mounting.

At a meeting in Soniaji's office, I intervened to pacify upset MLAs and MPs, and protect the Chief Minister. When asked to draft a statement for Deshmukh to issue to the press on his way out—which assured rehabilitation to those who had lost their houses and a review of the planned projects—I did it, and saved him. But he was not in the least grateful.

Indeed, this wasn't the only time I had to come to Chief Minister Vilasrao Deshmukh's rescue. On 26 July 2005, when unending rain brought death and destruction to Mumbai, the Chief Minister, dressed in crisp clothes and cocooned in his office, went on TV to call on people to stay calm and remain indoors. His interviews were condemned by all sections. People wanted the government to act and reach out, not offer advice from the comfort of offices. I was flooded with calls from all sides, even as the Central government rushed aid. I directed Deshmukh and his Ministers to get out and lead rescue and rehabilitation operations. Soon after, I personally visited the affected areas and met party workers, activists and citizens on the ground. The devastation was unbelievable—there had been landslides; houses had collapsed; shops were flooded; and bloated bodies were strewn on streets. Yet Mumbai was back to work almost immediately. Such was the spirit of its people.

In the meantime, the government found itself in the middle of a huge controversy involving the illegal transfer or sale of Wakf[69] properties in

---

[69]Wakf can be described as a religious endowment made in the name of Allah for the benefit of the poor and needy in the Muslim community. See Saba Naqvi, 'Allah's Left the Building', *Outlook*, 21 September 2009.

the state. The details that were coming out suggested the involvement of politicians and Wakf Board officials. The issue rocked the Assembly. I was compelled to submit a report of the proceedings to Soniaji. I also forwarded a detailed report prepared by Anees Ahmed, the Minister in charge of Wakf and Minority Affairs. I highlighted that one of the Wakf properties—meant for the welfare and education of Muslim orphans—had been sold cheaply to the Chairman of a high profile company.[70] Shortly after, the Minister in charge of Wakf and Minority Affairs was shifted out. The Mumbai bosses had their way. Since then, the issue has been raised in vain by the press and in the party, but no follow-up action has been taken.

On 26 November 2008, when Bombay was ravaged by serial terror attacks, I was in Bangalore with Manira. When I saw the news flash on the television screen, I rushed to Mumbai, arriving before anyone from Delhi could. The Prime Minister and Soniaji came in later that night. The scenes were tragic—limbs and blood on railway platforms, and loud wails in hospital corridors, as the wounded and the dead came in ambulances and taxis. There were crowds, police cars and screaming sirens. My head reeled; tears rolled down my cheeks as relations wailed for the dead and maimed. The actions of misguided extremists made me angry—but to what end?

◆

Notwithstanding all the antagonism I faced in Maharashtra's political arena, I continued doing my bit to strengthen the Congress in the state. Prabha Rau and I carefully put together a team of leaders to lead different regions— Narayan Rane for Konkan; Gurudas Kamat for Mumbai; Suresh Kalmadi for Western Maharashtra and Pune; Ashok Chavan and Sushilkumar Shinde for Marathwada; and a team of Nitin Raut (an SC), Satish Chaturvedi (a Brahmin) and Anees Ahmed (a Muslim) for Vidarbha. The arrangement worked well.

When Narayan Rane of the Shiv Sena joined the Congress with his followers in 2005, there were great expectations. After all, Rane is known to be a crowd-puller, a great organizer and a generous leader. We believed he would help strengthen the Congress not only in the Konkan and Mumbai but also in other areas. But efforts were made right from the start to

---

[70]One of the emails received by the Congress after the Mumbai blasts of 26/11 specifically mentioned this land deal, and threatened revenge.

marginalize him and cut him down to size—possibly because his rivals were afraid of his mass appeal. Despite all my efforts, Rane's role was limited to that of a Cabinet Minister. His frustration became obvious with time, with occasional outbursts. Instead of addressing his concerns, he was only advised by the High Command to remain patient and imbibe 'Congress culture'! For how long will he wait?

In the meantime, as the AICC General Secretary, I faced immense pressure on multiple counts. Vishram G. Patil—President of the Jalgaon District Congress Committee—was hacked to death in September 2005. His wife, Rajni Patil, claimed that her husband had defeated G.N. Patil—the brother of Pratibha Patil—in the District Congress Committee elections and that G.N. Patil had ordered his murder due to political rivalry.

Rajni came to Delhi to meet Soniaji, demanding justice and action. She was sent to me. She produced all the evidence she had, including the tape of the narcotics test conducted on the suspect, which I still have. She swore not to dispose of her husband's ashes until justice was done. In fact she had tied them in a bundle to a tree in her compound. I now found myself firefighting for the Congress as there were charges and counter-charges. I submitted a detailed report to the Congress President, even as the matter went to court. An ad hoc DCC President was appointed by me.

Then there was the 'rasta roko' agitation of farmers, who halted traffic on the Mumbai-Pune highway, protesting against the acquisition of 10,000 hectares of their fertile land in Raigad for an SEZ for a powerful business house.

I met the delegation of agitating farmers who insisted, 'We will die but will not budge from our land.' They added, 'This was a wasteland when we got it. We struggled for years and got a mini-dam erected—which gives us three crops and a decent income—so we can send our children to school and college. Now, the state government, to please this corporate house, is taking away our land. This land was given to us by Indira-tai; it cannot be taken away by Sonia-behen. Tell her she is doing an injustice to us!'

I sent a strongly-worded report to the Congress President, and this made me an immediate target of the company's wrath and tireless efforts to get me out of Maharashtra. Soniaji's advisors, in the meantime, asked me not to interfere. But the court did intervene and ordered a vote to check the claim that the agitators' leaders had accepted the deal for compensation worked out by the company's agents. The rest is history. The overwhelming majority of those affected voted against the acquisition of their land, and it had to be returned to them. What the Congress had failed to do, the courts did. This was the tragedy.

I must add that, throughout this chequered period, Soniaji refused to bow to the pressure to shift me out. She knew I was fair and honest, and that I only fought for the interests of the party.

◆

As AICC General Secretary, in charge of Maharastra, I had the opportunity to pay tribute to a rare endowment—the legacy of the Alvas. Thanks to Murli Deora and his team in the Municipal Corporation, two chowks near the Gateway of India were named after Joachim and Violet Alva—freedom fighters, MPs, lawyers and journalists who started their political life from the city. The boards carrying their names, installed on either side of the Taj Hotel, survived the 26/11 attack. There were impressive functions to mark the event, attended by the Chief Minister, Ministers, MLAs, friends, journalists and the family.

I also organized two events to mark the centenary of Joachim Alva. The first was the unveiling of a portrait of him and Violet Alva, the first couple in India's Parliament, at a glittering ceremony in Central Hall in Parliament, attended by the Speaker, the Vice President, the Prime Minister, the Congress President, L.K. Advani, several Chief Ministers, MPs and MLAs across parties, educationists, journalists, family and friends. The Parliament staff was astonished at the turn out—Central Hall was filled to capacity as many stood for want of seats.

This was followed later in the year by the release of a stamp by President Pratibha Patil in their honour at the Rashtrapati Bhavan. We were told that it was the first stamp in the country of a couple. While Telecom Minister A. Raja had sat on the file for months despite several reminders, Madhavrao Scindia's son, Jyotiraditya Scindia, as MoS, got it cleared within a week, making it possible to commemorate the first couple of the Indian Parliament with a stamp and a cover.

◆

My mother took ill with hernia for the second time at the end of June 2005. She was operated on and recovered remarkably for an eighty-nine-year-old. I was with her all along, but went for urgent party work to Delhi and Mumbai—at which point she was shifted back home. She passed away on 10 July—my sister's birthday. To me—nursed, mentored and motivated by her all my life—it was an irreparable loss. I still miss her and regret having left her at that crucial time, when she needed me most. She had a really big funeral, with leaders from adjoining states and Karnataka joining family and friends to pay their respects.

◆

Born in 1979 and the baby of the family, Nivedith—or Babu, as he has been called—was growing tall. In fact, I was so worried about his rapidly increasing height that I consulted a doctor to make sure that there was nothing unusual about it. He graduated from St Stephen's College, Delhi, after completing schooling in St Columba's and Delhi Public School. He was a great athlete, winning multiple medals at annual sports events, but mathematics was his blind spot.

Babu worked for Miditech before going on to Goldsmiths College, University of London for an MA in TV Journalism, and returned to continue his career in the media. He represented India at the Millennium Youth Parliament of CPA at Manchester in 2000. He was pampered by the family while I went through the busiest years of my career between 1984 and 1996 as a Minister with an active role in the party.

In Delhi Public School he had met Meera Haran—a Tamil Brahmin, a talented dancer and singer, and the only daughter of Indira and E.G.P. Haran (working with WHO [World Health Organization]). She went to King's College, London, after her MA in Clinical Psychology, for a PG (Postgraduate) Certificate in Child and Family Therapy, at the same time as Nivedith. This was where their romance blossomed. They were married in January 2005 with Hindu and Christian rituals, and had a reception on our lawns at 12, Safdarjung Lane, which saw leaders including the Vice President, the Prime Minister, Sonia Gandhi, L.K. Advani, Arjun Singh and several Congress people from the states, as well as stalwarts of the Left and regional parties. Sheila Dikshit, the Chief Minister of Delhi, proposed the toast. Nivedith and Meera are now settled in Bangalore, with Nivedith plunging into politics and Meera pursuing her professional work. They have two children—Manini, arriving on 10 October 2006, and Nithanth, on 23 November 2009.

◆

My years in the AICC were action-packed—I travelled, campaigned, won elections for the party, toppled governments and unmade Ministers. Soniaji once suggested that I take up the Chairmanship of the Khadi and Village Industries Commission, but I declined the offer. For one, I was happy with what I was doing. For another, it would mean moving to Mumbai.

In 2007, following an internal reorganization of the AICC, I was given charge of more than eight PCCS—Maharashtra, Punjab, Chandigarh, Haryana, Goa, Daman and Diu, Nagaland, Meghalaya and Mizoram, plus Chhattisgarh, West Bengal, and the Andaman and Nicobar Islands for some time.

I would spend long hours in the AICC, meeting leaders and workers from these states, and even from states I didn't handle. Listening solved half their problems. This job required a great deal of patience and empathy, and also came with a lot of responsibility—for, people approached us with hope and faith that Soniaji would solve their problems if they got her (or anyone close to her) to hear them out. All my day was consumed working for the party—which, I must say, the Congress took for granted.

Added to this, as a member of the Central Election Committee, I faced endless pressure from potential candidates for tickets. I helped countless people during the years I was a member, yet could not get a ticket for my son, Nivedith, for three successive elections—despite his work in my constituency; his track record in the Karnataka Pradesh Youth Congress as General Secretary and in the KPCC as Secretary; and his educational and professional qualifications, including a degree from London.

I was helped by a team of four smart, dedicated, committed and hardworking secretaries, who always accompanied me when planning and reporting sessions were held by the Congress President. I put them in charge of some of the states I handled and let them function independently, asking them to give me regular reports. By the time their terms with me ended, they had all been promoted—B.K. Hariprasad became General Secretary, AICC; Bharatsinh Solanki became the PCC President of Gujarat; Ajay Maken, the Delhi PCC Chief; and Siddharth Patel, the Chief of the Gujarat Congress later.

I toured most of my states and union territories extensively, met workers and leaders, and sorted out internal differences, with a firm hand against indiscipline. I was both respected and feared. Thanks to the time I invested in each state, the Congress won most of the local body elections it contested.

In Goa, with my support, the Congress managed to topple the Parrikar government and defeat the BJP in 2007. I was popular here since I speak Konkani and the senior Alvas are still remembered. I also handled Assembly elections in Meghalaya and Nagaland, and prepared the ground for elections in Punjab, Haryana and Mizoram by attending district conventions that offered a clear idea of possible candidates, besides bringing the factions onto a common platform.

Put in charge of Bengal, I had to handle the Assembly elections of 2006. Pranab Mukherjee was the PCC President, running party affairs from Delhi (where he was a Union Minister) through Somen Mitra. Pranabda and I had a couple of serious clashes over the candidates to be fielded. His supporters kept demanding change after change in the names of those cleared by the Central Election Committee. I could not allow this. When I objected to his demands, Pranabda threatened to resign and told me, 'You may run the election yourself!' To this, I responded, 'Why should you go, Dada? I will go!'

I promptly wrote to the Congress President, asking to be relieved of this responsibility. Soon after, I received summons from 10, Janpath. When I arrived, I saw Pranabda, who seemed to have calmed down. Together, we went in. Soniaji asked what the problem was. Pranabda looked at me, bewildered. When I recounted our spat, he patted me on the back and said, very nonchalantly, 'You are like my sister. You know me. I lose my cool and then forget. I am sorry. Please forget the episode.' Soniaji also told me to let the matter rest, and so that's what happened, and we walked out together.

But there was more to follow. Mabel Rebello (an MP from Jharkhand) and I spent hours with Mamata Banerjee trying to broker an understanding. She was not prepared to have an alliance with us as her party was part of the NDA. Finally, we drafted a statement to be issued by her, which said, 'The TMC is part of the NDA at the national level but not in the state.' This would pave the way for us to work out a seat-sharing formula, by which we would not field strong candidates against each other.

When we took the draft statement to the Congress President for a final approval, she hesitated. As for Pranabda, he was furious. He would not hear of it.

We now found ourselves confronting the West Bengal elections solo, with limited funds. Irate candidates refused to battle it out; they found the sum of one lakh rupees offered by the Congress wholly inadequate. Given the dearth of money, Mabel, Siddharth Patel, Solanki and I chose to stay on the outskirts of Calcutta—in a Marwari choultry serving good vegetarian food—while sharing cars and seeking funds from other states. Complicating the situation was the fact that sitting MPs and MLAs were inclined to work only in their own constituencies. When I visited a few areas, workers confessed that I was the first 'leader' to set foot there. Although Soniaji addressed several meetings, we knew we were fighting a losing battle.

As expected, we were routed. The TMC won 30 seats, the CPM won 176 seats, while we won 21 seats.[71] Defeated, exhausted and depressed, we packed our bags and left. The results clearly proved that if the TMC and the Congress had had an alliance, we, as a combined force, could have formed the government. But since we had let that opportunity slip, the field was left wide open for frustrated Congress leaders and workers to move to the TMC. In the next Assembly elections of 2011, Mamata emerged victorious and formed a government of her own.

The North-east was a special challenge, and flying by helicopters was a hazard. In 2008, elections in Nagaland and Meghalaya took place simultaneously. We had to organize six rallies in ten days—three in each state, with two for the Congress President and one for the Prime Minister. Our non-stop schedule demanded hopping from one hilltop to another— beating bad weather, cloudy skies and early sunsets. My knees began to feel the strain of uphill climbs and quick strides down muddy knolls, and leaps in and out of helicopters. I must say, my knees have never been the same since! But this was a small price to pay in exchange for the warmth extended to me by our people. I enjoyed their food; went to church with them; and, at times, stayed in their homes which sparkled with cleanliness. I was surprised to notice that everything—from the linen, carpets and kitchenware, to the household goods—in their homes was Chinese. 'These goods are better, cheaper and easier to get than those from India,' they told me honestly. Despite hearing many stories about underground outfits, I faced no trouble from them—though our candidates kept demanding extra funds to pay them off and ensure peaceful polling. By and large, these elections were incident-free.

---

[71]*West Bengal Assembly Elections 2006*, in < http://www.elections.in/west-bengal/assembly-constituencies/2006-election-results.html>, accessed on 9 November 2015.

However, I do remember our hotel rooms in Shillong being raided by the Election Commission on a complaint by Sangma (NCP) that money was being distributed by us. ₹30 lakh was found in Captain Daver's room (despite my specific orders not to bring money to the hotel), but I was able to account for every rupee with receipts for permitted amounts paid and to be paid to candidates. This closed the matter, though the raids made headlines and caused a great deal of embarrassment. I packed the 'suitcase men' back to Delhi the next morning.

Soniaji made a trip to Meghalaya for the campaign. A huge rally was organized in Tura where the Indian Idol finalist, Amit Paul, came to sing. There were two helicopters in operation—with Soniaji and the PCC President in one, and Chief Minister Lapang and me in the other, flying from Shillong to Tura. Our helicopter was diverted to a different helipad (on the instructions of the SPG), while our cars waited at the main helipad. We landed and rushed to the waiting motorcade only to realize that it was waiting for Sangma. When he saw us stranded, he most graciously gave us his van, and made sure that his generosity to the 'stranded Congress leaders' hit headlines the next day.

After the rally ended, the singing went on as the crowds kept asking for more. It looked like the party could celebrate victory with that response. But when the results came, the NCP had swept the Garo Hills. We won 28 of the 60 seats—the other seats went to the NCP (15), and smaller parties and independents. Despite my getting Lapang sworn in as Chief Minister—after pleading our case with the Governor as the single largest party—he had to resign as he could not manage to rally together the three extra MLAs he needed to prove his majority. The NCP formed a coalition government with the others, but in two years made way for a Congress-led coalition.

In 2008, Soniaji and I made a full-day trip to Mizoram, covering eleven districts severely affected by draught following the bamboo blooming calamity. Every twenty years, they bloom and the scent of the flowers attracts rodents of all sizes and strains from the hills. They devour the flowers, the pulp and shoots of bamboo and then attack crops, foodstock, and the bamboo floors and roofs of people's houses—causing draught and disaster. The starvation and despair in the villages had to be seen to be believed. The food and funds sent from Delhi for draught relief had not reached the rural areas. The people were angry with their elected leaders and their government led by Zoramthanga.

The Assembly results showed precisely how angry the people were. The Congress won 32 of the 40 seats, with the Chief Minister losing from both the constituencies he contested.[72] I had done all the planning and the selection of candidates, even appointing observers. But circumstances kept me out of the campaign as I had resigned as General Secretary by the time the campaign began.

Interestingly, the North-east followed me to Delhi in the strangest manner conceivable. One day, a young man walked into my house, telling my PA that he was a Minister in Nagaland for any number of departments. Thinking that he was a part of the Neiphiu Rio government, I met him, served him Christmas cake and coffee, and started a conversation on the state and its problems, only to realize that he was part of the underground government in exile! We had long arguments over his 'cause' till he finally left, wishing me a merry Christmas. I was quickly put under Y-category security.

After my long history with election campaigns, I thought Haryana would be easy to handle. After all, it was a small state, close to Delhi, with a proactive Chief Minister, a lot of political activity and galvanized workers. I attended conventions in every district, mobilizing the cadres. Soniaji, too, made several visits, launching schemes while addressing massive rallies. But soon internal dissidence emerged. I tried to stem this by arranging meetings of all the unhappy leaders with the Chief Minister at my residence. My efforts bore fruit in the 2009 Assembly elections, even though I was no longer in charge. A divided opposition, and a spirited campaign under Bhupinder Singh Hooda's leadership, supported by the High Command, ensured the party's victory, giving Haryana a Congress government for a second consecutive term.

Punjab, unlike Haryana, was a more difficult state to handle. The divisions in the Congress were open and obvious. The key Congress leaders, Rajinder Kaur Bhattal and Amarinder Singh, could never agree. Despite trying to intervene and broker peace, the public spats continued, with each group trying to prove its might. Little wonder that the party lost in 2007 and again in 2012!

◆

---

[72]See *Statistical Report on General Elections, 2008, to the Legislative Assembly of Mizoram,* in <http://eci.nic.in/eci_main/StatisticalReports/AE2008/Stats_report_MZ2008.pdf>, accessed on 11 April 2016.

I made many trips with Soniaji to the states I handled, and came to know her better, even as we developed a relationship of mutual trust. This bond was strong enough to withstand the many stories conveyed to her against me. In the early days of our travels together, I became painfully aware of her speed of walking, and the impossibility of keeping pace with her. She seemed to never tire, even after long trips on the campaign trail, while the rest of us were ready to collapse.

I also came to recognize her attention to detail; she'd often ask me about places and occurrences in Indian history that I was unfamiliar with, and astound me with dates and events I knew nothing about. At all times, she was quick to decipher situations and react, sometimes surprising one with her generosity. I remember one incident, in particular, during the Maharashtra campaign. A senior Minister had promised to give me a lift in his helicopter to the next venue, from where I was to fly back with the Congress President. Suddenly, for personal reasons, which I will not mention, he changed his programme and I was abandoned with my bag at the helipad gate. At this point, Soniaji's motorcade whizzed past. She noticed me standing helplessly, stopped, put me in her car and took me in her helicopter, back to safety.

I came to appreciate the times when Soniaji let bygones be bygones. I remember the case of a certain Congresswoman who wanted to be a Minister after the Assembly elections. She kept calling me, wishing to know what the Congress President thought of her. I told her in all honesty that the only remark that she had made was that she ought to be spending more time in her constituency. The Congresswoman promptly reached out to Soniaji to update her regarding the work she had done, adding that following a conversation with me, she felt she had to explain herself. Soniaji put two and two together, and was naturally upset. She admonished me for my indiscretion. I apologized but offered no excuses. I knew that my position asked for circumspection at all times. Soon after, I was sitting all alone at a Congress luncheon. She noticed me, called me and made me sit next to her, stunning all those around her. It was her way of telling me to forget what had happened.

◆

I made quite a few attempts to get Rahul on to a public platform. I met him often, and discussed several issues with him. We shared a good rapport. I offered him advice—often urging him to become part of the government set-up—but he remained noncommital. He was pleasant, always smiling and willing to listen, but it was clear—he had a mind of his own.

That he preferred to remain a low-key figure was made evident by a number of events—for instance, when I asked him to accompany us to a massive rally organized at Shivaji Park, Mumbai, for which his posters had been printed and kept ready, he said he would ask the Congress President and let us know. We received no response. The same story repeated itself during the Goa, Meghalaya and Nagaland election campaigns. When Prime Minister Manmohan Singh publicly invited him to join the Cabinet—and I further nudged him to become an MoS in the PMO to get acquainted with government functioning, and become a link between the party and the government—his response was, 'There is time for that.'

I did, however, get to see the leader in him during two visits. The first occasion arose when I accompanied him on a two-day trip to the suicide belt of Vidarbha. We did the journey by road from Nagpur, and the eminent journalist, P. Sainath, explained the tragedy unfolding there. It was a learning exercise even for me. We visited farms, interacted with distressed farmers and local officials, met widows and families that had lost those closest to them, and joined the Prime Minister and the Chief Minister, who were visiting the area on a fact-finding mission. Everywhere we went, there was anger over administrative indifference.

Even before my visit to Vidarbha, I had been pleading for a moratorium on small agricultural loans for two reasons—over 80 per cent of farmer suicides were the result of their inability to repay loans under one lakh rupees, while families received two lakh rupees as compensation when there was a farmer suicide. This was an incentive to die. Why not save lives, I pleaded, and let small loans go?

I reiterated that argument in Vidarbha, and it was here that a final decision was taken to do so.

I also visited Punjab with Rahul to push the IYC membership drive. Soniaji had asked me to go with him despite the fact that he had given clear instructions that no one, other than IYC office bearers, were to be present. I mobilized senior leaders to organize receptions in their districts; and got Rahul's meeting at the Chandigarh University cleared through the Governor's office (with the caveat that only students and Rahul would enter the hall). This was a most successful interaction. Everywhere he went, he was greeted by crowds, posters and slogans of welcome. At the press conference at Ludhiana, too, he shone. He enjoyed mingling with the local people—despite my repeated pleas that it was best if he remained within his security cordon—drinking lassi and tea offered by strangers, and sharing the food he was given along the way. By the time the day ended, I was exhausted. But Rahul was still alert, discussing party affairs and asking me questions about the Emergency, Sanjay's role, etc.

After dinner, he decided to visit a Harijan colony, and invited Ambika Soni and me to join him. The streets were dark and unpaved, with open drains criss-crossing paths. He went into homes, sipped tea while sitting on charpoys and listened to people's complaints and problems. They were thrilled.

During the course of this trip, I cautioned Rahul about the dangers of open membership in the IYC—which he was pushing for. I told him there could be infiltration, manipulation and sabotage from within unless we were cautious. He was not happy with my advice. Soniaji told me later that he was trying his best to bring new life and new blood into the IYC through a democratic process, and that I ought to encourage, not discourage, him.

However, it bears mentioning that everything I warned Rahul about has come to pass, with money and the clout of local politicians deciding elections and destroying loyal youth cadres—forcing the party to rethink its strategy.

◆

I held charge of Chhattisgarh for a brief period, during which time I got Charan Das Mahant appointed as the PCC President. But Ajit Jogi, the former Chief Minister, openly challenged the appointment and created a ruckus at the public function meant to welcome the new President. He declared: 'No General Secretary stays in this state without my support!' When the Prime Minister came to address the party workers, he created an even bigger scene, claiming that he had been insulted since no seat had been placed on the stage for him (this was actually not true as we had left a gap for his wheelchair in the front row on the stage). I had to threaten action against him and his followers before calm was restored. I was, however, replaced as General Secretary of the state shortly after—the fourth to be relieved in one year!

I had an opportunity to speak on the economic resolution at the AICC session in Delhi in 2007. I spoke about the party's commitment to the people, and the ideology that had guided it since the days of the freedom struggle. I called for food security through domestic self-sufficiency, the protection of the fertile land of farmers and a cautious analysis of the latest craze for SEZs—by acquiring from our farmers the land they had been made landowners of by the reforms of 1960s. I finally pleaded for the Women's Reservation Bill to be passed, and for the rights of tribals and forest-dwellers to be protected. Many were unhappy about my comments. One great economic ideologue even told me, 'You are the last of the socialists in the party!' Another added 'It is cheaper to import food than to grow it!'

On 29 and 30 January 2007, the Congress organized an international conference on peace, non-violence and empowerment. It was attended by many international personalities. I was nominated as the Leader of the Indian delegation, with Rahul and several Gandhians as members. I was also asked to work with Ambika Soni to arrange and assist with meetings for foreign delegations calling on the Congress President. Even as I fulfilled all my duties, it struck me as strange that I was never given an opportunity to speak either in the plenary or in the committees, though I sent my name twice to the Chairman of the committee, Jairam Ramesh.

As a follow-up to this conference, Soniaji and Rahul attended the UN Special Session on non-violence. India moved a resolution for 2 October— Mahatma Gandhi's birthday—to be declared 'non-violence day' by the international community, which was adopted unanimously.

In 2008, I was nominated by the Congress President to represent the party at the Congress of the Socialist International, in Athens, Greece. I chose to speak on 'the challenge of food security'. I began by quoting President George Bush, who had, during his visit to China, attributed the emerging situation of food scarcity to China and India consuming greater quantities of food! Then, I said, 'Yes, we are consuming more, and will keep consuming more! Our public distribution system, mid-day meal schemes in schools, and special nutrition programmes for adolescents and pre-school children will keep expanding. We want our people to consume more. It would be good if this wise gentleman looked at the food wasted in his dustbins, and the corn fed to his cattle, before pointing fingers at us!' There was loud laughter and a round of applause from the delegates.

It was at this Congress that I met Asif Ali Zardari, President of Pakistan, and told him of my friendship with his late wife, Benazir Bhutto, whose

New Year card had reached me after her death. Over lunch we shared many memories of her. I also got to renew my friendship with Margaret Papandreou, the former First Lady of Greece and a close friend, who drove to the conference venue to have tea with me.

While I had planned an extended trip from Greece to Turkey with Niru and Niret, Soniaji suddenly asked me to go to South Africa for an international women's meet. The dates clashed with our trip and I was unable to go. This was the second time I was declining an invitation to South Africa. Earlier, I was invited to join a meeting of The Elders[73] by Richard Branson, to be chaired by Nelson Mandela. But since the Goa elections were on, I was refused permission to go. Despite working closely with the ANC for many years and being honoured with the Nelson Mandela Award for Minority Empowerment and also by the President of South Africa on a visit to India, I regret the fact that I have yet to visit that country.

Apart from Athens, I attended, on behalf of the party, the Congress of the ruling party in Moscow—where Putin was re-elected President of the party. Niru and Niret went with me. It was a very formal assembly, with various organizations proposing and accepting his nomination. Then, he came, spoke and accepted the request of the party to continue for another term. There were no other speeches. I attended meetings of delegations from different countries and participated in discussions on the new world order that was emerging.

Then we undertook a sightseeing trip arranged by an Indian friend. We had an escort from the Embassy to help us get to Lenin's mausoleum. But the queue was long and we had to wait in line. To our utter surprise, our Indian friend came to us with a policewoman who saluted us and took us ahead of everyone. We presumed that she had been told by the Embassy who we were. Pleased with ourselves, we came out, only to confront the angry glances of the waiting public. The Embassy official was nowhere around. It was only then that our Indian friend told us that a few roubles to the lady had done the trick.

We flew to St Petersburg for two days before returning to Moscow, attending a function at the Embassy and then flying back. I had made

---

[73]The Elders is an international NGO of statesmen, peace activists and human rights advocates—brought together by Nelson Mandela in 2007—committed to working together for peace and human rights.

many trips to the old Soviet Union and the change was now obvious. Russia under Putin was a new country—for better or for worse, only time will tell. But many common people we spoke to, even old friends, remembered the past with nostalgia. They admitted they had more freedom now—'But for what?' they asked.

During this time, I also went to the fourth General Assembly of the International Conference of Asian Political Parties (ICAPP) on Peace and Prosperity in Asia organized by the Uri Party in Seoul.

In December 2006, I was back in Cuba for the third time as the party's representative for the fiftieth anniversary celebrations of Cuba's Revolution and the eightieth birthday celebrations of President Fidel Castro, which was postponed due to his illness. In fact, he did not attend any of the functions. India was represented by a three-member delegation—the General Secretaries of the CPM (Prakash Karat), of the CPI (A.B. Bardhan) and of the AICC (me). I was given the special honour of being hosted by the Cuban government and being put up with the Communist Party's VIP guests. I was invited to speak at the inaugural function in preference to the two Communist Party leaders from India. Africa and Latin America dominated the show, with hundreds of young doctors, nurses and teachers trained by Cuba. It was a charged atmosphere with battle lines clearly drawn. Fidel Castro was hailed as their friend and saviour. Later, our Ambassador hosted the Indian delegation to a fantastic cultural show at Tropicana in Havana, Cuba—the only one allowed to continue despite its American origins.

I was invited to the famous Salzburg Global Seminar in Vienna in 2006 on 'Women, Political Power and Next Generation Leadership'. I spoke on 'Women in the Panchayats', conducting a three-hour session with two short films shown by Manira on successful elected women at the grassroots who had made a difference. There was great interest in and admiration for our initiative, with countless questions. But the most exciting feature of the event was the fact that we were housed at the Von Trapp family mansion, made famous by *The Sound of Music*. The ambience of the small town, with quaint houses, streets and shops, and with the old fort for a backdrop, was unforgettable.

The Women's Forum for the Economy and Society held its Women's Forum Global Meeting at Deauville, France, in October 2008, to which a large Indian delegation was invited, as India was the guest nation that year. There were programmes fixed for us in Paris before and after the official forum meetings. It was a great experience, with women from varied fields and backgrounds—including Nandita Das, Tavleen Singh, Rohini Nilekani and Zia Mody—exchanging views, debating issues and suggesting the way forward so that women could become equal partners in progress. I was invited to speak at two of the main events—presenting the Indian point of view and detailing the challenges we were experiencing in our quest to mainstream women's development. The foundation of many lasting friendships was laid here. At the dinner on a barge along the River Seine I concluded my speech with 'under the bridges of Paris with you, we will make our dreams come true'—which received an emotional response.

◆

At the turn of the millennium, and in the year that followed, we lost three tall Congress leaders—Rajesh Pilot was killed in 2000 in a car accident; Jitendra Prasada died in 2001; and Madhavrao Scindia was killed in 2001 in a plane crash. Soon after I became AICC General Secretary came the loss of a fourth leader—P.V. Narasimha Rao.

While Pilot, Prasada and Scindia got all the honours due to them as Congress leaders—with shamianas erected at the AICC to receive their remains before the last rites—P.V. Narasimha Rao, the tallest of them all, was denied a state funeral in Delhi. His body was not even let into the AICC compound; instead, the gun carriage carrying the former Prime Minister and Congress President was parked on the pavement outside the gates, with chairs lined for party leaders. I was shocked to see this when I arrived. Ever since, I have regretted not protesting and walking away. Why was he humiliated in this manner? Was it because he was a South Indian? Even today, there is no picture of him on the AICC office walls, otherwise lined with Congress leaders—including those who left the party at crucial times. This, despite the fact that he was a freedom fighter, a Prime Minister who lasted a full term, a former Chief Minister, Congress President and AICC General Secretary, and a visionary who contributed to the nation's development.

◆

In 2007 came the question of finding a new President to succeed A.P.J. Abdul Kalam. Several names were making the rounds. Then, suddenly, there came the news that the Coordination Committee had decided to have a woman. I was flooded with phone calls from the press and friends, asking me to push for it. I refused to bite the bait. Then came the unbelievable choice of Pratibha Patil, who made it as a Rajput to challenge Bhairon Singh Shekhawat of the BJP, also a Rajput. Jayanthi Natarajan was chosen to assist her with the campaign, while the General Secretaries were asked to muster votes in the states they were in charge of. Pratibha Patil became the first woman President of India.

◆

August 2005 saw me receive the first Nelson Mandela Award instituted by the International Foundation for Minority Empowerment (with consultative status with the UN) at a simple ceremony at the UN Church Centre in New York, with Niru by my side. I made a hard-hitting acceptance speech, quoting Gandhiji and Mandela, and calling for justice and reconciliation in the face of violence and revenge. 'The causes of terrorism have to be understood,' I said, 'and remedial measures initiated by the international community to address the sense of injustice, alienation and hopelessness among large sections of people'. The result was that at every airport we checked into, for our trips to other cities in the US, we were stopped, made to step aside and undergo the most humiliating security procedures. I understood from my sources that our boarding cards automatically showed an XXX marking, which was a sign for special attention! So much for the right to free speech in a country that claims to be the greatest democracy in the world!

◆

In 2008, the Karnataka Assembly elections came up. My son, Nivedith, had applied for the Khanapur seat, which was part of my constituency, bordering Maharashtra. It had never been won by the Congress since Independence, since it was a stronghold of the Maharashtra Ekikaran Samiti (MES).

But R.V. Deshpande had other plans, and got Prithviraj Chavan, Jagdish Tytler and Vilasrao Deshmukh—who were in charge of the state—on board. Tytler came to me one day and said that Khanapur was a seat that the Congress traditionally lost, so I ought to consider an urban seat, such as Sarvagnanagar in Bangalore, which was minority-dominated and was also where I lived. I told him that since Jaffer Sharief wished to get that seat for his grandson, I had deliberately kept away. I added that I would gladly accept the seat if it was offered. He assured me that it was mine for the asking.

Soon after, the Central Election Committee met. I was not informed about this meeting on time and got there when the meeting was halfway through. In this list submitted to the Central Election Committee, Nivedith's name appeared against both Sarvagnanagar and Khanapur, but in both cases his name was listed with other candidates. Besides, despite the fact that he was well-qualified and had worked for the party in key positions, there was no mention of his experience; instead, his name came with only one descriptor—'son of Margaret Alva'!

And so, without any discussion, Sarvagnanagar went to K.J. George, who was shifted from Shanthinagar to make room for another Malayali, N.A. Haris. I objected. 'Why are only Malayalis contesting?' I asked. But there was no response. As for Khanapur, it went to a Muslim, Rafique Khanapure, who had lost earlier and lost once again by a much larger margin.

I was especially angry because the allocation of seats had been manipulated. While sons and daughters of many leaders in Karnataka and other states had been accommodated, Nivedith had been deliberately left out, in a bid to sideline me. Despite being AICC General Secretary, I had not been included in the list of star campaigners or been given a seat on stage when the Congress President had visited the state. While I could endure this, I could not accept the unfairness in the distribution of constituencies.

Needless to say, we lost the elections in Karnataka—a state we would have won had tickets been properly distributed. But I kept quiet.

Suddenly, one evening, journalists barged into my sitting room with a list of candidates of some other states. They pointed out that family members of several leaders had been included. I reacted sharply: 'Different rules exist for different people!' I said. On being questioned further, I said, 'That is how we lost Karnataka! We have complaints that tickets were sold at the local level. As for sons and daughters, Jaffer Sharief's grandson and my son are not smugglers or terrorists—why were they kept out?'

In no time, the channels were buzzing. My comments had made headlines! I refused to say anything more, nor did I deny the claims I had made. In the meantime, I went away for three days to attend a family function in Bangalore.

On my return to Delhi, I met Rahul. He told me not to take any action hastily, and urged me not to leave Delhi. I was then called by A.K. Antony, who was Defence Minister, to his residence. He tried to appear kind and helpful, and asked me what had provoked my comments. At the end of the meeting, he said that the Congress President wanted to meet me. As I got up to leave, I was surprised to see him tag along; this made me extremely suspicious and uncomfortable.

Together we entered 10, Janpath, and saw a grave Congress President seated at her table. I said, 'I feel like a schoolgirl summoned by the principal. Are you still angry with me?'

She smiled and asked us to sit down. 'Why did you do this, Margaret?' she enquired. 'And that too when elections are on?'

'I am sorry,' I replied. 'It was a sudden outburst. But what I said is true. I have proof—letters that reveal how much had been demanded from candidates!'

Now Antony tried to intervene.

'You stay out of this,' I told him, sternly.

Soniaji interrupted, 'I have always stood by you, even defended you, Margaret. But this time, the pressure on me is far too much. Everyone knows you are close to me. Why did you do this? You have let me down...'

I softly said, 'You brought me to the AICC. If you feel I have let you down, I will go. I need a day to finalize my letter of resignation. In fact, I have a draft ready. I will place on record all the facts that you need to know.'

'No, no, please do not say anything that will hurt the Leader!' Antony pleaded.

'You stay out of this, Mr Antony,' I said, firmly. 'This is between Soniaji and me. You have no place in our relationship!'

Soniaji put her hand on mine and said, 'Calm down. You will have to go for now, but I promise I will bring you back.'

I thanked her, apologized once again, and left my 'escort' behind.

I went home, redrafted my letter of resignation and sent it to the Congress President. Today, for the first time, I produce this letter:

11th November, 2008

My dear Soniaji,

I thank you for the patient hearing you gave me last night. I write this letter to you now in all honesty.

I write with a heart-filled with gratitude for what you, Rajivji and Indiraji have done for me; but also with a heart heavy with the hurt and humiliation, I have suffered silently.

I have worked in the Congress Party for over forty years. I came to Parliament in 1974 at the age of 32 and in all these years of public service, I have been able to hold on to what I believed in and have been appreciated for my forthrightness and sincerity of purpose, even when that did not translate into electoral victory. I acknowledge that it was you, who brought me to the AICC and the CEC at a time when I was defeated and at my lowest ebb. You helped me keep my accommodation when I had no place in Delhi to move into. You have shown your faith in me and given me important assignments which I have tried to fulfill with my heart and soul and even at the cost of my health, perhaps upsetting powerful people in the process.

I have given the best years of my life to the Party and Congress Governments that I served in. I have had a record for honesty, hard-work and total loyalty. I have always held my Party above personal gain and petty differences. However, the events of the last few weeks have rattled me deeply and led me to question the manner in which we have come to function.

After hours of discussions in the Central Election Committee and the many announcements made since the Karnataka elections that relations of leaders would not be given tickets to contest, it is indeed shocking to see the number of relatives that have been accommodated in the states going to the polls now. There was one set of guidelines for Karnataka presented by AICC representatives who have now sat on Selection Committees for these states, ignoring these guidelines. It is unfortunate that different criteria are followed for the southern states while those in the Northern States get away doing exactly what they wish. Winning candidates have been kept out because state leaders have chosen to divide seats among themselves with little consideration for their winning chances. The way in which genuine Congress workers have been ignored and even recommendations of CEC members rejected, I am afraid that the history of the Karnataka defeat is going to be repeated.

Times have changed and for the first time, I have come to feel like a misfit in an organization that I considered as precious as my own home. A look at our recent candidates lists show a distinct pattern of patronage to the wealthy and rich lobbies like mining, education and real-estate. A journalist recently asked me in Bangalore "Why does the Congress Party claim to be of the *Aam Aadmi* when it only fields rich candidates?"

The post of General Secretary was personally offered to me by you and one that I have worked very hard at. I understand there will be times that you will keep your own counsel and I accept and respect that. But the manner in which the change of PCC Presidents was effected in the states under my charge, hurt me. My opinion was neither sought, nor was I part of any discussion process before resignations were taken.

Pros and cons were not weighed collectively. In fact, I was merely asked to send a recommendatory note with pre-decided names for Maharashtra, Mumbai and Punjab saying they were your directions. In all my years in politics and Government, this is the first time that something like this happened to me and I was surprised that it was actually expected of me. But when I spoke to you, things changed. It is hard to function through intermediaries because we never seem to know when and which message is yours and what you want done.

I have now come to realize that I am out of tune with the decision-makers around you. My opinion is ignored or not called for ; my warnings brushed aside (though proved right later) and requests always turned down. My direct access and rapport with you has been resented by many for many reasons and they want me out.

I have been totally sidelined in matters related to Karnataka. The DCC President of Uttara Kannada District has not been replaced for 4 years despite repeated requests and promises. My son was refused a ticket because "relations" had to be kept out, while the son of a sitting MLC, who had openly worked against me in my constituency and is facing a murder charge, was given a seat as were so many other relations. As a Christian, I took my son and addressed public meetings for him. He won but he resigns to join the BJP and become a Cabinet Minister. Mr. Lad who pulled down our Government, gets an MLA seat even before joining the Congress, gets defeated, and we accept him as a Rajya Sabha nominee. Rama Krishna Hedge's daughter, never a Congress member is made a candidate and is routed. Shivmurthy is deliberately knocked out, to snub me and five seats are lost. The Khanapur seat is announced before the CEC meets and is lost by 16,000 votes.

The arrogance, indifference and over confidence of the campaign managers from outside, cost us the state. 25 seats were   cornered (bought ?) by one leader who lost them all, including his own, and he is rewarded !! Of the 65 sitting MLAs 36 lost. 15 "top leaders" were routed. Opinions of local people were ignored, despite   repeated   requests. I have letters to show   how things were '"managed". I have spoken the truth. I agree it was wrong for me to have done it publicly. It was not planned but provoked by journalists and they quoted me out of context. I apologize for that mistake.

I am a social activist more than a   political leader. I have had to keep   silent, avoid seminars and other platforms, because   I cannot publicly defer with Government policy.   But I have very strong   feelings about reversal of Congress policies as we learnt them under Pandit Nehru and Indiraji. And I know things are going to move much faster now for obvious reasons.

I do not seek fame or fortune. I came from humble origins. I have worked for forty years for the Party and my country. I have upheld the lofty traditions of my nationalist family whose association   with the Party is over 80 years. But the time has come for me to seek out public service of a different sort and give back to society through   non-political means.

I would like to be free to speak and work for causes I cherish. I wish to write, to travel, to join the struggle of women, the marginalized , my community that is persecuted in a secular state. I wish to spend time with my family and live life at my own pace.

It is a strange coincidence that my late mother-in-law Violet Alva resigned as Deputy Chairperson of Rajya Sabha in mid November, 1969 because of her humiliation and died 2 days later on 20th November, 69 of a stroke in her sleep God willing, I will live ....

I do not go in anger or disappointment. I go because I feel I have done my duty the best way I could. I have completed all tasks assigned to me and have put the 8 PCCs under my charge in election mode. I am now redundant. I have spoken the truth and questioned the double standards of a few. I thank you for what you have been and done for me. You once said, " I am very fond of you – You are always in my heart..." I hope I have proved myself worthy of your trust and affection. I am there If am needed, to help in any way I can.

I thank you for giving me the opportunity to work with you. I apologize since my words have caused you hurt. I know that you have held my interest at heart and stood by me even when I stood alone. You, Rahul and the family will always hold a special place in my heart and prayers and I will always wish you well.

God bless you, Madam.

warm regards,

Yours sincerely,

(MARGARET ALVA)

Smt. Sonia Gandhi,
President, AICC
New Delhi

◆

I came to learn from friends in the inner circle of the AICC that Antony, who had been asked to look into the entire controversy, had actually recommended my expulsion. While everyone else Sonia consulted ruled this out—recalling my years of unstinted service to the party—Antony's campaign against me finally yielded results.

I know why A.K. Antony pursued my removal with such determination. Back in 2004, when he had been the Chief Minister of Kerala, Soniaji was very upset about the defeat of the Congress in the state in the Parliamentary elections. All Congress candidates had lost; the only seat won was by an Indian Union Muslim League candidate as part of the UPA.[74]

She sent R.L. Bhatia and me to Kerala as observers to meet MLAs and party leaders and produce a factual report on what went wrong. We met everyone individually over two days and prepared a brief but clear report for the Congress President. The almost unanimous demand was for a change in leadership. The complaint was that A.K. Antony cared only about his image, to the exclusion of all else. He neglected the party. Soniaji marked the report with: 'For immediate follow up'. Then she deputed Pranab Mukherjee, Ahmed Patel and me to take the next steps in the state. We went. A.K. Antony was replaced by Oommen Chandy.

Antony never forgave me for this (even though the decision was Soniaji's) and used every opportunity he could to get even.

◆

Soon after resigning as the AICC General Secretary, I was in Goa with Nivedith to attend a wedding. There I had a fall in the bathroom; I broke a hand and slit the side of my scalp. Bleeding, bruised and shaken, I was flown back to Delhi by Manira, after preliminary treatment at Apollo Hospital, for a three-hour operation. I was advised complete bed-rest for at least a month.

I then shifted to Bangalore, hoping to settle down. But fate willed otherwise. I had not applied for a seat for Parliament in 2009, as I was depressed and upset with the party leadership over the recent events. But suddenly, Soniaji phoned, asking me to consider contesting from Karwar, as all senior leaders were running. I hesitated. But when she phoned again, in a moment of weakness, I agreed, despite strong opposition from my family. Yet they all rallied around me the moment they saw that I would not reconsider my decision.

In Karwar, with my hand in a sling, I was overwhelmed by a wave of

---

[74]See *Constituency-wise Results of Indian Parliament Elections, 2004, Kerala State*, in <http://keralaassembly.org/lok/winners.php4?year=2004>, accessed on 14 April 2016.

sympathy. Every report suggested that I would win. But R.V. Deshpande, using his money and muscle power, ensured last-minute manipulations. An independent Muslim candidate, Rahmatullah Qazi, his protégé—whom he fielded and funded—tilted the balance. I lost by 21,000 votes to Ananth Kumar Hegde of the BJP.

At the Centre, the UPA was back in power. Manmohan Singh became the Prime Minister for a second term—this despite the fact that Pranab Mukherjee had been elected to the Lok Sabha, while Manmohan Singh had opted to remain in the Rajya Sabha. I would have loved to stay on in Delhi at the BPST. In fact, Meira Kumar, who had become Speaker, promised to help me with another five-year term. But there were too many people lobbying for it, with Mani Shankar Aiyar, who had also lost the election, finally taking over.[75] Despite his best efforts, he could not get my former post of General Secretary of the AICC, but managed to bag a nominated Rajya Sabha seat in no time.

It was clear that the coterie around Soniaji wanted me out of Delhi at all costs, while she seemed to have forgotten her promise to bring me back.

One afternoon, while sleeping, I got a call from Soniaji to say that she had sent my name to the Prime Minister for the post of Governor. Before I could reply or refuse, the phone call ended. I got no appointment to meet her. The next call was from P. Chidambaram, who said that I was to be appointed Governor of Uttarakhand. This was against my wishes. But since refusing would have caused embarrassment to Soniaji, the government and the President, I reluctantly accepted it and moved.

It was a new beginning—one I hadn't bargained for—a Governor at sixty-seven years.

◆

Once I had made the mistake of saying: 'The Alvas are the only political family to have a member in Parliament without a break for almost half a century'. This statement sealed our fate. It was seen as a challenge.

And so, after sixty years, we prepared to move out of the capital. Shifting was a painful exercise. There were hundreds of books to sort out and pack, besides important files, albums and gifts. 'Do not move! Stay on. You

---

[75]Along with Mani Shankar Aiyar, who managed to get a nominated seat, many defeated favourites also got accommodated in the Rajya Sabha.

belong here,' my friends and well-wishers kept pleading. But I had already experienced the consequences of defiance, especially when helpless and alone. So I ignored their entreaties. I could not appear ungrateful or proud.

9 August—Quit India Day—was Niru's seventieth birthday. We hosted a big dinner on our lawns, not just to celebrate, but also to say goodbye to those who mattered. There were Governors and Chief Ministers, MPs and MLAs, bureaucrats and journalists, classmates and family, staff and friends from all walks of life. After toasts and prayers by the Archbishop of Delhi, the curtains came down on the Delhi durbar of the Alvas.

The Alvas are a family of freedom fighters, journalists, writers, trade unionists, lawyers and Parliamentarians. We have been respected for our honesty, high moral standards, secular values, socialist leanings and nationalist credentials—principles that had been passed from the third to the fourth generation.

I cannot say what the future holds—if we will be back in Delhi again; if we will, once more, have parties, 'open houses', festivals; if we will welcome, yet again, all those who knock at our doors in the capital.

For now, it seems, it's farewell to Delhi. If we have one solace it is that we've departed with our hands clean and our records unblemished—without an inch in this capital city to call our own, but with a capital of goodwill.

Chapter 28

IN THE GOLDEN CAGE:
THE RAJ BHAVAN DAYS

For the next five years, I lived with Niru in splendour in the Raj Bhavans of Uttarakhand and Rajasthan. They were years of loneliness but comfort, marked by visits by our children, family and friends. I also entertained VIPs, attended functions, toured extensively and was in the public eye all the time. Both the Presidents, the Prime Minister and Soniaji, besides leaders of all political parties, came to stay or visit, as did several foreign dignitaries. Festivals were celebrated, banquets hosted and meetings held. Children's Day brought kids from municipal schools, as also groups of rag-pickers, to Raj Bhavan. This repeated itself on Christmas Eve, which saw day-long celebrations with sports and dances, and food and gifts for each child. The Raj Bhavans were opened to all.

I did everything I could for the two states I was appointed to. I visited ancient shrines and pilgrimage centres, exotic tourist destinations and tribal areas. I addressed national training academies and convocations. I helped revitalize institutions—including the Red Cross Society and the Indian Council of Child Welfare—and got their functioning streamlined.

I visited jails, met prisoners and initiated steps to deal with their problems—including working on the rules governing parole; the money needed to help under-trials pay their fines for petty crimes; the release of terminally-ill life prisoners and those above sixty-five years of age, who had served fourteen years in jail; and the expansion of the existing open jails, so as to shift women serving life-terms there.

◆

The Dehradun Raj Bhavan—under construction when I arrived—was furnished from the cellar to the dome and came to be praised for its elegant splendour. It was inaugurated on 14 April 2010, which was also my birthday. The old guest house, that had served as a temporary Raj Bhavan, received a new look.

The Nainital Raj Bhavan—the 113-room castle built by the British—was in a shambles. It was restored with the help of a well-known heritage architect of Bombay, with funds from the Central government made available by the then Finance Minister, Pranab Mukherjee. Heritage furniture and chandeliers lying in the cellars were repaired and refurbished. The golf course was renovated, with a new club house added. The annual Governor's Cup Golf Tournament at Nainital began to acquire an all-India image. The old swimming pool was repaired and the banquet hall restored to its past glory. We spent some lovely times here, visited by leopards on a couple of occasions! Walks into the woods around us and games on the lawns kept us occupied outdoors all day.

The annual one-day flower show hosted by the Dehradun Raj Bhavan became a three-day spring festival—with cultural programmes, competitions for schools and special children, NGO stalls and a food court. We had thousands of visitors.

Uttarakhand has a whole community of retired senior officials, artists, writers and environmentalists, besides local women's groups, NGOs, national training and research centres, and educational institutions. I attended many meetings, seminars and festivals in different parts of the state, supporting causes that were dear to the local people.

It was during the bicentenary celebrations of Doon School that I raised the question of girls being kept out of this premier institution at a time when doors were (and are) being opened for women in different walks of life. There was an enthusiastic response from the student audience. President Pratibha Patil supported my stand in her Presidential address. Headmaster Peter McLaughlin responded positively, setting in motion the process of admitting girls into this all-male bastion.

I made it a point to repeatedly warn that the indiscriminate felling of trees, man-made forest fires and unplanned construction would wreak havoc on the ecosystem. I specifically called for a ban on blasting rocks for road construction as this would loosen the soil and cause landslides—the foothills of the Himalaya are fragile. The tragedy of June 2013, which saw unprecedented floods and landslides, and brought death and destruction to the state, and the massive forest fires of 2016 that have destroyed millions of trees, bringing an environmental catastrophe, only proved my point.

During the rains and floods, and even earlier, I appealed to schools to contribute generously. The response was immediate, and woollens, clothes, shoes and blankets poured into Raj Bhavan. The basement turned into a round-the-clock sorting centre, with volunteers and staff packing boxes for dispatch. Several truckloads were sent out till we were asked to stop further supply due to storage and distribution problems in the remote hilly areas.

While in Uttarakhand, I lost a very dear friend, Prabha Rau. Both of us had worked closely for many years, starting with our trip to Mexico in 1975. We were MPs together. We teamed up once more when she was the Maharastra PCC President and I was General Secretary in charge of the state. In July 2008, when she was appointed Governor of Himachal Pradesh, we spent a brief holiday with her. When I become Governor of Uttarakhand, and she was serving as Governor of Rajasthan, she decided to come with her family to Dehradun. We had planned a visit to Nainital as well. But fate willed otherwise. Even as we were preparing for her visit, there came the shocking news that she had died in her room in Jodhpur House in Delhi. I had lost a dear friend. I attended her funeral in her hometown to be with her family in their hour of grief. Strangely, I would go to Jaipur later to succeed her.

◆

The warmth of the people of Uttarakhand was heartwarming. The flowers were beautiful and the surroundings clean and green, with the lights of Mussoorie gleaming at night. But the climate did not suit us. Medical facilities were far from satisfactory and Niru had to be frequently admitted to Delhi hospitals. I mentioned this to Soniaji when she visited us. Soon after, I was offered Jaipur, which was vacant.

So began our stay in Rajasthan. There had been no full-time Governor in Jaipur for three years. As such, the Raj Bhavan was in a mess, the staff disorganized, with none of the systems operating. We stayed in the guest house for three months, and cleaned and refurbished the main building, before moving in. Everyone who visited us was astounded at the makeover. The sprawling gardens, which lay dry and bare, came alive with flower beds and relaid lawns. The two lakh rupees in our budget for buying flowers went towards producing them instead. The swimming pool became operational and many store rooms kept locked with junk were converted into bedrooms for guests.

The Summer Raj Bhavan at Mount Abu is a wooden heritage structure overlooking a lake with breathtaking surroundings. It was in a state of utter disrepair. Some much-needed restoration to revive its original ambience was undertaken. I spent a summer holiday there with the family, touring surrounding districts and interacting with local officials and residents.

Apart from reviving the West Zone Cultural Centre in Udaipur with innovative programmes, I saw first-hand the neglect caused by the diversion of tribal budgets. I submitted a report to the President, which resulted in his appointing an eight-member Committee of Governors under my Chairmanship to look into all issues affecting tribal districts. We made far-reaching recommendations for their efficient administration, all of which were discussed at a conference of Governors. The need to get universities in the areas involved in planning and executing programmes for employment generation and non-formal education was emphasized, and skill development among tribals received special attention and appreciation. In fact, the President had the Rajasthan model circulated to other states for replication.

The universities in the state received personal attention—VCs (Vice Chancellors) were appointed, staff vacancies filled, overdue government funds released, convocations made regular, and several issues sorted out through regular meetings of the Coordination Committee chaired by me.

But most of all, order and discipline was restored in the Raj Bhavan and its Secretariat, and redundant staff repatriated to parent departments. I do believe that the Governor's establishment is overstaffed, the thirteen-vehicle motorcade unnecessary and many customs of the past redundant.

◆

Many believed that Manmohan Singh would have been ideal for the top post at the Rashtrapati Bhavan, while Pranab Mukherjee would have made an excellent Prime Minister. I mentioned this to him once—his answer (which I will not quote) was frank and revealing.

When the race for the post of the President opened up in 2012, there was a lot of speculation. Despite the efforts of many to thwart his ambitions, Pranab Mukherjee made it, having quietly mustered support from several opposition parties. I was in the Raj Bhavan, but managed several non-Congress votes for him through intermediaries in Karnataka and Maharashtra, besides contacting a couple of Chief Ministers who were personal friends.

Most friends and admirers were happy to see him as President after his long years of service to the party and the nation—though the Congress has suffered greatly without his expert guidance and involvement with its decision-making processes.

I called on Prime Minister Narendra Modi soon after he took over, as did most other Governors. I had an interesting half-hour interaction with him at his residence, during which time I told him of my Gujarati connection—my mother-in-law was one! I told him I had come to pay my respects, not plead for an extension, adding, 'I am prepared to quit anytime.'

'There is no question,' he replied. 'You are doing a good job, please continue where you are.'

Soon after, I was given additional charge of Goa, followed by Gujarat.

◆

When I was offered the post of Governor of Rajasthan, friends and relations kept advising me not to go there as my two predecessors in that Raj Bhavan had died. I survived the 'jinx'.

In May 2014, friends and relations assembled at Jaipur for our fiftieth wedding anniversary—among them my younger brother, John. On the night of the 22nd, he slipped and fell while getting off a bus in the Raj Bhavan complex. He went into a state of coma and never recovered. He passed away on 30 May. It was my brother, instead of me, that the Raj Bhavan claimed as its third victim.

I was shattered, and kept waiting for my term to end. I left Rajasthan the day I completed my term, on 5 August 2014.

Between 2009 and 2014, I had seen governments change, sworn in three Chief Ministers and handled several controversies. But I never crossed the 'Lakshman Rekha' I had set for the Raj Bhavan. The ADCs, officials and staff were most cooperative, while the team of doctors and medical staff were always there to care for us.

In October 2012, to mark my seventieth birthday, I took my family on a thanksgiving pilgrimage to the Holy Land, covering Jordan, Israel and Palestine. While we were saddened by the divisions and tensions in these areas, the ten days we spent together were of prayer, bonding and love. We offered our gratitude to Christ for the blessings showered on us.

In August 2014, we returned home to Bangalore to settle down and enjoy our years of retirement. The family has expanded, with nine grandchildren. Niru and I have our health problems but are surviving. My life has changed drastically from Governor to Governess, focusing mainly on Niru's healthcare. I do enjoy the company of family and friends, and participate in socio-cultural events of interest to me. But these are limited. The children and grandchildren are always there to help and support me, but I carry the responsibility of ensuring that Niru is happy and comfortable, even as I pray and hope for his recovery.

The Congress party was routed in the 2014 General Elections, and reduced to 44 MPs in Parliament. Assembly elections, too, have yielded poor results. The regional parties are gathering strength and state satraps are dictating terms. Minority bashing and cultural cleansing is becoming the norm. Mind-boggling definitions of nationalism and patriotism are coined by fanatics who seek to rewrite history and reinterpret science. Even as claims are made that black money will not be tolerated, economic policies and taxation systems are constantly being fine-tuned to serve the rich and the powerful, even as the gap between the haves and the have-nots grows. The common citizen is fuming over rising prices and social tensions. The universities are in turmoil, with the youth challenging injustice and inequality. Women are demanding empowerment and an end to violence and discrimination. The Dalits are protesting against their exclusion and exploitation, even as tribals are fighting to save their lands. Farm distress is leading to suicides, and minorities are crying out for the protection of their Constitutional guarantees. The opposition is gradually uniting and the judiciary is asserting itself.

My active political life may have ended, but I have seen history made—Prime Ministers and governments come and go, policies and programmes change—sometimes for the better and sometimes for the worse. I have lived through victories and defeats, assassinations, despair and new hope. I have walked the corridors of power in Lutyens' Delhi, sat in Parliament for almost thirty years—on Treasury and opposition benches, and in the chair presiding over sessions in both Houses and in Central Hall.

Indian democracy has evolved; the voter has matured; women and youth in their millions have become politically aware. Media outreach influences citizens even in the remotest corners of the country. India is changing.

The future remains a mystery. But as I shut the window on my past, I have no regrets. I have lived my life my way. And will continue to do so, whatever the odds.

ACKNOWLEDGEMENTS

My thanks to:

Niret, Nikhil, Manira and Nivedith, for their invaluable inputs and advice;

Arpuda Rajan, for the long hours of work at the computer, helping incorporate editorial changes;

Kumdruddin Puttur, for his immense patience while transcribing my handwritten drafts;

C. Latha, for the research support;

Ritu Vajpeyi-Mohan and Rupa Publications, for help and guidance in publishing this book.

INDEX